Ultimate Adventures with Britannia

ULTIMATE ADVENTURES WITH

$\mathscr{B}$RITANNIA

Personalities, Politics and Culture in Britain

Edited by Wm. Roger Louis

I.B. TAURIS
LONDON · NEW YORK

HRC · HARRY RANSOM CENTER

Published in 2009 by I. B. Tauris & Co Ltd
6 Salem Road, London W2 4BU
In the United States of America and Canada, distributed by
Palgrave Macmillan, a division of St. Martin's Press
175 Fifth Avenue, New York NY 10010
www.ibtauris.com

Harry Ransom Humanities Research Center
University of Texas at Austin
P.O. Drawer 7219
Austin, Texas 78713-7219

The paper used in this publication meets the minimum requirements of
American National Standard for Information Sciences—
Permanence of Paper for Printed Library Materials

ISBN 978-1-84885-152-8 hardcover
ISBN 978-1-84885-153-5 paperback

Library of Congress Control Number 2009929265

Print production by Studio Azul, Inc., Austin, Texas

Table of Contents

List of Authors

Julian Barnes is the author of ten novels, two books of short stories, two translations, and two collections of essays: *Letters from London* (1995) and *Something to Declare: Essays on France* (2002). His novels include *Flaubert's Parrot* (1984) and *England, England* (1998). His most recent work is the memoir *Nothing To Be Frightened Of* (2008), an exploration of death, religion, and family.

Roby C. Barrett is a Scholar at the Public Policy Center, Middle East Institute, and a Senior Fellow with the Joint Special Operations University and the Air Force Special Operations School. A former Foreign Service Officer, he is the President of C.COMM Corporation, a firm specializing in Middle East security and defense policy. He is the author of *The Greater Middle East and the Cold War* (2007).

Shareen Blair Brysac's first career was in modern dance. Later a prize-winning documentary producer at CBS News, she is the author of *Resisting Hitler: Mildred Harnack and the Red Orchestra* (2000). She is the co-author, with Karl E. Meyer, of *Tournament of Shadows: The Great Game and the Race for Empire in Central Asia* (1999) and *Kingmakers: The Invention of the Modern Middle East* (2008).

Sir David Cannadine, FBA and former Director of the Institute for Historical Research, is Whitney J. Oates Senior Research Scholar in the Council of the Humanities at Princeton University and Chairman of the Trustees of the National Portrait Gallery in London. Among his books are *The Decline and Fall of the British Aristocracy* (1990), *G. M. Trevelyan* (1992), *Mellon: An American Life* (2006), and *Making History Now and Then* (2008).

John Darwin is Beit Lecturer in the History of the British Commonwealth at Oxford and a Fellow of Nuffield College. His books include *Britain, Egypt, and the Middle East, 1918–1922* (1981), *Britain and Decolonisation* (1988), and *After Tamerlane* (2008). His life work will be published by Cambridge University Press in 2009: *The Empire Project: The Rise and Fall of the British World-System, 1830–1970*.

Saul Dubow, Professor of History at the University of Sussex, is an historian of modern South Africa. He has interests in the intellectual, institutional, and political development of segregation and apartheid as well as the history of colonial science and race. He is the author of several books, including *African National Congress* (2000) and his most recent, *A Commonwealth of Knowledge: Science, Sensibility, and White South Africa, 1820–2000* (2006).

Roy Foster, Carroll Professor of Irish History at the University of Oxford and a Fellow of Hertford College, is the author of books and articles about Irish history and culture, including the two-volume authorized biography *W. B. Yeats: A Life* (1997). He currently holds a Wolfson British Academy Research Professorship to work on the Irish revolution of the late nineteenth and early twentieth centuries.

Peter Green, Dougherty Professor Emeritus of Classics at the University of Texas at Austin, is the author of numerous books on ancient Greece, including *Alexander of Macedon, 356–323 B.C.: A Historical Biography* (1991). He is a dedicated aficionado of twentieth-century English literature, on which he has written for periodicals such as the *New York Review of Books* and the *New Republic,* where "Drink and the Old Devil" had its genesis as a review article.

Robert L. Hardgrave, Jr., a founding member of British Studies, is the Temple Centennial Professor Emeritus in the Humanities, in the departments of Government and Asian Studies at the University of Texas at Austin. His publications reflect a range of interests focusing on India. They include *The Nadars of Tamilnad: The Political Culture of a Community in Change* (1969) and *A Portrait of the Hindus: Balthazar Solvyns and the European Image of India* (2004).

Sir Brian Harrison's first book was *Drink and the Victorians* (1971; second edition, 1994). Then came books on British reform movements, feminism and anti-feminism, Oxford University's history, and the evolution of British political institutions since the 1860s. From 2000 to 2004, he edited the *Oxford Dictionary of National Biography,* then in 2009 published *Seeking a Role: The United Kingdom, 1951–1970* in the *New Oxford History of England.*

A. G. Hopkins holds the Walter Prescott Webb Chair in History at the University of Texas at Austin. He was formerly the Smuts Professor of Commonwealth History at Cambridge and is an Emeritus Fellow of Pembroke College and a Fellow of the British Academy. His publications cover African history, British imperialism, and the history of globalization. His most recent book, written with colleagues at the University of Texas, is *Global History* (2006).

Dan Jacobson is a novelist and critic. Born and brought up in South Africa, he holds an Honorary D.Litt. from Witwatersrand University. His autobiography, *Time and Time Again* (1985), won the J. R. Ackerley Prize. His other works include the memoir *Heshel's Kingdom* (1998), the criticism collection *Adult Pleasures* (1988), and the novels *The Confessions of Joseph Baisz* (1977) and *All for Love* (2005).

Richard Jenkyns is Professor of the Classical Tradition at Oxford and a Fellow of Lady Margaret Hall. He was an undergraduate at Balliol College and later a Fellow of All Souls College. He is the author of eight books, including *The Victorians and Ancient Greece* (1980), *Virgil's Experience* (1998), and *A Fine Brush on Ivory: An Appreciation of Jane Austen* (2004). In 2004, he was Oxford University's Public Orator.

Margaret MacMillan is the Warden of St. Antony's College and a Professor of International History at Oxford. Her books include *Women of the Raj* (1988), *Paris 1919: Six Months That Changed the World* (2002), *Nixon and Mao: Six Days That Changed the World* (2007), and *Dangerous Games: The Uses and Abuses of History* (2009). She was formerly Provost of Trinity College and Professor of History at the University of Toronto.

Roger Morgan, a Cambridge-educated historian turned political scientist, was a research director at Chatham House (1968–74) and later a member of its governing council. He has taught at universities in Britain, the United States, and Europe, including the European University Institute, Florence. He has written or edited a dozen books on historical and political subjects, including *The United States and West Germany, 1945–1973: A Study in Alliance Politics* (1974).

Sue Onslow has taught at the London School of Economics since 1994 and is a visiting lecturer in the Department of War Studies, King's College. Editor of *The Cold War and Southern Africa: White Power and Black Liberation* (2009) and author of *Backbench Debate within the Conservative Party and Its Influence on British Foreign Policy, 1948–1957* (1997), she is writing a book on South Africa and the Rhodesian Unilateral Declaration of Independence.

Jason Parker, Assistant Professor of History at Texas A&M University, is the author of *Brother's Keeper: The United States, Race, and Empire in the British Caribbean, 1937–1962* (2008), which received the 2009 Bernath Book Prize of the Society for Historians of American Foreign Relations. He is currently at work on *The Contest: Hearts, Minds, and the History of U.S. Cold War Public Diplomacy in the Third World* and on a comparative study of post-war federations.

Sir Adam Roberts is President of the British Academy and Fellow of Balliol College, Oxford. He was Montague Burton Professor of International Relations at Oxford University, 1986–2007. He jointly edited (with Dominik Zaum and others) *The United Nations Security Council and War* (2008). His latest book (jointly edited with Timothy Garton Ash) is *Civil Resistance and Power Politics: The Experience of Non-violent Action from Gandhi to the Present* (2009).

Dominic Sandbrook was educated at Balliol College, Oxford, the University of St. Andrews, and Jesus College, Cambridge, where he was awarded his doctorate. Formerly a lecturer at the University of Sheffield and Senior Fellow at the Rothermere American Institute, Oxford, he is the author of *Eugene McCarthy: The Rise and Fall of Postwar American Liberalism* (2004) as well as books on Britain in the 1950s and 1960s: *Never Had It So Good* (2005) and *White Heat* (2006).

Bernard Wasserstein has been Meyer Professor of History at the University of Chicago since 2003. He was born in London and educated at the High School of Glasgow and at Balliol and Nuffield Colleges, Oxford. Before moving to Chicago, he was Professor of History at the University of Glasgow. His books include *The Secret Lives of Trebitsch Lincoln* (1988) and *Barbarism and Civilization: A History of Europe in Our Time* (2007).

Geoffrey Wheatcroft is a former literary editor of the *Spectator,* a feature writer for the *Daily Express,* and a sports columnist for the *Financial Times.* He writes also for the *New York Times* and the *Times Literary Supplement.* His books include *The Randlords* (1985), *The Strange Death of Tory England* (2005), and *The Controversy of Zion: Jewish Nationalism, the Jewish State and the Unresolved Jewish Dilemma,* which won an American National Jewish Book Award in 1996.

Caroline Williams graduated from Radcliffe College and holds master's degrees in Islamic history and Islamic art. Author of *Islamic Monuments in Cairo: The Practical Guide* (2002), she writes on the Orientalist painters and photographers who discovered the nineteenth-century Islamic-Arab world of Cairo as well as on the evolution of Cairo's Islamic city. She taught at the University of Texas at Austin, where she was a member of the Middle East Center.

The editor, Wm. Roger Louis, is Kerr Professor of English History and Culture and Distinguished Teaching Professor at the University of Texas at Austin. He is an Honorary Fellow of St. Antony's College, Oxford. His books include *Imperialism at Bay* (1976), *The British Empire in the Middle East* (1984), and *Ends of British Imperialism* (2006). He is the Editor-in-Chief of the *Oxford History of the British Empire*. In 2001, he was President of the Amercan Historical Association. In 2002, he became Founding Director of the American Historical Association's National History Center.

Introduction

WM. ROGER LOUIS

The word "ultimate" implies finality, but readers of *Adventures with Britannia* throughout the world may rest assured that the end is not yet in sight. Between ultimate and death are degrees of suspense and connecting links, past and future. Is it not common sense to assume that the stage after ultimate is post-ultimate?

The present volume begins, as have its predecessors, with the continuity of G. H. Hardy's affirmation that the agony of having to repeat oneself is so excruciating that it is best to end the agony by offering no apology for doing so. In the spirit of the adventurous refrain—more, still more, yet more, ultimate, post-ultimate—I again follow his example. This book consists of a representative selection of lectures given to the British Studies seminar at the University of Texas at Austin. Most of the present lectures were delivered in the years 2007–09.

Lectures are different from essays or scholarly articles. A lecture presumes an audience rather than a reader and usually has a more conversational tone. It allows greater freedom in the expression of personal or subjective views. It permits and invites greater candor. It is sometimes informally entertaining as well as anecdotally instructive. In this volume, the lecture sometimes takes the form of intellectual autobiography—an account of how the speaker has come to grips with a significant topic in the field of British Studies, which, broadly defined, means things British throughout the world as well as things that happen to be English, Irish, Scottish, or Welsh. The scope of British Studies includes all disciplines in the social sciences and humanities as well as music, architecture, and the visual arts—for the second time, a *Britannia* volume includes paintings. Most of the lectures in this collection fall within the fields of history, politics, and literature, though the dominant theme, here as previously, is historical. The full sweep of the lectures will be apparent from the list at the end of the book, which is reproduced in its entirety to give a comprehensive idea of the seminar's evolution and substance.

In 2009, the British Studies seminar celebrated its thirty-fourth anniversary. The circumstances for its creation in the 1970s were favorable because of the existence of the Humanities Research Center, now known as the Harry Ransom Humanities Research Center, at the University of Texas. Harry Ransom was the founder of the HRC, a Professor of English and later Chancellor of the University, a collector of rare books, and a man of humane vision. Through the administrative and financial skill of both Ransom and the present Director, Thomas F. Staley, the HRC has developed into a great literary archive with substantial collections, especially in English literature. Ransom thought a weekly seminar might provide the opportunity to learn of the original research being conducted at the HRC as well as to create common bonds of intellectual interest in a congenial setting of overstuffed armchairs, Persian carpets, and generous libations of sherry. This was an ingenious idea. The seminar was launched in the fall semester of 1975. It had the dual purpose of providing a forum for visiting scholars engaged in research at the HRC and of enabling the members of the seminar to discuss their own work.

The sherry at the Friday seminar sessions symbolizes the attitude. The seminar meets to discuss whatever happens to be on the agenda, Scottish or Indian, Canadian or Jamaican, English or Australian. George Bernard Shaw once said that England and America were two great countries divided by a common language, but he understated the case by several countries. The interaction of British and other societies is an endlessly engaging subject on which points of view do not often converge. Diverse conceptions, which are tempered by different disciplines, help initiate and then sustain controversy, not end it. The ongoing discussions in British Studies are engaging because of the clash of perspectives as well as the nuance of cultural interpretation. Though the printed page cannot capture the atmosphere of actual discussion, the following lectures do offer the opportunity to savor the result of wide-ranging research and reflection.

The British Studies seminar has two university sponsors, the College of Liberal Arts and the Humanities Research Center. We are grateful to the Dean of Liberal Arts, Randy Diehl, for allocating resources to sustain the program of Junior Fellows—a half dozen or so assistant professors appointed each year to bring fresh blood, brash ideas, and new commitment to the program. We are equally grateful to the Director of the HRC for providing a home for the seminar. I wish also to thank Frances Terry, who has handled the week-by-week administrative detail from early on in the seminar's history. I am indebted to Kip Keller for the many ways in which he has assisted the publications program of the seminar.

The seminar has been the beneficiary of generous gifts by the late Creekmore Fath and Adele Fath of Austin, Mildred Kerr and the late Baine Kerr of Houston, John and Susan Kerr of San Antonio, Becky Gale and the late Edwin Gale of Beaumont, Custis Wright and the late Charles Alan Wright of Austin, the late Lowell Lebermann of Austin, Tex Moncrief of Fort Worth, and the two dozen or so members of the seminar who have generously contributed to its endowment. We are indebted to Dean Robert D. King for his help over many years. I again extend special thanks to Sam Jamot Brown and Sherry Brown of Durango, Colorado, for enabling the seminar to offer undergraduate and graduate scholarships and generally to advance the cause of the liberal arts. The students appointed to scholarships are known as Churchill Scholars. The Churchill Scholars, like the Junior Fellows, not only contribute to the vitality of the seminar but also extend its age range from those in their late teens to the early eighties.

The present volume includes an innovation. As a result of John Darwin's lecture, the graduate students in history at the University of Texas complied a list of 100 Top Hits of Imperial History. It has a certain subversive purpose. Traditionally, students pursuing Ph.D.s in the fields of the history of the British Empire and area studies (India, the Middle East, Africa) must read at least 500 major books. I have always resisted the suggestion that an article might have the same significance as a book. But such was the discussion of seminal or significant articles in the aftermath of Darwin's lecture that I have yielded. I am now prepared to admit that some articles may have lasting significance. Students may now read 400 books and 100 articles. I believe in any event that it is good for graduate students to reflect that an article written in the 1930s may be just as compelling today as an essay post-2001. The list itself is a useful curiosity, a tribute to the intellectual reach of today's graduate students.

THE CHAPTERS—MORE PRECISELY, THE LECTURES—are clustered together around certain themes. The first three focus on the 1950s
and 1960s. **Bernard Wasserstein** writes of a little-documented community, the Jews of Glasgow. They flocked to the city during its era
of prosperity from the 1880s, when shipbuilding on the Clyde made
the area one of the major British industrial centers and a wonder of
the Victorian age. Today the shipbuilding industry has collapsed,
and for that reason and many more, Jews along with many others
have fled, leaving the city with a population about half its size in
the 1950s, when it still stood at more than a million. As a study in
urban decay, Glasgow has much to offer. It is one of the poorest cities in Britain. With more gangs than London, Glasgow is perhaps as
dangerous as Detroit, with which it has certain similarities because
of dependence on a single industry. Wasserstein spent his youth in
Glasgow in the 1950s, when his father was an assistant lecturer in
Greek at Glasgow University. He would have been astonished at the
time to know that stone buildings could have any color other than
black. He recalls the quite separate lives of Catholics and Protestants, a high degree of class consciousness, and the virtual absence
of anti-Semitism. Despite a specific traumatic experience that gave
him insight into human capacity for evil, it was a happy 1950s childhood. He returned in 2000 to teach at the university, which now en-
rolls 20,000 students compared with the 6,000 of the 1950s. He discovered the black stone had been restored to its original colors of
orange and cream. Despite a motorway that seems to have destroyed
much of the city rather than merely providing access, the renewed
Glasgow of the twenty-first century holds out hope—as symbolized
by the River Clyde: once a chemical cesspool, it now attracts human
swimmers as well as fish.

When did the decade of the 1960s begin and when did it end?
Brian Harrison points out that many of the turbulent events of
the time seem to be even more intense in retrospect. Like other
decades, the 1920s are a good example, the 1960s as a concept
took shape only when people began to reflect on the temper of the
times—at the expense, perhaps, of the 1950s, because in Britain
a radical mood had existed at least since the Suez crisis. Not until
1964 or thereabouts did political radicalism and the impression of
"youth in revolt" begin to capture the public imagination. In Britain as in America, painful honesty came into vogue. Strident self-
righteousness as much as miniskirts and the music of the Beatles
seemed to characterize "swinging London." The revolt against prevailing conventions eventually reached the highest level of government. In 1974, in the last year of the fading decade, members of

the Labour Cabinet decided to address one another by first name: Harold Wilson referred to Michael Foot as "Michael." According to Barbara Castle, "The whole atmosphere seemed transformed by that simple gesture." But there were also enemies of more relaxed social conventions and what many believed to be the drift toward a "permissive society." Isaiah Berlin said that students in his time had had "some respect for knowledge and intelligence," while those of the 1960s were "complacently ignorant." One thing at the time seemed clear to critics as well as those embracing the social revolution: the moralistic edge, or "new puritanism," seemed to take a different and ultimately less intense form in Britain than in the United States, where it was stoked by the civil rights movement and the war in Vietnam.

The backlash against the permissiveness of 1960s, argues **Dominic Sandbrook,** came quickly at the time, and it had a lasting impact in subsequent decades. Britain was still a conservative and cautious country with common views: for example, that too few murderers were hanged, too many students were addicted to pot and sex, and far too many colored immigrants had been allowed to infiltrate into the country. Such diverse figures as Mary Whitehouse and Malcolm Muggeridge denounced the corruption of British society and education. Whitehouse, a former schoolteacher, quite often and indefatigably explained the principles of the Moral Rearmament movement, which generally upheld a Christian way of life and specifically stood against promiscuity and drinking. Moral Rearmament had an apocalyptic fervor to it, not unlike its American equivalent of religious conservatism. But though she had a specific appeal, she also repelled a large part of the public with her moralistic hectoring. For example, Hugh Greene, the Director of the BBC, took pride in possessing a painting of a nude Whitehouse with no fewer than five breasts. Muggeridge had a wider influence because of his intellectual vitality, his sense of the ludicrous, and his graphic mental images: for example, of birth control pills being handed out with free orange juice. The students of the 1960s, according to Muggeridge, believed that the image of life was not God, but pigs in a trough. He held that Britain was in spiritual as well as economic decline. Another of Sandbrook's subjects, the radical-turned-conservative novelist Kingsley Amis, condemned the decade comprehensively when he pronounced himself sick of the whole "abortion-divorce-homosexuality-censorship-racialism-marijuana package." Such comments may appear comical in retrospect, but at the time there were real public anxieties, especially about the undermining of authority in university and secondary schools. A substantial part of the British public recoiled from student revolution. The 1960s may now seem to be a radical decade, but the enemies of the permissive society often held the upper hand and perhaps still do.

Roy Foster, who is known throughout the world for his work on the literature and poetry of Ireland, comments on Scotland—on the Scotland that existed in the mind and imagination of Hugh Trevor-Roper (1914–2003), Regius Professor of Modern History at Oxford and later Master of Peterhouse, Cambridge. Trevor-Roper was a polemicist who waged many of his historical battles in the public eye, for example in *Encounter,* which used to be the foremost intellectual journal before its CIA subsidy was revealed. With rare clarity and power of intellect, he wrote devastating critiques of fellow historians, including Arnold Toynbee, whose reputation never recovered from Trevor-Roper's onslaught. One of his first books, *The Last Days of Hitler,* revealed his talent for historical detective work and remained in print for the rest of his life. It has a bearing on *The Invention of Scotland.* Throughout his life, Trevor-Roper pursued the intricate relationship between myth and history, in Scotland as in Nazi Germany. Foster makes clear the roguish line of investigation and the deliberately insulting tone—as when Trevor-Roper with antiquarian correctness uses the word "Scotch" rather than "Scots" to refer to the Scottish people. He is out for blood, demonstrating to his own satisfaction at least that the constitutional, literary, and sartorial traditions of Scotland are mainly nineteenth-century inventions. Projected back in time, they thus suggest an ancient and medieval Scotland of kilts and bagpipes, poetry and legal traditions, that simply did not exist. There is obviously a strong line of mischief that runs throughout Trevor-Roper's work on Scotland, and it may explain why he decided not to publish the book in the wake of the catastrophe of his career. In 1983, he vouched for the authenticity of a forged set of Hitler's diaries. Had he published the book on Scotland then or later, critics might have called into question his judgment on Scottish traditions and might even have thought that the book, like Hitler's diary, was a hoax. But as Foster demonstrates, there is a great deal to be learned from Trevor-Roper's knowledgeable and maliciously witty interpretation.

Assessing the history of the Royal Institute of International Affairs, **Roger Morgan** deals with what Elie Kedourie called "The Chatham House Version" of history. Kedourie referred to the "establishment," the collection of civil servants, journalists, bankers, and military officers who supposedly ruled Britain and whose views found expression in the institute's discussions and publications. Morgan, who worked there as a resident scholar and director of programs for many years, presents an insider's account. He points out that at the time of the institute's creation—in the wake of the First World War, the same time as the founding of the Council on Foreign Relations in New York—the Foreign Office mistrusted the new body of mandarins who might try to interfere with foreign policy. In fact, Foreign Office officials eventually participated fully in Chatham House discussions, taking the opportunity to float ideas and win support. They were usually but not always successful. Arnold Toynbee, a central figure for some thirty years, criticized the Foreign Office for supporting Mussolini but defended the appeasement of Hitler. Toynbee, perhaps more than anyone else, provided an underlying or consistent rationale of the official mind, including a pro-Arab outlook. Morgan believes that the golden age of Chatham House was the period of the 1960s and 1970s, when both leadership and financial resources enabled extensive research as well as vigorous discussion and the publication of high-quality books in collaboration with the Oxford University Press. Since then, Chatham House has operated on slender resources. And it has not always been the voice of the establishment. Much to his credit, the recent Director, Victor Bulmer-Thomas, gave a valedictory address in December 2006 in which he condemned the invasion of Iraq as "a terrible mistake."

Adam Roberts provides an historical perspective on the study of international relations by asking whether the purpose of the discipline is to allow policy makers to predict the future. Can abstract reasoning and scientific methodology help officials foresee emerging patterns of conflict or reconciliation? He himself believes—in the tradition of the "British School of International Politics"—that a more humble approach of understanding languages, personalities, and cultural traditions at least allows us better to understand the recent past and the present, even if not the future, and especially to comprehend the aftermath of the Cold War. He accepts that the Western alliance played a major role in ending the Cold War, both through commitment to defense and through skillful diplomacy. But he is notably skeptical about single-cause explanations. Western scholarship has neglected to take into account the way the collapse of the Soviet Union was perceived by influential Russians at the time. This new generation of Russian leaders held a view of the world quite different from that of those locked into the Stalinist mentality. They believed that internal changes in Russia were far more important than external concerns. On the American side, the end of the Cold War led many to believe that people throughout the world were essentially the same and wanted U.S.-style democracy.

On the contrary, the Cold War in its last stage revealed that the conflict was not only about tension between the Soviet Union and the United States but also about the conflict of views on the place of post-colonial states in the future world order. Post-colonial states in Asia and Africa, and for that matter the countries of the former Soviet Union, do not necessarily want American-style democracy. Events after September 11, 2001, have demonstrated that we still live in a world shaped by the breakup of the Soviet Union and, it might be added, the end of the apartheid era in South Africa.

Robert Hardgrave captures the spirit and details of eighteenth-century Calcutta by tracing the life and career of François Balthazar Solvyns (1760–1824), a Flemish artist whose paintings and etchings uniquely portray Indian life and culture of the era. Solvyns portrayed the everyday life of peasants, craftsmen, and street vendors. He had been trained as an artist in Antwerp and Paris but, given the unstable political conditions of the Low Countries, decided to pursue his fortune in India. Though never part of the British elite in Calcutta, Solvyns nevertheless won a certain distinction. He produced a series of etchings in Calcutta in 1796, and later, in Paris, he published a lavish folio of 288 plates, *Les Hindoûs,* but the project ended in financial ruin. Today, Solvyns's depictions remain a rich source for knowledge and understanding of the people of India more than two hundred years ago. Among other reasons for his enduring significance, he was probably the first European to provide a systematic portrayal of the caste system. Hardgrave traces his own commitment to the Solvyns project, which has extended over four decades. Through detective work in India, Europe, and America, he has identified, collected, and described the corpus of Solvyns's work and was able to present a comprehensive collection of his paintings, drawings, and etchings in a volume published by the Oxford University Press. Four of Solvyns's paintings are reproduced in this volume.

Another artist, John Frederick Lewis (1804–76), is presented by **Caroline Williams** against the background of nineteenth-century Egypt. Lewis was the first British professional painter to live in Cairo. In the decade of the 1840s, when the British public was beginning to take note of Egyptian and Islamic culture, Lewis took on Orientalist subjects—Orientalist in the old-fashioned, pre–Edward Said sense of dealing with Eastern or Oriental peoples and themes. William Makepeace Thackeray visited Lewis in 1844 and found him living entirely in "Oriental fashion." When Lewis returned to London in 1850, he brought with him sketches and drawings that he used for the rest of his life, but in the context of nineteenth-century

England. In the 1850s, the word "Victorian" was increasingly used to describe respectable family life. The period was also one of industrial achievement and economic ascendancy. A new class of patrons liked paintings that presented understandable or life-like subjects placed in richly symbolic settings. Lewis's art chimed in well with these new, largely middle-class preferences. He used an Oriental setting but gave it a Victorian subtext. What is remarkable, according to Williams's deciphering of the paintings, is the extent to which Lewis himself and his family figured into them. For example in a portrait of the bey, the bey resembles Lewis himself. In short, his work combines an Orientalist's view of Cairo with a vision of the spiritual and social issues of modern, industrial Britain. Four of Lewis's paintings are reproduced in this volume.

Richard Jenkyns reassesses the career and writing of Arthur Conan Doyle (1859–1930). Though forever known as the creator of Sherlock Holmes, Doyle wrote significant historical novels and came to believe that the Holmes stories were a distraction. Doyle was a Scot, though he always referred to himself as obviously English. He practiced medicine for several years before his success with Sherlock Holmes allowed him to devote full time to his writing. Part of the Holmes phenomenon can be explained by Doyle's skill in borrowing ideas and styles from other writers and adjusting them for his own purposes, rather as J. K. Rowling has done in our own time. There is a good deal of Doyle in Dr. Watson, who is more complicated than Holmes's near caricature of him as simple, stolid, and not especially brainy. In fact, Watson is chivalric as well as solid, adventurous as well as bluff. Holmes by contrast is much more inconsistent. Though always quick to see things not obvious to others, and ingenious in the solution of a wide variety of crimes, he is usually indifferent to literature but occasionally seems to be supremely cultivated. He has a powerful but narrow mind, but is his personality self-controlled or close to neurosis? In the last part of his life, Doyle became a global evangelist for the cause of spiritualism. So it is much to Doyle's credit that he allowed Sherlock Holmes to express skepticism: "This Agency stands flat-footed upon the ground . . . No ghosts need apply."

With a comparison that will probably startle many readers, **Dan Jacobson** believes that the two great poets in the English language during the twentieth century were T. S. Eliot (1888–1965) and Thomas Hardy (1840–1928). Hardy is remembered mainly because of his fiction, while his poetry is often dismissed as simplistic and tortuous. Yet he wrote over 900 poems, ranging from lyrics, ballads, and sonnets to poems on public issues and events such as the sinking of the *Titanic* as well as the wars in South Africa and Europe. His poetry also included tributes to Shelley and Keats. From 1898, the date of his first collection, to the time of his death, his poetry, though uneven, revealed individuality and intellectual curiosity. Except for a discerning few, his contemporaries did not receive his poems enthusiastically. Eliot certainly did not: "He wrote sometimes overpoweringly well, but always very carelessly." Jacobson traces his own responses to the two poets. At first, as a student at Witwatersrand University in the late 1940s, he held Hardy in low esteem and was overwhelmed by Eliot. Yet his feelings about the two eventually underwent something like a revolution. He increasingly appreciated Hardy's sharp sense of the absurd, his wit, and his irony. While still fully appreciating Eliot's inspiration and genius, he now believes that Hardy is the superior poet because of his attention to detail, his tenderness, and the "steel" of his verse.

Julian Barnes thematically reviews a selection of George Orwell's essays, including "Such, Such were the Joys," to provide perspective on Orwell's social and political priorities. Orwell detested Bloomsbury and its preoccupation with precious friendship and pretentious literature; E. M. Forster was one of his frequent targets. On the other hand, he admired Dickens. To Orwell, Dickens stood in a class of his own for ferocious attacks on repressive and unjust institutions. Orwell himself directed his animating rage toward the Empire, Britain's class-ridden society, and the long arm of the state. There was a streak of the social engineer as well as the puritan in Orwell. He feared excessive state control but believed that a "British Revolution" might strengthen guarantees of individual liberty, thus helping avert the catastrophes described in *Animal Farm* and *Nineteen Eighty-Four*. By the end of the inter-war period, Orwell had emerged mainly as a political writer and a democratic socialist. He was an effective pamphleteer, already famous for his nonconforming brand of patriotism. In Barnes's summation, he denounced the Empire, which pleased the Left; communism, which pleased the Right; and the misuse of language, which pleased everyone. He was known for straight thinking and honest writing. Yet he once wrote that all art or writing to some extent is propaganda. Did Orwell live up to his own standards of accuracy, or did he too sometimes succumb to his own party line? Take, for example, his essay "Shooting an Elephant," which his biographer Bernard Crick subjected to verification. At the time it seemed almost heresy to question Orwell's literary integrity. According to his widow, Sonia Orwell, whose words Crick repeated several times during his visit to the University of Texas in 1996, "Of course he shot a fucking elephant. He said he did." But not quite in the circumstances Orwell himself described. It is not the same as if the story were fictional. Orwell prided himself on the accuracy of his political and social reporting. His writing must thus be held to highest standards, but perhaps bearing in mind his own injunction that all writing, in his telling phrase, is to some extent subjective.

Peter Green, a founding member of the British Studies seminar, begins his assessment of Kingsley Amis (1922–95) by reflecting on Evelyn Waugh, comparable as a satirist and tippler. Both Waugh and Amis proved that alcohol could be a hazard to the writer's profession. Both were alarmed when Amis was hailed in London literary circles as Waugh's successor. *Lucky Jim* was published in 1954. Green read it on the way to his Ph.D. examination, causing him to reflect on the radical lecturer who was at once anti-pretension and anti-establishment, virtues that Green himself exemplifies. But there the comparison ends, with Jim Dixon as well as Kingsley Amis, who became known as one of the angry young men of the 1950s. The social revolution of the subsequent decade seemed to pass Amis by, though swinging London became the subject of several of his novels. Adopting the pose of a garrulous misogynist and prodigious drinker, he caused the pose to become a reality. He progressively took a more hostile view of contemporary life and manners, and entrenched his reputation as a serial adulterer. His first wife, Hilary Bardwell, left him in 1963. His second, the novelist Elizabeth Jane Howard, helped restore his creativity, which is perhaps most marked in *Jake's Thing* (1978); but the demon drink increasingly took hold of his life. He drank a bottle of whisky a day, not including wine at meals. His life revolved around pubs and clubs. Yet until his last years he maintained discipline over his writing, usually composing 500 words every morning. Green takes full measure of Amis's personality as well as his writing by surveying recent biographies by Eric Jacobs, *Kingsley Amis* (1995); Richard Bradford, *Lucky Him* (2001); and Zachary Leader, *The Life of Kingsley Amis* (2006). If not an entirely likeable personality, Amis emerges from Green's pen portrait as a great comic novelist and a master of the English language—as can be seen in his posthumous triumph, his guide to good writing, *The King's English* (1997).

Just as Peter Green makes the connection between Evelyn Waugh and Kingsley Amis, so **Margaret MacMillan** contrasts E. M. Forster and Paul Scott. Forster's "loathing for the sahibs and memsahibs" reduced the British to caricatures in *A Passage to India* (1924). Scott's *Raj Quartet* (1966–75) on the other hand reveals a perceptive understanding of the British missionaries, civil servants, and army officers, including their families. The lecture celebrates Hilary Spurling's achievement in an edition of the *Quartet* that includes all four parts in two volumes.* I am proud myself to have played a minor part from the mid-1970s onward in helping make the historical significance of his work more widely known, though I did not go as far as Max Beloff, who said that one could learn more about the British in India by reading Paul Scott than by reading all of the historians on the subject. One of Scott's figures has present-day significance. Few of his readers at the time believed that the monster Ronald Merrick, the police chief, could have been capable of such vicious and depraved interrogations while an officer in the British Raj. In fact, he stands, in Margaret MacMillan's words, as "one of the great villains of literature." In view of what we now know of torture in such places as Kenya during the Mau Mau and Iraq during the American occupation, Scott was ahead of his time in portraying institutional brutality. His connection with the British Studies seminar is historic. He gave the very first lecture, in 1975. He later recalled Austin as "hotter than Bombay" and thought not only that he had received a hostile reception from the members of the seminar but also that he had been exposed as an amateur historian. This is not my recollection. I remember him as slightly drunk but given a warm and sympathetic hearing. The revelation was that Peter Green was the model for the hero of the series, Guy Perron. In view of the previous lecture, it will be of interest, I believe, to record Hilary Spurling's comment to me:

> Guy Perron is clearly based on Peter Green: both Green and Perron had an outstanding Cambridge record, an analytical intelligence and a powerful curiosity. Both are professional historians with the historian's impartial stance, methodical approach to evidence, broad perspective and emphasis on what Paul called lucidity and the calm rhythms of logical thought.

MacMillan's lecture helps remind us that there are areas of the mind and the imagination beyond the historian's reach but captured in literature, not least in *The Raj Quartet*.

Geoffrey Wheatcroft reflects on Churchill's Zionism. Contrary to the romantic view held by American cultists, Churchill's ideas were complex and sometimes reactionary, even by the standards of his own time. He held consistent but ambivalent views on the possibility of a Jewish state. He was committed to the Zionist cause from the time of the First World War, but he always posed a basic question: would a Jewish state be a benefit or a liability to the security of

---

*Paul Scott, *The Raj Quartet*, 2 vols. (Everyman's Library, 2007).

the British Empire? He was well aware of the danger of certain Jews "who take it for granted that the local population will be cleared out to suit their convenience." Churchill himself held the Palestine Arabs in the same contempt as he did Indians and Egyptians, while he regarded the Jews as "the most remarkable race which has ever appeared in the world." But his views underwent a substantial change toward the end of the Second World War. In 1944, Lord Moyne, the British High Commissioner in the Middle East, was assassinated by Jewish terrorists (or freedom fighters, depending on one's point of view). Churchill as always was emotional and loyal. Moyne had been one of his friends. Churchill's views toward Zionism were never again the same. He now spoke of Zionism as producing "a new set of gangsters worthy of Nazi Germany." But in this case he was not a political chameleon. He remained a Zionist, though less enthusiastic in his embrace of the cause. In Wheatcroft's analysis, Churchill consistently and clearly defined the British dilemma: Should the Jews be backed in the creation of an independent state? Or should the British hand over the country to the majority of the people who actually lived there? In Churchill's own words, "You cannot do both."

Sue Onslow portrays Julian Amery (1919–96) not only as a significant British politician on the radical Right but also as the foremost champion of the British Empire in his generation. Julian was the son of Leopold Amery, whose own career in the history of the Empire extended from the Boer War to the Second World War, when he served as Churchill's Secretary of State for India. One of Julian's critics quipped that he was born with a silver grenade in his mouth, a reference to his involvement in secret intelligence operations from 1940 onward. As a man of gifted intelligence and ability, he never fulfilled the promise of his youth, but as a Member of Parliament for nearly half a century he was knowledgeable, influential, and well connected—in 1950 he married Harold Macmillan's daughter, Catherine. To the British public, Julian Amery represented the diehard view of the Suez crisis of 1956, when he protested against the ignominious British withdrawal. In his judgment, it was a betrayal, and he regarded Anthony Eden as a fainthearted leader who had lost his nerve. Defeat at Suez came to him as a revelation of the decline and fall of the British Empire. Yet Amery continued to fight a rearguard action by maintaining that the Empire was not to be liquidated but sustained, nurtured, re-created, and defended. He emerges from Onslow's account as a remarkable, indeed formidable figure in British public life who, in his later years, became a caricature of a Tory imperialist, admitting that he had been largely frustrated in his efforts to sustain the British Empire.

David Cannadine questions the preconceptions of peace and order that are usually associated with British colonies' achieving independence. The most famous event of all, "freedom at midnight" in India on 15 August 1947, was stage-managed to create the impression that the British left with dignity and prestige as well as Indian feelings of goodwill. The ritual invented at the time of Indian independence set the precedent for subsequent celebrations, with many—but by no means all—of the former dependencies becoming members of the Commonwealth. Yet despite the impression of friendship and order, it was a deliberately contrived image. From the murder of Gandhi to the assassination of Benazir Bhutto, violence rather than civil order has characterized much of the history of the new states, including many others besides India and Pakistan. Across Asia and Africa, statues of British monarchs and proconsuls were toppled and left abandoned in obscure places. Streets were renamed. Parliamentary democracy became transformed into one-party rule or military dictatorship. There often occurred abuse of human rights as well as economic collapse, as is apparent in today's Zimbabwe. On the British side there was an unmistakable sense of retreat and disillusion, even recessional. In the 1960s, colony after colony achieved independence, or seized it, often in circumstances of civil war. In 1967, the British withdrew under fire from Aden, the departure marking the nadir of the British Empire's reputation. Yet such was the power of the deliberately crafted image of the "transfer of power" that most people to this day have a positive impression of new states achieving independence.

Jason Parker asks why federations failed in some cases and succeeded in others. In the Caribbean, plans for an economic and political union—a union of what critics called a gaggle of small and fragmented islands—made compelling sense to virtually all involved. West Indian nationalism had long roots. The argument for a Caribbean state stretching from Jamaica to Trinidad had been put forward for nearly half a century. But geography proved to be a major hurdle. The plan for the federation was launched in 1958, and the northwestern tip of Trinidad was to be the capital—at Chaguaramas, one of the key U.S. naval bases in the region (along with Guantanamo), thus seeming to tilt the geographical focus of power to Trinidad, at the eastern extreme. The United States was willing to transform the base into a political capital (though, typically, the U.S. Navy asked the blunt question: did the U.S. government want the federation to succeed or fail, the latter solution holding out the prospect of indirect domination of the islands). But the transfer of the base raised wide-ranging political questions, a further hurdle.

The setting up of the West Indian federation took place at the same time as Castro's rise to power. From the point of view of the U.S. government, the Prime Minister of Trinidad, Eric Williams, might prove to be "another Castro." It is true that Williams had his own ambitions as well as an anti-British and anti-American streak in his character. But he supported federation, and it might have worked had it not been for reaction in Jamaica, the last and fatal hurdle. In Jamaica, the Prime Minister, Norman Manley, seemed to be a bulwark of stability and common sense. He championed the cause of federation, but the Jamaican people themselves rejected it in a referendum of 1961. Jamaica would have wound up providing most of the budget for the otherwise unviable island groups. In 1962, Trinidad withdrew essentially for the same reason, thus sounding the death knell of the federation. What a different place the Caribbean would be today had the federation succeeded!

The 1950s and 1960s are also the focus of **Saul Dubow** as he critically probes a major work by Sir Keith Hancock, one of the distinguished historians of the twentieth century. Hancock devoted nearly two decades to writing the biography of J. C. Smuts of South Africa. The biography is famous because it is one of those rare works that actually can affect the sensibility of general readers as well as scholars by causing them to look at the world in a slightly different way after reading it, or at least by becoming a permanent part of one's intellectual furniture. But it has long been referred to as a flawed masterpiece. Hancock was an Australian, the first Australian to be elected to a fellowship at All Souls College. In a celebrated phrase, he declared himself in love with two soils, British and Australian. He established his reputation in the late 1930s and early 1940s with a survey of the British Empire and Commonwealth, though the survey actually consists of pioneer case studies on demography, economics, and politics, for example, in Africa and the Mediterranean. Late in his career, he took on the writing of the Smuts biography. Smuts engaged Hancock's historical imagination both as a Boer general who became one of the principal figures in the British Commonwealth, and as a South African statesman and world leader who drafted the preamble to the Charter of the United Nations. But Hancock brought with him to the task a set of assumptions that he failed sufficiently to challenge—for example, that South Africa and Australia shared similar attributes. In any event, he did not examine rigorously one of the most important dimensions of Smuts's thought, his attitude toward Africans. The biography thus has a blind spot, or at least a blinkered view, for what Smuts referred to as the "animal savagery" on the part of the "barbarians" who constituted the vast majority of the population. By no stretch of the imagination did Hancock share the assumptions of apartheid, but he was, as Saul Dubow argues, probably too uncritical of Smuts's underlying views about race.

John Darwin deals with famous historians, such as Sir John Seeley, who analyzed the British Empire. The emergent theme is that the Empire became an effective and coherent economic and military power in Asia in the early decades of the nineteenth century. By the 1820s or 1830s, the lead in the industrial revolution and the harnessing of Indian resources gave the British economic strength and the military capacity to break into markets throughout the world, not least in China. The result was a system of indirect as well as direct control over vital parts of the international economy. The chronological point is significant. As an effective power, the British Empire lasted about 150 years. But it was only toward the end of this period, in the 1950s, that historians began to take full measure of the indirect as well as direct nature of British imperialism. In 1953, John Gallagher and Ronald Robinson published a seminal article entitled "The Imperialism of Free Trade," which brought about an historiographical revolution by describing an interlocking world system. Regardless of whether one agrees or disagrees with their argument, no one can look at the subject in quite the same way after reading it. Such is the article's fame—reputed to be the article with the greatest number of references in social science literature—that it raises a further intriguing question: what constitutes a seminal or at least highly influential article? Darwin's lecture provoked such an intense discussion that it led to the creation of the list "100 Top Hits of Imperial History," which is attached to his lecture.

In the first of a concluding trilogy on Iraq, **Shareen Brysac** draws a pen portrait of Gertrude Bell (1868–1926), who played a leading part in the creation of the country previously known as Mesopotamia, or in British lingo, Mess-Pot. During the First World War, Bell befriended two ex-Ottoman officers who helped shape the destiny of Iraq up to the time of the revolution in 1958. Jafar Pasha served twice as Prime Minister, Nuri Pasha a record fourteen times, and was still active until his violent death during the revolution, when he was stripped, castrated, killed, and dismembered. Bell's early life helps explain how she came to exert such influence not only on the two Pashas but also on the King installed by the British in 1921, the Emir Faisal. Part Victorian, part new woman, she studied history at Oxford and traveled extensively in the Middle East. Her languages included Arabic, Persian, and Turkish. Recognized as "a remarkably clever woman with the brains of a man," she made her way in a man's world, eventually becoming the key expert on Iraqi politics in the early British administration. With Paris frocks, Mayfair manners, a pet gazelle, and an intellect as acute as T. E. Lawrence's—the two shared similar characteristics, including the exact height—she cut a remarkable figure. One of her main responsibilities was to provide political intelligence, but she also helped shape the state itself, including the boundaries and the structure of government. Many of the subsequent features of Iraq can be traced back to Gertrude Bell. She calculated that the three provinces could be held together under a collaborative regime—with Sunni leadership securing the oil fields and strategic airfields for the British. She became disillusioned with Faisal, and she probably would not have been surprised at the violent end of the era in 1958, or at the problems facing Iraq today—and it is certainly fair to say that there is no latter-day equivalent of Gertrude Bell in American-era Iraq.

Roby Barrett focuses on a critical moment in Iraqi history, the revolution of 1958 and its immediate aftermath. The revolution signified the end of the British era as well as that of the Hashemite dynasty in Iraq. After an initial speculation on the prospect of trying to reverse the revolution by an invasion, Harold Macmillan's government responded pragmatically. The British discovered that the new leader, Brigadier Qasim, would be willing to guarantee the oil agreements, and they placed their bets on being able to do business with the new regime. But it was by no means obvious what Qasim represented. Would he be pro-communist, leading Iraq into the danger of a communist takeover and even of becoming a Soviet satellite? Or, equally alarming to the British, might he become an ally of Nasser or fall under Nasser's dominance? To the Americans, there was never any question about the greater danger. A communist regime in Baghdad would change the very nature of the Cold War in favor of the Soviet Union. In Washington, at one point the Vice President, Richard Nixon, seemed to prevail in the view that action had to be taken to prevent Qasim from becoming a communist puppet. But President Eisenhower rejected the possibility of intervention except as a last extremity. The former Supreme Commander of the Allied Forces believed that American interference would lead to anti-U.S. sentiment throughout the region and would endanger American access to Middle Eastern oil. His instincts against direct intervention stand today as political wisdom. The combination of British pragmatism and the American principle of nonintervention served as a successful political formula for more than four decades from 1958 until the American invasion of Iraq.

A. G. Hopkins examines the supposition that there might be emerging, in Iraq and elsewhere, an American empire comparable to the British. The United States certainly had a similar empire, though on a much smaller scale, in 1898, but not in 1945, when the Americans either threw off or incorporated dependencies in the Pacific and Caribbean. After 1945, the United States became an aspiring hegemon, not an empire. The country thus shares characteristics of all great powers, but these attributes are not those of an empire similar to the British, which was an informal empire of trade and commerce as well as a territorial empire. The proof can be established by examining the two periods of modern globalization: from 1800 to about 1950, an era that favored the creation and expansion of empires and was dominated by Britain; and from the second half of the twentieth century, when the United States expanded globally but with the aim of achieving hegemony by controlling key states rather than by attempting to incorporate them. The conclusion is that the United States in the world today is not the successor to the British Empire, nor is there an American empire in any meaningful sense comparable to the old European empires.

1

Glasgow in the 1950s

BERNARD WASSERSTEIN

Dawn on New Year's Day 1952: I was not even four years old, but I can still recall the horror I felt at my first glimpse of Glasgow from the soot-speckled windows of the night sleeper train from London as it passed through the exposed underbelly of the city on its way to the terminus. In 1726, Daniel Defoe called Glasgow "one of the cleanliest, most beautiful, and best built cities in Britain."[1] Admittedly, few cities look their best when approached by rail, but what confronted me as I gazed into the dingy back windows, abutting the railway track, of homes in the Gorbals, known at the time (though not yet to me) as the worst slums in Europe, was a veritable image of hell. Peering through the fog of smoke, dust, and fumes, I had a terrifying vision of human degradation, urban squalor, and every kind of mineral, vegetable, and animal filth. In the inter-war period, another writer, less favorably disposed than Defoe, called Glasgow "the vomit of a cataleptic capitalism."[2] If I had been old enough to know what that meant, I would certainly have endorsed it as the steam engine pulled our train into Central Station on that grey dawn.

My father had been appointed to his first job, as an assistant lecturer in Greek at Glasgow University. My parents, my newborn brother, and I had left Euston shortly before midnight with a champagne toast to the New Year. After my initial shock wore off, I became deeply attached to what I regarded as my hometown. In spite of the city's dangerous criminal reputation, my parents wisely permitted me to wander alone at a young age by foot, tram, and bicycle. As a result, I grew to know Glasgow so well that the city became, in a way, my best friend.

In 1960, my family left Glasgow. I returned to live there again only in January 2000. Forty years on, Rip Van Winkle could not have been more amazed by the changes that I encountered. For the greater part of my childhood I simply had not known that stone could be any color other than black. But now, thanks to the Clean Air Acts and large-scale deindustrialization, the black city of my youth had returned to its original hues of cream and orange. The population had fallen from 1.1 million to not much more than half that. Of Glasgow's traditional Italian cafes (*oor Tallies*), only the University Cafe on Byres Road still sold homemade ice cream and burnished its old-style Neapolitan decor. The St. Enoch station and hotel had been demolished, and the enameled advertisement on the wall of its forecourt—with the famous jingle that had so fascinated me as a child, "They come as a boon and a blessing to men, the Pickwick, the owl, and the Waverley Pen"—had disappeared. (What exactly, I used to wonder, was the Pickwick? On investigation recently, I discovered that, like the owl, it was a pen nib.)[3]

Glasgow in the early 1950s was indeed in many ways a terrible place. It had the highest infant mortality rate in Britain and the highest death rate from pulmonary tuberculosis. Housing conditions were the worst in Britain. A quarter of the population still lived more than two to a room. More than half of all households in the city had no private bath, and nearly a third of the population had to share a lavatory with neighbors, often a stinking water closet on the tenement landing or an outdoor privy.

By the time I returned in the early twenty-first century, things had improved—but not all that much. Glasgow was still the poorest major city in Britain by almost any measure. More than half of all retired people in the city received income support to supplement their pensions. Forty-six percent of all households with dependent children in Glasgow were one-parent families. A third of the working-age population received unemployment benefits. Glasgow had the lowest life expectancy of any city in Britain for both men (69) and women (76). In some areas of the city, it was as low as 54 for men. Thanks to slum clearance, housing in Glasgow was much less overcrowded than it had been a half century earlier. Yet according to the census measurement of housing density known as "occupancy rating," Glasgow's housing stock was still by far the most overcrowded in Scotland and probably in the UK. And it was still a dangerous place: the murder rate was said to be higher than in Palermo.

Underlying all this was a downward economic spiral. Glasgow's foremost industry, shipbuilding, had been in decline since the First World War. In 1949–51, Clydeside still produced 13 percent of the world's shipping output. But by the 1970s, in spite of huge injections of government money, shipbuilding had virtually collapsed. Instead of promoting modernization, vast public investment in the 1960s and 1970s propped up an antiquated industry that was overtaken by competitors in countries like Sweden, Japan, and South Korea. Only a few vestiges survived, engaging in naval or oil-platform construction. Of course, the end of Clydeside shipbuilding was part of the larger collapse of British shipbuilding as a whole. But Glasgow was more heavily dependent on this industry than any other city and proved less able than most others to diversify.

The so-called upas-tree theory of the decline of Glasgow, advanced by the economic historian Sidney Checkland, stresses the primacy of shipbuilding in Glasgow's stupendous ascent and in its precipitous decline. The poisonous upas tree of heavy engineering, Checkland maintained, killed anything that sought to grow under its branches. Then, when the upas tree itself became diseased and died, all the ground around it had been contaminated and nothing new could grow.[4]

Overdependence on one major industry is, of course, often a recipe for urban decline, as in Detroit and Glasgow. Cases such as Chicago and Pittsburgh over the past few decades show, however, that diversification can arrest and even reverse decline. I have no special theory of urban decay to offer here. Instead, I propose to share with you some memories of my childhood and, in particular, of three institutions with which I was intimately involved—Glasgow University, the High School of Glasgow, and the Garnethill synagogue—and each of which, in its own way, may provide not an explanation but a parable that can help us understand the striking changes that have come over the city since the 1950s.

Glasgow, when we arrived there, was still recovering from the war. Seven years after V-E Day, homeless people were still living in air-raid shelters. Poor people still came round the backyard every day and rummaged in our rubbish bin, looking for edible leftovers. The ornate cast-iron railings around houses, terraces, gardens, and squares had mostly been torn out during the war on orders from Lord Beaverbrook, supposedly to build fighter planes, leaving unfilled gaping gashes, like missing teeth. In a few cases, they were replaced by cheap, utility-style metal fences that only emphasized the grievousness of the defacement of the urban streetscape. Some aspects of life were hangovers from a bygone era: the sound of horses' hooves could still be heard on the cobblestones outside our first

home, on Highburgh Road; milk, coal, and wooden logs were all delivered by horse and cart, and the rag-and-bone men also called out
their familiar, unintelligible cries from behind their decrepit nags.

The welfare state was securely established, as I knew from my
daily dose of government-supplied orange juice and glutinous-
tasting cod-liver oil. Spindly-legged children suffering from rickets
and other nutritional deficiency diseases, a common sight in the
1930s, were no longer to be seen, thanks to rationing, Aneurin Be-
van, family allowances, and school milk. Even under a Conservative
government, welfarism remained very much part of Glaswegian social consciousness, even if there was a paternalistic ring to some of
its propaganda.

While allowing me to wander, my parents warned me not to go
near the gangs of apparently feral "street children," who, as I understood it, slept by night in the drains and sewers, emerging in the
daylight to gather in packs at street corners. My first instruction
in the menace of other children came on the day after my fourth
birthday when I emerged proudly in the street with a prized gift,
a London policeman's helmet, made of cardboard. I should have
known better. In Glasgow, the police wore peaked caps not helmets,
and the *polis* were widely regarded as the enemy. Donning this head-
gear, I marked myself out as both a *Sassenach* and a Fauntleroy. A
neighbor's child did what came naturally: he took the helmet off my
head and pissed into it. Thus, fifty-seven years ago to this day, began
my education in the human capacity for evil.

In the winter it got dark at between three thirty and four in
the afternoon (Glasgow is on the same latitude as the Alaska pan-
handle). On the way home from school by tram, I would watch the
corporation lamplighters with their poles, kindling the gas lamps
in the street: the last ones in our part of town were not replaced by
electric lights until 1959.

The trams, all double-deckers, were of two types: the older models, which allowed one to sit in a separate compartment in the front
upstairs and observe the driver through an open space below; and
the more modern "Coronation" models, which had completely
closed tops and had first been introduced in 1938. Both types permitted smoking upstairs but carried signs with severe injunctions
to abstain from spitting on pain of fine. The latter was no doubt
mainly directed at tobacco chewers. But we schoolboys indulged in
the enjoyably wicked habit, in the older style of tram, of sitting in
the upstairs front compartment and spitting gleaming, half-chewed
lumps of licorice or "gobstoppers" on the head, preferably bald, of
the driver. Robert Douglas's recent memoir of his Glasgow child-

hood, *Night Song of the Last Tram* (2005), evokes better than anything I could say the romance of the Glasgow trams. They stopped
running in the west end in 1960, their departure deeply mourned.
When I returned in 2000, they remained for me ghostly presences
in streets that otherwise seemed little changed.

GLASGOW IN THE 1950S WAS STILL IN MANY WAYS a Christian city.
The spirit of the established Calvinist church hovered over the city,
affecting many aspects of its life. The Lord's Day was still observed
strictly. The only singing permitted was of religious verses, preferably psalms—though in a city of song and singers, inventive ways
around such restrictions were sometimes found, notably by the leg-
endary Glasgow Orpheus Choir, directed, until its disbandment in
June 1951, by Sir Hugh Brotherton. Pubs, cinemas, dance halls, and
all other places of entertainment were closed on Sundays. The only
food store in the west end of the city that was permitted to open was
Sidney Shaw's Jewish grocery shop on Woodlands Road, enjoying a
dispensation under the provisions of the Sunday Trading Act.

My family lived at the highest point of Gilmorehill, close to the
university. We were near enough for my father to sit at the breakfast
table until he heard the bell in the university's great tower begin
to chime the hour, whereupon he would rise, reaching the class-
room in time for his nine o'clock lecture. The university was proud
of its medieval origin, owing its foundation to a papal bull granted
in 1451, but in architectural and other terms it was really a Victorian institution. Its great central core, designed by George Gilbert
Scott and constructed between 1866 and 1872, was my childhood
playground. The academy of Adam Smith and Lord Kelvin was, in
those days, still literally the home of its professors, who lived in assigned houses around a quadrangle near the main gate.

A large house with a turreted tower occupied one end. That was
the home of the Principal and Vice Chancellor, Sir Hector Hetherington, by all accounts a benevolent and kindly man, but to me a leg-
endary and forbidding figure. On the only occasion that I encountered him directly, I elicited a voluble and memorable expression
of wrath. I happened, as was my wont, to be cycling illegally at high
speed in the wrong direction round the professors' quadrangle, with
my hands in the air, when a frighteningly majestic figure suddenly
appeared at an open window in the turret of the Principal's Lodging
and roared down at me, "Will ye git off that bike!" Hetherington's
quarter century as head of the university transformed it and tripled
its student body, but his reputation, at any rate among the matrons
of Hillhead, was scarred by the unpardonable actions of his two

sons. I recall the clucking disapproval when one of them opened what was seen as a veritable house of ill repute within a stone's throw of the university: the location of this affront to local morals, the "Papingo" coffee bar, within sight of Hetherington senior's domain, was regarded as a flagrant violation of the fifth commandment. The younger son, Alastair, did even worse: he went to England, which was pardonable; became editor of the *Manchester Guardian,* which was questionable; but then did something unforgivable—he boldly opposed the government's policy during the Suez crisis, incurring the wrath of a large part of respectable society.

The other leading figure in the university was the Professor of Humanity (that is, Latin) and Clerk of the Senate, Christian Fordyce. He "ruled Glasgow University for more than thirty years with a rod of iron."[5] His power derived not from any scholarly eminence (his sole scholarly production, a heavily bowdlerized edition of Catullus, thirty-three years in the making, was finally published, we are told, "to widespread contempt")[6] but from force of personality, which conveyed itself somehow even to a schoolboy observing him cross the professors' square, his gown billowing in the wind. Fordyce was a passionate collector of railway tickets—so obsessive, indeed, that "he had a criminal conviction for breaking into a railway station and stealing tickets for his collection."[7] He was one of the last exemplars of the old-style British provincial (by which I mean non-Oxbridge) professor-dictator, already a somewhat archaic figure when satirized in 1954 by Kingsley Amis in the grotesque character of Professor Welch in *Lucky Jim.*

In the late 1950s there were fewer than six thousand students at the university. Today there are more than twenty thousand, reflecting, of course, the vast growth in British higher education over the past half century. All the universities suffered growing pains, but Glasgow's transition was in some ways peculiarly troubled.

Let me isolate three problems: first, limited horizons. It was not that the university was particularly xenophobic. In the nineteenth century, it awarded the first medical degree ever granted anywhere to an African American. In the 1950s, the scarified faces of West African students were a common sight in Hillhead. But the university was still mainly a regional rather than a national or international institution: the overwhelming majority of its students came from Glasgow or its immediate environs. The university was slow to realize the desirability of recruiting students nationally, from the UK, rather than just regionally, from west of Scotland. Even in 2006–07, 47 percent came from Glasgow or nearby—a big change, but still the highest proportion of local students for any major university in the UK. By contrast, a majority of Edinburgh University's students, as early as 1900, came from outside Scotland. The Snell Exhibitions that sent Glasgow graduates (including Adam Smith) to Balliol College, Oxford, where they frequently did first degrees all over again, were regarded as the pinnacle of achievement at Glasgow; yet by their very nature they seemed an implicit acknowledgment of Glasgow's second-rank status.

Problem number two: the physical environment. With the massive post–Robbins Report expansion of British universities in the 1960s and 1970s, nearly all of them embarked on ambitious construction programs. Glasgow was by no means alone in this. But few other universities started off with anything approaching the grandeur and unity of the Gilmorehill campus. During Hetherington's reign, which ended in 1961, university planners largely respected the existing structure and scale of the architecture. But in the 1960s and 1970s, that harmony was shattered by monstrosities of New Brutalism, such as the miserable brick-and-concrete Adam Smith Building for the social sciences, the mean-spiritedness of which would surely have made its eponym weep. Most dreadful was the new eleven-story university library built in 1965–68 on a site on the summit of Gilmorehill made available by the demolition of Victorian row houses. I feel deeply about this, since the third floor of the library occupies air space that formerly constituted my bedroom on the upper floor of 13 Bute Gardens.

The university tore the heart out of the surrounding area of domestic architecture just as the new municipal tower blocks, designed by Sir Basil Spence, that replaced the old tenements in the redeveloped Gorbals tore the heart out of that working-class community and created instant new slums. Some of these were so dreadful that they were demolished barely two decades later. The university, unfortunately, did not follow suit. Only toward the end of the twentieth century did it and the city fully recognize the catastrophic series of mistakes that had been made and begin to build in a less destructive and barbaric style—as in the case of the justly acclaimed new medical-faculty building opened by the university in 2002 and the award-winning Crown Street regeneration project in the Gorbals, designed by Piers Gough, the first stage of which was constructed between 1993 and 2000.

To the defects of parochialism and architectural philistinism were added a third, of particular interest to historians and literary scholars, the unfortunate consequence of another decision taken more than a century earlier. In 1836, the university surrendered a privilege, which it had enjoyed under the Copyright Act since 1709, of the right to demand a free copy of any book published in Britain. In return for the surrender, the library was allowed by the government a compensation fund for book purchases amounting to £707 per annum. Even at Victorian prices, that was a colossal blunder. Thus it came about that Glasgow University Library, founded in 1451, today holds about two million books, whereas the University of Chicago Library, founded in 1892 holds eight million—or for a comparison closer to home, the library of Trinity College, Dublin, which did not commute the privilege and, extraordinarily as now a non-British institution, retains it to this day, holds four million. Here too, perhaps, we have a parable for Glasgow's more general failure as a city until too late to recognize and exploit existing competitive advantages.

OUR RESIDENCE AT THE DOORSTEP of my father's workplace meant that, in a sense, I went to university before I went to school. I certainly felt equally at home in both. The High School of Glasgow, which I attended between 1954 and 1960, is one of the oldest schools in Britain, founded in 1123, originally as the cathedral choir school. It is the only school in Britain, apart from Eton, to have produced more than one Prime Minister in the twentieth century: Campbell-Bannerman and Bonar Law. The school's four houses were named after its most distinguished former pupils: Bannerman; Law; Sir John Moore, hero of the battle of Corunna in the Peninsular War; and Lord Clyde, another military man, better known as Sir Colin Campbell, a commander in the Sikh War, the Crimean War, and the Indian Mutiny. The school song encouraged us to take inspiration from these heroes of the past:

> O, Alma Mater, glorious,
> So great, so grave, so good,
> We hail thy name victorious
> With joy, with gratitude.

In my day, the school had a curious and unusual status: it was run by the Glasgow Corporation, but unlike other corporation schools, it charged fees and operated selective entrance procedures. Perhaps reflecting the Labour-controlled corporation's ambivalence at this ideological anomaly, the fees were lower than those charged by fully private schools: the charge was £23.2s. per session, compared with £81 at Glasgow Academy. Although the high school still reaped an impressive tally of academic honors, I had a vague feeling that its best years were behind it, although I did not suspect that it might not be long for the world. A decade after I left, the city council decided that maintenance of a fee-paying school was repugnant to its principles. After a vigorous tussle, during which it almost closed altogether, the school seceded from municipal control in 1976 and became a private, fee-paying entity. Relocated to its spacious sports grounds at Anniesland on the western edge of the city, close to the suburbs of Bearsden and Milngavie, to which a large part of the Glaswegian middle class had migrated, it enjoyed immediate success, quickly reestablishing its reputation as one of the best schools in Scotland. Thus, doctrinaire rigidity, applied with insufficient regard to outcomes, reinforced rather than alleviated class differences—and that too is a parable for other self-defeating policies pursued by the local authority, particularly in regard to housing.

At least seventy out of the thousand or so pupils in the high school were Jewish, but I don't remember any Catholic presence at all. Most Catholic boys in the area attended St. Aloysius College, on nearby Garnethill. Around a quarter of the city's population was Catholic, descendants of the great Irish and Italian immigrations of the nineteenth and early twentieth centuries, but I don't recall consciously meeting a single Catholic in my nine years in Glasgow, except perhaps our cleaning lady, Mrs. McCluskey. Catholics and Protestants lived quite separate lives, went to separate schools, and, of course, supported different football clubs, Celtic and Rangers respectively. I do not know of any institution in the city that did not admit Jews (anti-Semitism was almost nonexistent in Scotland at the time), but the Western Baths, a private swimming club in the west end, notoriously would not admit Catholics.

Clifford Hanley, an acquaintance of my father and as a result the first real-life novelist I ever met, wrote in his autobiographical novel *Dancing in the Streets* in 1958 that Catholic-Protestant intermarriage was "a thing that goes on and on happening in Glasgow, in spite of the tuts of the ministers and the thunderings of the priests, and every time it does happen, Glasgow people shake their heads as if it was an original catastrophe, the first of its kind and the beginning of the end of the world." Actually, the intermarriage rate was still quite low in the 1950s, though it rose rapidly thereafter. In 1966, only 26 percent of Catholics who married in Glasgow wed non-Catholics; by 1977, 44 percent did so. A similar trend toward increased intermarriage was evident among Jews. The Glaswegian Jewish novelist Chaim Bermant, in his memoirs, recalls that his mother's entirely predictable first question when he telephoned her from London to report that he had decided to get married was, "Is she Jewish?" He replied in the affirmative, thereby immediately achieving, he writes, "all that a Jewish mother may reasonably expect of a Jewish son."[8]

Glasgow's fifteen thousand or so Jews in the 1950s were mostly second- or third-generation descendants of immigrants from Russia in the heyday of Glasgow's prosperity, between 1881 and 1914. The community was in many ways a microcosm of British Jewry as a whole. Whereas the latter had its paper of record in the shape of the venerable *Jewish Chronicle,* Glasgow had its own *Jewish Echo.* Heir to the daily *Yidishe Abendtsaytung,* founded by immigrant journalist Zvi Golombok before the First World War, and a monthly, the *Yidishe Shtimme,* founded in 1921, the *Echo* was established in 1928 and edited by Golombok until his death in 1954, whereupon his son Ezra took over. For a tiny provincial paper of a minuscule community, the *Echo* in the 1950s and 1960s was an impressive production, edited with flair by Golombok, who doubled for a time as the editor of *Scottish Opera News.* Bermant's first published pieces appeared in the *Echo.* At its peak in the 1950s, the paper's circulation reached 5,000. Thereafter, it gradually declined as the Jewish population dwindled. In the early 1960s, the *Echo* found itself thrust into a lilliputian press war when a disgruntled former employee set up a rival paper, backed by a few communal bigwigs. There was barely a market for one such paper, and the *Echo* soon saw off its competitor. The *Echo*'s editorial offices at 252 Crown Street, in the Gorbals, were the first newspaper offices I ever visited, and I found the smell of printer's ink a source of great excitement. Actually, I am now informed that the odor was not ink at all, since no actual printing took place there. The smell I recall probably came from molten metal in the linotype machines. Still, the whiff of Fleet Street was so inspirational that I decided to start my own newspaper in the high school, one impressively professional-looking issue of which Golombok produced for me on his press—my first venture into print.

We were members of Garnethill synagogue, the oldest in the city, opened in 1879, and the only one north of the Clyde. As in London, Leeds, and Manchester, the old Jewish immigrant area near the city center rapidly emptied in the early post-war period. The grim pre-war world of the Glasgow Jewish ghetto portrayed so vividly by Ralph Glasser in his bitter and moving autobiographical account, *Gorbals Boy* (1988), was disintegrating as the children and grandchildren of immigrants moved up the social ladder and out to suburbs such as Giffnock and Newton Mearns or, like Bermant, took the high road to England—in Glasser's case, to Oxford, though extreme poverty forced him to cycle all the way there.

Unlike the synagogues on the south side of the Clyde, where Yiddish remained the lingua franca until the inter-war period, Garnethill was a decorous, sometimes stuffy sanctuary that prized decorum and respectability. In the most prestigious pew of the congregation, wearing top hats, sat distinguished communal figures such as Lord Greenhill, a municipal worthy, and Sir Maurice Bloch, a whisky distiller. He had had the misfortune to be mentioned in the proceedings of the Lynskey Tribunal of 1948, which investigated government corruption. Bloch had made gifts (small-scale stuff—the odd hogshead of sherry) to a junior minister at the Board of Trade in the naïve hope of securing concessions regarding the importation of sherry casks.[9] He had not been prosecuted, and was permitted to retain his knighthood, but his name was erased from the list of Justices of the Peace. He spent the rest of his life atoning for his venial sin by making much larger gifts to worthier causes: Glasgow University, the Jewish Board of Guardians, the State of Israel—and me: I was one of the pupils in the Hebrew School who lined up to receive, from Sir Maurice himself, presentation copies of the Singer's prayer book, the back cover of each embossed with Sir Maurice's name in gold leaf to commemorate his generosity. I still possess the *siddur,* though I must confess I use it only rarely.

A symptom of what Freud calls the "narcissism of small differences" was the factionalism and petty communal quarrels that were faithfully recorded each week in the pages of the *Echo.* The most famous of these was the bitter feud between the two leading rabbis of the city: Kenneth Cosgrove, minister of Garnethill, and Wolf Gottlieb, head of the *Beth Din,* or rabbinical court of the city. As spiritual leader of the old-established "cathedral" synagogue, Cosgrove was the more anglicized of the two, one might almost say the more anglicanized, since he not only wore a dog collar but was maliciously and falsely reported to wear episcopal-style gaiters—a double offense (had the allegation been true) against both Jewish tradition and the Scottish prejudice against bishops. Cosgrove had earned a doctorate but not *semichah* (rabbinical ordination). Gottlieb, in consequence, refused to grant him membership in the Beth Din. While regarding himself as Orthodox, the clean-shaven Cosgrove took a more relaxed, modernist view of Jewish law than the bearded, strict-constructionist Gottlieb. The conflict took a number of symbolic forms. Thus it was, for example, that Garnethill was the only Orthodox synagogue in Glasgow, and one of the very few in the country, that boasted a mixed choir—in which I sang to the Lord in the company of female fellow sopranos and older and deeper male voices.

The rivalry between Cosgrove and Gottlieb was deeply acrimonious: they detested each other. At first it took the form of occasional disputes over common issues of contention in the post-war Jewish diaspora, especially concerning marriages and conversions. But shortly after we left Glasgow, the conflict came to a head as a local reflection of the so-called "Jacobs affair." This row pitted the British chief rabbi, Israel Brodie, who was backed by the Glasgow-born millionaire Isaac Wolfson, the boss of Great Universal Stores and lay head of the United Synagogue, the main federation of Orthodox communities, against Louis Jacobs, an Orthodox rabbi allegedly too liberal in outlook. Jacobs split away from the United Synagogue and founded his own congregation, tending toward the American centrist model of Conservative Judaism. Garnethill considered following Jacobs's lead. The fierce debate there attracted wide interest, since it was felt that if Garnethill too split from the chief rabbi, other communities would follow and an avalanche of defections might destroy the Orthodox dominance of British Jewry. The result of the vote, recorded in a banner headline in the *Jewish Echo,* was a very narrow defeat for the secessionists. Garnethill remained nominally within the Orthodox fold, but the congregation aged and dwindled. It survives today only as a tiny fraternity of elderly people.

In Glasgow, as elsewhere through much of their history, the Jews may be seen both as swallows whose arrival heralded socioeconomic spring and as rats whose departure indicated a sinking ship. The city's Jewish population has shrunk over the past half century, mainly through southward migration. Today it is less than a third of its size in the 1950s and has a very high age profile. The *Echo* closed in 1992, and many other Jewish institutions that gave the community cultural vibrancy in the 1950s, such as the Jewish Institute, the Avrom Greenbaum Players (a theatrical group whose fascinating archives are now in Glasgow University Library), and Geneen's kosher restaurant, have disappeared. The dozen or so synagogues of the 1950s have been reduced to six—and most of those have empty pews even on Yom Kippur (the Day of Atonement). On Saturday mornings, Garnethill can barely summon up a minyan (the quorum of ten men required for services). But its magnificent synagogue building has nevertheless found a new vocation as an archive center and historic monument. Here too, perhaps, we have a parable for the city in which it is embedded, which embraced its designation as European Cultural Capital of 1990 and as UK City of Architecture and Design in 1999 as opportunities for a new self-definition, rediscovery of its past, and, perhaps, a new beginning.

GLASGOW TODAY REMAINS A DEEPLY TROUBLED metropolis with terrible social problems. In 2006 there were said to be more criminal gangs in Glasgow than in London, a city more than twelve times its size. In March 2008, one-third of the entire population of Glasgow was reported to be subsisting on sickness benefits.[10] And the city still lives with the consequences of ruinous decisions taken in the 1960s and 1970s. One of those was the insensitive motorway construction that led, in the case of the Charing Cross area near the former high school, to what the late David Daiches described as almost "the destruction of a city in order to facilitate the means of reaching and leaving it." [11]

But there have also been other changes. The sharp edges of class consciousness and conflict that were so evident in my youth have softened. Kelvinside and the Gorbals are still different worlds, but they speak to each other, and their accents are no longer quite as different as they were in the 1950s: dialectologists at the university not so long ago reported that "Estuary English" (that is the Thames estuary), otherwise known as "Radio One English," has begun to infect all forms of Glaswegian, particularly among children, who now speak a new hybrid dialect known as "jockney." [12]

Some of the alleged improvements were empty puffery, like the "Glasgow's Miles Better" advertising campaign in 1983, promoted by a smiley cartoon figure, "Mr. Happy." Others had greater substance. The Clyde and the Kelvin, lifeless chemical cesspools in the 1950s, are now clean enough to support piscine and even human swimmers. And after decades of rat-infested dereliction, the old wharves and quays of the Clyde are being transformed with a £5.6 billion, fifteen-year regeneration plan for a new waterfront. Resuming its practice, in its glory days, of welcoming immigrants, Glasgow has not merely admitted a new generation of arrivals but has positively encouraged them, signing successive contracts with the government to take in asylum seekers. The latest official demographic estimates suggest that for the first time since the 1950s, the population has stabilized and may even be growing modestly.

Glasgow when I was a child was Britain's grimmest and most romantic city. Today it has shed much of the grime and most of the romance. In this brief trip down memory lane, I have tried to temper nostalgia with realism. But in the words of the city's unofficial anthem (inspired, according to its creator, Will Fyfe, by a drunk he met at the place where my own acquaintance with the city began, Central Station), I still feel that I belong to Glasgow and Glasgow belongs to me.

Spring Semester 2009

I am grateful to Ezra Golombok, Shirley Haasnoot, Colin Kidd, Ian Stewart Mac-Millan, Harold Strecker, and David Wasserstein for their help with this paper.

1. Daniel Defoe, *A Tour thro' the Whole Island of Great Britain* (London, 1738; 2nd ed.), Vol. III, p. 259.

2. The writer was Lewis Grassic Gibbon (also known as Leslie Mitchell) in Lewis Grassic Gibbon and Hugh MacDiarmid, *Scottish Scene; or, The Intelligent Man's Guide to Albyn* (London, 1936), p. 136.

3. Adrian Room, *Dictionary of Trade Name Origins* (London, 1983), p. 137. Room quotes a wartime variant by U.S. servicemen stationed in the UK: "They come as a boon and a blessing to men: the Blackout, the Torch, and the cute little W.R.E.N."

4. Sidney G. Checkland, *The Upas Tree: Glasgow, 1875–1975 and After, 1975–1980* (Glasgow, 1981; 2nd rev. ed.).

5. Oswyn Murray, *Times Literary Supplement,* 9 Feb. 2007.

6. Ibid.

7. Ibid.

8. Chaim Bermant, *Coming Home* (London, 1976), pp. 167–68.

9. *Parliamentary Debates,* Commons, 3 Feb. 1949, Vol. 460, cols. 1843–962.

10. *Sunday Times,* 30 Mar. 2008.

11. David Daiches, *Glasgow* (London, 1982), p. 246. Actually, Daiches wrote that it was *not* that: but he was a subtle writer and here clearly meant the opposite of what he wrote.

12. *The Times,* 20 Feb. 1999. But the researcher, Jane Stuart-Smith, later issued a semi-disclaimer; see http://www.phon.ucl.ac.uk/home/estuary/glasgow.htm

2

Historiographical Hazards
of Sixties Britain

BRIAN HARRISON

Any attempt to write the history of a decade is bound to fail. In Britain since the 1850s, most decades have lacked distinctiveness because they were fractured by war, political overturn, or both. In 1964, the sixties too experienced electoral overturn, but less in substantive policy than in the government's party label. In 1964 as in 1951, there was much continuity across the party political divide, and the sixties were at least as significant for social as for political change. Like the 1840s, the 1890s, the 1920s, the 1930s, and the 1980s, the sixties soon developed a distinctive image. Whereas the first and fourth of these decades came to symbolize scarcity and poverty, the other three symbolized rejection of hitherto prevailing convention. The 1980s discarded a constricting set of economic attitudes, whereas the 1890s and 1920s repudiated constricting conventions on morals and manners, and it is with the last two decades that the sixties belong. But even when a decade seems distinctive, its unity or coherence can be only retrospective: its history will concern not events as experienced, but subsequent attitudes to those events. Nobody living through the sixties, or through any other decade, could know that they were living through a distinctive period until they had got to the end of it. So the first sixties historiographical hazard is the danger of projecting on to sixties people a self-consciousness that they did not and could not experience. An additional hazard follows in each of the six sections that follow.

THE PHRASE "THE SIXTIES" CONJURES UP at least five images, each with a strong moralistic component. The first four are youth in revolt, relaxed manners, political radicalism, and puritanism repudiated. Puritanism is protean as a set of attitudes, however: it continuously evolves, and the sixties generated a "new puritanism" at least as austere as its precursor, with champions at least as self-righteous.[1] Yet if these images were relatively salient in the sixties, both individually and as a cluster, the second of the sixties hazards is to assume that such images were individually absent from other decades. All five appeared in Britain well before 1960. To age, youth is or seems perennially in revolt, and there are many earlier and later echoes of Lady St. Helier's complaint in 1909 that "society and modern life are run to-day on lines which conduce more to the enjoyment and amusement of the young people than of their elders."[2]

Here she brings the second sixties image into play: relaxed manners. A prolonged and cumulative erosion of aristocratic values undermined the formal manners and respect for privacy and hierarchy that had accompanied an earlier and relatively stable social hierarchy. In 1958, Earl Waldegrave referred in the House of Lords to the "terrible habit growing up among some of the young, whose response when asked to do or not to do something, respond with 'So what?'"[3] Already in the 1930s, relaxed discipline percolated from educational policy-makers hoping to harmonize with the libertarian and creative instincts spontaneously pushing up from below: the curriculum had to substitute "activity and experience" for accumulating and learning facts.[4] From there it was an easy though not necessary transition to the egalitarian idea that democracy entails repudiating "standards." The electronic media accelerated the process after the mid-1950s through pursuing "ratings," with the added attractions of informal manners and sometimes even recreational rudeness. "Anything properly done is out of date today," Harold Macmillan complained in his diary in 1954: "—like hand-made clothes or furniture, it is 'reactionary'. To finish your sentences; to put in verbs; to worry about neat turns of phrase or apt and appropriate adjectives—all this is 'undemocratic' and 'Victorian.'"[5] Even the new fashions seducing the young seemed at first disrespectful: the miniskirt, for example, which was promoted (from the mid-1960s) by fashion models who gloried in lacking what earlier generations called "background." Religion, too, was vulnerable. To the humanist public schoolboy of the 1960s, compulsory chapel seemed provocative: "During these years," wrote John Rae, Westminster School's headmaster from 1970 to 1986, "there were few headmasters who did not have to face some sort of protest in chapel."[6]

Political radicalism, the third of the sixties themes, also predates the 1960s. Although the Conservatives were continuously in government from 1951 to 1964, their pursuit of the center ground enabled the Labour Party and the labor movement to prescribe much of their agenda. Meritocratic values, owing much to the social radicalism of the Second World War, were invigorated by the Suez fiasco of 1956: "Suez, that was when we lost the intellectual vote," Iain Macleod recalled.[7] From the early 1960s, this radical mood moved toward its brief apogee at mid-decade before the disappointments and disillusionments of the Wilson government: devaluation, a failed National Plan, a divisive incomes policy, and further slippage in Britain's international status.

Puritanism repudiated, the fourth sixties theme, was also no novelty. From 1600 to 1660, Puritanism as a public attitude was advancing in England, and the term was eventually extended to denote "a member of any religious sect or party that advocates or aspires to special purity of doctrine or practice." After 1660, the dominant national outlook on personal conduct relaxed till the mid-eighteenth century. Then puritanism, in the sense of the public pursuit of purity in personal conduct, reappeared in force during the evangelical revival, only to go into reverse a century later. The First World War revived the ancient association between national self-defense and a puritan appeasement of the Almighty, which, after the hedonism of the 1920s, reappeared during the Second World War. Then in the 1950s, the hedonistic and materialistic reaction in Britain against wartime puritanism began. It owed much to American influences, and could not be neatly slotted into a single decade.

Fluctuations in attitudes to personal conduct are at least as central as economic fluctuations to a nation's daily experience, but are less easily measured. Yet if conduct could be precisely assessed, it would probably be revealed as more stable than public attitudes to it. Fluctuations in public attitudes masked a continuous culture of sexual liberation, at least for men, that had been amply exemplified in Victorian London's club land, home to "Walter," the author of the lengthy sexual diary *My Secret Life* (1888–94). To the 1960s, so liberated in public discussion, Walter's inquisitive and uninhibited outlook seemed "a significant anticipation of what is generally thought of as the modern, liberal, and liberated conception of sexual morality."[8] Then there was Bloomsbury, whose frankness on sexuality was advertised in 1967–68 by Michael Holroyd's two-volume biography of Lytton Strachey, and by the abundant material then accumulating on Virginia Woolf and her circle. The philosopher Bertrand Russell had been only on Bloomsbury's fringes, but his *Marriage and Morals* (1929) had been still more radical, though less widely discussed: moving beyond personal practice to universal prescription, it fearlessly drew out birth control's implications for the separation of sexuality from conception. Earlier feminists sought equality in sexuality through elevating male to female requirements of abstinence, but Russell sought the same end by a different route: through requirements as relaxed for women as for men. When in the early 1960s the contraceptive pill became widely available, women's segregation seemed less necessary, co-education could be extended, and (helped by the thalidomide tragedy) abortion could be more freely discussed. As for homosexuality, the Wolfenden report of 1957 built upon a long sequence of research and reflection that had been quietly educating opinion since the late Victorian period. So social change is not sudden, nor does it coincide precisely with arbitrary conventions for apportioning time: in both Britain and America, the twentieth-century permissive trend was continuous, and the 1920s and 1960s did no more than accelerate or publicize it.

The politicians were beginning to respond to the puritan retreat in other areas well before the 1960s. Calling in 1956 for Labour to move on from the personal austerities of the Webbs, Anthony Crosland, in his influential *The Future of Socialism*, urged a "greater emphasis on private life, on freedom and dissent, on culture, beauty, leisure, and even frivolity"; heightened exports and old-age pensions might be needed, but so also were "more open-air cafés, brighter and gayer streets at night, later closing-hours for public houses, more local repertory theatres."[9] Harold Macmillan, conscious as Chancellor of the Exchequer (1955–57) and then as Prime Minister (1957–63) of the need for the Conservatives to hold the middle ground, prompted a sequence of reforms, from the introduction of premium bonds to the relaxation of licensing laws; if, on occasion, Macmillan held back, his colleague R. A. Butler pressed further forward. And where the political parties feared to tread, backbenchers and writers (Roy Jenkins, Leo Abse, David Steel, Sydney Silverman, J. B. Priestley, Victor Gollancz, and Arthur Koestler, to name only a few) were advancing the antipuritan frontiers in such areas as censorship, abortion, illegitimacy, suicide, and capital punishment.

The fifth sixties image, not clearly distinct from the fourth, draws them all together: the "new" puritanism that succeeded the old. Two polarities must be distinguished here. The distinction between hedonism and puritanism old-style concerned attitudes to personal conduct, whereas the "new" puritans were distinguished from the hedonists by their political priorities, which nourished a reproachful, sectarian, and intense defense of sixties values. With shams torn aside, a painful honesty became the vogue, confronting consciences with sudden crises and imperiled careers. The mood of a movement of the late 1950s, the Campaign for Nuclear Disarmament (CND), chimed in with erosion in the hierarchies that had grown out of war and empire. These now retreated before a new romanticism that was more egalitarian and participatory in nature. What the sixties achieved for the UK was to concentrate and advertise all five sixties images, thereby carrying them to a higher power.

A THIRD SIXTIES HISTORIOGRAPHICAL HAZARD involves exaggerating the significance of national boundaries. Even the 1920s acquired a "permissive" image in both America and Britain: still more so the sixties, given the massive intervening growth in cross-cultural communication through the media. Sixties images owe much to U.S. shaping of British youth culture from the 1940s through the mass media, mass politics, and a preoccupation with civil rights. Colin MacInnes noted in 1957 how British pop singers aiming at prowess in the charts had become bilingual, "speaking American at the recording session, and English in the pub round the corner afterwards."[10] American priorities on civil rights influenced the outlook and tactics of the CND, the temporarily diminished enthusiasm after 1964 for the British majoritarian approach to democracy, and, later in the decade, the transfer (seldom appropriate) of American student priorities to British universities. In his parliamentary attack on American graduate-student leaders of the strike then disrupting the London School of Economics, the Minister of Education, Edward Short, pointed out (to cheers) how small was the radical minority, "the thugs of the academic world": out of 3,000 students, 300 were activists, fewer than 30 led them, and (to "renewed cheers") at least 4 of those, subsidized by the British taxpayer, came "from the United States."[11]

Germany was an overseas influence that, through Berthold Brecht, had by then long since breached the cozy country-house conventions of the London stage, which had dominated the early 1950s. The descent upon London of the Berliner Ensemble in 1956 with *Mother Courage* and *The Caucasian Chalk Circle* dissolved the distinction between the musical and the well-made play, and promoted the sixties virtues of political commitment and preoccupation with big issues; this carried further the sincerity and spontaneity of Stanislavsky's "method" acting, which had arrived from Russia via the United

States. Scandinavia, too, was a major influence during the sixties on areas as disparate as design, governmental structures, and sexuality. "If we want contemporary design," Viscount Samuel told the Lords in June 1964, "we must go to Scandinavia. The word 'modern' to-day is largely taken by buyers and consumers to mean Scandinavian."[12] British negotiations to enter the European Economic Community enhanced respect for European political institutions, and both France and Sweden strongly influenced British civil-service reform plans of the 1960s: Swedish open government, ombudsmen, and agencies won a new respect, as did the French civil service's professionalism and meritocratic structures. As for sexuality, Denmark was prominent among the countries supplying pornography to Britain in the 1960s, and was important for edging what was then called the National Council for the Unmarried Mother and Her Child toward including all one-parent families. The House of Commons debate on maintenance orders in 1967 prompted reactionary thoughts from some Conservative MPs. "I hope that we shall not introduce a Scandinavian society here," said Ronald Bell. More forthright was Quintin Hogg: "Sweden should be abolished."[13] The "days of May" in 1968, followed by de Gaulle's departure, however, helped to moderate hitherto uncritical enthusiasm for French governmental institutions and for Marxian glamorization of revolution while simultaneously reinvigorating Britons' long-standing tendency to congratulate themselves on political continuity.

National boundaries were irrelevant for the diffusion of sixties images at a second level, for within the UK their reception was highly diverse. The chronology and geography of change in each dimension of national life proceed at their own pace; only clumsily can the politician, the administrator, the lawyer and the opinion former coordinate opinion behind practical responses. Sixties values seem to have gained more support from the young and the middle-class living in the southeast than elsewhere. When Philip Larkin (writing from Hull) read Christopher Booker's *Neophiliacs* (1969), subtitled *A Study of the Revolution in English Life in the Fifties and Sixties,* "it made me realise how little in touch I have been w[ith] the world since 1945. I don't think I have ever read a copy of *Private Eye,* seen a performance of *Beyond the Fringe, That Was The Week That Was,* or whatever David Frost does. I have registered the Beatles and the mini-skirt, but that's about all."[14] It was from Birmingham in 1964 that the Midlands schoolteacher Mary Whitehouse launched her campaign to clean up TV; many years later, she recalled that on sexual permissiveness, "a very small group of people with particular determination and commitment found sympathy within broadcasting and had the opportunity to express themselves . . . At the same time you had a silencing, a censoring by ignoring, of the other voices in the country which could have put them into proportion."[15]

Minorities inevitably gravitate to the big city, especially when liable to persecution, and in London they could combine a safe anonymity with searching out others displaying like proclivities. As the journalist Anne Sharpley pointed out in 1964, "time and again homosexuals have told me the relief and delight they felt at first coming to London from country districts to find 'there were hundreds like me, all more than understanding.'"[16] It has been claimed that "the British drug scene of the 1960s was overwhelmingly a London scene," and it was from London that the BBC under Hugh Carleton Greene risked offending provincial sensibilities through working with the grain of "Swinging London."[17] Minority fashions, too, had their best chance if launched from London, whose latest innovations were promoted from Carnaby Street and Chelsea's King's Road. It was to London, too, that the Beatles inevitably gravitated when seeking national fame; Lennon recalled that when later returning to Liverpool, they "worried that friends might think we'd sold out. Which we had, in a way."[18]

HENCE THE FOURTH HAZARD: that preoccupation with sixties values will conceal the equal-and-opposite reaction that they evoked, whether regionally or not. It would have been surprising if no such reaction had occurred, given that sixties values threatened to reshape the intimacies of day-to-day private life. Gallup polls illuminate such controversy. Asked in 1965 whether schools should require boys to keep their hair cut short, the noes were outnumbered by 5 to 1; asked in 1966 whether homosexual behavior, if conducted between men aged 21 or older in private, should be a criminal act, 44 percent of the sample thought it should, 39 percent thought not.[19] The protesting tone of Bishop John Robinson might have caught public attention, but the "grating voice" of this enfant terrible became "rather more grating" to those who heard him in Anglican assemblies.[20] It is salutary to be reminded that whereas the most popular of the Beatles albums, *Please Please Me,* was in the top ten for forty-three weeks, *South Pacific* was in the top place for forty-six weeks, and was in the top ten for more than three years; it is also probably correct to say that "during the supposedly radical sixties, the majority of Britain's fifty million people led quiet and somewhat dull sex lives, with one or two sexual partners over a lifetime."[21] Many who were not just nonplayers or indifferent bystanders at the sixties game were (like Mary Whitehouse) infuriated by it.

On the cultural front, Noel Coward was a vituperative critic, and for *The Times* in May 1970, commenting on an interruption when the Foreign Secretary addressed the Oxford Union, declared that "the extreme student left is at its worst one of the nastiest political phenomena that Britain has experienced in this century."[22]

Sixties reformers themselves testified to the opposition's strength by tacking on to their reforms constraints that would ease them through Parliament. Opponents of pornography ensured that the Obscene Publications Act (1959) accompanied its newfound freedoms with an enhanced power to search, seize, and destroy. The law was tightened up further in 1964, and several high-profile prosecutions circumscribed the triumph in 1960 of *Lady Chatterley*. Likewise the Licensing Act (1961) accompanied relaxed opening hours with raised penalties for drunkenness. For all its benefits to women, the Abortion Act (1967) entrenched the medical profession's powers: male doctors rather than female backstreet abortionists were henceforth the gatekeepers, deploying their expertise to retain and even extend their discretion. And while the Sexual Offences Act (1967) legalized homosexual acts in private, it tightened up restrictions on what could be done in public. Its aim was to replace public control by self-control, leaving the respectably discreet undisturbed but complicating the lives of those who lacked privacy: in 1967–77, the recorded incidence of indecency between males roughly doubled, and the number prosecuted trebled. Opposition successfully blocked some sixties proposals for reform, two of them in 1968, for example: the private member's bill to establish a national lottery, and the recommendation by Lady Wootton's committee to legalize cannabis. The committee's aim was to shield those who used "soft" drugs from drifting into illegality and hence getting ensnared by traders in harder drugs. James Callaghan, playing to the gallery as Home Secretary, found himself in alliance with Quintin Hogg when calling for a halt "in the advancing tide of so-called permissiveness."[23]

A FIFTH HAZARD LIES IN THE THREAT to the historian's prized objectivity from the fact that the sixties reforms have remained controversial ever since. This is partly because the five components of sixties values by no means disappeared in 1970, and partly because Conservatives occasionally hoped to benefit by attacking them. During the 1970s, feminists, sexual minorities, and defenders of sixties reforms came out into the streets when Christians of the evangelical and Roman Catholic varieties attacked them. On 9 and 25 September 1971, protest groups in London disrupted the Festival of

Light demonstrations against moral pollution, and in Liverpool on 30 April 1972, scuffles between feminists and anti-abortionists left the anti-abortionist procession "silent and implacable."[24] Most novelists in the 1970s and early 1980s who wrote about the sixties were hostile, especially Malcolm Bradbury in *The History Man,* which he wrote in a depressed mood and later saw as "certainly my bleakest book."[25] He had earlier been "pretty sympathetic" to radical movements, but "my rising sympathy with sixties radicalism became more and more qualified."[26]

The Conservatives in 1969–70, still pursuing the center ground, conducted no sustained assault on sixties values, which were not discussed in the party's manifesto: only 2 percent of Conservative candidates in 1970 opposed the "permissive society" in their election addresses.[27] Moral reform was still then seen as a nonparty area, but in May 1969, Quintin Hogg already scented the potential for Conservatives of appealing to law-and-order traditionalism. Electors could be confronted by a frightening package: "We are fed up with the drug peddlers, the sex exploiters, the wildcat strikers, the parasitical students who live on Government grants for work they do not do and insult as irrelevant the elected representatives of the people who provide the money. We are tired of lecturers who support lawlessness and university authorities who cannot keep order."[28] Norman Tebbit, too, was early in the field. His speech when standing in 1969 for selection at Epping as a Conservative candidate expressed "the heart of my political beliefs," he recalled. There he condemned the "permissive society," whose sexual dimension he thought "part of a cycle of fashion" that would "turn back before long," with pornography becoming "a bore."[29] By the mid-1980s, Tebbit's attack had become shriller: linking bad art, bad grammar and bad spelling to contempt for family life, he referred to "the era and attitudes of post-war funk" as having given birth to the "permissive society," which, "in turn, generated today's violent society."[30] In the following year, he thought the permissive society had become a "poisoned legacy" for which socialists could offer no remedy: "sympathy for wrongdoers" had "slipped towards sympathetic tolerance of the wrong itself. Love for the sinner slipped into love of the sin."[31] In the course of rebutting the Church of England's report of 1985 on the inner cities, Kenneth Baker attacked sixties values from a rather different direction, associating them with the well-intentioned welfarist public expenditures that had created the moral desert of a council-owned, council-run, ill-designed, slum-cleared "mad folly of comprehensive redevelopment." Baker's aim was to throw the socialist enemy on to the defensive by demonstrating that "injudicious public expenditure," far from constituting a solution, could become "a cause of the problem." This morally damaging environment was man-made and deliberate: "The bulldozer relentlessly wiped out familiar neighbourhoods and whole communities. We lost the essential warp and weft of family relationships and friendship."[32]

Such a stance offered Conservatives some hope of detaching Labour's traditionalist mass following from its high-minded, progressive, middle-class humanitarians while harvesting recruits for a low-tax, libertarian program. Unsurprisingly, Margaret Thatcher took up Baker's architectural theme in her party conference speech of 1987 with an attack on "the worst form of post-war town planning—a sort of social vandalism, carried out with the best of intentions but the worst of results." The prizewinning architectural schemes were, she said, "a nightmare for the people," cutting them off from neighbors, making unsafe homes for children, discouraging enterprise, and foisting both crime and dependence on the local authority.[33] Her attack on the sixties ranged far more widely. Already by March 1982 she was assaulting "the fashionable theories and permissive claptrap" that, she claimed, undermined "the old virtues of discipline and self-restraint": the attacks on the police by Labour leaders, the teachers striking for higher pay, the trade unionists explaining away theft, the councillors urging people not to pay full fares. "The time for counter-attack is long overdue," she said; "we are reaping what was sown in the sixties."[34] Throughout the 1980s, her speeches repeatedly touched upon the need for schools and parents to inculcate politeness and discipline, conjoined with a populist attack on the sixties for subverting such conduct. "This business of breaking the rules began in universities," she told the *Daily Mail* in April 1988, "where most of these theoretical philosophies always start. They never start with ordinary people"; the young people who embraced them "did a whole generation a great disservice."[35] In her interview of 1987 with *Woman's Own*, usually "distorted beyond recognition" by being truncated and quoted out of context, she championed mutual responsibility within a pluralist society: "It's our duty to look after ourselves and then, also, to look after our neighbour."[36] In her last address as leader to the Conservative Party conference, in October 1990, she once more tried, while discussing educational aims and methods, to tar Labour with the sixties brush: "Labour's tattered flag is there for all to see, limp in the stale breeze of sixties ideology."[37] Recalling the political climate of the sixties in her autobiography, she saw British society as having "entered a sick phase of liberal conformism passing as individual self-expression. Only progressive ideas and people were worthy of respect by an increasingly self-conscious and self-confident media class."[38]

Yet what is surprising about Thatcher's attack on the sixties is how restrained it was, especially by American standards. There were several explanations. First, many in her own party, including her mentor, Sir Keith Joseph, had at the time gone along with many sixties fashions. Her subsequent self-distancing from her predecessors' centrist strategies would, if too forcible, stir up trouble with colleagues. More importantly, by the 1980s strong vested interests had grown up round the changed family patterns that sixties values had fostered: Conservatives, with public opinion doubtful about their economic strategy and with what then seemed a serious centrist challenge from the Social Democratic Party, could not risk making unnecessary enemies. Furthermore, because secularization had proceeded much further in Britain than in the United States, Conservatives feared getting too close to overtly Christian pressure groups—Catholic anti-abortionists, moralistic evangelicals, and the like—nor was Muslim restiveness under the newly established British family patterns sufficiently articulate or electorally powerful to compensate. Whereas Conservatives had in practice been attacking the culture of the "underclass" throughout the decade, the word had not yet been imported from America in this sense, and when Charles Murray's campaign did impinge on Britain after 1990, its American moralistic edge was blunted.

The drawbacks of John Major's "back to basics" platform in 1993 illustrated the dangers. John Redwood, the Welsh Secretary, in a speech on 2 July urged the need for children to be brought up within a two-parent family, and for fathers to assume "their natural responsibilities." Immediately running into difficulties, he explained that he wanted teenagers pressed "to form suitable relationships before having children," and expressed himself "surprised this is a radical suggestion. Any politician saying otherwise 30 years ago would have been hounded out of public life."[39] Major did not pick up the danger signals. When launching the "back to basics" strategy at his party conference on 8 October, he championed "sound money; free trade; traditional teaching; respect for the family and the law," with an overriding campaign against crime, and "did not think of the speech as remotely controversial."[40] Conservatives were soon pressed, however, on whether the campaign entailed a crusade for individual sexual morality, and could hardly deny it. The strategy then became embarrassingly vulnerable to every alleged moral lapse by a Conservative politician. In truth, the aim had been far more limited, as Major later explained: "I was seeking to articulate a mood in society at large which had lost confidence in the permissive, politically-correct, value-free society which had its roots in the Sixties."[41] The strategy "set out to confront and overturn a range of ideas that had led policy—in crime, health, schools, social work—down blind alleys" to the point that "professional wisdom had become divorced from public sentiment and from reality."[42] Redwood and others at the party conference in 1993 soon got into further difficulty by questioning whether unmarried mothers should receive priority for council housing. When Archbishop Carey defended the mothers, Redwood hoped Carey would share his view that "there is a small minority who need encouraging to form stable relationships and marriages before having children," given that this, "I would have thought, is also good Christian doctrine."[43]

As for Labour, its MPs had in the 1960s been more closely aligned with sixties values, but individually rather than collectively. The party had distanced itself from the necessary nonparty legislation and did not later think it would benefit by rising to its defense, especially given the party's ongoing moralistic traditionalism. The reaction against the sixties was among the Conservative rhetorical devices that Tony Blair imported into his speeches when seeking the center ground as Labour leader after 1994, though he showed none of Thatcher's virulence when doing so. Explaining in June 1995 "why the Left has been losing general elections for the last 16 years," he espoused what was in effect a "back to basics" policy on teaching methods, though without using the phrase.[44] Seeking in 2004 to strengthen social discipline within the inner city, Blair urged an end to "the 1960s liberal, social consensus on law and order," and that resources be switched from offender to victim. A "society of different lifestyles spawned a group of young people who were brought up without parental discipline, without proper role models and without any sense of responsibility for others," but now "people have had enough of this part of the 1960s consensus. . . . They . . . want rules, order and proper behaviour. They want a community where the decent law-abiding majority are in charge."[45] These were sentiments highly acceptable to the *Daily Telegraph,* for which the sixties were "a low, dishonest decade," but even the *Telegraph* was keen to move on: "Rather than making a scapegoat of the 1960s, we need to learn from its mistakes."[46]

"THE LAW TOUCHES US BUT HERE and there, and now and then," wrote Edmund Burke in 1796. "Manners are what vex or sooth [*sic*], corrupt or purify, exalt or debase, barbarize or refine us, by a constant, steady, uniform, insensible operation, like that of the air we breathe in. They give their whole form and colour to our lives. According to their quality, they aid morals, they supply them, or they totally destroy them."[47] A sixth sixties hazard lies in the difficulty of precisely locating or dating where some of the most significant shifts occurred. Such changes are gradual, anonymous, initially unobtrusive, and only half conscious—at least until they have accumulated sufficient force to evoke comment. Their historian will thirst for dates, names, and events, but will rarely find them.

At the level of social convention, the etiquette book is a poor guide to conduct at the best of times, but in periods when "manners" are repudiated, this major historical source dries up. We know that from the 1950s onward, the sportsman's respect for the rules, his style of play, and his relations with spectators were changing: how can these be adequately documented? Philologists detect long-term twentieth-century changes in how words are pronounced, and most notably the late-century rise of "Estuary English": how, when, and why did this occur?[48] As for shifts in attitudes to privacy and familiarity, Stephen Spender knew well enough that during his lifetime the young had become far bolder in phoning up the famous.[49] There were marked but imprecisely dated changes in the occasions when people could address one another by first names: Leonard Woolf dated the relaxation to the Edwardian years, but among Oxford undergraduates, the transition was still in progress in the 1940s, though by the late 1960s it had become "almost universal."[50] Still less clear is the significance of this change for social-class, sex, and friendship relations. By 1974, this informality had consolidated sufficiently for the politician's dates to become relevant. At its Cabinet meeting of 5 March 1974, the Labour government adopted Tony Benn's earlier suggestion that ministers should address one another by first name; according to Barbara Castle, "Harold [Wilson] was soon calling on 'Michael' [Foot] to give us his report on the mining dispute. The whole atmosphere seemed transformed by that simple gesture."[51]

The fashion among middle-class schoolboys and students for adopting working-class speech patterns and (as far as they dared) clothing can at least be vaguely dated to the late 1960s and early 1970s, but who knows how the habit spread or why? We know that fashions even for men became far more diverse in the 1960s, when uniforms and most occupational types of clothing went out of fashion, but it would be hazardous to link such changes with the decline of empire, though commercialization must at some level be relevant. Trends in the wearing of beards have been scrupulously documented from the evidence provided by the *Illustrated London News* from 1842 to 1972—evidence that brings out the distinctiveness in the late 1950s and early 1960s of the CND's bearded supporters. Frank Parkin thought it "fair to claim that the decision to grow a beard may be taken as a token of the individual's desire to make a personal statement about himself and his individuality—that he is not to be equated with the common herd."[52] Perhaps the most notable among the unplanned, only half explicable sixties changes was the retreat of the national anthem from public gatherings: was respect for the Queen better preserved by persisting with it amid a flurry of upturned seats and reachings for hats, or by reserving it for special occasions? From theatres, cinemas, and concert halls, it was in the late 1960s on the way out in two senses. The decline of empire and the associated decline of respect for hierarchy may explain its disuse at one level, but so does the race to be first out of the parking lot.

Perhaps most elusive among the changes culminating in the sixties occurred in that no-man's-land between history and political theory that Bernard Crick called "the theories of the untheoretical . . . the general prejudices or principles by which even the most practical men, consciously or unconsciously, select from the infinity of possible facts to make some order out of their environment."[53] Especially striking was the increasingly utilitarian and pragmatic mood shaping public debate on moral questions. Integral to it was the high contemporary prestige of the natural and social sciences, but behind that were secularizing trends going far back. With ample backing from admired intellectuals—Bertrand Russell, A. J. Ayer, Karl Popper, Isaiah Berlin, Barbara Wootton—the humanitarian reforms of the 1960s rested on no overarching contemporary text, and were seldom articulated in abstract terms; the supportive argument emerges from rival approaches to particular issues. For example, from the 1940s to the 1960s the debates on abolishing hanging and legitimizing abortion saw utilitarian styles of argument gaining ground over preoccupation with principle. On 24 March 1969, *The Times,* discussing the debate on euthanasia (which it opposed), thought an absolute morality condemning the taking of human life in all circumstances no longer universal. Hence the need "to examine the proposal from a moral position closer to that of its proponents. From that point of view human happiness, the avoidance of suffering, compassion, and the full realization of human capacities are the chief goods to be sought in inter-personal behaviour." Sixties humanitarians placed the immediate and tangible happiness and welfare of the individual human being at the center of their universe, and to this they subordinated long-term and less predictable social priorities, let alone transcendent but intangible and speculative theological concerns; indeed, they wished to dispense with the clergyman as a guide to social and moral conduct altogether. Their combination of empirical research and logical reasoning emphasized the sheer complexity of moral decision making and—to quote *Sex and Morality* (1966), the influential report to the British Council of Churches—"the new psychology has . . . focussed attention on immediate personal relationships, so that we now tend to think of the individual primarily as child, lover, friend or parent, rather than as citizen or creature with responsibilities to society at large and to God."[54]

THE SEVENTH AND FINAL HAZARD for the historian lies in the limited reach of sixties rationality in crucial areas. The lack of any literary classic to encapsulate sixties values for posterity reflects the decade's predominantly populist and classless pursuit of popular culture. In important areas, it favored the ephemeral, the oral, the visual, the communal, the irrational, and even the surreal. The written word, by contrast, wrote George Melly, "represents permanence of a sort. Thought is trapped there . . . A man who reads is alone with the author. A serious book demands sustained concentration: the retention of an argument."[55] There is a serious shortage of reflective, lucid, balanced, and sustained published discussions of such subjects as popular music, design, the arts, youth culture, sport, and even radical protest. Nigel Whiteley, discussing Pop design in the 1960s, claims that "Pop produced few theoretical statements. Indeed, some writers have remarked on Pop's anti-articulate and often anti-literate character"; it rejected the Modernist's scientific rationalism.[56] Indeed, together with pop music, it interacted with the drug culture, whose classless pursuit of living for the day did not seek permanence of any kind.

Irrationality so extreme and yet parasitic tended to inspire a furious irrationality in its critics too, as Barbara Wootton realized when trying to introduce reason into the highly emotional debate on regulating cannabis sales. "The causes for this hysteria are quite familiar to students of social psychology," she declared. "They . . . are always liable to occur when the public senses that some critical and objective study threatens to block an outlet for indulgence in the pleasures of moral indignation."[57] Likewise with sixties political radicalism, especially in student politics. Given that the meritocratic and rationalistic attack on amateurism, and the desire to mobilize the masses against "the system," were central to the radical protest of the decade, there was a deep irony in the fact that the protesters adopted so dilettante an approach to the political process. Tactically, they could often be sophisticated and dedicated, but in strategy, they could be almost willfully counterproductive. Sixties student politicians operated from narrowly schismatic groupuscules with visions and aspirations that were so impracticably broad that the man in the street felt better represented by the established political parties, however inadequately.

The student politician's self-regarding eagerness to take a stand on all the big issues, along with his zest for commitment to principle, showed all too little concern with practical consequences. Seeking freedom and experiment in personal life, he sought conformity in intellectual matters, shunning coalitions and banning or barracking disapproved speakers. "Is truth so weak that it has to be aided by the forceful suppression of argument?" asked the distinguished psychologist H. J. Eysenck, physically attacked in May 1973 as an alleged racist when delivering a lunchtime lecture at the London School of Economics.[58] Intolerance was yoked to terrorism. The "Angry Brigade" emerged from North London communes of young people with European revolutionary (especially Situationist) connections in the late 1960s, and abandoned any attempt to influence either politicians or their constituents.[59] This short-lived, pale British imitation of West Germany's Baader-Meinhof terrorist gang planted twenty-five bombs in all, including bombs at the houses of two Cabinet ministers; nineteen of them exploded. Its convicted leaders were drawn from radical students who were disillusioned with the Wilson government, who had dropped out from university into welfare and protest movements, and who felt completely alienated from established institutions. The brigade's leaders, the *Guardian* pronounced, "have yet to demonstrate even one of the three basic ingredients of a viable political group: a coherent philosophy; an intelligible analysis of the present system; or a coherent social programme of its own."[60]

There could be little dialogue between radicals of this type and the more constructive radicals of the 1930s, now influential. In 1968, Isaiah Berlin felt that "the revolutionaries of my day had some respect for knowledge and intelligence and tried to learn from the enemy . . . This generation is complacently ignorant, uses mechanical formulae to dispose of anything that may be difficult or complicated, hates history on the whole, wishes to throw off the past."[61] In May 1968, R. H. S. Crossman, Secretary of State for Health and Social Security, felt depressed that the fashion for revolution seemed to be superseding his lifelong parliamentarism: the "new forces from below . . . have little care for the concept of parliamentary democracy as we know it."[62] In February 1969, he thought the new generation of youthful idealists less capable than its precursors of fruitful dialogue with the authorities: they were mere "sentimentalists with no understanding of power," obstructing reform by "adopting revolutionary methods but without any prospect of a revolution."[63] The protesters, when concerned with university matters, merely alienated the ministers of education deploying public funds and frustrated private fund-raising.

The more seasoned spokesmen of left-wing protest gave little help. Little could be learned from the so-called angry young men of the 1950s, given their indignant but marginal and ultimately marginalized repudiation of the manners, language, and symbols of class. In his trenchant survey (1960) of fifties socialist literature, Bernard Crick found the strident and self-righteous essays Norman Mackenzie collected in *Conviction* (1958) "embarrassing, superficial, and in parts, alas, even silly." Like E. P. Thompson's New Left collection *Out of Apathy* (1960), the book gave less attention to making converts than to point-scoring among the converted. Practicalities and the art of politics (always of major concern to British Labour's pioneers) were neglected and even despised. Thompson's collection, said Crick, "represents a complete rejection of political values. All is denunciation and sectarian polemic. It is, brothers, the revolution or nothing."[64] A Marxian indifference to the means that would advance the (ill-defined) end, and a preference for theory rather than practicalities, pervaded much socialist writing in the sixties. Thompson held his nose while fastidiously reviewing Harold Wilson's *The Labour Government, 1964–70* (1971): it was "a record of one accident and eventuality after another trooping into the cabinet room," so that "one rises from this book with an enhanced contempt for parliamentarians."[65] The universities were not dependable as allies of reason. When George Carmody, his student at Watermouth University, asks the somewhat sinister sociology professor Howard Kirk in Bradbury's *The History Man* (1975) whether he must share his views in order to pass his course, the reply is equivocal: "It's not required, George. But it might help you see some of the problems inside this society you keep sentimentalizing about"[66].

When the protesters did receive sensible advice—from the seasoned feminist Mary Stocks, for example, in 1973—they were unlikely to accept it: "If Women's Lib will keep off sex, and avoid joining in processions and demonstrations which include anarchists, Maoists, Trotskyites, gay people, student bodies, strikers and other such irrelevant groups who do no good to their 'image', much remains for them to do for the cause which they (and I) have at heart."[67] "Antony Grey," who had done so much for homosexual law reform, found the Gay Liberation Front counterproductive: "Street theatre, however spectacular," he wrote, "is no substitute for the prosaic, colourless daily grind of political persuasion which in the end depends upon knowledge, competence, integrity and good repute. Self-discipline, though sometimes tedious and frustrating, is necessary in personal, social and political life."[68] The Fabians' anti-histrionic prescription for political success needed to be relearned.

In the outcome, the authorities once more applied the well-tried devices of conciliation and participation, lowering the voting age and the age of majority to eighteen in 1969 and co-opting leading figures within the National Union of Students. The more extreme forms of sixties irrationality could then be left slowly but ineluctably to cure themselves. The retreat from reason through the growing media-inspired cult of publicity and celebrity, however, was more insidious, and alarmed two close observers of the political scene in 1968: Richard Crossman and Tony Benn. The trivialization of politics through the advance of visual over oral and written comment prompted sensationalism, an undue preoccupation with gossip, and a fragmented attention span, they claimed.[69] Instead of fuller and more considered treatment of important (rather than merely topical) issues, said Benn, "almost all we see of trade union or business leaders are hurried little street interviews when they are pinned against a wall by a battery of accusing microphones, wielded by interrogators who have just come from covering an air crash and are on their way to the hospital where some quins have been born."[70]

In the late 1950s, ITV had set out to break with the BBC's undue deference and publicly to subject politicians to House of Commons–style irreverence, and the BBC followed suit. In such a climate, cynicism about politics made strides. In his Worsley speech of 1972, Roy Jenkins found "cynicism about politics and politicians . . . already widespread"; democracy would benefit only if Labour dissociated itself from seeing politics "as a mere game of 'ins' and 'outs', an arcane affair of House of Commons tricks and manoeuvres."[71] Lunching with media people in September 1964, Benn sniffed a mood that "wasn't anti-political in the way that CND or the real Left is anti-political. It was anti-political in a scornful and contemptuous way." Five years later, in a television program on a by-election, he attacked the presenter Alastair Burnet for speculating that the candidates were looking worried at the election count because they had taken out a bet on the result: "I just went for him and said this cheapened, vulgarised and denigrated politics," at which Burnet allegedly "crumpled."[72] The journalist Paul Johnson rounded off the decade in June 1970 by expressing disgust at "the spectacle of TV professionals—not notorious for the gravity or sincerity of their opinions—attempting to corner politicians into admitting that they are liars, manipulators or even scoundrels," whereas in his experience, the great majority were "honest, with genuine convictions, trying to serve their country to the best of their ability."[73] Here was an important theme that resonated throughout the rest of the century and beyond.

Fall Semester 2008

1. These four features are fully elaborated in chapter 9 of my *Seeking a Role: The United Kingdom, 1951–1970* (Oxford, 2009).

2. Mary Jeune, Lady St. Helier, *Memories of Fifty Years* (London, 1909), p. 65.

3. *Parliamentary Debates*, Lords (hereafter *HL Deb.*), 15 May 1958, col. 384.

4. Quoted from the Board of Education's consultative committee on primary education (1931) in J. S. Maclure *Educational Documents, England and Wales: 1816 to the Present Day* (London, 1955; 3rd. edn., 1973), p. 192.

5. Harold Macmillan, *The Macmillan Diaries: The Cabinet Years, 1950–1957* (ed. Peter Catterall; London, 2003), entry for 22 Feb. 1954, p. 294.

6. John Rae, *The Public School Revolution: Britain's Independent Schools, 1964–1979* (London, 1981), p. 102.

7. Robert Blake quotes this remark made to him in his "Anthony Eden," in John P. Mackintosh, ed., *British Prime Ministers in the Twentieth Century*, Vol. II: *Churchill to Callaghan* (London, 1978), p. 115.

8. Steven Marcus, *The Other Victorians: A Study of Sexuality and Pornography in Mid-Nineteenth Century England* (New York, 1966), p. 151.

9. Charles Anthony Raven Crosland, *The Future of Socialism* (London, 1956), pp. 524, 521.

10. Colin MacInnes, *England, Half English* (1961), p. 14, reprinting an essay on Tommy Steele first published in *Encounter*, Dec. 1957.

11. *Parliamentary Debates*, Commons (hereafter *HC Deb.*), 29 Jan. 1969, col. 1372; for reactions to the speech, see *The Times*, 30 Jan. 1969, and (for a less sympathetic view) Richard Bourne in the *Guardian*, 7 Feb. 1969.

12. *HL Deb.*, 11 Mar. 1969, col. 1221.

13. *HC Deb.*, 8 Dec. 1967, cols. 1877–78.

14. Philip Larkin, *The Selected Letters of Philip Larkin, 1940–1985* (ed. Anthony Thwaite; London, 1993), letter of 14 Jan. 1970, p. 426.

15. Mary Whitehouse, interviewed by David Dimbleby, *Listener*, 5 July 1979.

16. *Evening Standard*, 22 July 1964.

17. John Davis, "The London Drug Scene and the Making of Drug Policy, 1965–73," *Twentieth Century British History*, 17, 1 (2006), p. 30; Asa Briggs, *The History of Broadcasting in the United Kingdom*, Vol. V: *Competition* (Oxford, 1995), pp. 353, 366.

18. Quoted in Hunter Davies, *The Beatles* (London, 1968; rev. edn., 1985), p. 247.

19. George H. Gallup, ed., *The Gallup International Public Opinion Polls: Great Britain, 1937–1975* (New York, n.d.), Vol. II, p. 833 (Oct. 1965); p. 874 (July 1966).

20. Eric James, *A Life of Bishop John A. T. Robinson: Scholar, Pastor, Prophet* (London, 1987), p. 81.

21. Dominic Sandbrook, *White Heat: A History of Britain in the Swinging Sixties* (London, 2006), p. 472.

22. *The Times*, 12 May 1970.

23. *HC Deb.*, 27 Jan. 1969, cols. 958–59.

24. *Guardian*, 1 May 1972.

25. D. J. Taylor, *After the War: The Novel and England since 1945* (London, 1993), p. 198.

26. Malcolm Bradbury, interviewed (Oct. 1984) in John Haffenden, ed., *Novelists in Interview* (London, 1985), pp. 26, 35.

27. David Butler and Michael Pinto-Duschinsky, *The British General Election of 1970* (London, 1971), p. 438.

28. *The Times,* 5 May 1969.
29. Norman Tebbit, *Upwardly Mobile* (London, 1988), p. 80.
30. Norman Tebbit, First Disraeli Lecture, *Guardian,* 14 Nov. 1985.
31. *The Times,* 10 Apr. 1986.
32. *HC Deb.,* 11 Dec. 1985, cols. 938–40.
33. Margaret Thatcher, *Collected Speeches* (ed. Robin Harris; London, 1997), speech of 9 Oct. 1987, pp. 286–87.
34. Thatcher, speech at Harrogate, *Observer,* 28 Mar. 1982.
35. *Daily Mail,* 19 Apr. 1988.
36. Quotations from Margaret Thatcher, *The Downing Street Years* (London, 1993), p. 626; *Woman's Own,* 31 Oct. 1987, p. 10.
37. Thatcher, *Collected Speeches,* party conference speech, 12 Oct. 1990, p. 439.
38. Margaret Thatcher, *The Path to Power* (London, 1995), p. 130.
39. *Guardian,* 3 July 1993 (speech at Cardiff); *Sunday Times,* 11 July 1993.
40. John Major, *The Autobiography* (London, 1999), pp. 554–55.
41. *Sunday Telegraph,* 20 Oct. 1996.
42. Major, *Autobiography,* p. 387.
43. *Guardian,* 12 Oct. 1993.
44. *Daily Telegraph,* 24 June 1995.
45. *Independent,* 20 July 2004; *Daily Telegraph,* 18 Oct. 2004.
46. *Daily Telegraph,* 18 Oct. 2004.
47. Edmund Burke, "First Letter on a Regicide Peace" (1796), in Burke, *Writings and Speeches,* Vol. IX (ed. Robert B. McDowell, Oxford, 1991), p. 242.
48. *Guardian,* 10 Sept. 1998.
49. Brian Harrison, "The Public and the Private in Modern Britain," in Peter Burke, Brian Harrison, and Paul Slack, eds., *Civil Histories: Essays Presented to Sir Keith Thomas* (Oxford, 2000), p. 345.
50. A. S. C. Ross, with R. Brackenbury, "U and Non-U Today. 1. Language," *New Society,* 22 Aug. 1968, p. 265.
51. Barbara Castle, *The Castle Diaries, 1974–76* (London, 1980), entry for 5 Mar. 1974, p. 36.
52. Dwight E. Robinson, "Fashions in Shaving and Trimming of the Beard: The Men of the *Illustrated London News,* 1842–1972," *American Journal of Sociology,* 81, 5 (Mar. 1976), pp. 1135–38; Frank Parkin, *Middle Class Radicalism: The Social Bases of the British Campaign for Nuclear Disarmament* (Manchester, 1968), p. 52.
53. Bernard Crick, foreword to David Paul Crook, *American Democracy in English Politics, 1815–1850* (Oxford, 1965), p. x.
54. British Council of Churches, *Sex and Morality: A Report to the British Council of Churches, October 1966* (London, 1966), p. 13.
55. George Melly, *Revolt into Style: The Popular Arts in Britain* (London, 1970), p. 205.
56. Nigel Whiteley, *Pop Design: Modernism to Mod* (London, 1987), p. 7.
57. *HL Deb.,* 26 Mar. 1969, col. 1308.
58. See Eysenck's letter to the *Guardian,* 30 Apr. 1974.
59. Gordon Carr, *The Angry Brigade: The Cause and the Case* (London, 1975), pp. 17–24. The Situationist International, consisting mainly of artists and intellectuals, had been formed in 1957 round Guy Debord's theory of the spectacle: the world we see is not real but what we are conditioned to see.
60. *Guardian,* 7 Dec. 1972.
61. Quoted in Michael Ignatieff, *Isaiah Berlin: A Life* (London, 1998), p. 254.

62. Richard Howard Stafford Crossman, *The Diaries of a Cabinet Minister,* Vol. III: *Secretary of State for Social Services, 1968–70* (London, 1977), entry for 26 May 1968, p. 77.

63. Ibid., entry for 25 Feb. 1969, p. 385; R. H. S. Crossman, *The Role of the Volunteer in the Modern Social Service* (Sidney Ball Memorial Lecture, 1973), p. 11.

64. Bernard Crick, "Socialist Literature in the 1950s," *Political Quarterly,* 1960, pp. 363, 371.

65. *New Society,* 29 July 1971, pp. 200, 202.

66. Malcolm Bradbury, *The History Man* (1975; paperback edn., 1985), p. 134.

67. *Woman's Journal,* Sept. 1973, p. 49.

68. Antony Grey [pseud. of Anthony Edgar Gartside Wright], *Quest for Justice: Towards Homosexual Emancipation* (London, 1993), p. 266.

69. See Richard Crossman's Granada lecture in *The Times,* 22 Oct. 1968.

70. Tony Benn, speech at Bristol, *The Times,* 19 Oct. 1968.

71. *Observer,* 12 Mar. 1972.

72. Tony Benn, *Out of the Wilderness: Diaries, 1963–67* (London, 1987), entry for 8 Sep. 1964, p. 138; Benn, *Office without Power: Diaries, 1968–1972* (London, 1988), entry for 30 Oct. 1969, p. 209.

73. *New Statesman,* 19 June 1970, p. 858.

3

Against the Permissive Society: The Backlash of the Late 1960s

DOMINIC SANDBROOK

I throw out a challenge. Men and women who believe in the decent way of life step forward and say so. Provoke the newspapers and the BBC to show where they stand. Let it clearly be seen that all that is immoral and "sick" in our society is not to be tolerated, let our leaders in all walks of life speak out before it is too late.
Dr. S. E. Ellison, letter to *The Times*, 11 October 1969

Although the 1960s are stereotypically seen as years of tremendous change and liberation, even a cursory glance at any newspaper from the final years of the decade, when the so-called permissive society was supposedly at its height, suggests a very different picture of popular attitudes and behavior. At the end of 1969, when the magazine *New Society* conducted a detailed poll of 1,000 adults to mark the end of the decade, the results suggested a much more cautious and conservative Britain than is commonly remembered. All social groups—rich and poor, young and old—agreed that there was "too much publicity given to sex," that "murderers ought to be hanged," and, by an enormous margin, that there were "too many coloured immigrants in the country now."[1]

By this stage, in fact, what we commonly consider the "backlash" against the permissive sixties was already underway, and in this essay I propose to look at four individuals who came to personify the conservative reaction against the liberal reforms and social changes of the decade. Mary Whitehouse, Malcolm Muggeridge, Lord Long-ford, and Kingsley Amis were a diverse group: a West Midlands schoolteacher, a controversial journalist, a high-minded peer, and a disputatious novelist. But their angry responses to the changes of the 1960s clearly struck a chord with thousands of ordinary British people. And although they were often seen at the time as backward-looking, reactionary figures, in many ways they laid the foundations for the Thatcherite counterattack in the decades to follow.

ONE MORNING IN MARCH 1963, at the secondary modern school in Madeley, Shropshire, a group of fourth-year girls accosted their Senior Mistress, Mary Whitehouse. Whitehouse was responsible for teaching their sex-education lessons, and she was appalled to hear that on the previous evening, the television program *Meeting Point* had hosted a discussion about sex before marriage. "I know what's right now, miss," one of the girls said confidently. "I know now I mustn't have intercourse until I'm engaged." Whitehouse was hor-rified, for she had taught them that any sexual contact before mar-riage, whether the participants were engaged or not, was entirely wrong. It never occurred to her, of course, that they might be wind-ing her up.

Worse was to follow. A couple of months later, Whitehouse rep-rimanded three girls and two boys who had, according to their classmates, been "doing things they shouldn't do," in emulation of Christine Keeler and Mandy Rice-Davies. "Well, miss," the ring-leader explained, "we watched them talking about girls on TV and it looked as if it was easy and see how well they done out of it miss, so we thought we'd try." Finally, not long afterward, came the last straw. One evening a distressed mother told Whitehouse that her daugh-ter had "gone off with a boy." The miscreant had apparently been watching a play on television—and then, the mother said, "when it got to the sexy part I could see her getting redder and redder in the face, she was so worked up. Then she got up and ran straight out of the house and went off with this boy."[2]

This was the background to Mary Whitehouse's long battle against what she saw as the permissive society. Born in Warwickshire in 1910, she had trained as a teacher and worked in a school just outside Wolverhampton. There she met and fell in love with a mar-ried man sixteen years her senior, although, she said, "there was no misbehaving."[3] Eventually, Mary broke off the relationship, but the episode left her in great emotional turmoil, made worse by the news that her parents had separated. At the age of twenty-five, therefore, she turned to religion, joining the Wolverhampton branch of Moral

Rearmament. Founded by an American evangelist, this movement demanded "Absolute Honesty, Absolute Purity, Absolute Unselfishness and Absolute Love." The purpose of Moral Rearmament, according to its founder, was "the remaking of the world. We remake people; nations are remade."[4] Certainly Mary seems to have found in Moral Rearmament the solace she craved: it was there that she met her future husband, Ernest Whitehouse, and in 1940 they were married.

Ernest Whitehouse worked for his father's flourishing manufacturing business, earning enough money for Mary to give up work and raise a family. For the next twenty years, then, she was a housewife. But she was not, as she often claimed, an "ordinary" housewife like millions of others. Unlike most housewives, she was both confident and familiar with the media. At the Queen's accession in 1952, she wrote to the BBC with suggestions on how people could help the new monarch in her duties, and she even delivered a talk in the special coronation edition of *Woman's Hour*. And she was also exceptionally religious. Every day began with a Bible reading in bed, after which she would complete a series of physical exercises and then have a formal morning prayer, all before breakfast. Unlike most women her age, she was completely convinced of the presence of the divine in her life. Her work, she wrote, was about "fulfilling God's purpose"; she had "day by day, a sense of meaning and a sense of faith that God was in [it]."[5]

In the summer of 1963, worried that her children were being "won over to a sub-Christian concept of living," Whitehouse began her career of writing angry letters to the BBC.[6] On 27 January 1964 she announced the launch of the Clean-Up TV campaign, in collaboration with her friend Norah Buckland, the wife of a Staffordshire vicar and a fellow member of Moral Rearmament. "We women of Britain believe in a Christian way of life," began their manifesto, which urged women to "fight for the right to bring up our own children in the truths of the Christian faith, and to protect our homes from the exhibitions of violence." From the outset, their target was the BBC, which they accused of peddling "the propaganda of disbelief, doubt and dirt" as well as "promiscuity, infidelity and drinking." Instead, they argued, the BBC should be broadcasting programs that "encourage and sustain faith in God and bring Him back to the heart of our family and national life."[7]

On 5 May 1964, Clean-Up TV held its first public meeting, at Birmingham Town Hall. Seventy-three coachloads of people filled the hall to capacity, and the BBC sent a camera crew to record its critics. "Most of the audience," wrote one observer, "were middle-aged women." Indeed, all but five of the twenty-seven speakers were women, too, and almost all shared the view that television was corrupting the morals of the nation. There were messages of support from the Mothers' Union, the Catholic Women's Organisation, the Women's Institute, the Townswomen's Guild, and all manner of church and youth groups. "In view of the terrifying increase in promiscuity and its attendant horrors," read a telegram to the Queen drafted by Buckland and Whitehouse, "we are desperately anxious to banish from our homes and theatres those who seek to demoralize and corrupt our young people." By the end of the evening, it was evident that Clean-Up TV was off and running. "There are those who will find it easy to laugh at the women who were here tonight," commented an article in *The Times*, but the scoffers little knew what they were dealing with.[8]

For Mary Whitehouse, the argument about television was really an argument about a bigger issue, namely, the apparent erosion of Christian values by modern consumerism and mass culture. She picked on the BBC because it was seen as the preeminent national cultural institution, "an additional established church," as one writer puts it.[9] But she was not the first to do so. There were clear links between Clean-Up TV and Moral Rearmament, on which she drew for friends and supporters. Indeed, Moral Rearmament campaigners had been complaining for years that the BBC, especially in its factual programs, was "a corrupting influence" and "a spiritual sewer [that] flows out into the homes of Britain."[10] Whitehouse told audiences that people watched BBC programs "at the risk of serious damage to their morals, their patriotism, their discipline and their family life."[11] A report prepared for the Birmingham meeting listed the "objectionable" features of recent BBC programming: "sexy innuendoes, suggestive clothing and behaviour; cruelty, sadism and unnecessary violence; no regret for wrong-doing; blasphemy and the presentation of religion in a poor light; excessive drinking and foul language; undermining respect for law and order; unduly harrowing and depressing themes," and so on.[12]

In the spring of 1965, Whitehouse and Buckland decided to replace Clean-Up TV with a new organization that would speak for the entire television audience and would work harder at influencing BBC executives. They also decided to tone down some of the fiercer evangelical rhetoric in order to attract more supporters. The new group was the National Viewers' and Listeners' Association (NVALA). During the next few years, few programs escaped its scrutiny, and even escapist fantasies were not immune. Whitehouse was especially critical of *Doctor Who*, which she solemnly attacked for its reliance on "strangulation—by hand, by claw, by obscene vegetable matter."[13] This was perhaps her greatest weakness: very few programs, however innocuous, passed muster. Had she concentrated on a handful of genuinely controversial productions, she might have wielded greater influence. But many people who shared some of her anxieties were undoubtedly put off because she appeared so extreme.

The BBC, not surprisingly, was intensely suspicious of Mary Whitehouse from the beginning. An internal report on the Birmingham Town Hall meeting described it as "comical," "sinister," and "menacing."[14] She exercised no real influence over programming or policy in the sixties; indeed, programs rapidly became more controversial and sexually explicit, not less. In a letter to the *Church Times* in August 1964, one senior BBC official explained that they had to "recognise and give expression to the growing points of society," and insisted that "serious and creative writers of this generation must be free to write about society and its problems as they see them."[15] This was an opinion shared by the BBC's liberal Director General, Hugh Carleton Greene, who utterly detested his conservative critics. After retiring as Director General in 1969, he made the curious decision to hang in his home a full-frontal nude painting of Mary Whitehouse with no fewer than five breasts. According to some accounts, he would occasionally amuse himself by throwing darts at it—a task presumably made easier by the proliferation of breasts—squealing with pleasure at every strike.

Greene was not the only person who thoroughly disliked Mary Whitehouse. She was bombarded with hundreds of threatening telephone calls and letters, and attempts were made to lure her sons to orgies on the pretext that they were Christmas parties. The Conservative backbencher Sir Gerald Nabarro told a television audience that she was "a hypocritical old bitch."[16] On the other hand, she also had her defenders, especially within Nabarro's own party. In 1974, Sir Keith Joseph hailed "that admirable woman, Mary Whitehouse," calling her "a shining example of what one person can do single-handedly when inspired by faith and compassion." She even claimed an endorsement from the unlikely figure of Mick Jagger, whom she had met on a television panel. "He said he expected me to be the wrong kind of person," she confided, "and, well, I wasn't at all—and he felt we had a rapport."[17]

As many observers remarked at the time, the NVALA was a militantly antiradical movement, opposed to what Whitehouse called "the secular/humanist/Marxist philosophy."[18] Her husband, Ernest, told an interviewer that what had first disturbed them was the "pressure from the left-wing" to "destroy the Christian faith," and a family friend observed that their "dread of communism really surprised me."[19] This no doubt owed much to the influence of Moral Rearmament, which was fiercely anticommunist, and it is hard to imagine a similar dread among many other Shropshire housewives. Whitehouse insisted that there was a deliberate communist conspiracy to undermine British morality. "The enemies of the West," she said in 1965, "saw that Britain was the kingpin of Western civilisation; she had proved herself unbeatable on the field of battle because of her faith and her character. If Britain was to be destroyed, those things must be undercut."[20] She even hinted that the BBC itself had fallen under the control of communist agents. "They've infiltrated the trade unions," she explained. "Why does anyone still believe they haven't infiltrated broadcasting?"[21]

Other commentators, however, argued that the NVALA was essentially a religious movement. Whitehouse herself thought that during the early sixties, "religion, the idea of God, Christianity in particular, were very much under attack."[22] She was bewildered by her lack of support from the Church of England, and blamed "soft permissives" and "left-wing humanists."[23] According to one account, her object was "to recolonise social life for God," turning Britain into "a cross between a wet Sunday in Wales and eternal *Songs of Praise*."[24] Indeed, to many observers, her campaign looked like a kind of religious revival, opposed not only to homosexuality, abortion, and divorce, but also to liberalism, humanism, and moral flexibility. In this sense, it was not unlike American religious conservatism during the same period, rooted in small towns and the countryside, deeply informed by anticommunism, and bitterly resentful of the dismissive indifference of educated elitists like Hugh Carleton Greene and his colleagues at the BBC.

More than any other person, Mary Whitehouse popularized the issues of permissiveness and moral corruption, and she was undoubtedly one of the best-known and most controversial women of the sixties and seventies. In some ways, she anticipated the appeal of Margaret Thatcher, another dutiful mother from the provincial English lower-middle class, steeped in Protestant values, dedicated to the family, and driven by a sense of her own rectitude and righteousness. Both called for a return to traditional values, both believed that the country was on a path of corruption and decline, and both rejected the liberalism they associated with the permissive society. Such similarities suggest that Whitehouse was much more than an evangelical revivalist. Her attack on the permissive society was also a response to many of the major post-war political and social changes: the creation of the welfare state, the growth of consumerism, the rise of the working classes, the militancy of the unions, and so on. Like Thatcher, she appealed to a middle class that felt threatened by socialism and social change, and worried that its values were being eroded by collectivism and permissiveness. Unlike the leading politicians of the sixties, she was not prepared to accept economic materialism and cultural liberalism as acceptable national goals. Instead, she presented a worldview based on zealous antiradicalism and moralistic Christian rigor, and informed by a powerful sense of loss and nostalgia. As the historian Jeffrey Weeks notes, she was "far from being a crank"; she was a portent of the future.[25]

AT THE FIRST NVALA CONVENTION, the principal speaker was the Conservative backbencher William Deedes. At the second convention, in May 1967, the speaker was the journalist Malcolm Muggeridge, and he did not disappoint the audience: "I am absolutely convinced that our civilisation will rush down the Gadarene slope which others have slipped down before, if we adhere to the notion that the image of life is not God but pigs in a trough. If life is pigs in a trough . . . then of course it does not matter much what you show on TV. If that were life, if *Till Death Us Do Part* is life, I cannot see that there would be anything to do but to commit suicide."[26]

As one watching journalist remarked, Muggeridge's appearance at the NVALA convention would have been "widely welcomed by connoisseurs of strange events and weird juxtapositions."[27] By any standards, he was an extraordinary character. A former Marxist who had changed his mind after visiting the Soviet Union in the thirties, he had been the editor of *Punch*, had courted controversy by publicly mocking the monarchy in the mid-1950s, and had become one of the most prominent television interviewers in the country, famous for his clowning behavior as well as his sardonic wit. But what many of his friends did not know, and what gradually became evident during the sixties, was that Muggeridge also had a deep sense of spiritual longing. After spending an evening drinking with friends, he would then sit at home reading the works of Christian mystics until the small hours. By the early sixties, surrounded by conspicuous consumption, he was becoming a fierce critic of modernity and materialism, opposed to "wealth, ambition, celebrity, sexual liberation." Like his great hero St. Augustine, he converted to Christianity and began transforming himself from a libertine to an ascetic. He became a vegetarian, gave up smoking, and

delightedly told interviewers that he had given up sex, which he
called "a trivial dream of pleasure which itself soon dissolves into
the solitude and despair of self-gratification."[28]

In November 1966, Muggeridge was elected Rector of Edinburgh
University, a ceremonial position in which he was supposed to represent the interests of the students to the university authorities.[29]
It was a fairly meaningless accolade, but when Muggeridge was formally invested, on 16 February 1967, he used the occasion to launch
a sensational assault on the values of modern Britain. He complained that the government was bent on "raising the school age,
multiplying and enlarging our universities, increasing public expenditure on education until juvenile delinquency, beats and drug-
addicts and general intimations of illiteracy multiply so alarmingly
that, at last, the whole process is called into question." If this were
not enough, he predicted that "permissive morality" would soon
come into question, too: "When birth pills are handed out with free
orange juice, and consenting adults wear special ties and blazers,
and abortion and divorce—those two contemporary panaceas for
all matrimonial ills—are freely available on the public health, then
at last, with the suicide rate up to Scandinavian proportions and the
psychiatric wards bursting at the seams, it will be realized that this
path, even from the shallow point of view of the pursuit of happiness, is a disastrous cul-de-sac."[30]

Unsurprisingly, this did not go down well with the students, and
within a few months the Rector had irreparably fallen out with his
electors over drugs and contraception. By the beginning of 1968,
the university magazine *Student* was pressing him to resign, and it
even printed a cartoon showing Muggeridge as a rotting skull with
worms crawling into his sockets. Anyone who knew Muggeridge
knew that he was unlikely to give in, but his response surpassed
even his own iconoclastic standards. He was already due to deliver
the annual rectorial address from the pulpit of St. Giles', the High
Kirk of Edinburgh, on 14 January 1968, and when the day came, the
cathedral was packed with an expectant crowd that included representatives from Fleet Street and a television crew from the BBC, all
eager to hear his oration.[31]

Muggeridge did not disappoint. He gave not an address but a
sermon, and began by comparing modern Britain to the Roman
Empire in its last days, which he called an age of fantasy, materialism, and spiritual decay. Then he turned on his critics, "the students in this university," whom he called "the ultimate beneficiaries
in our welfare system." They were "supposed to be the spearhead
of progress," and he would welcome any sign of "rebelliousness or

refusal to accept the ways and values of our run-down, spiritually impoverished way of life . . . up to and including blowing up this magnificent edifice in which we now sit." But he detected no such signs—they were too busy wallowing in the detritus of the affluent society: "How sad, how macabre and funny it is that all they put forward should be a demand for pot and pills. It is the most tenth-rate form of indulgence ever known. It is the resort of any old slobbering debauchee anywhere in the world at any time—"dope and bed". The feeling raised in me is not so much disapproval as contempt. This, as you may imagine, makes it difficult, indeed impossible, for me as rector to fulfil my function." [32]

As Muggeridge stepped down from the pulpit, he also stepped down from the post of Rector, the first person ever to do so. Even when the student union voted to support his return—itself a hint that the students were more conservative than many people imagined—he refused to heed them, but continued on his long, lonely march toward greater conservatism and, eventually, Catholicism.

OF ALL THE ANTI-PERMISSIVE CAMPAIGNS, perhaps the most notorious example was the Longford Commission on Pornography, convened in the early summer of 1971 by the elderly Labour peer. Longford was a Catholic convert, a sentimental idealist, and a dogged advocate of unpopular causes like penal reform, as well as one of Muggeridge's oldest and closest friends. He had been completely unaware of the existence of pornography until 1970, when it came as such a shock to him that he immediately decided to destroy it. In April 1971, he initiated a debate in the House of Lords about the "incipient menace of pornography in Great Britain," and prepared for the occasion by visiting a strip club, the Soho Stokehole, as well as by sitting through "an exhausting course of prurient films" and visiting a "sex supermarket." [33] This was only a taste of what was to come. In May he released the names of an extraordinary collection of people who had agreed to join his inquiry into pornography, including six peers, an archbishop, three bishops, and three professors, as well as Jimmy Savile, Cliff Richard, and, inevitably, Malcolm Muggeridge.

The commission was supposed to examine the link between pornography and sexual violence, and Longford's approach to the problem was unconventional to say the least. In August, he took five other commission members to Copenhagen to investigate Danish obscenity laws. The trip kicked off with a visit to two sex shows: women were paired with men, with other women, and with animals, but Longford found it all rather too much. He lasted only five minutes in the first club, walking out in disgust with the manager trailing behind him, saying: "But sir, you have not seen the intercourse. We have intercourse later in the programme." The second club was even worse. Here, according to an amused reporter, "a half naked girl thrust a whip into Lord Longford's hand and invited him to flagellate her. He declined and after she had playfully mauled him by thrusting the whip around his neck and pulling violently on it, he got up and left." By contrast, his colleagues stuck it out rather longer, and disagreed with Longford's verdict that this kind of thing was likely to encourage sexual violence. Gyles Brandreth even announced that he would like to see the Danish laws introduced back home.[34] Not surprisingly, this all made splendid reading, but it also made it hard to take Longford seriously. When his report finally came out the following year, many people found it hard to banish the image of the elderly peer being strangled with a whip in the clubs of Copenhagen.

ONE OF THE MORE UNLIKELY MEMBERS OF LONGFORD'S COMMISSION on pornography was the novelist Kingsley Amis, who knew a good deal about the subject and privately thought that Longford was a "fucking fool."[35] But Amis, too, found much to dislike in the cultural climate of the late sixties, and in his own way he too anticipated the conservative reaction of the years to come. As an adolescent, he had been a communist, like Muggeridge, and when he rose to prominence in the 1950s, he was still a strong Labour supporter. In 1957, however, he wrote a pamphlet on socialism in which he declared that the best political motive was "self-interest" and attacked "the professional espouser of causes, the do-gooder, the archetypal social worker."[36] By 1960, his relationship with the party had reached "the name-calling and walking-out stage," and in 1964 he voted Labour for the last time.

In 1967, utterly disillusioned by Harold Wilson's government, Amis wrote an article for the *Sunday Telegraph* entitled "Why Lucky Jim Turned Right," and followed it up with a pamphlet for the Conservative Political Centre called *Lucky Jim's Politics*. He had abandoned Labour, he said, because he hated idealism so much, and had converted to "grudging toleration of the Conservative Party because it is the party of non-politics, of resistance to politics." Amis thought that the "evils of life" were "ineradicable by political means, and that attempts to eradicate them are disastrous." He was sick of progressive education, sick of socialist improvement, and sick of the appeasement of communism abroad; and above all, he was sick of the whole "abortion-divorce-homosexuality-censorship-racialism-marijuana package."[37]

Amis was not the only prominent writer who advertised his contempt for the Wilson government and the supposedly permissive society: other writers moving to the right or becoming increasingly critical of modern values included Donald Davie, John Braine, Robert Conquest, and Anthony Powell, many of whom used to meet at Bertorelli's restaurant on Charlotte Street for "Fascist lunches." And although Amis's best friend, Philip Larkin, the most accomplished poet in the country, was not a Bertorelli's regular, he still dashed off letters to his friends dripping with contempt for trade unionists, immigrants, students, and socialists of all kinds. One factor pushing Amis and his friends to the right was the war in Vietnam, which they saw as a vital crusade against international communism. Even without Vietnam, however, it is likely that they would have moved rightward, pushed by their fierce populism and contempt for idealism. The fashionable intellectual values of the late 1960s, which emphasized sensation and spirituality, were very different from the pragmatic detachment they had celebrated in the fifties, and their moral values were affronted by what they saw as the excesses of the permissive society. Both Amis and Larkin had been brought up in reserved middle-class households in the twenties and thirties, and although they often defied their parents' values, they still respected them. Amis, for example, was a womanizer, but did not regard promiscuity as an inherently good thing, and even though he owned pornography himself, he still joined Longford's commission.

Like Donald Davie, Amis was appalled by the expansion of higher education, and he consistently argued that "more will mean worse."[38] Even in *Lucky Jim* there is a scene in which two lecturers discuss the increasing pressure to "chuck Firsts around like teaching diplomas and push every bugger who can write his name through the Pass courses."[39] While Labour's Anthony Crosland was arguing passionately for greater egalitarianism and opportunity in higher education, Amis insisted that "there must be an elite, and there can't be equality."[40] In April 1965, he wrote mockingly to the *Observer*:

> Perhaps only you could have published a whole article on university failures that laid no weight on the almost invariable cause of failure: *insufficient ability*, or, alternatively, *excessive stupidity.*
>
> I was glad to learn from you, however, that as many as 14 per cent of people do fail. Evidently not all standards have been fully lowered everywhere yet. But your fashionable brand of sentimental mercy will hasten the process.[41]

The educational reforms of the sixties were instrumental in pushing a considerable number of older intellectuals toward the antipermissive right. To the likes of Amis and Davie, Labour's commitment to comprehensive schools and polytechnics was probably the single most unattractive feature of modern politics. Two men who agreed were C. B. Cox and A. E. Dyson, both university lecturers in English and the founders of the literary magazine *Critical Quarterly.* Cox and Dyson were lower-middle-class men who had won scholarships to Cambridge and regularly voted Labour. They also edited a second periodical, *Critical Survey,* aimed at teachers of English, and in March 1969, they devoted a special issue to a discussion of progressive education, comprehensive schools, the expansion of universities, and student unrest. They called it their Black Paper.

The essays in the first Black Paper had two common themes: educational standards were falling, and a misguided egalitarianism was undermining British education and culture. The issue had an apocalyptic tone, with talk of "the progressive collapse of education," "anarchy becoming fashionable," and the rejection of "discipline and work."[42] The new Education Secretary, Ted Short, was furious, and rather wildly claimed that the publication of the Black Paper was "one of the blackest days for education for the past hundred years" and "the crisis of the century."[43] Delighted at the ensuing publicity, Cox and Dyson published four more Black Papers in the next six years, all attacking comprehensive education, the collapse of standards, and progressive methods of teaching. Within the Labour Party and in the pages of liberal newspapers like the *Observer* and the *Guardian,* the authors were regarded as "fascists" who were trying to destroy opportunity and equality; but in the columns of Conservative newspapers and among the Tory rank and file, they were heroes.

The controversy also reflected the increasing politicization of education. The introduction of "progressive" teaching methods, often based on play rather than instruction, alarmed many parents, who worried that their children were being used as guinea pigs in some harebrained Hampstead experiment. Changes such as the abolition of grammar schools and the introduction of comprehensives ensured that education became one of the most divisive political issues in the country from the late sixties onward, and were crucial in alienating former Labour supporters like Cox and Amis. Education was also the area in which arguments about the cultural legacy of the sixties were most obviously politicized. Even though student disturbances in Britain were pretty minor compared with those elsewhere, they became a symbol linking the indulgence of idealistic socialist ministers with the degenerate promiscuity of modern consumer culture. In this context, they connected the moralistic outrage of Whitehouse and Muggeridge on the one hand, with the rebellion of former Labour supporters like Cox and Amis on the other. What this all amounted to, therefore, was both a cultural and a political critique, a countermove against falling moral standards as well as a denunciation of Labour's social engineering. It was to provide excellent ammunition for a new generation of Conservatives in the years to come.

In between denouncing the government and contributing to the Black Papers, Kingsley Amis also found the time to continue his literary career. By the end of the decade, he was the leading exponent of what the critic D. J. Taylor calls "the anti-1960s novel," a savage social satire attacking the liberal values associated with the period.[44] Amis's first novel along these lines was *I Want It Now* (1968), the very title of which expresses the impatient self-indulgence that he associated with the late sixties. The central character is a shallow television interviewer who falls in love with a promiscuous but unsatisfied society girl, providing an excuse for Amis to satirize fashionable liberalism and social snobbery. At one point, the hero hosts a television discussion about cultural freedom with a theatrical producer and a novelist, both of whom agree that Soviet writers are "significantly freer" under communism than British writers are under capitalism.[45] On another occasion, he glances at a newspaper and sees the headlines "*Export Gap Widens—Britain Loses £22m Arms Order—Textile Strike Spreads—Malta: Agreement Hopes Fade—Two Shipyards To Close.*" "The forces of progress," he thinks to himself, "were really gaining ground at last."[46]

Three years later, Amis published *Girl, 20* (1971), which has a good claim to be his funniest book. Its narrator, Douglas Yandell, is a music critic and a good friend of the eminent conductor and composer Sir Roy Vandervane. Vandervane is the quintessential middle-aged progressive desperately trying to "arse-creep youth": he takes a dreadful seventeen-year old mistress, drags Douglas around a succession of hideous boutiques and nightclubs, and finally disgraces himself completely by performing the ludicrous piece "Elevations 9" on stage with a rock band called Pigs Out.[47] This performance, which forms the climax of the novel, takes place at a giant disused tramway depot before an audience of around a thousand people. Only "here and there" can Douglas see "an ordinary human being: journalist, performer's parent or ill-instructed queer." Around him there is "a prevailing hairiness," and one member of Pigs Out is likened to "a degenerate descendant of Charles II." All in all, "it smelt of tennis shoes, hair and melting insulation, and was fearfully hot."[48]

Plenty of other writers shared Amis's concerns about the direction of modern life, from A. S. Byatt and Piers Paul Read to Simon Raven and Malcolm Bradbury. Perhaps the outstanding example of anti-permissive satire, though, is Anthony Powell's *Hearing Secret Harmonies* (1975), the final volume of his sequence *A Dance to the Music of Time*. *Hearing Secret Harmonies* presents one of the most ludicrous spectacles in an anti-sixties novel when the despicable Kenneth Widmerpool, a recurring figure in the cycle, transforms himself from a Labour peer and the chancellor of a new university into "Ken," an absurd polo-necked apologist for student revolution. In a nice parody of the "radical chic" of the late sixties, Widmerpool even disrupts a prize-giving ceremony by publicly condemning "the wrongness of the way we live, the wrongness of marriage, the wrongness of money, the wrongness of education, the wrongness of government, the wrongness of the manner we treat kids like these." He finally ends up as a wretched member of the "Harmony" commune, chanting meaningless mantras and prancing about in blue robes.[49]

IN THE YEARS TO COME, CRITICS OF PERMISSIVENESS from Mary Whitehouse to Kingsley Amis became great admirers of Margaret Thatcher. This was no coincidence: their interpretation of recent history had an obvious appeal to the Thatcherites of the late 1970s and 1980s. By presenting the sixties as a decade of excess, self-indulgence, and national decline, the Conservatives hit on a deceptively simple explanation for Britain's woes, one that could easily be blamed on Harold Wilson and the Labour Party. But they did not invent the anti-permissive case, and its appeal transcended partisan boundaries. Plenty of working-class Labour voters agreed that liberalism had gone too far, and plenty of ordinary people preferred the bluff cultural conservatism of "PC Jim" Callaghan to the elegant liberalism of Roy Jenkins.

Of course, the anti-permissive version of the sixties was a caricature, exaggerating the changes of the period at the expense of the continuities, presenting a vision of decadence and excess that often bore little relation to the realities of daily life. All the same, modern writers who dismiss with casual superiority the supposed ignorance or hypocrisy of Mary Whitehouse and her supporters are missing the point. Whitehouse, Muggeridge, Amis, and the others spoke for millions of people who felt frightened or threatened by social and cultural change. Millions of people were unhappy that British power was so clearly in decline, felt let down by the Wilson government, and worried that the country they loved was changing beyond recognition. Millions were troubled that while church attendance was falling, the figures for divorce, abortion, delinquency, and violent crime were all on the rise. Millions saw the sixties not as years of liberation, but as an age of anxiety. And in the decade to come, they would find their champion: a middle-aged middle-class grocer's daughter from Grantham.

Spring Semester 2009

1. *New Society,* 27 Nov. 1969.

2. Mary Whitehouse, *Who Does She Think She Is?* (London, 1972), ch. 5; Max Caulfield, *Mary Whitehouse* (London, 1975), pp. 19–23.

3. *Daily Telegraph,* 24 Nov. 2001.

4. Michael Tracey and David Morrison, *Whitehouse* (London, 1979), p. 59.

5. Ibid., pp. 198, 55.

6. Ibid,, p. 40.

7. Ibid., pp. 42–43;

8. *The Times,* 6 May 1964; Caulfield, *Mary Whitehouse,* pp. 68–70; Tracey and Morrison, *Whitehouse,* pp. 43–44.

9. Anthony Smith, *British Broadcasting* (Newton Abbott, 1974), p. 62.

10. A. W. Gordon, *Peter Howard: Life and Letters* (London, 1969), p. 302.

11. Tracey and Morrison, *Whitehouse,* p. 44.

12. Ibid., p. 46

13. Quoted in John Tulloch and Manuel Alvarado, *Doctor Who: The Unfolding Text* (London, 1983), p. 158.

14. Quoted in Asa Briggs, *The History of Broadcasting in the United Kingdom,* Vol. V: *Competition* (Oxford, 1995), p. 334.

15. Quoted in Tracey and Morrison, *Whitehouse,* p. 45.

16. Quoted in Caulfield, *Mary Whitehouse,* p. 110.

17. Ibid., pp. 1, 4.

18. Mary Whitehouse, *Whatever Happened to Sex?* (London, 1977), p. 72.

19. Tracey and Morrison, *Whitehouse,* p. 64.

20. *Daily Telegraph,* 24 Nov. 2001.

21. Caulfield, *Mary Whitehouse,* p. 140.

22. Ibid., p. 56.

23. Whitehouse, *Who Does She Think She Is?* p. 11.

24. Tracey and Morrison, *Whitehouse,* pp. 188–89.

25. Jeffrey Weeks, *Sex, Politics and Society* (London, 1989), p. 277.

26. Quoted in Caulfield, *Mary Whitehouse,* p. 99.

27. *The Times,* 22 May 1967.

28. Gregory Wolfe, *Malcolm Muggeridge* (London, 1995), p. 326; Malcolm Muggeridge, *Tread Softly for You Tread on My Jokes* (London, 1966), p. 57.

29. *The Times,* 11 Nov. 1966.

30. *The Times,* 17 Feb. 1967.

31. Wolfe, *Malcolm Muggeridge,* p. 352.

32. *The Times,* 15 Jan. 1968.

33. *The Times,* 20 and 21 April 1971.

34. *The Times,* 25, 26, and 27 April 1971.

35. Eric Jacobs, *Kingsley Amis: A Biography* (London, 1995), p. 12.

36. Kingsley Amis, *Socialism and the Intellectuals* (Fabian Society pamphlet: London, 1957), reprinted in Gene Feldman and Max Gartenberg, eds., *Protest: The Beat Generation and the Angry Young Men* (London, 1959), pp. 267–68.

37. Kingsley Amis, "Why Lucky Jim Turned Right," reprinted in Kingsley Amis, *What Became of Jane Austen?* (London, 1970), p. 217.

38. Jacobs, *Kingsley Amis,* pp. 187–88.

39. Amis, *Lucky Jim,* pp. 169–70.

40. Morrison, *The Movement,* p. 261.

41. Amis to the editor, *Observer,* 18 Apr. 1965, in Zachary Leader, ed., *The Letters of Kingsley Amis* (London, 2000), p. 660.

42.   See C. B. Cox and A. E. Dyson, *The Black Papers on Education* (London, 1971).

43.   *The Times*, 9 Apr. 1969.

44.   D. J. Taylor, *After the War: The Novel and England since 1945* (London, 1993), p. 198.

45.   Kingsley Amis, *I Want It Now* (London, 1968), p. 218.

46.   Ibid., p. 248.

47.   Amis, *Girl, 20* (London, 1971), pp. 126–27.

48.   Ibid., p. 201.

49.   Anthony Powell, *A Dance to the Music of Time* (London, 1997), Vol. IV, p. 641.

4

Trevor-Roper's Scotland

ROY FOSTER

Hugh Trevor-Roper seemed to be an Oxford don supplied by central casting. An erect Northumbrian with a distinctly patrician air, he commanded a grandee position impregnably within the establishment. He became Regius Professor at Oxford, Master of Peterhouse in Cambridge, and—as Lord Dacre of Glanton—a member of the House of Lords; he possessed a country house in Scotland, built for Walter Scott's family; he married the daughter of Field Marshal Earl Haig; his recently published letters to Bernard Berenson are effortlessly snobbish. But Trevor-Roper also maintained a highly developed sense of the ridiculous. After making his reputation with a subversive biography of Archbishop Laud, he turned to investigating the lives of mythomanes, eccentrics, and deceivers. (*The Hermit of Peking*, his study of the forger Edmund Backhouse, is one of his most delightful books.) Equally unpredictable was his fascination with the banality of evil as reflected in the Nazi high command, which inspired *The Last Days of Hitler*, his groundbreaking and engrossing account of life in the Führer's bunker.

Trevor-Roper was a master of the interrogative essay, which in his youth he used as a billhook to slash the reputations of erring colleagues. It was also the weapon used to powerful effect in some enduringly important historical debates, such as controversies concerning the rise of the Tudor gentry, the general crisis of the seventeenth century, and "the invention of tradition" in the age of romanticism and nationalism. That last idea was also the name of a landmark collection of essays edited by Eric Hobsbawm and Terence Ranger a quarter century ago, in which a variety of historians explored the surprisingly recent origin of myths to do with, inter alia, the British monarchy, the construction of colonial Africa, and the institution of Welsh bards, asking pertinent questions about the issues at stake, the interests involved, and the compensatory psychological effects of such intellectual and literary maneuvers.

As an historiographical concept, the invention of tradition proved equally attractive to Marxists (old and new), skeptical liberals, and cynical Tories; and it rapidly entered the lexicon. Trevor-Roper's contribution to the book was an urbane dissection of "the Highland Tradition of Scotland." It proved (to his own satisfaction at least) that the culture of the Highlands—bagpipes, kilts, clans, and all— was a Victorian fantasy attached retrospectively to an area that was "racially and culturally . . . a colony of Ireland." This unnerving notion, which was not universally welcome, forms the subject of his latest, though posthumous, book, a lively salvo from beyond the grave.

Trevor-Roper died in 2003, but his habit of accumulating unpublished essays and his taste for writing many things at once have enabled him to have a prolific afterlife. A substantial biography of a pioneering Calvinist court physician has already appeared since his death, and more essay collections are in the pipeline. This would not be possible without the affection and commitment of his friends and ex-students, most of whom loved and revered him. One of them, Jeremy Cater, has skillfully edited Trevor-Roper's lectures on Scottish myth and history, originally delivered at Emory University, in which he further developed his understanding of the invention of tradition. It is a beguiling, witty, and elegant volume. While leaving wide open the enduring question whether Trevor-Roper was a Whig or a Tory, it shows him at his skeptical Gibbonian best.

The Trevor-Roper style is not precisely Gibbon's, though he uses footnotes with a similar blend of savagery and mischief. The very first one in the book begins, joyfully: "The cannibalism of the Scots—a very sore point with later Scotch antiquaries—rests on a single statement of Jerome in his *Adversus Jovinianum*. For the discomfort which this text caused later, see, for example, the several pages of intellectual writhing over the topic by Sir Thomas Craig." His own prose does not writhe. It has a clarity and a pungency that suggests several Scots exemplars (Hume, Cockburn, Stevenson); and Scotland was one of his preoccupations. This book investigates the political, literary, and sartorial trappings of "Scottishness," building on earlier writings about Scottish historians and the surprisingly recent

creation of clan tartans. It provides a consistently witty and beauti-
fully written demonstration of the political uses of history, the un-
appeasable appetite of nation builders for self-referring myths, and
the harmless fun provided by the human desire to make ourselves
into what we are not.

This was how the "Sobieski Stuarts," two English brothers who
began life in the early nineteenth century as John and Charles Allen, ended as claimants to the throne of Scotland. They sum up
the syndrome for Trevor-Roper, in his inimitably empathetic way.
The brothers were indulged and feted by a whole gallery of Jacobite
wannabes, and devoted themselves to the creation of marvelously
complex genealogies and secret documents, constructing arcane
connections to the royal houses of Central Europe. (Like many ma-
gicians, they spent some time in Prague.) Even after exposure, they
retained a corpus of true believers, appealing to Queen Victoria to
relieve their poverty on account of their royal blood. "Their policy
had been that of all successful mystery-men. . . . They simply played
their part as if they believed it, and left others to speculate—and by
their speculation to build up the myth."

But mythmaking raises other questions, too, questions not pursued in this book. Trevor-Roper brilliantly evokes the sixteenth-
century scholar George Buchanan, who moved from being "a migra-
tory cosmopolitan intellectual" in the Erasmian mode to tutoring
the future King James VI. Along the way, Buchanan constructed the
case against James's tragic mother, Mary, Queen of Scots, and created an historical pedigree for an independent Scottish monarchy.
The Invention of Scotland then moves on to another piece of mythmaking two centuries later: the 1760s forgery by an obscure Scots writer
named James Macpherson of a great corpus of "ancient" bardic poetry, supposedly authored by "Ossian," a Scottish Homer lost in the
mists of time. The book ends, more or less, with the endorsement
of the sartorial myth of kilts, tartans, and the whole iconography
stage-managed by Walter Scott. This was symbolized by the visit of
King George IV to his northern kingdom in 1822, where he was
kitted out hilariously in full stage garb. What followed was the do-
mestication of the Highlands into theme-park history, passionately
endorsed by Queen Victoria and her successors.

At the end of it all, one wonders: why Scotland? And how did
"Caledonia" get away with it, when the Victorian stereotypes attached to the other Celtic elements of the United Kingdom were
tarred with such damaging stereotypes by the metropolitan arbiters
of opinion: the Welsh as mendacious, hypocritical, sexually incon-
tinent; the Irish as dirty, brutish, stupid, and disloyal. In point of

fact, Scotland no less than Ireland was marked by endemic poverty, excessive drinking, traumatic emigration patterns, brutal violence, and a history of dispossession; self-pity, religious bigotry, and all sorts of social introversion were no less rife. Yet Scotland the brave emerged as a jewel of the Empire, combining robust moral independence with support for the best of British: a reservoir of bonny, brainy, humorous, talented empire builders. ("Scotty" the engineer remains a classic component of imperial and post-imperial adventure stories, culminating in the character played by James Doohan on *Star Trek*.)

Religion, of course, has a lot to do with it; Scottish Catholicism is conveniently airbrushed from the stereotype, and the dominie remains a much less threatening figure than the Irish priest. Nor did the Irish Union of 1800 operate as advantageously as the Scottish Union of 1707. In the end, one is forced to conclude that the Scots did it all better, and more ruthlessly. They kept vital freedoms in religion, law, and education. They used (and invented) their history to advantage. They jumped onto the Union bandwagon, infiltrating the metropolitan government (right down to Gordon Brown) as well as the empire. Poor as they were, they had an industrial revolution at the right time. But they were also welcomed in, and allowed access, in ways denied to the Irish—partly owing to ethnic and religious prejudice, partly because Irish resistance to incorporation took a different course. And the interesting question at the beginning of the twenty-first century is whether Scotland will follow Ireland into complete independence (within Europe) or stick with the experimental version of home rule that it currently enjoys.

The Invention of Scotland reminds us of several suggestive issues behind these developments, notably the enduring contrast between Lowland and Highland Scotland, which differ profoundly in economics, culture, and political history. The sensitive question of Irish-Scottish connections features here. The original "Scots" were in fact Irish invaders who, after the Romans left Britain, colonized present-day Argyllshire, then known as the kingdom of Dalriada. Instead of gradually being absorbed by the native Pictish stock, the Dalriadans succeeded in "Scoticizing" them (Trevor-Roper's word). The process tends to be submerged by the way in which nationally minded historians invented pedigrees for imaginary Scottish kings—forty of them, to be on the safe side. (The fact that this was exposed as a fantasy by a jeering Welsh antiquary, Humphrey Lhuyd, may be significant.) The Ossian cult revived the troubled question of Irish influence, since the originating fables recorded in these reconstituted epic poems were in fact Irish, as was pointed out by outraged Irish antiquaries.

The whole question of Ossian has been examined by several penetrating recent studies, but none is as entertaining as Trevor-Roper's, which is written in the spirit of a detective story. The cloudy poetic romances published by James Macpherson, capturing the ear of polite England and Europe (notably the Napoleonic court) and winning endorsement from some authorities who rapidly came to regret their ingenuousness, were certainly based on some Gaelic fragments, though not the great Homeric panoply that Macpherson claimed. But even with the residue of authentic material, there has always been an intriguingly bad fit between the awkward and unpopular medium-figure of Macpherson, who clammed up in later life, and the rolling, romantic verbosity of his bardic productions. Trevor-Roper, by brilliant sleuthing, uncovers a sort of committee of forgers clustered around Macpherson's cleverer cousin, a Highland laird who died inconveniently soon, leaving his cloddish relative with an uncomfortable inheritance. It is a marvelous story, delivered as a kind of sucker punch from beyond the grave, and it should have exactly the detonating effect its author so much liked to produce.

It also suggests that enduring Scots theme of doubleness, doppelgangers, Jekylls and Hydes: the containment of multitudes within a single apparently well-organized organism. Trevor-Roper writes sympathetically of Walter Scott: "Within him there were two—at least two—souls. At one time he would be the Augustan man of letters, the practical Unionist, the well-balanced, scholarly heir of the eighteenth-century Enlightenment who edited Dryden, saw through Ossian, and brought gas to Abbotsford; at another he would be the romantic Jacobite, the poet who would allow himself to be carried away by his own too sympathetic vision of an archaic Highland past." Trevor-Roper credits Scott's Jacobite novel *Waverley* (1814) with starting the tartan craze and with instigating the fetish of the kilt. Even more suggestively, he asserts that the British Army's Highland regiments really began the study of stirring traditions based on rickety foundations. The Sobieski Stuart brothers also played an important part, writing *The Costume of the Clans* and unwisely publishing in 1842 an elaborately edited "ancient" text about traditional Scottish dress, the *Vestiarium Scoticum,* which was exposed as yet another invention. But one of the enduring pleasures of this book, as of the study of national tradition in general, is the discovery of how little hard fact actually matters.

How inevitably an indulged and self-created and often fantastic "national tradition" leads to full-blown nationalism is a large and open question. The Scottish National Party, whose platform is based on an independent Scotland in Europe, is currently in the ascendant and threatens to overcome the Labour Party in Scotland, the

Conservatives already having been liquidated. SNP ideologues tend to fulminate against the Scotophilia created by Victorian Romantics, promoting instead the gritty values of post-industrial Glasgow, the patois of "Lallans" (a Lowland Scots dialect), and Robbie Burns above Walter Scott, the skirl of the bagpipes, or the ruined castle keeps outlined on a million shortbread tins. But these icons of radical authenticity may owe more than they realize to preceding inventors, who helped create the sense of difference and superiority on which the germ of nationalism thrives.

There is a final irony about this wonderful little book. Trevor-Roper is remembered most vividly in the popular mind for being himself the victim of a hoax: late in his career, he unwisely authenticated the supposed discovery of Hitler's missing diary, which turned out to be a forgery. Rushed into a snap judgment by a newspaper, the great historian lived to regret bitterly his credulity. Perhaps this is why he held back in his lifetime from publishing a book that deals so brilliantly and authoritatively with the readiness to believe in constructions that are entertaining, edifying, or—most potent of all—comforting, and that cast a compensatory glamour over harsh realities and foregone conclusions.

Spring Semester 2009

A version of this lecture appeared in the *New Republic*, 3 December 2008.

5

Chatham House and All That

ROGER MORGAN

The Royal Institute of International Affairs, also known as Chatham House (after the institute's venerable building in St. James's Square, London), has sometimes been portrayed by suspicious critics as a component of the British establishment, a sinister and conspiratorial organization where the holders of corporate, military, and political power meet to determine the course of British foreign policy. Sometimes the criticism has been sharp and specific. For instance, the eminent scholar Elie Kedourie, in a celebrated polemic against the "Chatham House Version" of the Middle East, argued that the pro-Arab bias of the institute's research (especially the work of Arnold Toynbee, its Director of Studies for thirty years) was directly connected to a fundamentally misguided British policy in that region. To place such criticisms in perspective, it will help to recall the reasons why the institute was created in the first place.

The Royal Institute of International Affairs was founded in 1920. What was it for, and what is it for now? During its nearly ninety-year existence, the institute can be said to have pursued five distinct though interrelated aims: first, to promote knowledge of international affairs with a view to improving the state of the world; second, to provide information and ideas for its members (originally a few hundred, now about five thousand); third, to act as a learned society that would play a leading role in the study of what its royal charter called "the sciences of international politics, economics and jurisprudence"; fourth, to educate British public opinion on international affairs, through its publications and the media; and fifth, to play a part in the making of British foreign policy.

The plan to establish a British Institute of International Affairs, like the planning for the Council on Foreign Relations in New York, took shape during the First World War and its aftermath. One reaction to the war was a "liberal internationalist" viewpoint, which held that if decision makers and "public opinion" were provided with better information about world affairs and foreign countries, misunderstandings and miscalculations could be prevented and conflicts averted.

The Paris Peace Conference of 1919 was structured in such a way that for long periods the huge assembly of delegates had little to do while they waited for the "Big Four" Allied leaders to conclude the necessary deals behind closed doors; this encouraged many of them to discuss ways and means of running the affairs of the world differently. At a meeting held on 30 May 1919, leading British and American delegates, including Lord Robert Cecil and General Tasker Bliss, were brought together by a caucus organized by Lionel Curtis, an internationalist who had served in Lord Milner's "Kindergarten" in South Africa. The meeting resolved to establish "an Anglo-American institute of international affairs" in order to promote understanding of these affairs, and to "provide libraries and research facilities."[1]

In the event, the proposal for a single Anglo-American institute, with branches in London and New York, proved impracticable, partly for legal reasons. The American participants in the Paris meeting joined forces with the newly established Council on Foreign Relations, while the British group proceeded to set up a separate British institute in London. Transatlantic contact and cooperation between the two organizations has normally been fairly close from that day to this, but not as organic as originally envisaged.

The British Institute of International Affairs was formally established at a meeting in London on 5 July 1920. The motion to create it was proposed by a former Foreign Secretary, the Liberal Viscount Grey, and seconded by another, the Conservative Lord Balfour. These were elected as two of the Presidents of the new institute, the third being the Labour politician J. R. Clynes—a tripartite arrangement that has continued, symbolizing the nonpartisan nature of the institute. The institute was "to encourage and facilitate the study of international questions, to promote the exchange of information and thought on international affairs, with a view to the creation of better-informed opinion, and to publish or arrange for the publication of works with these objects."[2] It was decided that membership should be limited to one thousand and should be by invitation only. This arrangement gave the institute from the beginning the image of a self-perpetuating and even conspiratorial elite—an image that it has still not wholly dispelled, despite radical changes in its composition and procedures. The men invited to become members (British citizens only) included officials, journalists, politicians, academics, and a limited number of bankers and businessmen. The 756 original members or invitees included 106 military officers, 174 officials (including 42 from the Foreign Office, whose special position will be discussed later), 31 Members of Parliament, and 113 academics (mainly teachers of law, history, or colonial affairs at Oxford or Cambridge). The establishment composition of the membership is indicated by the fact that 88 of those in the above categories held either peerages or knighthoods.[3]

The institute began its life in temporary accommodations (from 1921, in rooms in Bloomsbury rented from London University's Institute of Historical Research), and soon developed an active program of lectures and discussions. In this connection it is worth mentioning the well-known Chatham House Rule, which was introduced in 1927, shortly after the institute moved to its new address. In its original form, the rule, designed to ensure a fuller exchange of views between visiting speakers and the audience, stated: "In order that speakers may feel free to express their opinions, all meetings of the Institute shall, unless otherwise stated, be strictly private. Members shall be free to use information received at any meeting of the Institute but . . . the speaker's name shall not be quoted nor the fact mentioned that the information was obtained at a meeting of the Institute." The rule still applies to some meetings, but not to all.

As for the new institute's first publications, they included what was to become an annual *Survey of International Affairs,* written in large part by Arnold Toynbee. This followed the advice Viscount Grey had given in his address to the inaugural meeting of 1920, that the institute should "try to do for the present something like what history does for the past." As he put it, "if year by year it will . . . produce something like an annual register of foreign affairs . . . , it will be doing a most important service. It will not interfere with policy, but provide materials from which politicians, statesmen and journalists can form sound opinions in regard to policy."[4]

Grey's hint that the new institute's work should not "interfere with policy" no doubt reflected the strong fears of senior Foreign Office officials that the intrusion of a number of meddlesome outsiders might hinder the delicate work of diplomacy, particularly if the diplomats were expected to discuss this with the outsiders. A rule was thus established that members of the Foreign Office, while they could become members of the institute and attend its events, were not allowed to speak at them.

In the mid-1920s, the institute experienced three major changes: it appointed Professor Arnold Toynbee as Director of Studies, a post he was to hold for thirty years; second, it was provided, thanks to a Canadian benefactor, with the building in St. James's Square that has been its home ever since, and that, having once housed William Pitt the Elder, 1st Earl of Chatham, took the name of Chatham House; and third, the grant of a royal charter in 1926 made it the Royal (rather than the British) Institute of International Affairs.

The first of these events, the installation of Arnold Toynbee as Director of Studies, ensured that Chatham House came to be regarded as a major source of significant and sometimes authoritative publications on international affairs. The centerpiece of the publications program was the annual *Survey,* which Toynbee and his small staff produced from the 1920s to the 1950s. Although interrupted by the Second World War, which changed its publication rhythm and the form of its coverage of events, the series continued to appear, despite mounting difficulties, until the 1970s. Meanwhile, some of Toynbee's efforts were devoted to producing his monumental ten-volume *Study of History,* which appeared between 1934 and 1954. Toynbee and his team also issued a steady flow of substantial monographs on many aspects of world affairs, as well as shorter commentaries and journal articles.

As for the institute's new location, its move to 10 St. James's Square placed it close to Whitehall and to Westminster, respectively the executive and legislative branches of British government. This proximity helped the institute get eminent public figures, British and foreign, to address its meetings. It also facilitated a closer relationship with the Foreign Office—as time went by, the restrictions on diplomatic participation in Chatham House events were greatly relaxed—and with other governmental departments. The cost of maintaining the large and antiquated building in central London was always considerable. It was only during the exceptional circumstances of the war that the institute received really substantial financial support from the government; and the maintenance of Chatham House and its manifold activities has required sustained efforts to ensure support from corporate supporters and research-funding bodies.

As for the granting of the institute's royal charter in 1926, this recognized that it formed part of what journalists and scholars were later to identify as the ruling establishment of the United Kingdom.

It confirmed that the institute was prestigious, like the Royal Historical Society, without of course making it part of the machinery of the state, like the Royal Courts of Justice or the Royal Navy.

DURING THE 1930S, AS THE INTERNATIONAL SITUATION worsened and British foreign policy faced mounting challenges, the relations between Chatham House and the policy makers became more complex. Hitherto, Toynbee and his team had rarely criticized governmental policy, and Foreign Office officials were regularly asked to write or to comment on sections of the annual *Survey*. However, there was now a dramatic change. Toynbee's *Survey* for 1935 contained a virulent attack on the Baldwin government's policy of appeasing Mussolini, which included conniving at his conquest of Abyssinia. Although the authorities of Chatham House issued the standard explanation that this study represented only the personal views of the author, controversy was inevitable. It must be added that Toynbee's views on the appeasement of dictators were ambiguous, even equivocal. In contrast to his condemnation of the Hoare-Laval Pact on Abyssinia in 1935, he was closely aligned with the dominant section of the British establishment that sought to appease Nazi Germany. In 1938, when the Chamberlain government was pressing Czechoslovakia to cede the Sudetenland to Germany, Toynbee was even prepared to tone down the pro-Czech arguments of a Chatham House book by the expert Elizabeth Wiskemann in order to avoid hampering this policy of appeasement.

The outbreak of war in 1939 was radically to transform Chatham House's nongovernmental situation. Just as the First World War had indirectly caused the institute's creation, the second brought about a fundamental change in the work it was doing and in the main addressee of its analyses and reflections. This addressee now became the British government.

As soon as war broke out, Chatham House implemented a plan that had already been worked out in detail with the Foreign Office. Arnold Toynbee and the majority of the institute's research staff left London for Oxford, where they were installed in Toynbee's old college, Balliol, and linked up with a network of diplomats, Oxford academics, and others to form the government's Foreign Research and Press Service, of which Toynbee was the Director. The tasks of this agency were varied. Originally, they included, as well as collecting and analyzing information from the world's media, writing propaganda material, some of it to be scattered over Germany by the Royal Air Force. However, the work that was most congenial to Toynbee and his associates (such people as Oxford's Professor of

International Relations, Alfred Zimmern) was the preparation of policy briefings offering advice to the Foreign Office, and to the Cabinet as a whole, on what should be done to win the war and to shape the post-war settlement.

In 1943, as victory for the Allies seemed increasingly likely, the government decided to strengthen its capacity for post-war planning by merging Toynbee's Foreign Research and Press Service with the Political Intelligence Department of the Foreign Office to form the Foreign Office Research Department, of which Toynbee was to be the Director until 1946.

If we can identify any period in Chatham House's history when its work had a direct causal effect on British foreign policy, it must be this wartime period, when the institute's research efforts were largely devoted to the production of studies for the attention of decision makers. Regrettably, this interesting period has not yet received the scholarly attention it deserves. The recent study *Think-Tanks and Power in Foreign Policy* by Inderjeet Parmar contains much information on Chatham House's wartime role, but it stops short of a systematic evaluation of the documentary evidence available. The fact that, as the author shows, persons associated with Chatham House played a significant role in British foreign-policy actions—for instance, Lord Lothian in Anglo-American negotiations in 1939–40, or Professor Charles Webster in the drafting of the UN Charter—is not evidence that Chatham House as such had any particular influence.

In some cases, the documentary evidence does show a direct input from Chatham House (in its wartime guise as the FRPS) into the policy of the British government. For instance, Churchill's despairing proposal of June 1940 for a Franco-British Union arose directly from work done in 1939–40 by Toynbee, Zimmern, and other Chatham House figures with their French counterparts: this work was personally encouraged and used by R. A. Butler, Lord Halifax's Under-Secretary, who reported to the Foreign Secretary that he had asked the "two learned gentlemen" to develop their project "in their leisure hours at Chatham House."[5] Again, research and recommendations by Chatham House experts, including C. A. Macartney and R. W. Seton-Watson, played an influential part in shaping the UK's wartime policy toward southeastern Europe. Churchill and Eden disagreed sharply on the future of the Balkan states: should these be restored to full national independence after the Allied victory (the view of Eden and the Foreign Office), or should they be grouped together in some kind of "Danubian Federation" (a course strongly advocated by Churchill, who had nostalgic memories of the old

Austro-Hungarian Empire)? Toynbee's Chatham House researchers gave expert backing to the latter view, and this became the official British position until the Soviet Union's post-war hegemony in Eastern Europe made it unattainable.

After the Second World War, the institute entered a period that was undramatic in comparison with its wartime hyperactivity. Arnold Toynbee and the Director-General, Ivison McAdam, who both returned to St. James's Square after war service, had been in place since the 1920s, and it was natural that much of the work of the institute—for instance, the writing of the annual *Survey*—should be passed on to their younger colleagues. Toynbee, indeed, was occupied with the concluding volumes of his *Study of History,* and the institute's output of other publications, though regarded as worthy, was criticized as being somewhat uninspired. In 1954, there was a major crisis of confidence in Chatham House's management: junior members of the research staff were dissatisfied with their jobs, and several of the institute's members were critical of the quality of the meetings and discussions. This was followed by a change of leadership: the post of Director-General was taken over by a gifted author and former intelligence officer, "Monty" Woodhouse, until his election as Conservative Member of Parliament for Oxford in 1959, and the editorship of the *Survey* was taken over by the eminent medievalist Geoffrey Barraclough and later by Donald Cameron Watt.

In connection with the *Survey,* we may note one of the most serious criticisms to have been made of the work of Toynbee and his associates. Although Professor Elie Kedourie's celebrated attack, *The Chatham House Version,* was published in 1970, it expressed a fundamental critique of the whole of Toynbee's interpretation of Middle Eastern affairs since the early 1920s. In the context of castigating British policy for what he regarded as its cardinal error of attempting to befriend and appease Arab nationalism, Kedourie condemned Toynbee's "scientific" (to Kedourie, profoundly "unscientific") studies of the Middle East for misguidedly positing the existence of an authentic "Arab civilization." This civilization, according to Toynbee, which was emerging from Ottoman domination, was being threatened by the aggressive force of Zionism encouraged by the British commitment to a Jewish National Home, as embodied in the Balfour Declaration of 1917. It was true that Toynbee had sharply criticized the Balfour Declaration and had a low regard for Judaism as a civilization. Despite his attempts to maintain a balance, much of what was written about the Middle East by himself and his colleagues (notably Harold Beeley and George Kirk) leaned toward the Arab point of view.

The two decades from the end of the fifties to the late seventies were particularly active and fruitful ones for the institute. The high standards set in this period have been maintained, with some ups and downs, ever since. The Director from 1959 to 1971 was Kenneth Younger, a Labour politician who had served as the Foreign Office's Minister of State (at times, in effect, as acting Foreign Secretary) in 1950–51, at the end of Clement Attlee's premiership, and who gave up his parliamentary career to direct Chatham House. As Director of Studies, Younger recruited Andrew Shonfield, a brilliant journalist and author on economic and international affairs, who was to succeed Younger as the institute's Director from 1972 to 1977.

Chatham House intensified its collaboration with institutes abroad, especially in continental Europe as well as the United States, and at the same time continued to produce a flow of substantial publications. Its expanded research staff included, in international economics and political economy, Andrew Shonfield, Susan Strange, and Caroline Miles, and, in international law, Rosalyn Higgins and James Fawcett. Notable works in area studies dealt with Russia, China, Africa, and Latin America; and, in the field of international relations, I can mention my own contributions (I was the deputy to the Director of Studies from 1968 to 1974), in the form of books on Anglo-German relations and U.S.-German relations, and the edited volume *The Study of International Affairs: Essays in Honour of Kenneth Younger* (1972). As well as book-length studies, we all contributed articles to the institute's two journals (the quarterly *International Affairs* and the monthly *The World Today*) and commented on current events through the press, radio, and television.

In the latest phase, the thirty years since the 1970s, the nature and balance of Chatham House's output of publications have somewhat changed. The *Survey* has disappeared, and there are fewer book-length studies altogether, while the output of shorter and more topical commentaries, paperbacks, and briefing papers has greatly increased. Under a series of Directors (including one eminent journalist, two retired senior officers from the armed services, and two leading academics), the research staff, including a number of part-time research fellows, has continued to grow. One way in which the institute measures its external impact is by the number of mentions of Chatham House in the media (many of them relating to articles or broadcasts by the staff): the 2007 *Annual Report* records that while the aimed-for target for such "media mentions" in 2006–07 was 1,500, the number achieved was 6,371. In the same year, when the target for hits on the Chatham House Web site (where publications and reports of presentations can be downloaded) was 600,000, the number achieved was 1,104,000.

BEFORE CONCLUDING, I WOULD LIKE TO RECORD a few impressions of what it was like for me to work there when I became Assistant Director of Studies in 1968. My appointment allowed me to pursue my own research, including the completion of a book on the relations between the United States and post-war Germany. My other duties included helping the Director and the Director of Studies, Kenneth Younger and Andrew Shonfield, plan and manage the research program of the institute. I thought, and still think, that we made a good team for this purpose. Younger, as a former intelligence officer, parliamentarian, and government minister, had all the interests and contacts provided by that experience. Shonfield, a celebrated journalist, broadcaster, and author on economic and international affairs, was held in high regard by a vast circle of influential people, both in the UK and abroad. My own, subordinate contribution came from the fact that after teaching International Relations for ten years in British and American universities, I knew the academic field and those who tilled it. Combining our complementary perspectives and contacts, we were able to bring a wide range of useful participants together for Chatham House discussions and publications.

Part of my job amounted to running a specialist publishing operation. Chatham House produced at least a dozen substantial books a year, some of them written by the in-house research staff, others commissioned from external experts, and all published as a matter of course by Oxford University Press. My role was to help identify subjects deserving study, and appropriate authors, and then to submit the proposal to the institute's Research Committee for approval (often after intensive discussion) and for the grant of any necessary funds for travel, documentation, or research assistance. The Research Committee was an impressive body. Chaired by the Oxford historian Alan Bullock, it included several other weighty representatives of the academic world (including Hugh Seton-Watson and Bernard Lewis), a senior editorial manager from Oxford University Press, and a member of the Planning Staff of the Foreign Office.

Sometimes a Chatham House book was produced by a lone author who would sooner or later send in a manuscript. Other books would have contributions by several authors, directed and edited by one of the in-house experts. In yet other cases, a book would be produced by an author working together with a study group of experts that met periodically to discuss the work in progress: this was the case for Kenneth Younger's little book on British foreign policy, *Changing Perspectives in British Foreign Policy*, published in 1964, and for a larger-scale treatment of the same subject that I organized in the early seventies and that produced complementary volumes by Professors Joseph Frankel (*British Foreign Policy, 1945–1973*) and William Wallace (*The Foreign Policy Process in Britain*). In other cases—this was a further way in which Chatham House's output differed from that of a conventional publishing firm—a two- or three-day seminar or conference would be convened, and the contributions to it would be revised, following the conference discussions, to form chapters of an edited book. This was the case, for instance, for a comparative study of British and German policy-making that I organized with Professor Karl Kaiser, the director of research at Chatham House's sister institute in Bonn, and that led to book publications both in English (*Britain and West Germany: Changing Societies and the Future of Foreign Policy*, 1971) and in German.

There were also frequent conferences designed to assess current world events, particularly by meeting with colleagues from other countries. One of the first Chatham House events I helped organize was a conference planned in late 1968 with the Institute of Defense Analyses in Washington, D.C., to consider how Anglo-American relations might or should develop after the inauguration of a new administration in early 1969.

My years at Chatham House were occupied with writing, managing research, discussing world affairs at a variety of levels and places, lecturing in the UK and elsewhere, and a good deal of broadcasting for the BBC. Sometimes I would go to the World Service studios in Bush House and offer my comments—on events in Brussels, say, or Willy Brandt's eastern policy—in French and German as well as English. All these activities formed part of the normal contributions of Chatham House's senior researchers to the overall functions of the institute.

I NOW TURN, IN CONCLUSION, to the question of how far, and how successfully, the institute has achieved the objectives its founders and their successors have defined for it. To reiterate, these included five distinct though partly overlapping aims: understanding world problems, with a view to helping solve them; providing information and ideas for the institute's members; functioning as the British learned society for the academic study of international affairs; informing public opinion about foreign affairs; and playing some kind of role in the making of British foreign policy.

As regards the first objective—to contribute to the understanding and the amelioration of international problems—Chatham House has a long record. The way it feels free to criticize British foreign policy was illustrated in a valedictory address by the former Director, Professor Victor Bulmer-Thomas, given in December 2006, in which he described the 2003 invasion of Iraq as "a terrible mistake."[6]

A consideration of the institute's second aim—the provision of information and other services to its members—must start by asking who today's five thousand members are. About half of them belong as individuals, the traditional mix of academics, former and serving officials, businesspeople, and journalists. The remaining members represent the institute's corporate subscribers: business firms, banks, government departments, and foreign diplomatic missions. In great contrast to the old days of a strictly all-British membership, members of London's diplomatic corps, or of foreign banks and other corporate bodies, as well as qualified individual foreigners, now make up one-third of the membership. Further changes include a noticeable increase in the number of younger participants: members younger than thirty-five now make up 20 percent of the total. The steady growth in membership must reflect appreciation of the services Chatham House provides.

The institute's third aim, to function as a learned society for the academic study of international affairs, was certainly a worthy and necessary one when Chatham House was founded. In the 1920s, the academic field of International Relations was in its infancy, and Chatham House's role as a promoter of research and publication gave it an important impetus. It could be said that of the significant British books on international affairs published in the twenties and thirties (and perhaps for longer), the majority appeared under Chatham House's auspices. By the closing decades of the century, much had changed. University centers of advanced research in international affairs—not least Oxford's St. Antony's College and the University of London's School of Oriental and African Studies, as well as the Centre for International Studies at the London School of Economics—were publishing their own impressive series of books in the field. The spirit of the times called for the institute to see itself as one of London's growing number of foreign policy think tanks and to restrict its former role as a learned society.

A fourth objective has been to create a better-informed public opinion on foreign affairs by disseminating the results of the institute's research as widely as possible. This was a reason for getting publications out as soon as possible after the events they described, and the institute also set great store by providing an information service that allowed members and enquirers to keep up to date with world events. Chatham House's media contributions included a weekly article by Toynbee in the *Economist,* and there were also strong links with *The Times* and the *Observer.* Radio and, later, television also provided Chatham House researchers with new channels for their mission of public enlightenment, and the development of the BBC External Service, which broadcast during and after the Second World War in other languages as well as English, allowed them to contribute to public opinion across frontiers. As noted earlier, Chatham House can now employ such yardsticks of its influence as the number of media mentions it receives annually, many of which are related to radio or television broadcasts by the staff or associates, as well as their contributions in the printed press. Judging by the high annual totals of these mentions, as well as by the growing popularity of the institute's Web site, this educative ambition of Chatham House's founders is still being pursued with some success.

I turn finally to the institute's fifth aim, that of playing a part of some kind—and in practice, of several kinds—in the making of British foreign policy. The officeholders responsible for foreign policy reacted to the creation and development of the institute in sharply divergent ways. At the political level, it was given a fairly warm welcome: Robert Cecil, Edward Grey, and Arthur Balfour all participated in its establishment; Lord Curzon became one of its trustees; and during the inter-war years, a practice developed by which the incumbent Foreign Secretary would address Chatham House's annual dinner, usually offering detailed suggestions for research. In contrast, the Foreign Office's official level, from Permanent Under-Secretaries downward, regarded the new institute with great suspicion, as a meddlesome body likely to interfere in the work of diplomats, and one with which their contacts had to be severely regulated. In practice, it was not long before this attitude was modified. Foreign Office officials at various levels found Chatham House useful in a number of ways, and it is worth considering what these ways turned out to be.

For a start, on certain occasions and in certain circumstances, Chatham House was able to feed into the policy process some ideas that had an influence on what the practitioners did. This was certainly true of the two wartime issues cited above, and there were later cases as well. An example of how the Foreign Office commissioned from Chatham House a study of a specific (and sometimes new and challenging) policy issue to supplement the work of its own Research Department and Planning Staff was its request in the eighties for a study of the political implications of space research;

this work was carried out by the Director, Admiral James Eberle, and Dr. Helen Wallace. More research is needed on the question of what input Chatham House has made to the substance of British foreign policy, and it will not be easy to carry out, partly because of the multiplicity of other causal factors at work, and perhaps partly because foreign-policy practitioners may not readily admit to the effect of outsiders' efforts on their own. The very least that can be said is that generations of British diplomats have found it useful to participate in Chatham House discussions in order to clarify and try out their own ideas concerning the issues facing them.

The Foreign Office has also found Chatham House a useful partner in the practice of what has come to be called "Track Two Diplomacy," the pursuit of quasi-diplomatic exchanges at a level less formal than that of official negotiations. An example is the Anglo-American conference of 1968, already mentioned, in which Chatham House and its American partner convened a meeting of officials and non-official experts from the two countries, an operation considered important enough by the Foreign Office to receive considerable financial support. This followed in a tradition established before the Second World War: Chatham House was the British participant not only in conferences of Commonwealth countries, but also in such bodies as the Institute of Pacific Relations, of which Chatham House constituted the British national section. After the war, the Foreign Office frequently turned to Chatham House to animate and manage bilateral meetings, sometimes with friendly states, such as our Western European partners (Chatham House played a central role in the Anglo-German Koenigswinter Conferences, launched in 1950), and sometimes with states behind the Iron Curtain: Chatham House contributed much to the "round tables" organized in Eastern European countries (where the British Council was banned from operating) by the Great Britain–East Europe Centre, established by the Foreign Office in the 1960s, and to the later British-Soviet Forum.

This list of Foreign Office–Chatham House interactions could be prolonged. Andrew Shonfield, when Director of Studies, was invited to join a top-level group, the Duncan Committee, reviewing the conduct and organization of the UK's representation abroad. When the Foreign Secretary, Sir Alec Douglas-Home, visited China in 1973, he took with him not only Chatham House's Chairman, Lord (Humphrey) Trevelyan, but also, as a governmental present for the Chinese People's Institute of World Affairs, a long reading list we had compiled. In addition, Chatham House experts have been much in demand as lecturers in training courses for diplomats and other civil servants; as speakers at the Foreign Office's international conference center at Wilton Park, in Sussex; and even—in the days when the Foreign Office's budget provided for such things—as envoys on lecture tours to foreign audiences, like the tour of the United States and Canada that I was invited, and financed, to undertake in the seventies.

In several ways, then, the interaction between diplomats and outsiders that was manifest at the Peace Conference in 1919 and that led to the creation of Chatham House lives on. And it is probably true to say that Chatham House can indeed be described as part of Britain's establishment.

Spring Semester 2008

1. Quoted in Deborah Lavin, *From Empire to International Commonwealth: A Biography of Lionel Curtis* (Oxford, 1995), p. 166.

2. Quoted in C. E. Carrington (revised and updated by Mary Bone), *Chatham House: Its History and Inhabitants* (London, 2004), p. 49. I have drawn heavily on this essential source of information.

3. Inderjeet Parmar, *Think-Tanks and Power in Foreign Policy: A Comparative Study of the Role and Influence of the Council on Foreign Relations and the Royal Institute of International Affairs, 1939–45* (Basingstoke, 2004), p. 32.

4. Roger Morgan, "'To Advance the Science of International Politics . . . ': Chatham House's Early Research," in Andrea Bosco and Cornelia Navari, eds., *Chatham House and British Foreign Policy, 1919–1945* (London, 1994), p. 123.

5. Quoted in Andrea Bosco, *Federal Union and the Origins of the Churchill Proposal* (London, 1992), p. 148.

6. Victor Bulmer-Thomas, *Blair's Foreign Policy and its Possible Successor(s)*, Chatham House Briefing Paper No. 06/01 (Dec. 2006), p. 1.

6

The Study of International Relations in Historical Perspective

ADAM ROBERTS

I had the privilege of being the Montague Burton Professor of International Relations at Oxford from 1986 to the end of 2007—for the last gasp of the Cold War and the first two decades of the post–Cold War era. The end of the Cold War is arguably the most significant development in international relations since 1945, and the most difficult to interpret. This is a glimpse at the causes and consequences of the events whereby the Cold War ended, and their implications for the study and practice of international relations in the post–Cold War period.

What follows is an unashamed defense, even celebration, of a pluralist approach to both the conduct and the study of international relations. This is a pluralism that accepts the relevance of many different views of international relations: not just the proper emphasis on power and interest that is found in realist theories, but also those views that stress the significance of ideas and norms, the impact of domestic political and economic structures on international politics, the roles of transnational movements and international organizations, and the existence of new challenges. It is a pluralism of theories, a pluralism of political systems, a pluralism of different cultures and mindsets, a pluralism of methods of analysis, and a pluralism of academic disciplines. While eschewing simple linear visions of progress, such a version of pluralism does not reject evidence of, or ideas about, progress. Pluralism in these senses is a strength of International Relations studies in British universities generally. (I follow here the odd custom of using lower-case throughout when referring to actual international relations, and capital initials when referring to the academic subject of International Relations. No priority of the academy over actuality is implied.)

I feel a special obligation to focus on, even celebrate, diversity. In 2006, the Foreign and Commonwealth Office (FCO), shockingly, sought to bring an end to that respected institution of British diplomacy, the valedictory dispatch customarily written by UK ambassadors on leaving their posts. Indeed, I may have had something to do with it. I am not an unreserved enthusiast for all aspects of target setting and other bureaucratic devices, whether in the university or in the conduct of foreign policy. I was encouraged in my doubts about five-year plans when I came across a truly robust response to the pressure to set targets, courageously and successfully expressed in the immortal words of the USSR Deputy People's Commissar for Foreign Affairs, Maxim Litvinov, in 1929:

> Unlike other Commissariats, the Commissariat for Foreign Affairs cannot, unfortunately, put forward a five-year plan of work, a plan for the development of foreign policy. It is not difficult to see why. In putting forward control figures and drawing up the plan of economic development we start from our own aspirations and wishes, from a calculation of our own potentialities, and from the firm principles of our entire policy, but in examining the development of foreign policy we have to deal with a number of factors that are scarcely subject to calculation, with a number of elements outside our control and the scope of our action. International affairs are composed not only of our own aspirations and actions, but of those of a large number of countries, built on different lines from our Union, pursuing other aims than ours, and using other means to achieve those aims than we allow.[1]

There has yet to be an equally well-argued and robust statement from the FCO or the Ministry of Defence in response to the stream of demands for departmental targets and plans that swept through Whitehall in the Thatcher, Major, and Blair years. I have a special reason for mentioning Litvinov's statement, quite apart from its explicit recognition that different countries have different structures and values. For better or worse, I happened to mention it to Sir Ivor Roberts, now President of Trinity College, Oxford, when he was British Ambassador to Italy, and he in turn cited Litvinov's statement in his valedictory dispatch from Rome in September 2006.[2] Immediately upon receiving it, Sir Peter Ricketts, the Permanent

Under-Secretary of the FCO, abolished the whole institution of the valedictory dispatch. This was one of several matters on which Sir Ivor had some crisp comments to make in evidence to the House of Commons Foreign Affairs Committee in July 2007.[3] The committee agreed with him, and called for the reinstatement of these dispatches.[4] My sin of having contributed in a small way, and involuntarily, to a foolish government decision requires an act of atonement. This is it.

The reinstatement of valedictory dispatches would be one means of showing respect for the different cultures and mindsets that make up our world. Alas, not only has it not happened, but an FCO mission statement adopted in 2008 makes no mention of understanding foreign countries and cultures as a core FCO task. The apparent neglect of this core task undermines the FCO's Britannia-like vision of the UK as "a global hub in the 21st century," which is conjured up in the same mission statement.[5] An understanding of the complexity of the world—of how different experiences and thought-patterns have shaped both the past and present of different societies—is a necessary basis for policy making that we would be unwise to downplay. To know where we are, we have to know where we, and others, have come from.

What were the processes of change that led to the end of the Cold War? What, in particular, can we learn from the memoirs of participants and documents of the period now available? Do these sources change the pictures that each of us may have built up about the nature and causes of these events?

My own experience may have distorted my understanding. It is a strange fact of my academic career that I spent the first days of my first teaching post, as a lecturer at the LSE in September 1968, in post-invasion Czechoslovakia. Then in April 1986 I spent the first days of my Montague Burton professorship in the Soviet Union. In between, in May 1972, I spent some time doing research in Yugoslavia. I have always been attracted by lost causes, but to lose three countries smacks of carelessness. On the other hand, there is much to celebrate in these events and in the ending of the Cold War, with which they were associated.

The events of 1989–91 in Eastern Europe and the Soviet Union are the most remarkable case of large-scale peaceful change in world history. True, they were followed by tragedy in some of the successor states, and they led to hubris in the United States. Yet these events shaped much of what came after for the better, especially in the unification of Germany and the subsequent consolidation of democratic systems of government in many Eastern European countries.

The transition was and remains a cause for celebration—and also for careful consideration of how and why it occurred so peacefully. Excessively simple views of this process have had a baneful effect in the years since 1991. The factors that led to the ending of communist rule throughout Europe, and to the collapse of the great communist federations, are numerous and complex.

It is sometimes said that scholars of International Relations failed to predict the end of the Cold War. There were indeed some notable cases of a failure not only to predict, but even to observe what was going on in front of our eyes. In 1992, the historian John Gaddis memorably criticized International Relations specialists for failing to see the end of the Cold War coming.[6] Although he did not explicitly note this fact, the academics he was targeting were overwhelmingly American—for certain U.S. specialists in International Relations made the boldest claims of being capable of foreseeing and influencing the future, and their supposedly scientific methodologies have tended to be parsimonious, seeking to explain outcomes from a limited range of considerations. With their emphasis on states and international systems, they have often played down the domestic and human dimensions of decision making. They have tended to place more reliance on abstract reasoning and hard facts than on understanding foreign languages, histories, and cultures. They have often missed the uniqueness of particular individuals, situations, and moments. Not surprisingly, the end of the Cold War caused particularly deep soul searching among some colleagues in International Relations, especially in the United States. It contributed to the emergence of the "constructivist" school, which—while unfortunately creating a new ism for an approach the essentials of which would not seem strange to many historians—at last took proper account of human consciousness and how perceptions of the world are shaped by each person's, and each country's, lived experience.[7]

The very idea that International Relations is a science, and stands or falls by its ability to predict the future, would have been rejected strongly by many, perhaps all, of my predecessors in the Montague Burton chair. When Alastair Buchan took up the post in 1972, he was clear about what could and could not be claimed for the subject:

> If through an orderly study of the recent past we can achieve some comprehension of the contemporary international system, can we claim any predictive value for our judgements? Clearly not in any detailed fashion, or for the whole complexity of international or

transnational interaction. If we attempt this we risk either vague-
ness or misleading dogmatism. But we can, as Mill said, indicate
"an order of possible progress". . . . I believe in the validity of a
plural international system of many different kinds and sizes of
nations and civilizations as the one most conducive both to justice
and to order, difficult though it may be to manage.[8]

This use of John Stuart Mill's phrase was an impeccably liberal
way of indicating that we should be cautious about linear ideas
of progress. I heartily agree. As a former student of the historian
A. J. P. Taylor, who famously emphasized the influence of chance in
history, I am diffident of making any predictive claims. Such cau-
tion has been widespread in British universities and had a notable
exponent in Alastair Buchan's successor in the chair, Hedley Bull,
who was to be equally emphatic that what the academic subject of
International Relations aspires to achieve is understanding, not
prediction.

Both Buchan and Bull, with their pluralistic approaches, recognized that by the 1970s the Cold War had lost much of its ideological sting. Both saw that some of the major causes of conflict
in the era we now think of as the Cold War had little to do with
Soviet-U.S. rivalry and involved instead the inherent difficulties
of establishing new political orders in and between post-colonial
states, a subject that is still today at the heart of most conflicts. Both
Buchan and Bull recognized that change could be peaceful as
well as violent—indeed, Buchan's 1973 Reith Lectures were titled
"Change Without War."[9]

In fact, some scholars and writers did see not exactly how the
Cold War would end, but some of the pressures and forces that
could lead to that outcome—"an order of possible progress." After
Alfred Zimmern retired from the Montague Burton chair in 1944,
he continued to support international organizations, as he had done
with an excess of devotion in the League of Nations era, but he did
so with some interesting twists. In a little-known and curiously staccato book, *The American Road to World Peace* (which, not surprisingly
given its title, was published in the United States and not the UK),
he wrote in 1953 that the persistent Soviet use of the veto on UN Security Council action was a mere temporary phenomenon, because
the Soviet Union itself could not last: "In fifty years' time—and this
is a very generous reckoning—the Soviet Union will be a historic
memory."[10] Not bad: actually, it was just under forty years before the
Soviet Union disappeared.

Those of us who followed the events in Czechoslovakia in 1968
always had in the back of our minds the idea that other ruling

communist parties might embark on major reform projects. It would
not have been clever for westerners to express this idea too openly.
In Prague in April 1969, I heard several Czechoslovak academics express the thought—at the time it seemed a wan hope—that one day
there might be a serious reform movement in the Communist Party
of the Soviet Union. As we now know, there were many similarities
and connections between the Prague Spring and events in Moscow
two decades later. My distinguished Oxford colleague Archie Brown
had more than an inkling of a possible "Moscow Spring." In a paper
for a high-level meeting at Chequers in September 1983 that helped
shape UK policy toward the Soviet Union, he wrote:

> That the party intelligentsia can play a decisive part in introduc-
> ing not only <u>piecemeal reform</u> but also <u>more fundamental change
> was demonstrated by the case of Czechoslovakia</u> in the years
> <u>1963–68</u>. The Soviet Union is a very different country with differ-
> ent historical traditions and it would be rash indeed to predict an
> <u>early "Moscow Spring"</u>. But in principle it is clear that a movement
> for <u>democratising change</u> can come from within a ruling Commu-
> nist Party as well as through societal pressure. It would be carry-
> ing an historical and cultural determinism too far to say that this
> could *never* happen in the Soviet Union.[11] (underlining by Prime
> Minister Thatcher)

Many generalists also correctly recognized the troubles of the Soviet system. Raymond Aron said to Hedley Bull in 1982, at their last
meeting: "It is my view that the most important and indeed most
neglected question in contemporary international relations scholarship is: what will the West do when and if the Soviets decline? How
we answer that question will perhaps determine whether there will
be war or peace in our time."[12] This statement draws attention to
the common failure to foresee that the process of Soviet collapse
could possibly be as peaceful as it eventually turned out to be. It
shows that there were some who got a great deal right without ever
presuming, still less claiming, that they were engaged in a scientific
and predictive academic discipline. Indeed, there seems to be an
inverse relationship between claims to scientific prediction and capacities to sense the direction of events.

What exactly were the factors that led to of the end of the
Cold War? The historical evidence suggests a multifaceted explanation encompassing what might easily be seen as ideological op-
posites and logical incompatibles: both force and diplomacy; both
pressure and détente; both belief and disbelief in the reformability

of communism; both nonviolent resistance in some countries and guerrilla resistance in others; both elite action and street politics; both nuclear deterrence and the ideas of some of its critics; both threat and reassurance; both nationalism in the disparate parts of the Soviet empire and supranationalism in the European Community. A worrying possibility is that the Cold War would not have ended but for two myths: that Soviet-style communism could be reformed and that Star Wars could work. The very complexity— indeed indigestibility—of this mix of factors helps explain why they have not attracted the same attention as have the ideas of the great simplifiers.

Of the many simplifying views of the end of the Cold War, two merit special comment because they cast a shadow into the future. The first is the idea that the USSR was forced into change by Reagan's arms buildup in the 1980s. As one would expect, key Soviet decision makers are critical of this interpretation, suggesting that events could have unfolded faster without some of Reagan's early policies and rhetoric. More importantly, some of the key U.S. figures involved—including George Shultz, Secretary of State, and Jack Matlock, Ambassador to the Soviet Union—while supporting a mixture of strength and diplomacy, resist simple conclusions about the role of external pressures.[13] The documentary evidence now available indicates that the pressures for change felt by the Soviet leadership were of many different kinds: most came from within the Soviet Union; some came from Europe rather than the United States; and some dated back to long before Reagan's presidency. Many came from generational change.

The second simplifying view saw the end of the Cold War as the end of history. This reinforced the deep American sense that if only tyrannies around the world can be deposed, peoples will live in freedom and peace. One could blame it all on Rousseau, with his beguiling statement "Man is born free, and everywhere he is in chains."[14] Many visions and policies, from the "new world order" invoked by President Bush in 1990 to the neoconservative dreams of imposing democracy in 2003, reflected a belief in universalism: that all peoples basically want the same political system, and the military force of democracies can assist the historical process. In the excitement and confusion of the Cold War's end, the spirit of imposed universalism fled from Moscow, but flourished as never before in its other favorite haunt, Washington, D.C.

The post–Cold War era has had many profound interpreters. Universities, including many in the UK, can be proud of the many thoughtful academic contributions to understanding the new circumstances in which we live. At the same time, however, in the public political realm there has been a Babel-like confusion, and no shortage of facile generalizing, about how to characterize the contemporary system of international relations.

American and British visions of world order were not, and are not, by any means identical. In these two countries there are different traditions of thought about how world order should be conceived and implemented. The United States is heir to a revolutionary tradition that sees the rest of the world as composed of monarchical, reactionary, and dictatorial systems of government, the departure of which would enable peoples, freed from their shackles, to pursue their common goals. In International Relations in the United States, an abstract cast of mind has tended to produce an abstract set of thoughts about world order. This is best illustrated by the World Order Models Project, which was established at Princeton University in the early 1970s. WOMP's history is instructive for thinking about world order today. This project was expressly devoted to the creation of "relevant utopias," a glorious aim that proved hard to achieve. By soliciting contributions from many different cultures and countries, the project came up with results that served to "render the original research scheme unfeasible."[15] In other words, it discovered the elementary and terrible truth that different societies and different countries do not share a common vision of how human life or world politics should be organized; nor do they have a common understanding of what constitutes the main obstacles to international order.

Yet the notion of world order does have substance, and is not tied exclusively to a particular set of Anglo-Saxon ideas for reforming the world in our image. Hedley Bull's magisterial study of the roots of international order, far removed temperamentally and analytically from the World Order Models Project, was entitled *The Anarchical Society: A Study of Order in World Politics* (1977). Bull accepted that the term "world order" was not vacuous:

> Since the late nineteenth century and early twentieth century there has arisen for the first time a single political system that is genuinely global. Order on a global scale has ceased to be simply the sum of the various political systems that produce order on a local scale; it is also the product of what may be called a world political system.[16]

Bull also pointed to the special value of the term "world order":

> World order is wider than international order because to give an account of it we have to deal not only with order among states but

also with order on a domestic or municipal scale, provided within particular states, and with order within the wider world political system of which the states system is only part.[17]

Throughout the period since 1945, and often in parallel with the language of world order, there has been a tendency among academics in International Relations and also, to a lesser extent, among policy makers to characterize world politics as uni-, bi-, or multipolar. Such characterizations imply that there is a single world order and that the overarching structure of that order has particular importance in shaping, and helping us explain, events. There are plenty grounds for skepticism about the adequacy of defining world order in polar terms.

Since the end of the Cold War there has been much talk of a "unipolar world," or at least a "unipolar moment," and a tendency to conflate the distinct ideas of the U.S. role and of international order. It is questionable whether it ever made sense to speak of a unipolar world. The pervasive belief that this is a single united world has been buttressed by the rhetoric of globalization; by the belief in the West that democracy is a panacea; and by a reluctance to understand the extent and depth of different worldviews.

Yet if unipolarity and its relative, globalization, are flawed as both descriptions and prescriptions, can any other "polar" characterizations do better? One distinguished scholar of International Relations, the late Samuel Huntington, defined the post–Cold War world as "uni-multi-polar."[18] This term, which sounds like a way to hedge one's bets, is more convoluted than illuminating. Huntington himself all but abandoned it. His conclusion (speaking in 2005) was that the United States should be much less aggressive in its management of international order and should especially avoid attempts to impose democracy on others. He noted the existence of "efforts to change the structure of global politics from what I have awkwardly called a uni-multi-polar world into a truly multi-polar world. That is the way in which inevitably the world is moving, and both the world and the United States will probably be much better off once we get there."[19]

"Multipolarity" does indeed have possible value as both description and prescription. It is free of the implicit arrogance and hubris of unipolar claims. It recognizes the changing facts of economic and military power. However, like other polar ideas, its weakness may lie in its implicit assumption that the world consists of something akin to magnetic poles and iron filings. Does this really fit the pattern of relations in the post–Cold War era? Perhaps the polar tradition of thought about world order has served its purpose, and other language needs to be found.

In the late 1980s and early 1990s, as the Cold War subsided, it sometimes seemed as if the waters of a reservoir were going down and old landmarks were reappearing. Some of the features that emerged into view, such as failed states, conflicts with an ethnic dimension, and the revival of spheres of influence, were only too familiar to historians. However, there were also some developments that were new or that continued processes already significant in the Cold War years. These included the worldwide move toward democracy; an emphasis on acting collectively that went far beyond previous practices such as the geographically and institutionally limited role of the Concert of Europe in the nineteenth century; the rapid growth of global communications; and a number of strong challenges to the previous dominance of European or Western ideas about how the world should be ordered.

The changes at around the time of the end of the Cold War seemed to some observers to offer hope for a new world order, one in which international law, great-power cooperation, international organizations, and democratic political systems would all play a larger part than they had been able to do for most of the twentieth century. There were several distinct visions of such an order. They had the strengths that derive from identifying significant new developments and possibilities—"a certain order of possible progress." However, they also had the weakness of assuming too easily that the suspicions held by great powers and small ones would be quickly overcome and that long-held differences of interest and intellectual perspective would decline in significance. All great causes need to be protected from their most zealous advocates, and ideas of a reformed international order are no exception.

Although the particular visions of the new world order that flourished in the first half of the 1990s ran into predictable and indeed predicted trouble, the idea that we are in a defining period of international relations still survives, influencing policy making in many countries. Even in a United States disillusioned by much of the experience of the 1990s, the idea of completely reshaping the world found new forms of expression. One of these was neoconservatism, a cluster of ideas that, at least to a benighted non-American, seems to be oddly misnamed and to have more in common with French revolutionary Bonapartism than with philosophical conservatism. The invasion of Iraq in 2003 was in part a product of that cluster of ideas; and some of the subsequent events in and around Iraq have cast doubt on the extent to which this body of thought relates effectively to the enduringly complex realities that it seeks to change.

The confusion about the nature of the present world order—and how it can be described—arises because of genuine complexities in the structure of power, the pattern of events, and the ways of thinking about them. While this confusion is not likely to be resolved quickly, the single phrase that best encapsulates the contemporary world order is still "the post–Cold War era." It has the merit of anchoring our understanding of international politics in the great change that occurred in 1989–91, of avoiding language that suggests a complete divorce from the past, and of recognizing that the events of 11 September 2001 did not, as some asserted, usher in a totally new era.

DESPITE THE SERIOUSNESS OF NEW CHALLENGES, international collaboration today is at a remarkably high level by almost any measure: the range of topics covered, the adoption of international standards in a wide range of technical matters, the movement of goods and people, and the extent to which cooperation involves societies as a whole and not just their foreign ministries. In the whole period since 1945, international wars have been fewer and, taken overall, less costly in human lives than in previous eras. The challengers to the present world order do not offer an ideology that is likely to be widely shared. International order appears to be sufficiently robust to be able to survive the temporary incapacitation of the United States because of Iraq and Guantánamo. Could it survive further major blows to U.S. power and prestige, whether self-inflicted or the result of the defiance of adversaries? This is doubtful. An essentially plural or even "anarchic" order, however well-functioning today, is not inherently a strong framework for addressing such challenges as nuclear proliferation, population movements, resource crises, and the effects of global warming: there has to be space within it for effective leadership, whether by major powers or international organizations.

What is the role of international organizations? Since the end of the Cold War, regional and global organizations have been the subject of exceptionally high hopes and occasional disappointments. In light of the difficulties experienced by the United States in its largely unilateral management of Iraq since 2003, there is a tendency (especially but not only in Europe) to argue that multilateral approaches are inherently better than unilateral ones. This sets up a false dichotomy: it fails to take account of the fact that there were some real problems of UN involvement in crises that contributed to the U.S. disenchantment with multilateralism. The Security Council had proved less capable of deciding on military means than on principles and goals, and had achieved a mixed set of results in the conflicts in which it was most deeply engaged. In public international discourse there is a need for a realistic appraisal of both the strengths and the weaknesses of multilateral approaches to security. The depictions of the UN as offering a system of collective security are themselves part of the problem, leading as they do to ill-tempered recrimination about why the desired system has not been achieved. At best, what the UN has to offer is "selective security."

The post–Cold War world has been the subject of an extraordinary series of prescriptions and characterizations: "new world order," "clash of civilizations," the "end of history," and "global chaos." It is more intellectually demanding to analyze and comprehend than the Cold War. However, it is not, or at least not yet, as dangerous, at least as far as the possibility of major war is concerned. On the nature of the post–Cold War order, as on other matters, we could usefully keep in mind the words of Colin Lucas, at the time Oxford's Vice-Chancellor, when speaking in March 1998 in the Great Hall of the People in Beijing at the centenary of Peking University: "The task of a university is to enable its members to distinguish that which is true from that which merely appears to be true." That is a particularly appropriate approach for explaining the end of the Cold War and also for understanding the world that has emerged since. The beginning of wisdom lies in recognizing the plurality of the causes of events, especially the end of the Cold War—and recognizing also the plurality of perspectives that endure in the post–Cold War world.

Fall Semester 2008

This lecture is an adapted and updated version of "International Relations after the Cold War," *International Affairs*, 84, 2 (Mar. 2008), pp. 335–50.

1.   "Report by Litvinov, Vice-Commissar for Foreign Affairs, to the Central Executive Committee," 4 Dec. 1929, *Protokoly Zasedanii Tsentralnogo Ispolnitelnogo Komiteta Sovetov*, Moscow, Bulletin 14, p. 1. The translation here is from Jane Degras, ed., *Soviet Documents on Foreign Policy* (London, 1952), Vol. II, p. 408.

2.   Ivor Roberts, valedictory dispatch on his departure from the ambassadorship in Rome and from the diplomatic service, 13 Sept. 2006. Partial text available at: http://grberridge.diplomacy.edu/Teaching/display.asp?Topic=IvorRoberts.

3.   Ivor Roberts, evidence to the House of Commons Foreign Affairs Committee, 17 July 2007, HC 795-III; available at: http://www.publications.parliament.uk/pa/cm/cmfaff.htm#reports.

4.   "We recommend that the decision to ban valedictory telegrams should be reversed, other than in respect of comments about the governments to which the outgoing Ambassadors or High Commissioners are accredited or comments likely to cause diplomatic embarrassment": House of Commons Foreign Affairs Committee, report on *Foreign and Commonwealth Office Annual Report 2006–07*, HC 50 (London, 19 Nov. 2007), p. 8.

5.   From the FCO's 2008 mission statement, *Better World, Better Britain*, available at: http://www.fco.gov.uk/en/fco-in-action/strategy.

6.   John Lewis Gaddis, "International Relations Theory and the End of the Cold War," *International Security*, 17, 3 (Winter 1992–93), p. 5.

7.   Peter J. Katzenstein, ed., *The Culture of National Security: Norms and Identity in World Politics* (New York, 1996), p. xi.

8.   Alastair Buchan, *Can International Relations Be Professed? An Inaugural Lecture Delivered before the University of Oxford on 7 November 1972* (Oxford, 1973), pp. 20–21, 26. Mill's phrase had also been used in Llewellyn Woodward's inaugural in 1945, p. 7.

9.   Alastair Buchan, *Change without War: The Shifting Structures of World Power; The BBC Reith Lectures 1973* (London, 1974).

10.   Alfred Zimmern, *The American Road to World Peace* (New York, 1953), p. 267.

11.   Archie Brown, "The Political System, Policy-Making and Leadership," paper presented to Chequers seminar on the Soviet Union and Eastern Europe, presided over by the Prime Minister, 8 Sep. 1983. Quoted in Brown, "The Change to Engagement in Britain's Cold War Policy: The Origins of the Thatcher-Gorbachev Relationship," *Journal of Cold War Studies*, 10, 3 (Summer 2008), p. 12.

12.   Quoted in Kurt M. Campbell, "Prospects and Consequences of Soviet Decline," in Joseph S. Nye, Graham T. Allison, and Albert Carnesale, eds., *Fateful Visions: Avoiding Nuclear Catastrophe* (Cambridge, Mass., 1988), p. 153.

13.   George P. Shultz, *Turmoil and Triumph: My Years as Secretary of State* (New York, 1993), pp. 159–71, 527–38; and Jack F. Matlock, *Autopsy on an Empire: The American Ambassador's Account of the Collapse of the Soviet Union* (New York, 1995), pp. 670, 671.

14.   Jean-Jacques Rousseau, *Du Contrat Social, ou Principes du Droit Politique* (Amsterdam, 1762), p. 2; English translation in Victor Gourevitch, ed. and trans., *Rousseau: The Social Contract and Other Later Political Writings* (Cambridge, 1997), p. 41.

15.   David Wilkinson, "World Order Models Project: First Fruits," *Political Science Quarterly*, 91, 2 (Summer 1976), p. 332.

16.   Hedley Bull, *The Anarchical Society: A Study of Order in World Politics* (London, 1977), p. 20; see also the third edition, with forewords by Stanley Hoffmann and Andrew Hurrell (Basingstoke, 2002).

17. Bull, *Anarchical Society*, p. 22.

18. Samuel Huntington, "The Great American Myth: There Is No US Empire, but There Is a Uni-Multi-Polar World," talk in Toronto, 10 Feb. 2005, available at: http://www.aims.ca/library/huntington.pdf.

19. Ibid., p. 4.

7

Balthazar Solvyns and
Eighteenth-Century Calcutta

ROBERT L. HARDGRAVE, JR.

Every book has its own story. Every research project has a genesis and evolution. François Balthazar Solvyns (1760–1824) was
a Flemish artist who, in the late eighteenth century, sought
his fortune in India and took as his consuming life work the production of a collection of etchings portraying Hindus in their costume,
work, and cultural life (see plate 1, Balthazar Solvyns attended by
servants).

What became for me the Solvyns Project began with a chance
encounter in the summer of 1966 in San Francisco when a friend
told me of some etchings he had seen in a shop that specialized
in Indian miniatures.[1] I was immediately drawn to them: here was
an artist genuinely interested in the people of India. The etchings,
clearly very old, were unsigned, and unlike anything I had seen
before. The most famous European artists to work in India were
Thomas and William Daniell, whose sumptuous aquatints in *Oriental Scenery,* published in London in six parts from 1795 to 1808,
portrayed the Indian picturesque in scenery, monuments, and ru-
ins. People, when they appeared at all, were tiny figures providing
little more than scale. The etchings in the San Francisco shop, in
contrast to the Daniells' refinement, were rough in their execution;
they were printed on thin handmade paper and then mounted
on a heavier paper, with a title pasted on below and a section

heading and number at the top. The sections were thematic, and the etchings depicted caste occupations, religious mendicants (see plate 2, Udbahu, a sadu), musicians with their instruments, boats, carts and palanquins, and, in larger size, festivals and scenes of city life—identifiable as Calcutta. Most striking was the focus on the human figure, each portrayed as an individual, a real person. The figures were intentionally elongated, in a mannerist style, and the facial expressions were dour, but in their portrayal there was an immediacy and a presence that was compelling. The collection was incomplete—various numbers among the different sections were missing—but my friend and I bought the lot and divided them among the two of us and several colleagues in Indian studies.

It was only later that I was able to identify the artist as Solvyns. In 1969, Mildred Archer, curator of prints and drawings at the India Office Library, London, wrote an article for the *Connoisseur* magazine on Solvyns, with illustrations from his *Collection of Two-Hundred and Fifty Coloured Etchings: Descriptive of the Manners, Customs and Dresses of the Hindoos.* The series, from which my own etchings came, had been published in Calcutta in 1799. In the *Connoisseur* article and in an essay on the little-known artist she had done a year earlier with her husband, Mildred Archer related what she had found out about Solvyns's life from sources in the India Office Library, including Calcutta newspapers of his time. I learned of his influence on Indian artists who painted Company School miniatures, works produced for European patrons and illustrating a range of Indian subjects, including caste occupations very much as Solvyns portrayed them. Archer wrote too of the pirated *Costume of Indostan,* published by Edward Orme in London in 1804 and 1805, a volume of sixty prints "after Solvyns." The Orme volume, its subjects prettified in soft pastel colors, had been highly successful, whereas Solvyns's own Calcutta etchings, rejected by the public as "rude" and lacking in the picturesque, had been a financial failure. On his return to Europe, determined to portray the people of India with fidelity, Solvyns took on the production of a new and lavish set of etchings, *Les Hindoûs,* published in Paris in four elephantine volumes from 1808 to 1812.

What I learned from the Archer articles reinforced my fascination with Solvyns and led me as a collector to search for the full, unbroken sets of the Calcutta and Paris etchings. I was fortunate to acquire the Paris edition, *Les Hindoûs,* from Maggs Bros. Rare Books, London, in the early 1970s. Although the bindings of the four volumes were tattered, the prints were in immaculate condition. Soon after that, I found a copy of Orme's *Costume of Indostan,* and a little more than a decade later, again in England, I acquired the volume of Solvyns's Calcutta etchings, with both the 1799 title page and the original leather binding.

In those days, the challenge for a collector of European prints and drawings portraying India was in finding them. Except for the Daniells' prints from *Oriental Scenery,* which commanded very high prices, most of what came on the market was reasonably priced. That changed in the 1980s, when prices climbed even as more items were drawn onto the market. I soon found myself priced out of any serious effort to collect, but my interest in the field remained, and on each trip to London—a regular venue for my research on Indian history, society, and politics—I sought out Mildred Archer to see new acquisitions in prints and drawings at the India Office Library. I also got to know Giles Eyre, a London art dealer who had made European artists in India his specialty. Indeed, it was Eyre who had first interested Mildred Archer in the works of Solvyns. Although the auction houses Christie's and Sotheby's periodically offered Solvyns items, as did the venerable dealer of Asian art Spink & Son, it was Eyre's gallery in St. James that, in 1978, gave Solvyns an exhibition that his work deserved.

Solvyns held a special interest for me, a university professor specializing in India, for what he reveals of India two hundred years ago. Most of the etchings constitute the first visual representation of their subjects, and the etchings and Solvyns's accompanying text thus provide an enormously rich resource for an understanding of Indian society. In the late 1980s, I proposed to my colleague Stephen Slawek, who is an ethnomusicologist and a sitarist, that we use Solvyns's thirty-six etchings of musical instruments for a long article for the journal *Asian Music.*

That publication launched the Solvyns Project—the commitment to publish a book that would reproduce all the Solvyns etchings, with commentary on each and introductory chapters on his life and work. For the next decade and more, juggling it with other commitments, I worked on Solvyns. The project took me several times to London, Paris, Antwerp, and Brussels, and twice to Calcutta. In London, my haunts were the India Office Library, the British Library, and the Victoria and Albert Museum, which held the original drawings from which Solvyns prepared the etchings. In Paris, it was principally the Bibliothèque nationale; in Antwerp, the Stadsbibliotheek; in Brussels, the Bibliothèque royale. In Calcutta, the Victoria Memorial provided my home base. But wherever I went in my search for Solvyns, I left no possible source unexplored, at least to my knowledge, and I sought out people with a range of specialties that might relate to Solvyns's life and work and to the Indian subjects he portrayed. In the United States, my pursuit took me to, among many institutions, Harvard's Houghton Library, the Yale Center for British Art, the New York Public Library, and the Peabody Essex Museum in Salem, Massachusetts, whose Solvyns collection includes two of his finest oil paintings.

During this research, Slawek and I revised the music article for a book, *Musical Instruments of North India: Eighteenth-Century Portraits by Baltazard Solvyns* (1997), and that was followed four years later by *Boats of Bengal* (2001).[2] Both books, published in India, reproduce etchings from *Les Hindoûs* in black-and-white. Each print is accompanied by Solvyns's descriptive text and by my detailed commentary on the subject portrayed. The two small books—inexpensive, though handsomely printed—were spin-offs of the larger Solvyns publication project. That volume, *A Portrait of the Hindus: Balthazar Solvyns and the European Image of India, 1760–1820* (2004), contains plates, many in color, from the Paris edition (supplemented by etchings from the earlier, Calcutta edition), along with Solvyns's text, my commentary on the art, and chapters on Solvyns's life and work.

The project, which I sometimes describe as a hobby that got out of control, was something of a detective investigation, involving, as is so often true in research, a combination of hard work and serendipity. There is comparatively little material on Solvyns's life, so my research began with Mildred Archer's article in the *Connoisseur*. I soon discovered mistakes and anomalies in her account and in the entries on Solvyns in various nineteenth-century biographical dictionaries, and all the errors went back to two essays on Solvyns, in French, published soon after his death in 1824. Sorting it out proved a major challenge, but gradually the contours of his life emerged.

BALTHAZAR SOLVYNS WAS BORN IN ANTWERP IN 1760, of a prominent merchant family. At the age of twelve, he won a drawing contest for admission to the Academy of Antwerp, where he pursued studies in marine painting. The young Solvyns soon came under the patronage of the Habsburg governors of the Austrian Netherlands, Marie Christina and her husband, Albert, and in 1776, at the age of sixteen, he was named captain of the Fort at Lillo, a sinecure to support his painting.

Solvyns was then sent to Paris to perfect his art at the Académie des Beaux-Arts, and was especially influenced by the work of Joseph Vernet, famed for his paintings of the ports of France. On Solvyns's return to Antwerp, Marie Christina commissioned him to paint views of the ports of Ostend and Antwerp in the manner of Vernet.

In 1789 there was a revolt against Habsburg rule, and Solvyns may have left with his patrons for Vienna. The paintings of Ostend and Antwerp went too, only to disappear from the royal collection after the First World War. A large engraving after Solvyns's view of Ostend is all we have of the paintings that won him distinction as a young artist.

If Solvyns did accompany his patrons to Vienna, he did not stay very long. Back in the politically unstable Low Countries in 1790, Solvyns decided to seek his fortune in India. Ostend at that time was under the commercial leadership of a colony of English merchants who traded round the world with ships of various flags. Some operated, illegally, outside the monopoly of the East India Company in Bengal. In 1790, Solvyns set out for India aboard the *Etruscan,* which sailed under an Austrian flag, but was captained by an Englishman, Home Popham. The ship arrived in Calcutta in 1791 with a cargo of trading goods, furniture, and a substantial amount of wine taken on at Madeira. Solvyns had not secured prior permission to arrive, but Calcutta authorities winked at these irregularities, and he settled in and was recorded each year in the register of residents of Calcutta until his return to Europe in 1803.

India in the late eighteenth century attracted a number of British artists who found a ready market for their works among the Europeans in Calcutta and Madras and among the royalty in the courts of the Indian princes. Thomas Hodges and, later, Thomas and William Daniell sold landscapes, but the handsomest profits were to be made in portraiture, and here such painters as Tilly Kettle, Thomas Hickey, and John Zoffany enjoyed the patronage of nabobs and nawabs alike.

Solvyns, trained as a marine artist, was adept at neither landscape nor portraiture, and upon his arrival in Calcutta, he became something of a journeyman artist. He provided decoration for celebrations and balls, cleaned and restored paintings, and offered instruction in oils, watercolor, and chalk. The decoration of coaches and palanquins apparently provided Solvyns his steadiest income, but hardly the success and sense of accomplishment he sought as an artist. In 1792, he did a watercolor drawing of two Andaman Islanders, which was the first portrayal of that people. He accepted commissions to portray the country houses of East India Company officials, as well as several ships, his forte. We don't know how many paintings he did, but several that have survived are in private collections and museums.

Solvyns moved several times during his thirteen years in Calcutta, but he always resided in the neighborhood of Tank Square and Lal Bazar, an area of governmental and commercial buildings where Europeans had first established their residences. The Great Eastern Hotel today is a convenient landmark. To the north was the "Black Town" of native Calcutta, with its mixture of palatial houses constructed by opulent Bengalis and huts of mud and straw. By Solvyns's time, the area where he lodged was no longer favored by the better class of English residents. Many, such as the Orientalist Sir William Jones, founder of the Asiatic Society, had airy houses in Garden Reach, and new houses were being built along Chowringee.

Solvyns lived on the margin both physically and socially. Despite his distinguished family background in Antwerp, he was never a part of elite European circles in Calcutta. In going through the lists of those attending the meetings of the Asiatic Society, I was unable to find Solvyns's name even once during the time he was there. And I suspect that few things could have been more frustrating or deeply humiliating for him.

There is no record to support the notion that Sir William Jones urged Solvyns to take up the project to portray the people and cultural life of Bengal in a series of etchings, as Archer supposed, but in 1794, surely inspired by Jones and perhaps spurred on by his own marginal position in Calcutta, Solvyns announced his plan to publish *A Collection of Two Hundred and Fifty Coloured Etchings: Descriptive of the Manners, Customs and Dresses of the Hindoos.*

After lining up a sufficient number of subscribers, Solvyns set out to record the life of the native quarter of Calcutta, or Black Town, as it was then called. He approached his task almost scientifically, drawing his subjects from life and with more concern for accuracy than aesthetics, though clearly with artistic intent and sensibility. By portraying the Hindus with fidelity, Solvyns provided an unrivaled ethnographic account of Bengal in the late eighteenth century. A particularly fascinating aspect of the series of etchings is that Solvyns organizes his subjects in a very Hindu way: by what he understands to be the hierarchy of rank or quality. Indeed, in his ordered portrayal of Hindu castes in Bengal, however problematic it may be, Solvyns may well have been the first European to provide a systematic ranking of castes.

Solvyns, though not a member of the Asiatic Society, shared much of the Orientalists' perspective and aspired to be recognized among them, but his India was the one in which he lived. He was closely observant, curious, and, even in a time of relative tolerance, less judgmental of Indian customs than most Europeans of his day. Indeed, he often found Indian culture and thought superior to much of what was to be found in Europe. Perhaps in part as a result of his own marginality, Solvyns reached out to the India around him, and his etchings reveal a sympathy with the Indians he portrayed. No other artist entered the Indians' world to the extent that Solvyns penetrated the heart of Calcutta's Black Town.

THE COLLECTION OF ETCHINGS WAS PUBLISHED in Calcutta in a few copies in 1796, and then in greater numbers in 1799. Divided into twelve parts, the first section, with sixty-six prints, depicts "the Hindoo Casts, with their professions." Other sections portray servants, means of transportation (carts, palanquins, and boats), modes of smoking, religious mendicants (sadhus and fakirs), musical instruments, and Hindu festivals and religious ceremonies. In the last section, four etchings depict suttee (plate 3).

The project proved a financial failure. The etchings, by contemporary European standards, were rather crudely done; the forms and settings were monotonous; and the colors were of somber hue. They did not, in short, appeal to the vogue for the picturesque. Indeed, in their nitty-gritty, the etchings conveyed an India that may have been all too real for the comfort of those British officials and merchants who led increasingly separate lives from the people among whom they resided and over whom they ruled.

In 1803, Solvyns left India for France. Near the end of the six-month voyage, his ship wrecked off the coast of Spain. He was able to save his notes, drawings, and etchings, but if he brought the copper plates, they were lost.

In November 1804, Solvyns married Mary Ann Greenwood, the daughter of an English merchant family resident in Ghent. The couple took up residence in Paris, and drawing upon his wife's resources, Solvyns prepared new etchings and produced a lavish folio edition of 288 plates, *Les Hindoûs,* published in Paris between 1808 and 1812 in four volumes (see plate 4, the title page for volume I.). The Paris edition, curiously, omitted several of the subjects depicted in the Calcutta collection, but it added others, such as the "Hindu Raja at his Prayers" and "Nations Most Known in Hindoostan," in which Solvyns includes himself.

In his introduction, Solvyns writes that while European scholars had done much "to dispel the darkness which enveloped the geography and history of India, . . . its inhabitants alone have not yet been observed nor represented with the accuracy which is necessary to make them perfectly known." To rectify this situation, he offered to the public *Les Hindoûs,* "the result of a long and uninterrupted study of this celebrated nation." He writes in the Introductory Discourse to volume I:

> The drawings from which are engraved the numerous plates . . .
> were taken by myself upon the spot. Instead of trusting to the

words of others, or remaining satisfied with the knowledge contained in preceding authors, I have spared neither time, nor pains, nor expense, to see and examine with my own eyes, and to delineate every object with the most minute accuracy. . . .

I admitted nothing as certain but upon the proof of my own observation, or upon such testimony as I knew to be incontrovertible. I have wholly neglected the testimony of authors who have treated these subjects before me, and have given only what I have seen, or what I have myself heard from the mouth of the natives the best informed and most capable of giving me true instructions upon the subject of my enquiries.

What I have said of the text, may also in some degree be applied to the prints themselves, in which I have purposely avoided all sort of ornament or embellishment; they are meerly [*sic*] representations of the objects such as they appeared to my view.[3]

The Paris edition was published with the assistance of a subsidy from the French Ministry of Culture. After the publication of the first volume in 1808, Solvyns pleaded with the ministry for additional support to enable him to complete the enormously expensive set of etchings. As the project neared completion in 1812, Europe was at war, and during preparation of the final volume, Napoleon was defeated in Russia. Royal libraries that had subscribed to *Les Hindoûs* canceled their orders, published copies of the set remained unsold, and Solvyns was financially ruined.

When the Kingdom of the Netherlands was formed in 1814, Solvyns returned to his native Antwerp. In recognition of Solvyns's artistic achievement and with concern for the artist's difficult financial position, King William appointed Solvyns as captain of the Port of Antwerp, a position he held until his death, ten years later. Following his death, efforts by his friends to commission a memorial statue for an Antwerp church failed when political turmoil again disrupted the lowlands that in 1830 would become Belgium.

SOLVYNS NEVER ACHIEVED THE RECOGNITION he had sought, and his legacy as an artist in portraying the Hindus was obscured in anonymity. Copies of Solvyns's etchings in early nineteenth-century books on India and in missionary tracts appeared without attribution. His depiction of suttee was frequently reproduced—even as a bas-relief for a gold-plated silver snuffbox—but without acknowledgment. By the late nineteenth century, Solvyns was almost entirely forgotten: virtually no references to him appeared in articles about European artists in India, nor was he recognized as a source for social history or ethnography.

For me, Solvyns is above all an ethnographic artist, providing a window through which we can view the world in which he lived. In all, Solvyns's Calcutta and Paris editions portray nearly 300 different subjects. For my commentary on each etching, I had to identify who or what Solvyns portrayed and to provide a description ranging from one to a half dozen paragraphs. Solvyns gave a name to each etching. A few were in English, but most were in either Hindustani or Bengali—idiosyncratically spelled as he heard them. Finding the correct name or word was often a formidable challenge, since many were obscure or archaic. With the right name and its variations established, I then set out to find as much as I could about the subject. Here I worked principally with sources from the period of Solvyns's years in Calcutta: memoirs and accounts of old Calcutta and of Bengali culture, and documentation on the castes and tribes of Bengal. In most cases, as I have noted, Solvyns's depiction was the first visual portrayal of a particular subject, and the image itself constitutes a rich source for our knowledge and understanding of the people of India more than two hundred years ago.

Successful research often turns on a chance meeting or discovery—something that can never be planned and to which the scholar must be open. In the course of my work on Solvyns, serendipity was often my muse. Let me share one such experience. Fairly early in my research, I was talking with a rare book dealer in London about Solvyns when his assistant broke in to say that she recalled one of their clients, a gentleman in Belgium, mentioning that he owned a house in Antwerp with a wall mural that he thought was by Solvyns. In my excitement, she promised to write to him and give him my address in London. Within a few days, I received an invitation to visit Belgium from Mr. Ernest Vanderlinden, a retired diplomat and distinguished art collector. The full story of this and later visits with the Vanderlindens is worthy of an extended account, but suffice it to say here that the wall painting was a Turkish scene, clearly not by Solvyns, though from the late eighteenth century. What led Mr. Vanderlinden to think that it might be by Solvyns was that the Antwerp house, originally that of the great Flemish painter Jacob Jordaens, had been purchased by the Vanderlinden family in 1823 from a Solvyns—not, as it turned out, from Balthazar, but from his brother Laurent's family.

To assuage any disappointment I might have had, Vanderlinden promised to put me in touch with members of the Solvyns family he knew in Brussels, the Baroness Solvyns and her sister-in-law, née Solvyns, a descendant of Balthazar's brother. The Solvyns ladies received me with great generosity, giving me access to unpublished

Solvyns family papers, which contained details on Balthazar's life, marriage, and family, and they gave me photographs of two oil paintings still held within the family: a self-portrait done after his return to Antwerp (to which there had never been published reference) and a large painting, *The Entry of William I, King of Holland, on his Yacht in the Port of Antwerp,* dated 1818. This painting, perhaps Solvyns's last, was with a branch of the family living in Australia. A few years later, in Sydney, I got to meet the Solvyns brothers, Laurence and John, and to see the painting.

Over the years of the Solvyns Project, I was able to turn up a number of previously unknown Solvyns paintings, often by such flukes of fate. I may yet, in my continuing search for Solvyns, find the views of the ports of Ostend and Antwerp, the two paintings that made Solvyns famous as a young artist. Who knows? If Solvyns was forgotten for 150 years and his great work in portraying the Hindus passed into obscurity, I hope that my work has redeemed his legacy.

Spring Semester 2008

1. The results of the Solvyns Project may be found in the following volumes: Robert L. Hardgrave, Jr., and Stephen M. Slawek, *Musical Instruments of North India: Eighteenth-Century Portraits by Baltazard Solvyns* (New Delhi, 1997); Hardgrave, *Boats of Bengal: Eighteenth-Century Portraits by Balthazar Solvyns* (New Delhi, 2001); Hardgrave, *A Portrait of the Hindus: Balthazar Solvyns and the European Image of India, 1760–1824* (Ahmedabad/New York, 2004).

2. "Baltazard" is the alternative spelling of his name that Solvyns used for the title page of *Les Hindoûs*.

3. Solvyns, *Les Hindoûs,* Vol. I (Paris, 1808), p. 21.

Figure 1.
John Frederick Lewis, *An Intercepted Correspondence*, 1869. Oil on panel, 74.3 x 87.3 cm (29.2 x 34.4 in).
Private collection.

Figure 2.
John Frederick Lewis, *A Lady Receiving Visitors (The Reception)*, 1873. Oil on wood,
63.5 x 76.2 cm (25 x 30 in).
Yale Center for British Art, Paul Mellon Collection.

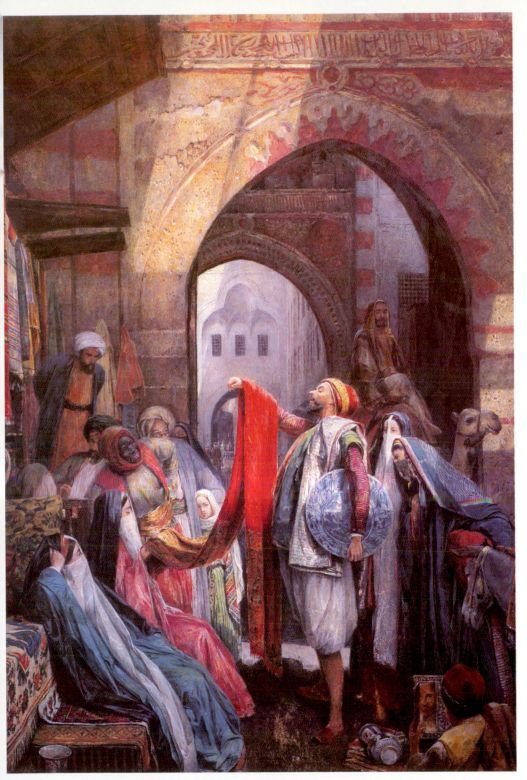

Figure 3
John Frederick Lewis, *A Cairo Bazaar: The Della'l*, 1875. Watercolor and bodycolor,
65 x 49 cm (25.6 x 19.3 in). Private collection

Figure 4.
John Frederick Lewis, *Life in the Harem, Cairo*, 1858. Watercolor and bodycolor,
60.6 x 47.7 cm (23.8 x 18.8 in). Victoria and Albert Museum, London.

8

John Frederick Lewis
and Nineteenth-Century Cairo

CAROLINE WILLIAMS

As an artist, John Frederick Lewis (1804–76) was renowned for the Orientalist subjects he painted for a contemporary Victorian audience. However, his personal biography is known only in broad outline. Nowhere is this discrepancy between critical acclaim and personal reticence more apparent than in *An Intercepted Correspondence* (figure 1), which he exhibited in 1869. On the surface, the painting is a splendid example of the Orientalist genre. But this subject contains two more levels: one in which Lewis highlights the main action for his British audience, and another, more elusive, in which Lewis perhaps hints at the personal. An unfolding description of these three layers—the apparent, the interpretative, and the speculative—is the concern of this essay.

The first level of meaning in *An Intercepted Correspondence* is the one in which its Orientalist nature is the most obvious. The scene takes place in a second-floor *qa'a*, or reception room, in the *harim* of an Oriental Cairene house and captures a dramatic moment in an upper-class family's life. In the alcove of the *mashrabiya*, or lattice window, the master, an old bey, sits cross-legged on a pillow-strewn divan. The sun's slanting rays highlight the central drama: a young harim resident (or perhaps the young fourth wife) has been caught red-handed with a message-laden bouquet of flowers, which the duenna, or harim custodian, presents as evidence to the bey. The old patriarch must decide what to do. Through the lattices of the window behind the duenna and the girl, the dome and minaret of a mosque are just discernible.

Lewis's extraordinary ability to depict the play of light and shadow, the overlay of one pattern upon another, and the textures and sheens of rich fabrics is fully evident. The details of furnishings and costume are all correct. Edward Lear, a fellow artist and visitor to Egypt, commented that Lewis's work was "perfect as representation of real scenes and people," and *An Intercepted Correspondence* seems to fit exactly this compliment.[1]

Lewis was the first professional artist to live in Cairo. He lived in a rented house somewhere in the Azbakiya district for nine and a half years, from November 1841 to May 1851. He left few letters and no diaries or journals, and practically all we know about the time he spent in Cairo comes from a long and amusing literary account written by William Thackeray.[2] While on a tour of the eastern Mediterranean, Thackeray visited Lewis in 1844 and found him living in complete Oriental fashion. Several of Lewis's paintings parallel the descriptions that Thackeray set down about his encounter with the painter, paintings that seem to fill the gap in the written record with visual hints about Lewis's Cairene life.

Hosh of the House of the Coptic Patriarch, exhibited in 1864, appears to illustrate Thackeray's description of the courtyard of Lewis's own house: "a broad open court, with a covered gallery running along one side of it. A camel . . . a gazelle . . . numerous brood of hens and chickens . . . pigeons flapping, hopping . . . fluttering and cooing about." Thackeray also mentions "the wooden lattices of arched windows through . . . which I saw two of the most beautiful, enormous, ogling black eyes."[3] Thackeray's account of the dinner that Lewis served him is depicted in *The Mid-day Meal* (1875). It was "excellent," and "put upon copper trays, which are laid upon low stools . . . We ended the repast with [fruit] . . . deliciously cool and pleasant . . . We put our hands into the dish and flicked them into our mouths in what cannot but be the true oriental manner."[4]

Lewis was in Cairo at a time (1841–51) when its Egyptian and Islamic cultures were being noted and described for the first time. Sir John Gardner Wilkinson and Edward Lane had just published volumes on "manners and customs," the former for the pharaonic world, the latter for contemporary Egyptian society. There was great interest in how people lived, and Lewis reflected this interest visually. When he returned to England in 1851, he did so with enough sketches and drawings to use as a basis for his work until his death, in 1876.

However, in Lane's great description of Egyptian life and mores there is no mention of flowers being used as a means of communication. Furthermore, *An Intercepted Correspondence* was painted many years after Lewis left Cairo, so there is another level at which this painting can be viewed and understood. Lewis uses the scene to interpret a foreign culture for his mid-nineteenth-century Victorian audience. He also tries to appeal to new patrons, a new morality, and new art fashions. In other words, the subject matter of his painting was affected as much by its intended audience as by the culture in which it was set.

Lewis arrived back in London from Cairo in 1851 to an England much changed since he had gone abroad in 1837. His return coincided with the Great Exhibition of 1851, a vibrant celebration of British industrial achievements and economic supremacy. The great tycoons of the industrial Midlands had become the new art patrons. They preferred pictures by living painters rather than the old masters collected by the aristocracy. They also preferred a narrative art that featured "real" subjects.

Lewis's paintings and style perfectly suited these preferences. He produced vignettes that fulfilled the demands of the new middle-class patrons who wanted a visual story without any complicated iconography. His bright palette and lavish fabrics, along with his experiments with light, evoked the glamour and luxury with which the Orient was associated in Western minds.

Lewis's expression of texture, form, color, and light is so detailed and realistic as to be almost scientific. The scene in *An Intercepted Correspondence*, so closely observed and rendered, suggests that Lewis, rather than fabricating an image, painted a true reconstruction of what he might have seen or heard about from female informants.[5] But for its intended British audience, it was also a dramatic evocation of social parallels.

Lewis returned to England at a time when Victorian gender roles mirrored those of the Islamic world in broad sweep, even if not in details. In England from the 1850s onward, the word "Victorian" was increasingly used as a new and self-conscious term to describe respectable and responsible family life. For all the apparent differences between the mores of the two worlds, there was a marked similarity between the Victorian middle-class milieu into which Lewis settled and the Ottoman upper-class Cairene surroundings that he had left. In both societies, masculinity and femininity were defined in relation to their spheres of activity and influence, in relation to the public and the private. Men—active, adult, commanding—were associated with the public world of business and politics, while women—

sheltered, compliant, and nurturing—were corralled within the protective privacy of the home. The middle-class Victorian woman, like the upper-class Muslim lady, was identified with home and was seen as its chief ornament. Her social life revolved around paying calls, attending "at homes," and taking tea. This was not very different in overall structure from the gender roles in Cairo, and in his harim paintings, Lewis made this point in minutely painted, brilliantly colored strokes (see figure 2, *A Lady Receiving Visitors [The Reception]*).

In the domestic setting of *An Intercepted Correspondence,* the women are artfully dressed and displayed against luxurious backgrounds. Lewis was portraying the quid pro quo of Muslim domestic life: these women, the bey's wives, in their sheltered, luxurious, pampered setting, are neither deprived nor unhappy. Furthermore, their presence as witnesses to the bey's decision stamps them as implicit participants in the drama. The Victorian audience could appreciate both aspects of the story: that women often make compromises for privilege, and that there is a double standard among men and women. The women of Lewis's harim scenes, in spite of their Middle Eastern provenance, are persons with whom Victorian viewers could understand and sympathize.

THAT LEWIS SAW HIMSELF AS AN ARTISTIC BROKER between the Egyptian world where he had lived so happily and the English world of which he was now a part can perhaps be illustrated by two market scenes he painted just before his death. In *The Street and Mosque of the Ghooreyah* (1876), the surface meaning seems straightforward. The architectural context frames the action in the street, where two young ladies lean toward a black-bearded *shaykh,* who sits crosslegged on a stone bench and examines something in his hand. But who is the man right of center? He seems curiously detached. Is this Lewis? In his paisley turban, the man looks remarkably like the subject of *Young Mamluk Bey* (1868), who is also in a paisley turban and who looks like the young man in Lewis's most famous picture, *The Hhareem* (1849), all of whom look like young Lewis himself in the miniature by Simon Jacques Rochard of 1826.

The same man (in *The Street and Mosque of the Ghooreyah)* also evokes the central character in *A Cairo Bazaar: The Della'l* (figure 3), painted a year earlier. A *dallal,* as Lewis explained by citing a passage from Lane's *Manners and Customs of the Modern Egyptians,* is an auctioneer-broker, one who acted as a middleman between the merchants who hired him and prospective customers. In this watercolor, the *dallal* holds out a shawl for the two ladies on the bench in front of him to inspect.

The Della'l offers an interpretation of the *Ghooreyah.* In the latter, the man in the center is a dallal, and the mistress and her maid, wishing to buy something from him, are asking the old man, a moneychanger, to certify a "doubtful coin," which he is examining. If Lewis depicted the dallal as a portrait of himself, then he, as a painter, also represented himself as a mediator offering an English audience the chance to buy his painted views of Cairo.

Between 1851, when Lewis returned to England, and 1869, when he exhibited *An Intercepted Correspondence,* Victorian art set off in new directions. Just after Lewis's return to England, William Holman Hunt, an acquaintance, displayed *The Awakening Conscience* (1853– 54), a painting full of hints and clues that enriched its main theme of a girl suddenly aware that her affair with a lover is at a dead end. Hunt's painting became the prototype for the many serious, often moralizing scenes from modern life that followed, all of them rife with "significant and symbolic details" that encouraged the viewer to look for deeper meanings and to "read" the painting like a book.

A close look at Hunt's painting reveals many symbolic details that give the story additional thrust: the gauntlet has been thrown down; there is no wedding ring on the girl's fourth finger; the cat under the chair toys with a bird; a ball of wool lies unraveled by the piano; the music above the open keyboard is titled "Oft in the Stilly Night"; above, the clock strikes twelve.

The use of symbolic representation, in which the main message is accentuated through a buildup of significant details, became a feature that Lewis incorporated into his own paintings. His Victorian audience would have readily understood the theme of *An Intercepted Correspondence.* In 1869, the year of the painting, a book called *The Language of Flowers* provided the symbolic meanings attached to flowers. The flowers in the painting are all carefully chosen for their significations. For example, the pansy, the anemone, and the roses in the bouquet stand for "think of giver," "giver feels forsaken," and love, while in the vase next to the bey, the larkspur, the rose, and the scarlet dahlia represent haughtiness, love, and instability. By giving a Victorian subtext to an Oriental setting, it is as if Lewis were making the point that women in both settings—in Cairo and in London—are subjects of a patriarchal order.

The central action is enhanced by other clues. In a niche above the cupboard by the side of the divan, there is a Japanese Imari vase decorated with a samurai warrior, and, next to it, a live pigeon roosts. This is an authentic touch—pigeons in Cairo often fly into rooms—but Lewis's Victorian audience would have interpreted the samurai warrior gesturing aggressively toward the huddling dove as an omen of the girl's fate. The cupboard refers to one of Lewis's own pictures: *Caged Doves* (signed and dated 1864), in which both the dove and the lady are captives. Another ominous note is conveyed by the fruit on the stand. These rounded forms full of seeds have, since Caravaggio and the seventeenth century, been associated with feminine attributes, and here, the green melon (a color that echoes the girl's green dress) has been cut open as a threatening omen.

These are the "significant details" that added to the painting's meaning and that the Victorian audience would have delighted in "reading." Among the hidden messages, however, there are three that are more puzzling. These are the Arabic inscriptions that Lewis inserted into his image. These inscriptions add an intriguing, and perhaps personal, meaning to the scene.

The most obvious inscription is located on the wall between the alcove and the cupboard, an area Lewis imbued with symbolic intent. The inscription brackets the space above the bouquet and the bey's hand, thus symbolically joining man and young woman. The easily legible words, from the Qu'ran, carry the following appropriate message: "For those who say: 'Our Lord! We do truly have faith, so forgive us our faults'" (3:16).

Another area of inscription frames the duenna and the young lady, and also the faint silhouette of the mosque glimpsed through the *mashrabiya* screen: "[For the righteous are in] Gardens with rivers flowing beneath them; therein they abide with spouses purified and God's good pleasure, and God perceives [His servants]" (3:15).[6]

This is the Qu'ranic verse that immediately precedes the one over the cupboard. In a Cairene house of the Ottoman period, such as the one in the painting, verses from the Qu'ran were often used at the base of the *shukhshaykha,* or the skylight well over the main *qa'a*. However, research currently being done in Cairo, in surviving Cairene domestic architecture, finds no other instance of the use of these specific Qu'ranic inscriptions (3:15–16). In fact, for the same parts of the room—that is, the parts rising up to and encircling the skylight—other verses are commonly used: the throne verse (2:255) or the victory verse (48:1–5 or 3:190–191).

Thus, both of these Qu'ranic verses referring to "repentance" and "mercy" appear to be a deliberately chosen part of Lewis's story. Even so, their presence is puzzling. Lewis created the painting eighteen years after returning to England, at the age of sixty-five, and he included Arabic inscriptions that few of his British viewers could have been expected to note or read.

The extent of Lewis's abilities in colloquial or classical Arabic is not possible to assess from surviving records. Lewis had an exact eye, and inscriptions he used in other paintings are also legible. He also had many acquaintances, including E. W. Lane and Joseph

Bonomi, who were good Arabists and who could have pointed him in the direction of these verses. We know also that he knew Hanafi Isma'il, an Egyptian who spoke fluent English. Hanafi accompanied David Roberts to the Holy Land in 1839, and had thereafter been a guide to other British clients. In 1846, he gave Arabic lessons to a guest living in Lewis's house. Thus Lewis, with access to these linguistic guides, might have copied the inscription while he was in Cairo and used it much later in *An Intercepted Correspondence.* The inclusion of these inscriptions could then indicate that Lewis had a greater sympathy and understanding of Islam than is commonly supposed. In 1857, he painted *Interior of a Mosque, Afternoon Prayer (The 'Asr),* in which the praying man is considered to be a representation of Lewis himself. In *An Intercepted Correspondence,* Lewis might be using the benign Qu'ranic verses to try to offset the cumulative and menacing impact of the visual clues set up for his British audience. Since few of his viewers would have been expected to interpret these references, his own inclination toward Islam would have been part of a private message.

This private or personal sphere is emphasized by the third inscription. It lies in the cartouche on the right wall. In Ottoman Cairene houses of the seventeenth and eighteenth centuries these cartouches were used as decoration and were filled with poetic inscriptions, which also served as chronograms, or alphanumeric systems of dating. In these systems, each letter is assigned a value, and the total for all the letters becomes the date.

The relevant inscription here reads: "Record here the glory that has dawned." The letters in this third inscription add up to the Hijra year 1241, which corresponds to 16 August 1825–5 August 1826 in the Latin calendar. In architectural chronograms, the date usually refers to the year in which the house or architectural element was created. This is not the case here, since the nineteenth-century reference postdates the Ottoman period. Lewis deliberately chose the year 1241, and in the milieu of Victorian England, he intended it to convey a message.

Apart from Thackeray's description of his visit to Lewis, and a few mentions in the correspondence between contemporary expatriate residents of Cairo, a real fact known about Lewis in Egypt was his marriage on 8 May 1847 to Marian Harper in Alexandria. Lewis was then two months away from his forty-third birthday, and Marian was two months shy of her twenty-fourth. Marian was beautiful, and Lewis often used her thereafter as a model for the women in his Oriental settings.

Lewis had used the phrase "Record here the glory that has

dawned" in a previous painting. It appears in *Life in the Harem, Cairo* (figure 4), in which a young woman looks down at the bouquet of roses ("love") and pansies ("think of giver") she holds in her lap. Michael Lewis, the painter's great-grandnephew and biographer, noted that the subject in "the Cairo harem-painting, done in 1858, bears a close resemblance to Marian."[7] The "glory that has dawned" seems here to be a discreet compliment to Lewis's model-wife.

Of his time in Cairo, Lewis kept no written records—no diaries, journals, letters, or personal accounts. Other references that might have survived disappeared after his death. There is thus nothing that suggests that his relationship with his beautiful and much younger wife was anything other than totally devoted. However, it is in his paintings that Lewis leaves clues to his life in Cairo, and in this painting there remain curious references and ambiguities.

THE INTERPRETATION THAT FOLLOWS is derived from the other "clues" that Lewis has incorporated into his painting. First, it is possible that the bey represents Lewis himself. He looks very much like the description left by Thackeray: "His beard curls nobly over his chest . . . and gives to him a venerable and Bey-like appearance."[8] An albumen-print photograph of Lewis in Oriental costume, taken a few years before the painting was executed, verifies this description. This was not the first or only time Lewis used himself as a model in one of his paintings, and it is thus possible that he placed himself again in the narrative of his imagery.

Second, the young woman resembles Marian, his wife. She has already been identified as the model in *Life in the Harem, Cairo,* who holds a floral love token and sits under the same inscription. There is a further link between the two paintings: both include a view of a mosque with an Ottoman minaret. The guilty inmate of *An Intercepted Correspondence* wears a green dress with a red sash around her hips. In another picture, *The Siesta* (1876), Lewis used the sleeping Marian as his model. It is a loving portrait. Balancing the sleeping lady is a table with three vases containing roses (love, beauty), red poppies (sleep, consolation), white lilies (purity, modesty, sweetness), and arum lilies (ardor), but the sleeping Marian wears the same green dress and red sash.

The number provided by the chronogram is more problematic. Lewis married Marian Harper on 8 May 1847. Marian was twenty-three. The letters in the chronogram, however, add up to the Muslim lunar year 1241, equivalent to August 1825 to August 1826, not to 1238 (18 September 1822–7 September 1823), which would be the birth year of the presumed object of "the glory that has dawned." It is possible that an unintentional mistake was made, that somehow the numeral 1238 was intended, but the calculation did not work. Noha Abou Khatwa, an epigrapher in Cairo, wrote: "I have encountered in many cases mistakes in *abjad* calculations."[9]

It seems possible that at this level—the mysterious, personal level—Lewis might have been referring to an incident, or fantasy, in his own life: that the young lady of the drama was his wife and that she had given him cause for jealousy. Now, years later, he has forgiven her, or her constancy has smoothed over his initial suspicions. The Qu'ranic inscriptions indicate this forgiveness. Lewis deliberately chose these texts, and he took great pains to make the Arabic legible. The texts creatively encode a record in a painting intended for general enjoyment in such a way that none of Lewis's English viewers would be aware of it.

If not meant as a personal reference or message, then why did Lewis choose those inscriptions? Why did he bother to render them so legibly? Who did he think would read them? Why do they appear in a painting executed eighteen years after Lewis left Egypt, one aimed at a British audience unable to read and appreciate their content? These are questions for which, at the moment, there are no firm answers, only hypothetical explanations.

In conclusion, at the personal level, John Frederick Lewis's message is hard to decode. We are left with only suggestive musings. On the interpretive level, this work is an example of the Victorian vogue for paintings dealing with spiritual and social issues relevant to modern, industrial Britain. It is also an example of the narrative genre in art, which became so popular in the nineteenth century. Finally, at the level of obvious meaning, *An Intercepted Correspondence* remains a brilliant evocation of a Cairene domestic interior in which the unfolding drama, in its luxurious and exotic setting, continues to both tease and please the eye.

Fall Semester 2007

1. Quoted in Michael Lewis, *John Frederick Lewis, R.A., 1805–1876* (Leigh-on-Sea, 1978), p. 33.

2. W. M. Thackeray, *Notes of a Journey from Cornhill to Grand Cairo* (Heathfield, 1991), p. 145.

3. Ibid., pp. 143–44.

4. Ibid., p. 145.

5. While Lewis would not have actually painted a harim scene, the details of the room and its furnishings would have been accessible to him because he lived in an "Ottoman" house in the Azbakiya district.

6. I have not had access to the original painting. In reproductions it is possible to decipher this verse. I thank Drs. Abd al-Karim Rafeq and Driss Cherkaoui, who read it: "janat tajri min tahtiha al-anhar khalidin fiha wa azwaj muttahira wa ridunu min Allah wa Allah basiru."

7. Michael Lewis, *John Frederick Lewis*, p. 39.

8. Thackeray, *Cornhill to Grand Cairo*, p. 145.

9. Noha Abou-Khatwa to the author, e-mail, 6 June 2003.

Plate 1.
Balthazar Solvyns attended by servants, in Calcutta.
Etching by Solvyns for the title page to *Les Hindoûs*, Vol. IV (Paris, 1812).
Collection of Robert L. Hardgrave, Jr.

AN OODDOOBAHOO.

Plate 2.
Udbahu, a sadhu, in Balthazar Solvyns
A Collection of Two Hundred and Fifty Coloured Etchings: Descriptive of the Manners,
Customs and Dresses of the Hindoos, sec. VII, no. 10 (Calcutta, 1796, 1799).
Collection of Robert L. Hardgrave, Jr.

Plate 3.
Sahagamana, sati, in Balthazar Solvyns, *Les Hindoûs*, Vol. II, sec. 11, no. 1 (Paris, 1808).
Collection of Robert L. Hardgrave, Jr.

LES HINDOÛS,

PAR F. BALTAZARD SOLVYNS.

TOME PREMIER.

PARIS,

CHEZ L'AUTEUR, PLACE SAINT-ANDRE-DES-ARCS, N° 11,

Et chez H. NICOLLE, rue de Seine, n° 12, à la librairie stéréotype.

DE L'IMPRIMERIE DE MAME FRÈRES.

1808.

9

Conan Doyle and Sherlock Holmes

RICHARD JENKYNS

Sir Arthur Conan Doyle could be described correctly though misleadingly as a versatile and almost entirely forgotten writer. He wrote lively historical novels set in the Middle Ages or in the seventeenth and eighteenth centuries. He wrote plays and poems and at least one novel of modern life that was thought somewhat risqué. He also wrote light sketches about three children called (alas) Laddie, Dimples, and Baby. He wrote science fiction and adventure stories and a history of the First World War in several volumes. For a literary career—and there was a good deal more in Conan Doyle's life besides writing—it was strikingly large and diverse.

Much of this might be worth reviving, and indeed a fair number of Conan Doyle's books lasted in the public eye a good while. His publishers kept the historical novels in print at least until the end of the fifties. And they were in the school library when I was a boy. Sherlock Holmes apart, at least one other corner of his oeuvre has survived. The two collections of Brigadier Gerard stories, *The Exploits of Brigadier Gerard* and *The Adventures of Brigadier Gerard,* are today in print in the lists of at least two publishers. The Professor Challenger stories are not quite forgotten, especially *The Lost World,* kept in memory, I suspect, largely through film treatments. But the Challenger stories are not, in my view, much of a success. Their hero is a variant on Holmes, a gruff, noisy scientist whom Conan Doyle tries rather too hard to make into an eccentric. He is meant to be likable for all his roughness, but he comes across as merely pleased with himself.

The brigadier is another matter. Conan Doyle had the bright idea of looking at the Napoleonic Wars—mostly the Peninsular War, though the saga extends into the Russian campaign and to Waterloo, and there is even a tale set in Devon, after the Brigadier has been taken prisoner—through the eyes of a French narrator, one who is both gallant and comic. Gerard, who tells the stories as an old man looking back from the middle of the nineteenth century, is brave, boastful, sporadically resourceful, and stupid. In the words of the Emperor himself, "I believe that if he has the thickest head he has also the stoutest heart in my army." The Irish historian Owen Dudley Edwards has claimed that the Gerard stories are the prime candidate for the greatest historical short-story series, just as *War and Peace* is for the title of greatest historical novel. That may seem extravagant, though I am not sure who Conan Doyle's rivals would be in this particular competition. The character of Gerard is drawn broadly, not subtly; but he is a lot of fun, the stories go with a swing and with plenty of invention, and the combination of comedy, swashbuckling adventure, and occasional horror has something original about it. This is perhaps Conan Doyle's most endearing work.

But of course the reason why his desk and papers, resident in Austin, Texas, are objects of pilgrimage is because of Sherlock Holmes. Holmes is the character who has made his author immortal: like his older contemporary Sir Arthur Sullivan, creator with W. S. Gilbert of the Savoy operettas, Conan Doyle is remembered for the sideline that distracted him from his more serious and (as he supposed) more durable work. For the same reason, much has been written about his life. But in 2007 there appeared a new chance to learn about him and his times from a book produced by Jon Lellenberg, Daniel Stashower, and Charles Foley (henceforth LSF). This is a collection of Conan Doyle's letters, linked by passages of short narrative—a life seen mostly though the man's own words.

As it happens, Conan Doyle had a more eventful life than most writers. His background was surprising, and reveals an unexpected kind of social and emotional mobility in Victorian Britain. He was born in Edinburgh. His mother was Irish, and evidently a vigorous and interesting personality. His father, a Scot of Irish ancestry, was an artist and illustrator, emotionally unstable. The family was Catholic, and Conan Doyle was sent in his teens to board at Stonyhurst in Lancashire, a well-known public school—what in America would be called a prep school—run by Jesuits. In middle life, Conan Doyle's mother converted to Episcopalianism. His own Catholic faith seems to have dropped from him fairly early. It seems unclear what replaced it—probably a kind of undogmatic Anglicanism, so he would, at a guess, have regarded himself as "C of E," more or less, at least until he took up the spiritualism that dominated his last years. Although he had not a drop of English blood, as far as I am aware, he referred to himself as English quite without self-consciousness, in contrast to his Edinburgh contemporary Robert Louis Stevenson, who once said that Bournemouth, on the English south coast, was the most foreign place in which he had ever lived. All this suggests a greater spiritual and emotional fluidity in Victorian life than is sometimes allowed.

After leaving school, Conan Doyle was trained as a doctor and worked in general practice for a number of years in Southsea, a district of Portsmouth on the Hampshire coast, until Sherlock Holmes's success allowed him to write full-time. He was an enthusiastic sportsman: cricket was his greatest love, but he was also a pioneer in the new sports of skiing and rally driving. He had a taste for adventure, and interrupted his medical career to sail north aboard an Arctic whaler; he also joined in the crew's other principal activity, clubbing seals. He thought it the best time of his life. During the Boer War, when he was already middle-aged and famous, he put his literary career on one side to go out to South Africa as a military doctor. The conditions were tough—one of his colleagues had to be sent home in a state of nervous collapse—but he saw it out. Back home, he campaigned for two victims of miscarriage of justice, in the face of official obstruction. In the First World War, he was back visiting the front again. And in the last decade of his life, up to his death in 1930, he championed the cause of spiritualism, traveling as far as Australia to spread his gospel and enduring a good deal of mockery ("Is Conan Doyle mad?" one newspaper asked). Besides great energy, he had both moral and physical courage.

However, it was no doubt a life more fascinating to live than to read about. To be frank, he is not a very interesting letter writer, and it is a further limitation that the vast majority of these letters were written to the same recipient, his mother. Perhaps conscious of this, LSF offer their book in part as "a window opening on to a bygone age," and that is fair enough. As I have already indicated, we can learn some interesting things from it about the milieu of his class and time. His private life was a period piece of a peculiar kind. His first wife caught consumption and spent many years of increasing invalidism before finally succumbing. Meanwhile, her husband had fallen deeply in love with another, much younger woman, Jean Leckie, who became a kind of platonic mistress to him for almost a decade, until the wife's death freed them to marry. Conan

Doyle never contemplated leaving his wife, for whom he seems to have retained a sincere though mild affection, and he was indignant at the suggestion that he and Jean had consummated their affair. This combination of passion and restraint, of infidelity and high-mindedness, does indeed seem to belong to a world distant from our own.

For all his virtues, Conan Doyle also reveals in these letters a self-complacency and an exaggerated view of his importance that are a little comic: one catches the accents of Mr. Toad and even of Mr. Pooter. And curiously, there is one other fictional character who may come to mind: his own Brigadier Gerard. He thought that his *Micah Clarke* was better than Stevenson's *Kidnapped;* his *White Company* was, he said, a "very good" book, and the first in English literature "to draw the most important figure in English military history, the English bowman soldier." He described another of his works, *The Stark Munro Letters,* as "vital and original": "I really don't think a young man's life has been gone into so deeply in English literature before." (So much for *David Copperfield* and *Great Expectations.*) Another book was "absolutely fresh and new," with "a quality of heart which is rare in English literature." His history of the First World War would amaze people and sweep the country because he was the only man who knew the facts. When he became a spiritualist evangelist, he compared himself to St. Paul. "There is no doubt that thought in Adelaide will never be the same again," he wrote after speaking in that city. Even his love affair, he said, showed a courage and heroism that were almost unique in history. He was heroic in financial matters too: "I don't suppose any man has ever sacrificed so much money to preserve his ideal of art as I have done." In fact, money is one of his favorite topics in the letters to his mother, and it is here that the flavor of Mr. Pooter can be felt.

In the earlier part of their book especially, LSF are on the look-out for pieces of Conan Doyle's life that may have found their way into his stories. For example, they have dug up a Dr. James Watson, one of his fellow physicians in Portsmouth. Is this the man from whom Conan Doyle took the name of Sherlock's friend? Probably not, since he notoriously had difficulty remembering whether Watson's Christian name was James or John. So Dr. Watson of Southsea was not, after all, like the ornithologist James Bond, the author of a book on birds of the Caribbean, whose name was recognized by Ian Fleming as fitting him for more exacting challenges. When Conan Doyle wanted a name for his creation, he seems to have looked for something solid, Anglo-Saxon, and inconspicuous, and "Watson" fit the bill.

But LSF have found a more telling connection between fact and fiction. In almost the last of the Holmes stories, Watson refers to "my old school number, thirty-one," and 31 was Conan Doyle's own number—allocated to him for things like lockers and coat pegs—at Stonyhurst. There does seem to be an implication here, at the end of his career, that Watson had been his alter ego. And here perhaps is the key to Dr. Watson, for he is the real stroke of genius in the Holmes saga, just as in P. G. Wodehouse's stories it is Bertie Wooster, the baffled narrator, who is the truly original (and oddly subtle and complex) invention, rather than the superhuman Jeeves.

Watson is often taken to be a simple, stolid John Bull, with not a lot of brain. "Good old Watson!" says Sherlock Holmes. "You are the one fixed point in a changing world." But those words come in "His Last Bow," perhaps the weakest of all the Holmes stories, written in a burst of wartime patriotism and at a moment when the author himself was starting to misinterpret his own creation. The real Watson is more complicated, if one may use the word "real" of a fictional character. When we first meet him, in *A Study in Scarlet,* he has returned from the North-West Frontier, where he was wounded by an Afghan bullet, and is newly arrived in London, restless and lonely. Watson is chivalric as well as solid, he is rather perceptive about Holmes, and he never loses a liking for adventure: his recurrent willingness to abandon his practice for a few days to follow Holmes on his latest escapade is more than a convenient narrative device. A reading of Conan Doyle's letters explains, if nothing else, why his Watson always seems authentic: he had only to represent himself, and a fully rounded figure would appear upon the page.

As a narrator imperfectly aware of the impression that he is creating, Watson bears some resemblance to Brigadier Gerard. If Gerard had been invented first, we could see Watson as a subtler, more understated version of an earlier idea. But in fact the Gerard adventures date from a few years after Watson's first appearance, and so it appears that we can tell a different story. There is a glorious unselfconsciousness about the invention of Watson; it is one of those cases—like Bertie Wooster again, for that matter—in which the author seems to have achieved more than he intended. It seems to me likely that Conan Doyle realized what he had done, and accordingly developed Gerard as a broader variant on a theme. Much as I like the brigadier, he is more crudely depicted than Watson, and Conan Doyle works a little too hard at making sure that we realize what a braggart and a clot he is. But Watson always seems natural.

Sherlock Holmes himself is a more problematic case. Many people would say that he is one of the most vivid characters in all literature. But his most famous attribute, his deerstalker hat, owes more to the illustrator than to the text, and is in any case a stage prop rather than a part of his intrinsic nature. And Conan Doyle's portrait is famously inconsistent. At first, Holmes's mind is powerful but narrow: he neither knows nor cares that the earth goes round the sun, and he is wholly indifferent to literature. But later he becomes superbly cultivated, letting fall allusions to Hafiz and Horace. The tension in his spirit between severe intellect and fierce passion runs pretty much through all the stories, though even here Conan Doyle does not quite seem sure whether Holmes is rigidly self-controlled or close to neurosis. The opium craving was perhaps a mistake, but having given him this attribute, Conan Doyle was stuck with it.

And yet as every reader knows, Sherlock Holmes somehow works. People think of him as a real person, a trap into which LSF themselves fall in one place. Rather sportingly, Conan Doyle quoted the wit who remarked that although Holmes might not have been killed when he fell over the cliff, he was never quite the same man afterward. LSF add a solemn footnote to point out that Holmes was not in fact killed at the Reichenbach Falls. This not only misses the joke, it is wrong: it would be true only if Holmes were a real person. The fictional Holmes did perish in his last struggle with Moriarty. ("Killed Holmes," Conan Doyle wrote in his diary at the time.) The alternative Holmes who lives on belongs to other, later stories.

PERHAPS ALL ONE CAN DO IS TO SAY, RATHER HELPLESSLY, that he has the quality of myth about him. Just as Odysseus remains Odysseus through all the varied and inconsistent stories that the Greeks told about him, so Holmes survives his contradictions. The time of his creation was indeed a mythic moment. I will take an indirect route to explain what I mean.

In analyzing great powers, it has become fashionable to distinguish between hard and soft power. It is arguable that by 1900 the hard power of Britain was already past its apogee; but what of its soft power? In one respect, the soft power of the nineteenth century's top nation was extraordinarily weak. In music, the high and middlebrow culture of today throughout the West, and even beyond, is still saturated with works from that century and with the story of their enduring influence, yet England plays almost no part in this. Sullivan and the earlier Elgar, rather late in the story, are the only participants. By contrast, the influence of Victorian Britain's idea of sport has been colossal. All the five sports most widely played and followed in the world—soccer, cricket, tennis, golf, and rugby— were codified in Britain in the second half of the nineteenth century. The very idea of sport as we understand it today is a British invention of this period.

And here I indulge in a digression. It is an indulgence that Conan Doyle, with his own sporting interests, would surely have granted. Was it the case that a few silly old men in London some time late in the nineteenth century took a decision that profoundly affected the United States in a way that endures to this day? The puzzle is this: what became of cricket in North America? In *Little Women,* cricket is the game that the young people play (and it is a curious fact that, conversely, the first reference to baseball recorded in the dictionaries comes in Jane Austen, in the first chapter of *Northanger Abbey*). The international sporting rivalry with the longest history is a cricketing one—between England and Australia—and it struck foreigners as bizarre that men would travel 12,000 miles to knock a ball around a field. Hippolyte Taine, in his *Notes on England,* describes the English passion for team sports as an anthropological curiosity and mentions the story that some Englishmen had gone to Australia to play cricket (with the implication that the story, though *ben trovato,* could hardly be true). It was indeed extraordinary, and the fact that it seems more or less natural to us shows how immense this form of British influence has been over the whole world.

The very first international competition of any kind was a cricket match, but it was between the United States and Canada. Later, the United States applied to join the community of cricket-playing nations. That request was refused because the country was not part of the British Empire (if you won't play with us, we won't play with you). Did that refusal kill off cricket in America? Did it permit the triumph of baseball and lead to one of the more curious forms of American exceptionalism, its reluctance to play the team games that the rest of the world plays? Perhaps some ambitious young historian can come up with the definitive answer.

The idea of sport as we know it is perhaps the most long-lasting and widespread way in which later Victorian Britain has shaped today's world. But its mythmaking has also been remarkably durable, for it is striking how much of our modern mythology was made in Britain in the last two decades of the nineteenth century: besides Sherlock Holmes, *Treasure Island, Dr. Jekyll and Mr. Hyde, The Jungle Books, King Solomon's Mines, The Turn of the Screw,* and *The Prisoner of Zenda* all originate in this short period; *Peter Pan* followed very early in the new century. And perhaps our own mythic instinct may explain why *The Hound of the Baskervilles* is easily Holmes's most famous case. At first blush that seems surprising, for the story does not make much sense and the denouement is an anticlimax: the large dog turns out to be a large dog. Conan Doyle himself, not one to under-rate his own works, thought the book "not as good as I should have wished." But the story has an archetypal quality: the great Grimpen Mire seems to have come out of the collective northern subconscious. T. S. Eliot borrowed the name to describe humanity "in a dark wood, in a bramble, / On the edge of a grimpen, where is no secure foothold"; and thus the *Four Quartets* became one of the more unexpected places to which Conan Doyle spread his influence.

However, *The Hound of the Baskervilles,* set in Devon, is not a typi-cal piece, for Sherlock Holmes is not only one of literature's great smokers but also one of its great Londoners. And he is a Londoner of a very particular era. The last of the stories was written in the 1920s, but just as Peter Pan never gets any older, so no reader really believes in his heart that Holmes exists beyond the 1890s. His, we feel, is the London of fogs and hansom cabs, of an East End where sinister lascars skulk and (to move from fiction to life) where Jack the Ripper, another mythic figure, goes about his ugly business. It is usually cold or damp or both. "It was a bright, crisp February morning, and the snow of the day before still lay deep upon the ground" is a typical sentence to set the scene in Baker Street. Or: "It was a cold morning of the early spring . . . A thick fog rolled down between the lines of dun-coloured houses, and the opposing win-dows loomed like dark, shapeless blurs, through the heavy yellow wreaths." The first of these quotations comes from "The Beryl Coro-net," the second from "The Copper Beeches," in which Holmes and Watson take the train to Winchester. Once they are in the country, the weather changes entirely, to "an ideal spring day" with a blue sky flecked with little fleecy clouds. Even the weather points up the distinctiveness of Holmes's London.

Conan Doyle's spiritualism also seems very "period" now. Here we need to distinguish, as Conan Doyle himself did not always do, between psychical research and the spirit world. In the early twen-tieth century, many intelligent people were ready to take psychic phenomena seriously. That was not in itself unreasonable: the world is full of very mysterious things—light, time, elementary particles—and it is not in principle absurd that mental transference might be among them. In practice, we have dropped the idea because after much searching, there has turned out to be no good evidence for it. Spiritualism, on the other hand, if it is to mean anything at all, is concerned with a supernatural realm and not with the physical realm at all.

No doubt the First World War had something to do with it: Conan Doyle noted that he had been able to put more than a dozen grieving mothers in contact with their dead sons. And his own nephew, Oscar Hornung, who had perished on the western front, also got in touch, for some reason using a working-class Glasgow family as intermediaries. Oscar turned up again just before Conan Doyle set out for Australia, to speed him on his way, this time accompanied by Conan Doyle's own son, who had died of the Spanish influenza.

Despite the natural feelings of the bereaved, it is hard now to understand how people could believe this stuff. Perhaps the affair of the "Cottingley fairies," to which LSF give only half a Delphic sentence, may offer a clue. Two Yorkshire girls claimed to have seen fairies and to have caught images of them on film. They looked exactly like pictures cut out from a modern book, which is of course what they were. Why then was Conan Doyle deceived? If we meet an angel, the one thing of which we can be sure is that he will not look like a figure from a stained-glass window; and if we find fairies at the bottom of our garden, we can be certain that they will not resemble the fancies of an Edwardian illustrator. But spiritualism seems to be a willful failure of imagination: it sees life after death not as utter transformation but as the continuation of earthly life with superior facilities. That indeed is a popular view of heaven today, it seems, but it ought not to survive serious reflection. "We carry on with our wisdom and knowledge," Conan Doyle wrote, "our art, literature, music, architecture, but all with a far wider sweep. Our bodies are at their best. We are free from physical pain. The place is beautiful." He added that there would even be whisky on the other side. Skeptics have often wondered why the dead are so erratic in their visitations to those of us who are still on this side of the veil and why, when they do turn up, they have so little of interest to say. Conan Doyle saw the problem: he knew one lady who had spent the first few years after her death trying to set up a bureau of communication to organize interchange between earth and the spirit world more efficiently. After a decade and a half, she abandoned the project, realizing, as Conan Doyle admitted, that most spirits are not interested in this world at all.

CONAN DOYLE IS IMMORTAL, BUT HIS IMMORTALITY rests on a small part of his output: the best of him is in Sherlock Holmes, and the best of Holmes is in the first two collections of short stories. In many ways, he was an accomplished magpie, somewhat like J. K. Rowling in our own time, borrowing ideas from other writers and adapting them for his own purposes. The historical novels do not disguise their debt to Walter Scott. The inspiration of *The Three Musketeers* is evident in Brigadier Gerard's character and adventures. "Charles

Augustus Milverton," in which Holmes and Watson do a spot of burglary—from the best of motives, to be sure—takes us toward the milieu of the gentleman thief Raffles, the creation of Conan Doyle's brother-in-law E. W. Hornung. "His Last Bow" takes its story, the capture of a German spy on the eve of the First World War, all too obviously from John Buchan's *The Thirty-nine Steps*. *The Lost World* (in which Professor Challenger finds an unknown land in South America) derives from Rider Haggard's *King Solomon's Mines,* though it lacks the intensity and indeed the sheer scariness of that remarkable book. *The Hound of the Baskervilles* owes a good deal to another Devon book, R. D. Blackmore's *Lorna Doone,* with Dartmoor replacing Exmoor as the sinister wilderness that finally swallows up the villain.

Sherlock Holmes, though, is fully Conan Doyle's invention, though his immense fame meant that he ultimately escaped his creator's complete control. One can contrast the fate of Professor Challenger: at the end of his life, in *The Land of Mist,* Conan Doyle had Challenger try to expose spiritualism, only to be persuaded of its truth by irrefutable evidence. However, some instinct of literary self-preservation told him that Holmes must not follow that path. In "The Sussex Vampire," written in 1924, when Conan Doyle's spiritualist mission was at its height, Holmes asserts his skepticism: "This Agency," he says, "stands flat-footed upon the ground, and there it must remain. The world is big enough for us. No ghosts need apply." It says a good deal for Sherlock Holmes's autonomy that although he would have been the most prestigious of all recruits to the cause, Conan Doyle knew that he could not convert him.

Fall Semester 2008

A version of this lecture appeared in the *New Republic,* 12 March 2008.

10

Eliot versus Hardy

DAN JACOBSON

Thomas Hardy has always been much better known as a novelist than as poet. This is hardly surprising. Novels are generally easier to read than poems (nursery rhymes aside), and can survive translation into other tongues more plausibly than poetry ever can. For much the same reason, novels lend themselves to adaptation into stage plays, musicals, and movies more readily than the general complexity of verse forms would ever permit. All that said, it is remarkable nevertheless that so many readers of Hardy's fiction, who must be numbered still in the hundreds of thousands, are virtually unaware of his achievements as a poet. Yet it is Hardy as a poet that I intend to write about here, and I do so for the most direct of reasons: namely, that I find the best of his poems far more affecting than any of his fictions.

To say that is not to dismiss him as a novelist: the best of his novels—among which I would include *Far From the Madding Crowd, Tess of the D'Urbervilles,* and *Jude the Obscure*—will always deservedly find responsive readers. Yet my conviction of his greatness as a writer springs essentially from what he wrote as a poet rather than as a novelist. In fact, I have no doubt that the two greatest poets in the English language during the twentieth century were Hardy and T. S. Eliot, however little either man might have cared to have his name and work yoked with the other's.

Obviously, I do not think it perverse to speak of Hardy as a "twentieth century poet." True, his novels were all written and published during the nineteenth century, the last of them, *Jude the Obscure,* coming out in 1895. Yet it was only after attempting to begin his career as a writer by sending poems to some of the journals of the day, and having them duly rejected by the editors of those journals, that he turned with much greater success to the writing of fiction. Throughout his subsequent career as a novelist, however, he continued to accumulate poems and drafts of poems. He was later to say that it had been the howls of outrage that greeted *Jude the Obscure,* on the grounds of the novel's supposed obscenity, that led him to abandon the writing of fiction altogether. Yet given his persistence in continuing to write poems "in secrecy" (his wife's phrase, purportedly, but widely believed to be his own) during the thirty-year period between the publication of his first novel and his last, one must wonder whether he made the change when he did because he felt that time was running out on him, and that if he failed to gather his poems together and publish them in the manner that he thought best, then the opportunity might be lost forever.

His first appearance as a poet before the British public was with a volume called *Wessex Poems and Other Verses,* which came out in 1898, just three years before the death of Queen Victoria. From then on there was to be no stopping him. By the time of his death, which took place just a few months short of his eighty-eighth birthday (and some ten years after the end of the First World War), he had brought out hundreds upon hundreds of poems: lyrics, love songs, and little squibs; ballads, sonnets, and drinking songs; poems on public issues and events like the sinking of the *Titanic* and the outbreak and ending of wars in South Africa (1899–1902) and Europe (1914–18); tributes to other poets such as Shakespeare, Shelley, and Keats; and extended dramatic pieces of a type that are almost impossible to define, the longest of these being *The Dynasts,* a mammoth poem about the Napoleonic Wars, which was eventually published in three separate parts. Constantly writing and rewriting, discarding, elaborating, and returning to the stock of poems accumulated during his adult life, he had in late middle age effectively begun what amounted to a second career that, in it public aspect, lasted for almost as long as his career as a novelist.

This time, though, no one thought of sending his poems back to him. Writers returning from the war, such as Siegfried Sassoon, Robert Graves, and T. E. Lawrence, admired and paid court to him; so did the half savage American expatriate Ezra Pound, who had settled in London and wrote warmly to Hardy about his work, adding for the recipient's perusal two of his own recent publications. (According to Michael Millgate's biography, Hardy responded to these gifts with "polite discretion": "I will not try to express my appreciation of their contents," he wrote, "as I am a very slow reader; & as, moreover, your muse asks for considerable deliberation in estimating her.") By contrast, T. S. Eliot, the other expatriate American poet who had recently settled in London, and whose fame as a poet was soon to outstrip not only Pound's but Hardy's too, had greeted the older man's fictions with an unmistakable chilliness. Admitting that at times Hardy wrote "overpoweringly well" (though without offering any illustration of what he meant by this, which by and large was unlike his usual practice), Eliot went on to condemn Hardy's novels for what he insisted they stood for, that is, "extreme emotionalism," "passion for its own sake," and "decadence." He also lumped Hardy together with D. H. Lawrence, saying that both men might have been better poets if they had not devoted so much of their energies to the novel.

These remarks appear in *After Strange Gods,* a short series of lectures delivered by Eliot in the United States in the early 1930s, which the author himself later withdrew from circulation. So far as these lectures are remembered today, it is probably because of the speaker's generous warning to his audience against the danger of admitting any large number of "free-thinking Jews" into "the society that we desire." (This within a year of Hitler's coming to power in Germany.) What is more to the point in the context of Hardy's work, however, is to say how extraordinary it now seems that while writing in generally denigratory terms about Hardy's fiction, Eliot managed to say not a word about his verse. For him, apparently, it simply didn't exist, though by then Hardy, who had died a few years before the lectures were delivered, had been an established figure on the British poetry scene for some thirty years. Instead, on the subject of Hardy in general, Eliot offered this kind of comment:

> The work of the late Thomas Hardy is an interesting example of a powerful personality uncurbed by any institutional attachment or by submission to any objective beliefs; unhampered by any ideas, or even by what sometimes acts as a partial restraint upon inferior writers, the desire to please a large public. He seems to have written as nearly for the sake of "self-expression" as a man well can; and the self which he had to express does not strike me as a particularly wholesome or edifying matter of communication. He was indifferent even to the prescripts of good writing; he wrote sometimes overpoweringly well, but always very carelessly.

And so the passage goes on, until it winds up in a manner characteristic of Eliot's criticism at this period of his life, with a general condemnation of Hardy's appeal to a "majority . . . capable neither of strong emotion nor of strong resistance" and imagining "passion

to be the surest evidence of vitality. This in itself may go towards accounting for [his] popularity."

It is difficult not to believe that Eliot's harshness here arose, in
part at least, from Hardy's tenacious rejection of religious belief in
any form. (Notice, among much else, the flat, meaningless phrase
about the older writer's indifference to "the prescripts of good writing" or "any objective beliefs," as though his readers would be bound
to know exactly what meaning such phrases were supposed to bear.)
It is also difficult to resist the conviction that in adopting this tone
in talking about Hardy, Eliot was in some degree led by snobbery
of a particular kind: the snobbery of one arriviste grown supremely
confident of his capacity to dispose of another.

Hardy himself never commented publicly on Eliot's work, though
according to his biographers, he did copy some passages from "The
Love Song of J. Alfred Prufrock" into his notebook as an example
of the "free verse" he reprobated in conversation. English social life
being what it was (and in some respects still is), it would seem that
Hardy never fully recovered from the humiliation of having had a
cultivated mother, whom he loved greatly, employed as a domestic
servant in other people's households, and a father who earned his
living as a stonemason. Like his fictional character Jude, Hardy was
tormented in his youth by the conviction that his own and his family's lowly social status had denied him many advantages, the chief
of these, perhaps, being the opportunity to get into Oxford. Yet for
all he could know, and for all we will ever know, and certainly for all
that T. S. Eliot ever knew, that enforced escape from Oxford may
in fact have been the making of him as an artist—the supposed absence from his life of "institutional attachment" or "objective beliefs"
notwithstanding.

In Hardy's verse, as in his prose, there is never any intimation of
a supernatural world that can be reached or should be strived for
beyond the common, earthly one that all humans inhabit. The "objective belief" that Hardy clung to throughout his life was that while
we bring to the world a variety of passions that help determine our
fates, our lives remain governed by a mixture of choice, chance, and
temporal succession from which there is no escape and to which we
have to submit as stoically as we can. For Hardy, it is precisely the
sense of a remorseless, blind successiveness ultimately governing
all human (and animal) experience that makes so heartbreaking
the crucially significant moments that many of his poems describe.
Such moments may change our lives at a stroke, yet whatever their
origins or outcomes, they remain indifferent to our hopes and incli-
nations and are incapable of responding to the meanings we impute
to them or may try to take from them. Indeed, in large part it is

our sense of their inscrutability, their "out-of-reachness," that helps make these moments as significant to us as they are.

Strangely enough, it is precisely in this connection that one can find a similarity of sorts between Eliot and Hardy, that is, they are both preoccupied with the unpredictability of whatever moments of illumination come our way, and hence with the consequences they may bring in their wake. Given the differences between the two men in background, character, taste, belief, modes of versification, and habits of mind, they obviously express this preoccupation in different ways and draw different conclusions from what any such visitation might suggest; nevertheless their openness to this kind of experience does make them brothers of a kind. Both men are obsessed with what Hardy called "the quality of time"; hence, as poets they share not only a capacity to describe in their verse moments of a truly transfiguring intensity, but also the compulsion to try to relate such moments to "the waste sad time stretching before and after," as Eliot calls it, with a note of despair and dismissiveness that is special to him, and that is seldom heard in even the most melancholy of Hardy poems, glum and despairing though the latter's poems often are—at times even half comically so, like a child kicking a bedstead. And all the poet's invocations to God, the Fates, the Spirits, the Immanent Will, Voices from the Graveyard, and countless other such capitalized Presences cannot conceal from the reader that references of this kind are never to be taken literally. Rather, they are no more than the words he uses to reveal our incapacities: never a mode of actually calling for aid from the processes that are forever going about their business around us and that we are, willy-nilly a part of. Whereas Eliot—certainly in what can be called his devotional poetry—writes out of hope and expectation, and never with more intensity than when he actually chides himself for daring to hope and expect.

> I said to my soul, be still, and wait without hope
> For hope would be hope for the wrong thing; wait without love
> For love would be love of the wrong thing; there is yet faith
> But the faith and the love and the hope are all in the waiting.
> *(East Coker, III)*

AT THIS POINT I SHOULD CONFESS THAT my enthusiasm for Hardy's poems came as a relatively late discovery, whereas I was simply overwhelmed by my first unaided attempt to read something of Eliot's. That event (it felt like nothing less than that at the time) took place in the library of Witwatersrand University, Johannesburg, when I came on two lines from his "Whispers of Immortality" in *Poems*

(1920): "And breastless creatures under ground / Leaned backward with a lipless grin"—a sequence of phrases that made it impossible for me to go on sitting at my desk; instead, I found myself wandering about the lawn outside, trying to get over what I had just read. I realize now that the power of the lines springs largely from their extraordinary assimilation of life and death to one another: the skeletons "lean backward," like people exchanging jokes with one another in a pub or at a party. But how can they behave in that fashion, given the loss and ruin they have already suffered? And to what end do they do it? From that moment I was hooked, a devotee, compelled for decades afterward to have lines and verses from one Eliot poem or another constantly passing through my head at random moments, as if nothing would ever be able to banish them. By comparison, Hardy, so far as I knew his verse, struck me as something of a simpleton, a bumpkin, a striker-off of jingles, of tortuous rhymes and phrases, an eager deliverer of solemn queries masquerading as deep thought.

Since then, my feeling about the two poets has gone through something like a revolution. It is plain to me still that many ineffective or substandard poems are included in Hardy's *Collected Poems,* something that cannot be said about the roughly comparable volumes by Eliot, which are much more finely winnowed. However, while remaining convinced that the best of Eliot's work will continue to evoke astonishment and even awe among readers for as many years ahead as one might care to guess, I now believe that Hardy, who was happy to declare that "all we can do is write on the old themes in the old styles," and who described critics as "parasites no less noxious than autograph hunters," is ultimately the more rewarding of the two poets. The combination in Eliot's early verse of bravura and desolation, of high spirits and self-doubt, of sexual humility and moral hauteur, of snobbery and self-abnegation—not to speak of the plaiting together of all these moods and appetites, and various others, with a hunger for both religious certitude and public success—was indeed revolutionary, as many critics in succeeding generations were eager to declare. And in the meantime, though Hardy's life on earth was long since over, his verse seemed to plod on indomitably, occasionally striking his readers with a fine line here and a worse one there while all too often revealing the author's remarkable gift for never seeming to know the difference between these two possibilities.

What I did not really notice in Hardy's poetry then, or dismissed glibly because it seemed to me so deliberately "unsmart," was how much steel there was in it. Nor did I pick up on its tenderness. Or its proud and close attention to detail. Or the poet's singular capacity, almost as if he were working in filigree, to create a sense of surprise and elevation by way of both his most elaborate and his most humble-seeming rhymes and rhythms, as he does also with the patterns constantly being drawn and redrawn on the page by the varying lengths of his lines. Yes, there are failures and occasional absurdities in the poems—how could anyone deny it?—but they are more than balanced by utterances that fuse the speaker, the reader, and the people figured in the poems into a unity from which none of them can escape. And from which they would not wish to escape, if only they knew themselves better.

> Woman much missed, how you call to me, call to me,
> Saying that now you are not as you were
> When you had changed from the one who was all to me,
> But as at first, when our day was fair.
>
> Can it be you that I hear? Let me view you, then,
> Standing as when I drew near to the town
> Where you would wait for me: yes, as I knew you then,
> Even to the original air-blue gown!

The subtlety of the versification is extraordinary, from the urgency of the opening line to the seesaw grammatical complexity of the next three, which force the reader to ravel out, as the speaker himself is doing, the wavering flow and recoil of the fractured relationship between the two lovers. And that brings in its tow the speaker's recollection of something that appears at first to be descriptive merely—yet in that single, astonishing phrase ("Even to the original air-blue gown") the poet has once more re-created the intensity and evanescence of the relationship they had shared. *Air-blue*? In that place, at that moment in the poem, the line is masterly, and I would never trust the ear or sensibility of anyone who thought it merely just another instance of Hardy's proneness to strange locutions.

The poem, entitled "The Voice," is surely one of the better known among the long sequence of memorial poems Hardy wrote after the death of his first wife. It goes on for a further two stanzas, the last of them following a different rhythm and rhyme scheme from those preceding it. Yet the note of distress in the six syllables of the last line of the poem ("And the woman calling") does more than repeat in compressed form the first line of the poem; it leaves the speaker with no way out of his loss. The woman's voice, and with it the sense of his own failure, will accompany him wherever he goes. However, to indicate in the briefest possible manner the range of tones to be heard in his verse, I will offer a remarkably short, witty poem which is hardly known at all, but which will, I hope, add substance to my remark about "the steel" that is never absent from his verse. This little poem is simply yet mysteriously called "Waiting Both":

> A star looks down at me,
> And says, 'Here I and you
> Stand, each in his degree:
> What do you mean to do, —
> Mean to do?'
>
> I say: 'For all I know,
> Wait, and let Time go by,
> Till my change come.' — 'Just so,'
> The star says. 'So mean I: —
> So mean I.'

It is a funny yet chilling little affair, that much cannot be doubted. Having read the two verses, we are left in no doubt about which of the two speakers in the poem is going to outlast the other. How then, as both comedy and warning, is it to be rated when compared with some of Eliot's sinister-jocular lines—with this exchange, say, from "Fragment of an Agon"?

> SWEENY: I know a man once did a girl in.
> Any man might do a girl in
> Any man has to, needs to, wants to
> Once in a lifetime, do a girl in
> Well he kept her there in a bath
> With a gallon of lysol in a bath
>
> SWARTS: These fellows always get pinched in the end.
>
> SNOW: Excuse me, they don't all get pinched in the end.
> What about them bones on Epsom Heath?
> I seen that in the papers
> They *don't* all get pinched in the end.

Given the differences between them, any attempt at a direct comparison between the two passages would be implausible; yet no one would wish to deny the power of the machine-gun rat-tat-tat of Sweeny's assertion of what any man has to, needs to, wants to, once in a lifetime do with a troublesome partner. Yet to my taste, "Waiting Both" is the funnier of the two passages—and much the grimmer, too.

Spring Semester 2009

11

Such, Such Was Eric Blair

JULIAN BARNES

You have to feel a little sorry for Mr. and Mrs. Vaughan Wilkes, or "Sambo" and "Flip," as they were known to their charges. During the first decades of the twentieth century, they ran St. Cyprian's, a preparatory school in Eastbourne, on the south coast of England. It was no worse than many other such establishments: the food was bad, the building underheated, physical punishment the norm. Pupils learned "as fast as fear could teach us," one alumnus later wrote. The day began with a frigid and fetid plunge bath; boys denounced one another to the authorities for homosexual practices; and daily morale was dependent on whether a boy was in or out of favor with Flip. In some ways, the school was better than many: it had a good academic record, Sambo nurtured contacts at the most important public schools, especially Eton, and clever boys from decent families of modest income were accepted on half fees. This was a calculated act of generosity: in return, the boys were meant to reward the school by gaining academic distinction.

Often, this worked, and the Wilkeses might have had reason to congratulate themselves, in the early years of the First World War, for having admitted on reduced terms the sons of Major Matthew Connolly, a retired army officer, and of Richard Blair, a former civil servant in the Opium Department of the government of India. The two boys, Cyril and Eric, each won the Harrow Prize (a nationwide history competition), and then took scholarships to Eton in successive years. The Wilkeses must have thought their investments had paid off, the accounts balanced and closed.

But Englishmen of a certain class—especially those sent away to boarding schools—tend toward obsessive memory, looking back on those immured years as either an expulsion from the familial Eden and a traumatic introduction to the concept of alien power, or else as the opposite, a golden and protected spell of time before life's realities intrude. And so, just as the Second World War was about to begin, the Wilkeses, much to their distaste, became a matter of public discussion and argument.

Major Connolly's boy, young Cyril—renamed "Tim" at St. Cyprian's and given the school character of an Irish rebel (although a tame one)—published *Enemies of Promise* in 1938. While describing in some detail the harshness and cruelty of the lightly disguised "St. Wulfric's," Connolly also admitted that as preparatory schools went, it had been "a well run and vigorous example which did me a world of good." Flip was "able, ambitious, temperamental and energetic." Connolly, who leaned toward Edenic memorializing (especially about Eton), recalled the vivid pleasures of reading, natural history, and homoerotic friendship. He devoted several wistful pages to the last subject. Connolly's book must have felt to the Wilkeses as damaging as the fire that burned St. Cyprian's to the ground the following year. Flip wrote him a "Dear Tim" letter about the harm he had done to "two people who did a very great deal for you," adding that the book had "hurt my husband a lot when he was ill and easily upset."

For the next thirty years, the debate continued about the true nature of the Wilkeses—diligent pedagogues or manipulative sadists?—and more widely about the consequences of sending small boys away from home at the age of eight: character building or character deforming? The photographer Cecil Beaton had been at St. Cyprian's at the same time as Connolly and Blair, surviving by charm and the ability to placate by singing "If You Were the Only Girl in the World and I Were the Only Boy." He applauded Connolly for having "seen through all the futilities and snobbishness of Flip and her entourage." Others joined in, like the naturalist Gavin Maxwell and the golf correspondent Henry Longhurst, a stout defender of Flip as "the most formidable, distinguished and unforgettable woman I am likely to meet in my lifetime." Connolly later came to regret what he had written. When Flip died, in August 1967 at the age of ninety-one, he turned up at her funeral, doubtless expecting sentimental reunion, the rheumy eye, and the forgiving handshake. Not a bit of it. The major's boy had turned out a bad egg and a bounder, as literary types often do. Connolly self-pityingly noted that "nobody spoke to me."

Yet Flip's death merely led to the most savage and contentious contribution to the debate. Ten years after *Enemies of Promise*, Eric Blair, by then George Orwell, wrote his essay "Such, Such Were the Joys" as a pendant to Connolly's account. It was never published in Britain during his lifetime, or Flip's, for fear of libel; but it did come out in the United States, in the *Partisan Review,* in 1952. Longhurst picked up a copy of the magazine in Honolulu and was "so shocked that I have never read it again." Forty years after it was first published in Britain, sixty years after it was composed, and now almost a century after the events it describes, "Such, Such" retains immense force, its clarity of exposition matched by its animating rage.

Orwell does not try to backdate his understanding; he retains the inchoate, emotional responses of the young Eric Blair to the system into which he was flung. But now, as George Orwell, he is in a position to anatomize the economic and class infrastructure of St. Cyprian's, and those hierarchies of power that the pupil would later meet in grown-up, public, political form: in this respect those schools were truly named "preparatory."

Orwell also writes with the unhealed pain of an abused child, a pain that occasionally leaks into his prose. He describes a younger pupil—aristocratic and thus entitled to privileges denied to half-fees Blair—like this: "a wretched, drivelling little creature, almost an albino, peering upwards out of weak eyes, with a long nose at the end of which a dewdrop always seemed to be trembling." When this boy had a choking fit at dinner, "a stream of snot ran out of his nose onto his plate in a way horrible to see. Any lesser person would have been called a dirty little beast and ordered out of the room instantly." Orwell's denunciatory fervor is almost counterproductive; readers may well feel sorry for the little chap whose hair color, nasal explosions, and accident of birth were none of his doing.

If Connolly was, by his own admission, a tame rebel at St. Cyprian's, Orwell was a true one: Connolly wrote that Blair "alone among the boys was an intellectual and not a parrot." And if the child is father to the man, the writer's account of his own childhood is often a sure guide to his adult mentality. (At St. Cyprian's, Blair denounced boys for homosexuality—"one of the contexts in which it was proper to sneak." Decades later, during the Cold War, Orwell sneaked on the politically unreliable to the British Foreign Office.) "Such, Such Were the Joys" is about life in an English preparatory school, but it is also about politics, class, empire, and adult psychology. And the writer's mature views on these subjects feed into his corrective vehemence: "Life was hierarchical and whatever happened was right. There were the strong, who deserved to win and always did win, and there were the weak, who deserved to lose and always did lose, everlastingly." The same typist who produced the final, fair copy of "Such, Such" also typed a draft of *Nineteen Eighty-Four;* both the cadences and the message of those two sentences must have made her feel the overlap.

THE QUEEN OF ENGLAND, ADVISED BY HER GOVERNMENT, appoints knights and peers; the nation at large, by more informal means, appoints national treasures. To achieve this status, it is not sufficient to be outstanding in your profession; you must reflect back some aspect of how the country imagines itself to be. (You also need to be seen not to be chasing the title too hard.) Typically, national treasures tend to be actors or sportsfolk or, increasingly, those made famous by television. It is hard for living writers to become NTs, but not impossible. Charm is important; so is the capacity not to threaten, not to be obviously clever; you should be perceptive but not too intellectual.

A most successful national treasure of the last century was John Betjeman, whose genial, bumbly appearances on television overcame the handicap of his being a poet. Someone like Betjeman's contemporary Evelyn Waugh could never have become a treasure: too rude, too openly contemptuous of those whose opinions he despised. Postulants for treasuredom are allowed to have political views, but must never appear angry or self-righteous or superior. In recent times, the two writers to attain unarguable NT status have been Alan Bennett and the recently deceased John Mortimer: both old-fashioned liberals, but managing to exude the sense that if confronted by a rabid cryptofascist Little Englander, they would offer a glass of champagne (in Mortimer's case) or a steaming mug of cocoa (in Bennett's) and then search for common ground in uncontentious topics.

When it comes to the dead, it is hard to retain, or posthumously acquire, treasuredom. Being a great writer in itself has little to do with the matter. The important factors are, first, an ambassadorial quality, an ability to present the nation to itself, and represent it abroad, in a way it wishes to be presented and represented. Second, an element of malleability and interpretability: the malleability allows the writer to be given a more appealing, though not entirely untruthful, image; the interpretability means that we can find in him or her more or less whatever we require. Finally, the writer, even if critical of his or her country, must have a patriotic core or what appears to be one.

Thus Dickens, as Orwell observed in 1939, is "one of those writers who are well worth stealing" (by "Marxists, by Catholics, and, above all, by Conservatives"). He also fulfills the last criterion: "Dickens attacked English institutions with a ferocity that has never since been approached. Yet he managed to do it without making himself hated, and, more than this, the very people he attacked have swallowed him so completely that he has become a national institution himself." Something similar has happened with Trollope, who—partly through relentless TV adaptations, but also because he invented the pillar-box—hovers on the edge of being a national treasure. This near status has been greatly helped by the public support of two Trollope-reading Tory Prime Ministers, Harold Macmillan and John Major, despite the fact that Trollope hated Tories.

And George Orwell? It would surprise, and doubtless irritate, him to discover that since his death, in 1950, he has moved implacably toward NT status. He is interpretable, malleable, ambassadorial, and patriotic. He denounced the Empire, which pleases the Left; he denounced communism, which pleases the Right. He warned us against the corrupting effect on politics and public life of the misuse of language, which pleases almost everyone. He said that "good prose is like a window pane," which pleases those who, despite living in the land of Shakespeare and Dickens, mistrust "fancy" writing. He distrusted anyone who was too "clever." (This is a key English suspicion, most famously voiced in 1961 when Lord Salisbury, a stalwart of the imperialist Tory Right, denounced Iain Macleod, the Secretary of State for the Colonies and a member of the new reforming Tory Left, as "too clever by half.")

Orwell used "sophisticated" and "intellectual" and "intelligentsia" as terms of dispraise, hated Bloomsbury, and not just expected but hoped that the sales of *Uncle Tom's Cabin* would outlast those of Virginia Woolf. He was scathing about social elites, finding the ruling class "stupid." In 1941, he declared that Britain was the most class-ridden country on earth, ruled by "the old and silly," "a family with the wrong members in control"; yet he also recognized that the ruling class was "morally fairly sound" and in time of war "ready enough to get themselves killed." He described the condition of the working class with sympathy and rage, thought them wiser than intellectuals, but didn't sentimentalize them; in their struggle they were as "blind and stupid" as a plant struggling toward the light.

Orwell is profoundly English in even more ways than these. He is deeply untheoretical and wary of general conclusions that do not come from specific experiences. He is a moralist and a puritan, one who, for all his populism and working-class sympathies, is squeamish about dirt, disgusted by corporal and fecal odors. He is caricatural of Jews to the point of anti-Semitism and routinely homophobic, using "the pansy left" and "nancy poets" as if they were accepted sociological terms. He dislikes foreign food and thinks the French know nothing about cooking, while the sight of a gazelle in Morocco makes him dream of mint sauce. He lays down stern rules about how to make and drink tea and, in a rare sentimental flight, imagines the perfect pub.

He is uninterested in creature comforts, clothes, fashion, sport, or frivolity of any kind unless that frivolity—like seaside postcards or boys' magazines—leads to some broader social rumination. He likes trees and roses and barely mentions sex. His preferred literary form, the essay, is, as George Packer observes in the introduction to the two-volume collection of Orwell's essays he edited, quintessentially English. He is a one-man truth-telling awkward squad, and what, the English like to pretend, could be more English than that? Finally, when he rebranded himself, he took the Christian name of England's patron saint. There aren't too many Erics in the lists either of saints or of national treasures. The only Saint Eric is Swedish, and he wasn't even a proper, pope-made saint.

"Getting its history wrong," wrote Ernest Renan, "is part of being a nation." Pointedly, he said "being," not "becoming": the self-delusion is a constant requirement, not just part of a state's initial creation myth. Similarly, getting its iconic figures wrong—and rebranding them at intervals—is part of being a nation. The Orwell whom the English have sanctified is a descendant of the stone-kicking, beef-eating, commonsensical Dr. Johnson (another malleable iconic construct). It is the Orwell who writes to the publisher Fredric Warburg in October 1948, "I think Sartre is a bag of wind and I am going to give him a good boot." It is the Orwell of straight thinking, plain writing, moral clarity, and truth telling.

Yet things are never so simple, not even in truth telling, and Orwell's line "All art is to some extent propaganda" might make us cautious (and reflect that the dictum applies a fortiori to journalism). Take Orwell's denunciation of St. Cyprian's. Despite being written three decades after young Eric Blair's grim experiences, it is much harsher than that of anyone else who wrote about the school. If Orwell had lived to show up at Flip's funeral, the revenge of the golf correspondents might have been worthy of St. Cyprian's itself. But was Orwell's account so unremitting because he saw more truth than all the others, because time had not sentimentalized him, because with hindsight he could see exactly how that kind of education system perverted young minds and spirits to the wider purposes of the

British establishment and Empire? Or was his thumb propagandistically on the scale?

ONE SMALL MOMENT OF LITERARY HISTORY at which many Orwellians would like to have been present was an encounter in Bertorelli's restaurant in London between Orwell's biographer Bernard Crick and Orwell's widow, Sonia. Crick dared to doubt the utter truthfulness of one of Orwell's most celebrated pieces of reportage, "Shooting an Elephant." Sonia, "to the delight of other clients," according to Crick, "screamed" at him across the table, "Of course he shot a fucking elephant. He said he did. Why do you always doubt his fucking word!" The widow, you feel, was screaming for England. Because what England wants to believe about Orwell is that, having seen through the dogma and false words of political ideologies, he refuted the notion that facts are relative, flexible, or purpose serving; further, he taught us that even if 100 percent truth is unobtainable, then 67 percent is and always will be better than 66 percent, and that even such a small percentage point is a morally nonnegotiable unit.

But the unpatriotic doubter must persist, as Crick did. And in the afterword to the paperback edition of his biography, he quotes a tape recording of an old Burma hand's memories of the incident Orwell recounted. According to the elderly witness, Orwell did indeed shoot "a fucking elephant." However, the elephant had not, as Orwell claimed, rampagingly killed a man (whose corpse he described in detail); further, since the beast had been valuable company property, not to be so lightly destroyed, its owners complained to the government, whereupon Blair was packed off to a distant province and a certain Colonel Welbourne called Blair "a disgrace to Eton College." Such external doubting might corroborate the internal doubts of literary genre. As Crick argues, twelve of the fourteen pieces in the issue of *Penguin New Writing* in which "Shooting an Elephant" first appeared were "similarly of a then fashionable genre that blurred the line between fact and fiction—the documentary, 'authentic' style."

The same skepticism—or critical research—may be, and has been, applied to Orwell's equally celebrated anti-Empire piece, "A Hanging." Crick, while admiring its six pages as having "the terror of a Goya coupled with the precise, mundane observation of a Sickert," was not convinced that Orwell had ever attended a hanging; or even if he had, whether it was this one—the hanging of the essay being by implication something confected. Whether or not this is the case, there is one interesting omission from Orwell's account: any stated reason why the man was being hanged. If, as a young journalist, you attended an execution and afterward drank whiskey with those in charge, you would surely have found out what crime the poor devil had committed. And if so, why not pass it on to readers? It is possible that the offense was so vile that Orwell suppressed it, lest readers conclude that there might, after all, be something to be said for capital punishment. Or he might have suppressed it as irrelevant, given his belief that any execution anywhere was an "unspeakable wrongness." Or, as Crick suspected, he might have been describing a typical execution rather than a specific one.

When Dirk Bogarde or Ronald Reagan exaggerates (or invents) his war service, we think him mildly (or seriously) deluded. We might, if sympathetic, imagine them stretching the truth once or twice, and then finding themselves stuck with the story. Why judge Orwell differently? Because he is Orwell. We could argue, as David Lodge has done with "A Hanging," that the value of the two Burmese essays does not rest on their being factually true. But this is a very literary defense, and possibly a case of cutting the writer slack because we admire him anyway. Yet we are hardly dealing with someone like Ford Madox Ford, who believed in the greater truth of impressions over that of mere grubby facts. Further, if the neglected Ford is sometimes classified as a "writer's writer," Orwell was the very opposite—a kind of nonwriter's writer. Many of those who admire him might lose respect or faith if he turned out not to have shot a fucking elephant, or not to have attended this specific fucking execution, because he, George Orwell, said he had, and if he hadn't, then was he not mirroring those political truth-twisters whom he denounced? If "all art is to some extent propaganda," then are we not to suppose that the laws of propaganda apply even if you are on the side of truth, justice, and the angels?

ONE OF THE EFFECTS OF READING ORWELL'S ESSAYS en masse is to realize how very dogmatic—in the nonideological sense—he is. This is another aspect of his Johnsonian Englishness. From the quotidian matter of how to make a cup of tea to the socioeconomic analysis of the restaurant (an entirely unnecessary luxury, to Orwell's puritanical mind), he is a lawgiver, and his laws are often founded in disapproval. He is a great writer against. So his "Bookshop Memories"—a subject others might turn into a gentle color piece with a few amusing anecdotes—scorns lightness. The work, he declares, is drudgery, quite unrewarding, and makes you hate books; while the customers tend to be thieves, paranoiacs, dimwits, or, at best—when buying sets of Dickens in the improbable hope of reading them—mere self-deceivers. In "England Your England," he denounces the left-wing English intelligentsia for being "generally negative" and "querulous": adjectives that, from this distance, seem to fit Orwell pretty aptly. Given that he died at the age of forty-six, it is scary to imagine the crustiness that might have set in had he reached pensionable age.

Nowhere is he more dogmatic than in his attitude toward writing: what it is for, how it should be done, and who does it badly. Auden is "pure scoutmaster"; Carlyle "with all his cleverness . . . had not even the wit to write plain straightforward English"; Rupert Brooke's "Grantchester" is "accumulated vomit." Even those he approves of have major faults: Dickens is really "rather ignorant" about how life works; H. G. Wells is "too sane to understand the modern world"; while Orwell's "defense" of Kipling is oddly patronizing. There are huge generalizations about how writers develop and age; and for all his moral clarity about totalitarian language, his own prescriptiveness is sometimes severe, sometimes woolly.

"All art is to some extent propaganda" looks striking, but is greatly weakened by the "to some extent," and what, finally, does it mean? Only that all art is "about" something, even if it is only about itself. "Art for art's sake"—a concept Orwell would abhor—is just "propaganda" for art itself, which the movement was well aware of. Then there is "A novelist who simply disregards the major public events of the moment is generally either a footler or a plain idiot." Since this dismisses both novelists of the private life and those who (as was common in the nineteenth century) set their stories a generation or two back, out go Austen, the Brontës, Flaubert, James, and so on, and so on.

"Good prose is like a window pane." As an instruction to cub reporters and old hacks—also as a self-instruction of the kind writer-critics issue to the world while actually describing their own procedures—it sounds reasonable enough. But it begs questions, as does Orwell's other key instruction, from "Politics and the English Language": "Let the meaning choose the word, and not the other way about." Together, these dicta presuppose, and instruct, that writing is a matter of examining the world, reflecting upon it, deducing what you want to say, putting that meaning or message into words whose transparency allows the reader, now gazing through the same window pane from the same position, to see the world exactly as you have seen it. But does anyone, even Orwell, actually write like that? And are words glass? Most writing comes from a more inchoate process; ideas may indeed propose words, but sometimes words propose ideas (or both transactions occur within the same sentence). As E. M. Forster, a frequent target of Orwell's, put it (or rather, quoted) in *Aspects of the Novel:* "How do I know what I think till I see what I say?" To Orwell, this might seem a piece of pansy-left whimsy; but it probably accords more closely to the experience of many writers.

IN *DOWN AND OUT IN PARIS AND LONDON,* ORWELL enumerated the things about England that made him glad to be home: "bathrooms, armchairs, mint sauce, new potatoes properly cooked, brown bread, marmalade, beer made with veritable hops." In "England Your England" he celebrated "a nation of stamp-collectors, pigeon-fanciers, amateur carpenters, coupon-snippers, darts-players, crossword-puzzle fans." In 1993, the Trollope-loving Prime Minister John Major, with his party split, the currency on the slide, and his own authority diminishing, found similar refuge in those seemingly eternal aspects of Englishness: "Fifty years on from now, Britain will still be the country of long shadows on cricket grounds, warm beer, invincible green suburbs, dog lovers and pools fillers [that is, bettors on football pools], and, as George Orwell said, 'Old maids bicycling to holy communion through the morning mist' and, if we get our way, Shakespeare will still be read even in school." Less than a third of those fifty years have elapsed, but many pools fillers now play the national lottery or log on to Internet gambling sites; global warming is giving the English a taste for chilled beer; while the bicycling Anglicans are being replaced by Muslims driving to the suburban mosque. All prophets risk posthumous censure, even mockery, and the Orwell we celebrate nowadays is less the predictor than the social and political analyst. Those born in the immediate post-war years grew up with the constant half expectation that 1984 would bring all the novel described: immovable geopolitical blocs plus brutal state surveillance and control. Today, the English may have their sluggardly couch-potato side; their liberties have been somewhat diminished; and they are recorded by CCTV cameras more often than any other nation on earth. But otherwise, 1984 passed with a sigh of relief, while 1989 and the fall of the Berlin Wall brought a louder one.

Orwell believed in 1936 that "the combines can never squeeze the small independent bookseller out of existence as they have squeezed the grocer and the milkman." That "never" was a risky call. And on a larger scale, he believed throughout the Second World War that peace would bring the British revolution he desired, with blood in the gutters and the "red militias . . . billeted in the Ritz," as he put it in private diary and public essay. And after the revolution: "The

Stock Exchange will be pulled down, the horse plough will give way to the tractor, the country houses will be turned into children's holiday camps, the Eton and Harrow match will be forgotten." One out of four on the vision thing—and tractors were hardly a difficult pick.

Against such a background, it would be rash to try to predict the continuing afterlife of Orwell's work. Many of his phrases and mental tropes have already sunk into the conscious and unconscious mind, and we carry them with us as we carry Freudian tropes, whether or not we have read Freud. Some of those English couch potatoes watch programs called *Big Brother* and *Room 101*. And if we allow ourselves to hope for a future in which all of Orwell's warnings have been successfully heeded, and in which *Animal Farm* has become as archaic a text as *Rasselas*, the world will have to work its way through a lot of dictators and repressive systems first. In Burma there is a joke that Orwell wrote not just a single novel about the country, but a trilogy: *Burmese Days, Animal Farm,* and *Nineteen Eighty-Four.*

Orwell shared with Dickens a hatred of tyranny, and in his essay on the Victorian novelist distinguished two types of revolutionaries. There are, on the one hand, the change-of-heart people, who believe that if you change human nature, all the problems of society will fall away; and, on the other, the social engineers, who believe that once you fix society—make it fairer, more democratic, less divided—then the problems of human nature will fall away. These two approaches "appeal to different individuals, and they probably show a tendency to alternate in point of time." Dickens was a change-of-heart man, Orwell a systems-and-structures man, not least because he thought human beings recidivist and beyond mere self-help. "The central problem—how to prevent power from being abused—remains unsolved." And until then, it is safe to predict that Orwell will remain a living writer.

Spring Semester 2009

A version of this lecture appeared in the *New York Review of Books*, 12 March 2009.

12

Drink and the Old Devil

PETER GREEN

What essential ingredients go to make up a satirist? In particular, what high-octane social gases are needed to fuel, and spark, his (seldom, till the feminist revolution, her) process of internal combustion? *Facit indignatio uersum,* snarled that poverty-stricken and *passé* gentleman place-seeker Juvenal two millennia ago: it's resentment that drives me to write. Cliché-ridden hack writing, jumped-up rich lower-class *arrivistes,* pushy aggressive women, trendy homosexuals, pretentious bores, above all Greeks (Juvenal's anti-Hellenic rant has all the qualities of later anti-Semitism): there is a timeless flavor about the list of his pet hates. Byron, too, a very different social animal, similarly pilloried fools, bores, bad literature, and bluestockings (who provoked, in *Don Juan,* one of his most ingenious rhymes: "But—Oh! Ye lords of ladies intellectual, / Inform us truly, have they not hen-peck'd you all?"). Jonathan Swift, who had time for individuals but detested mankind, was the same: "Hated by fools, and fools to hate, / Be that my motto and my fate."

Cruel wit, a delight in ridicule, a short-fuse temper, and a bottomless well of bile: these are the satirist's weapons, and they haven't changed much down the ages. It also helps to have a grievance. Gilbert Highet, in *The Anatomy of Satire* (1962), is not the only critic to have noted the number of satirists who "have been impelled by a rankling sense of personal inferiority, of social injustice, of exclusion from a privileged group." Hunger stimulates resentment and puts an edge on the appetite.

The twentieth century's supreme satirist in English fiction, it is now generally agreed, was Evelyn Waugh, who with an unremittingly caustic eye dispatched the odder habits of Britain's class-ridden society (not to mention American funeral practices) in light and witty Augustan prose. But in Waugh's case, an interesting and dangerous metamorphosis took place. The middle-class chronicler of upper-class follies himself fell—hook, line, and sinker—for the romance of English aristocratic Catholicism, with its great houses and recusant peerages. While this actually sharpened Waugh's attacks on left-wing trendies and the lower middle classes, especially the products of post-1945 political egalitarianism, it also let loose that streak of hagiolatric Pre-Raphaelite sentimentality—already detectable in *A Handful of Dust*—which was to turn too much of *Brideshead Revisited* into embarrassing mush. It is hard to tell at times whether Waugh is more enamored of God or the Marchmain family, and his correspondence makes it all too clear that this was no case of the author assuming a fictional persona. Waugh dearly loved a lord; and a global hierarchy based on Rome had the additional cachet of trumping all merely national snobberies, not least those that might keep him out.

His anxieties, memorably crystallized in *The Ordeal of Gilbert Pinfold,* were well grounded. The titled recipients of Waugh's adoration didn't reciprocate ("That vulgar little man in his awful check suits," was how one of them summed him up to me), and Waugh ended his days as a bloated, petulant blimp, playing the country-house squire, soaking up gin and chloral, arguing with Nancy Mitford about U and non-U, and writing testy letters to *The Times* about slumping standards in manners, morals, and education. J. B. Priestley, reviewing *Pinfold,* argued that the quite evidently autobiographical crack-up it described was the direct result of Pinfold (that is, Waugh) living a lie by falsely assimilating himself to the class he worshipped. That hit near the mark.

Waugh's career, in fact, offered several salutary warnings to an aspiring satirical novelist. Stay on the outside looking in; otherwise, you are all too liable to end up indistinguishable from what you started by satirizing. Watch out particularly if you become fashionable and successful: nothing is more calculated to disarm your radicalism. If the diehards can't beat you, they will adopt you. Above all, think twice about making your living as a writer. Wasting time and energy on hack journalism to pay the bills will be the least of your problems. Even best sellers have to cope with a far more serious deficiency: little or no experience of what, for the majority of the human race, is the chief business of life—a nine-to-five job, with all the demands, restrictions, threats, dangers, challenges, competitiveness, and unpredictable social relationships that come with it.

The instinct, too often, is to get out of the rat race as soon as possible (most often after a brief stint as some kind of teacher) in pursuit of that singularly elusive will-o'-the-wisp known as creative freedom. But those who spend all day in hard-working solitude at home, and then want to tie one (or several) on in good company at the end of it, tend not to be quite on the same wavelength as those who get their bellyful of company during working hours and welcome a return home for domestic peace and relaxation. Inevitably, the creative loners end up writing on what they know about; and what they know about, all too often, is limited to urban sexual adventurism (all those bored Updike housewives with husbands at the office), holidays abroad, and the shenanigans of other writers. Drink has always been a regular ingredient in the mix: the roll call of famous literary lushes is long enough to validate alcoholism as an endemic hazard of the profession. Waugh and Graham Greene also threw in the extra hot spice of religion: no accident, I have often thought, that some of the most powerful scenes in *The Power and the Glory* take place in the Mexican province of Tabasco.

It might have been thought that Waugh's career would have worked as an awful warning against over-close imitation; the facts, unfortunately, tell a different story. One of Waugh's best incidental critics was to prove a striking example of this, and not through any lack of insight. He defined *Decline and Fall*, brilliantly, as pessimistic romance presented as farce. He pinpointed the way in which, later in Waugh's career, "what had been an enlivening bitterness sank to defiance and jeering." He pilloried *Brideshead Revisited* (in a piece mischievously titled "How I Lived in a Very Big House and Found God") for numerous and appalling symptoms of radical decline, including the corruption of judgment by snobbery. "Throughout life"—this when reviewing the biography of Waugh by Christopher Sykes—"[Waugh's] rudeness in public was famous . . . but without this compulsion to say the unsayable he would never have come to be the writer he was." (Takes one to know one.) He saw Waugh's horror at the destruction of innocence, diagnosed his Catholicism as a self-insightful alternative to suicide (or liquor, though Waugh in fact kept himself going with liquor too). He praised Waugh's generosity and kindness to the unfortunate, his sense of honor. When he first burst upon the London literary scene, he was hailed—to the intense alarm of them both—as Waugh's successor. This, ironically, proved true in too many ways for comfort. The critic's name, of course, was Kingsley Amis.

KINGSLEY WILLIAM AMIS WAS BORN ON 16 APRIL 1922, in Norbury, a newish outer suburb south of London. When a rail line was put through in 1878, as Amis reports in his *Memoirs,* "the stretch between Streatham and Croydon was too long so they planted a station in between." Haphazard metroland expansion did the rest. The name was picked from a neighboring country house. Until young Amis came along, Norbury's nearest approach to literature was as the setting for one of Conan Doyle's Sherlock Holmes stories; marinated in a genteel atmosphere of tennis clubs, bridge parties, and stucco-fronted semidetached villas, it formed a natural breeding ground for upwardly aspirant lower-middle-class conservatism. Popular lending libraries abounded, encouraging a mild philistinism toward anything more literary than romances, whodunits, and the new *Pooh* books. Fake Tudor architecture, pseudo-Jacobean furniture, and imitation Turkish rugs were all the rage. This was the world in which Amis grew up, a world in which, as he later confessed, "I would as soon have expected to fall in with a Hottentot as with a writer," and the pretentions of which he started demolishing at an astonishingly early age.

When the poet Philip Larkin, Amis's closest friend, told an interviewer that he himself had begun writing "at puberty, like everyone else," Amis commented, in surprise, "He left it until puberty? I'd been writing for years by puberty." To his first biographer, Eric Jacobs, the author of *Kingsley Amis* (1995), he admitted, revealingly, "I wanted to be a writer before I knew what that was." Zachary Leader, who quotes these words early on in his own monumentally thorough biography, *The Life of Kingsley Amis* (2006), sidesteps their clear implication. Among the six dominant themes he lists as crucial for understanding Amis as man and novelist, he stresses, first and foremost, "the formative influence of Amis's early upbringing." There is a great deal of truth in that; but the fact remains that plenty of other only children grew up in lower-middle-class homes in Norbury between the wars without ending up, for good or ill, as the wealthy and world-famous fictional voice of their generation. When every other factor has been counted in, what sets it all in motion is still the inexplicable creative spark that strikes seemingly at random, and in the ancient world was externalized as a visitation by the Muse.

Amis's parents were typical of their background and period: anyone familiar with Charles and Carrie Pooter, in *The Diary of a Nobody,* will at once recognize their antecedents. His father, an export clerk with Colman's Mustard Co., turned down an offer to be the firm's representative in South America because his wife refused to go abroad; he was never offered a promotion again. Apart from some mild eccentricities (unfunny imitations, pretending to be a foreigner in pubs) inherited and sharpened up by his son, William Amis fitted in well. He played cricket and tennis well into middle age. Uncertain of his own social status, he believed in the lower orders, blacks included, "knowing their place." Both he and his wife, Peggy, thought of sex, even sex in marriage, as something dirty and not to be discussed in Kingsley's presence; what their son got instead were the usual inane lectures about masturbation thinning the blood and, if persisted in, leading to insanity. Kingsley's difficult birth was made the excuse not only for no more children but for the cessation of marital relationships altogether. When Peggy encouraged the seven-year-old boy to write, it is safe to say she didn't know she was encouraging a trend that would lead, ultimately, to vivid expositions of sexual dystopia. None of this (as I can testify from my own very similar metroland childhood) was in the least exceptional.

The good fairy who endowed young Amis at birth with both Juvenal's "incurable disease of writing" (*insanabile scribendi cacoethes*) and the talent and determination to make a success of it got considerable help from two related factors, both educational. The first was the existence of the great endowed British grammar schools. The second was the post-war expansion of Oxbridge and the university system as a whole, initially to accommodate a flood of ex-service students offered Further Education and Training (FET) grants, but in due course to extend tertiary education to sections of the population that had hitherto hardly been touched by it. At the City of London School, Amis was taught by top-class scholars (his headmaster had a double First in classics from Trinity College, Cambridge) who today would settle for nothing less than a professorship. From one teacher in particular, the Reverend C. J. Ellingham, he learned the value of memorizing literature by heart, astonishing his novelist son Martin by quoting, at random and often at length, from poets as varied as Shakespeare, Marvell, Pope, Byron, Kipling, Auden, "and of course Larkin."

Zachary Leader tells us a good deal about Ellingham and his influence on Amis: mostly, I suspect, with the wholly laudable aim of countering the vague (and fallacious) popular belief that Amis's alleged philistinism meant that he was also poorly read. Whatever his acerbic views about large numbers of authors from Chaucer to Virginia Woolf, these largely deriving from his strong and often strident antimodernism, Amis's detailed familiarity with the canon (not to mention offbeat areas such as sci-fi) would put many a contemporary academic to shame. Ellingham also taught him (another decidedly unfashionable view today) that, as Leader says, "one can disagree with a poem's ideas or politics and still admire it." For both Ellingham and his student, A. E. Housman was a classic case in point.

But the deepest impact that Ellingham had on Amis was through his brilliant and trenchant textbook, *Essay Writing: Bad and Good* (1935), of which Amis wrote, after rereading it in 1986, that he was struck by "just how much has stayed in my memory, and how much it has influenced me." That influence penetrated every aspect of his writing and much of the thought behind it. Once alerted, one cannot read a page of Amis without sensing Ellingham's guidelines and aphorisms in the background. On this, as on so many critical issues, Leader offers no direct judgment, preferring simply to lay out the evidence and let the reader draw his or her own conclusions.

In particular, though he would have hated to hear himself so described, Ellingham was a splendid sniffer-out of bullshit. "If you are describing a sunset," he wrote, "and feel that 'the sunset was beautiful' is not enough, it is bluff to write 'the sunset was amazingly beautiful'. You have not avoided the duty of describing the sunset. You have only made your task harder, for now you must show that it was amazing as well as beautiful." Any reader of Amis's posthumous *The King's English: A Guide to Modern Usage* (1997) will at once recognize the master's touch. "If you decide to use slang," Ellingham wrote, "never apologize for it with quotation marks. You cannot have it both ways." And again: "Be scrupulously honest . . . You cannot vamp up enthusiasm for the 'sublime masterpieces of English literature' if you read or enjoy nothing but Edgar Wallace or Angela Brazil. If it is a crime to enjoy Edgar Wallace, which I deny, do not be a furtive criminal." When Amis compiled *The James Bond Dossier* (1965), he must have felt he had his old tutor's full approval.

Thus, one by one the elements that went to make up the phenomenon we know as Kingsley Amis, novelist, poet, and polemicist, were being set in place: the lower-middle-class mores that, with irrepressible humor, he satirized but could never entirely discard; the ambivalent obsession with sex; the only child's tendency to see the world—in effect, other people—as not only hostile but also violent, alien, and inexplicable (a tendency exacerbated by three years in the army, for him a Kafka-like structure of looking-glass logic); energy and determination to a quite extraordinary degree; above all, a classics-based education, at school and Oxford, that gave him a powerful style and honed his critical intelligence. So far the good fairy. What the bad fairy threw in to balance things included the egotism of a spoiled only child, always inveighing against the egotism of others, especially women; an overmastering weakness for liquor and adultery; plus, most crippling of all, a quite staggering, and deliberate, narrowness of experience and interests. Abroad—literature, languages, cultures—left Amis cold except as a source of sunshine and cheap booze. Architecture, most of the visual arts, science, nature, Russian ballet, the business world, T. S. Eliot, and the modernist movement—all were ignored or derided. Vulgar provincial philistinism, sneered the elite. A new chapter in Britain's perennial class war was about to begin.

THE IDEA FOR *LUCKY JIM* WAS PLANTED in Amis's mind as early as October 1948, while he was still at Oxford. Larkin, degree in hand, had moved to a sub-librarian's post at University College, Leicester, where Amis visited him. On Saturday morning they dropped in for coffee at the college common room. Amis looked around—a cold-eyed anthropologist among the natives—"and said to myself, 'Christ, somebody ought to do something with this.'" He pinpointed the scene as "strange and sort of *developed,* a whole mode of existence no one had got on to from outside." The new world of provincial university life had found its fictional chronicler, though it would take more than six years, and several false starts and rejections, before Jim Dixon finally made his famous debut, in the publisher Victor Gollancz's trademark pus-and-permanganate-colored dust jacket. The effort of this prolonged literary birth seems to have cleared a block in Amis's psyche: from then on, he turned out books steadily and methodically, as though on a conveyor belt.

But back in 1948, Amis was in a very far from comfortable position. He had scraped a First in his finals, but this apart, his prospects looked less than encouraging. He had very little money. His girlfriend since 1946, Hilary ("Hilly") Bardwell, had got pregnant, and after first considering an abortion, they had had a highly unromantic shotgun marriage, gloomed over by all four parents. Throughout his noisy undergraduate career, Amis had made a point of targeting revered figures of English literature and the dons who taught them, with childish, highly public, and often obscene anti-Establishment rant: *Beowulf* got zapped as an "anonymous, crass, purblind, infantile, *featureless* HEAP OF GANGRENED ELEPHANT'S SPUTUM"; the Fellows of his college in procession had "*much less* dignity than a procession of syphilitic, cancerous, necrophilic shit-bespattered lavatory attendants." With lethal mimicry ("Shakespeare" emerged as something like *Theckthpyum*), he mocked the verbal affectations of the Goldsmith's Professor of English, Lord David Cecil: Cecil, who was not amused, subsequently ensured that Amis's B.Litt. thesis failed.

Normally, an Oxbridge First would be a sure passport to a good job; Amis's applications were turned down with monotonous regularity (the word had obviously gone round about him), and he got his University College of Swansea lectureship—offered as the result of a last-minute emergency—only after all other more desirable posts had been filled. Pay was poor, he had a heavy teaching load, and soon after her first baby was born, Hilly was pregnant again. The Amises were frequently broke. A heavily autobiographical first novel, *The Legacy,* never found a publisher. Then, over months of exchanges with Larkin, Amis began to work toward adapting to fiction the kind of down-to-earth realism that stamped their correspondence. A work initially entitled *Dixon and Christine,* and embodying a maliciously accurate, barely disguised portrait of Larkin's girlfriend, Monica Jones, began slowly to evolve.

One of the best things in Leader's lengthy biography is his subtle teasing out of this process: his assessment of what, and how much, the manuscript that became *Lucky Jim* owed to Larkin, his untangling of the two friends' intricate and improbable collaboration. His careful verdict, with which I basically agree, would seem to be that while Amis benefited enormously from Larkin's astringent suggestions, the overall debt wasn't as great as Larkin—discouraged by *Lucky Jim*'s huge success from writing further fiction himself— ultimately came to believe. The rumors that Larkin had virtually written *Lucky Jim,* boosted by his catty comment to Monica ("I refuse to believe that [Kingsley] can write a book on his own—or at least a good book"), and his claim to another girlfriend, Maeve Brennan, that Amis had "stolen" *Lucky Jim* from him, Leader dismisses, showing such comments to have been, at best, envious exaggerations. That particular canard has been around for a long time, and it is good to see it finally laid to rest.

I HAVE, FOR EMINENTLY PERSONAL REASONS, A VIVID RECOLLECTION of the literary furor that greeted *Lucky Jim*'s original publication, in 1954. I was due to undergo my Ph.D. orals, and at Paddington station stopped by the bookstall for reading matter to cheer me up on the train. The word had got out that *Lucky Jim* was, among other things, a hilarious riff on the scholarly world. Just what I needed. But by the time I reached my destination, I felt like canceling the whole thing, creeping away into a quiet corner, and cutting my throat. The universities were peopled with trendy malevolent half-wits. Most research was mind-numbingly platitudinous dreck. The real world was somewhere quite different, reserved for disorganized young drunks who burned holes in the bedclothes, passed out when giving a public lecture, insulted everyone in sight, and still ended up with the best girl and a cushy London job. I managed to pass my orals, but—not, I think, looking back, entirely by accident—spent the next decade or so as a literary journalist rather than as the professional academic I had long dreamed of becoming.

More than half a century later, my social hindsight reinforced by Amis's subsequent career and a mass of telling detail from Jacobs's and Leader's biographies, it is easy enough to put this landmark novel, and the effect it had on me, into perspective. The handsome young iconoclast photographed by *Vogue* was also, we now know, terrified both of flying and of the dark and liable, all his life, to panic attacks if left alone in a house or apartment overnight. What was taken at the time as a left-wing attack on the conservative British political and academic Establishment revealed itself in due course—when Amis changed tack and began targeting the radicals—as not even the classic swing from left to right brought about by success, but rather as an undifferentiated, for the most part apolitical, and often aggressively sophomoric distaste for authority figures of any sort. Amis's second wife, the elegant and talented novelist Elizabeth Jane Howard, told Leader, shrewdly, that what really interested Amis wasn't so much politics per se as the company of male political journalists, preferably in bars. The rodomontade against the academic world was fueled as much by insecurity as ambition: when he finally, in 1960, exchanged Swansea for Cambridge, Amis found the new cultural ambience so off-putting that after a couple of years he resigned his Fellowship.

Shortly before *Lucky Jim's* publication, Amis wrote to Larkin: "What I want, cully, is a chance to decide, *from personal experience,* that a life of cocktail parties, cars, week-ending at rich houses, wine, night-clubs and jazz won't bring happiness. I want to *prove* that money isn't everything, to *learn* that pleasure cloys." He soon got his chance, but the learning took a lifetime. Like some of the other so-called Angry Young Men—John Braine, John Osborne—with whom he came to be associated in the public mind, his attitude to money was that of every stereotypical nouveau riche: spend it by the handful on personal luxuries. As the cash and contracts began to pour in, and a week after the birth of his daughter, he took Hilly out to dinner in Swansea and ordered a bottle of Veuve Clicquot. ("Can you afford it, boy?" the Welsh waiter enquired amiably.) A good car and a TV set quickly followed. Amis was so impatient that he spent royalties before he got them, seldom made proper allowances for taxation, and began a lifelong tradition of dunning agents and publishers for ever-greater advances to deal with his spiraling debts.

Meanwhile, the London literati, gobsmacked first by *Lucky Jim,* and then a couple of years later by *Look Back in Anger* and Colin Wilson's *The Outsider,* were nervously trying to make cultural sense of it all. Trendy, but a tad short on intellectual background, they hailed *The Outsider* as England's cutting-edge answer to the French avant-garde, only to see it annihilated—to their acute embarrassment—by professional philosophers as an amateur scissors-and-paste ragbag culled from secondary sources. They labeled Jim Dixon, Jimmy Porter, and Joe Lampton (the antihero of *Room at the Top*) Angry Young Men, the spearhead of a social revolution: in fact, all three come across as ruthlessly on the make in the existing system, while Osborne's Porter drips nostalgia for the Edwardian perks of a lost colonial empire. They also became identified with their authors: Dixon's notorious crack about "filthy Mozart" became a standing reproach to Amis, who (as both biographers make clear) in fact cherished Mozart as his favorite composer.

But lower-middle-class UK intellectuals were on the march all right—part of the huge post-war social upheaval that had begun in 1945 by delivering a landslide Labour victory at the polls—and thumbing their collective noses at the traditional shibboleths and polite niceties of (as they saw it) the toffee-nosed craps and wankers whose turf they were invading. What is less often noted is how much of their own mores they brought with them. The Archie Bunker-ish racist pub chat about Jews, "nignogs," and foreigners generally was something that Amis, Larkin, and the rest inherited from their parents and never got rid of, along with an ineradicable social unease, something neither cash nor honors could wholly kill, in the presence of nobs. Before going to Buckingham Palace to be dubbed a knight, Amis put himself on a beanless diet for a week, so scared was he of accidentally farting in the royal presence.

The unease also bred mean and retributive ingenuity. In old age, Amis arranged for Hilly and her impecunious third husband, Lord Kilmarnock, to become, in effect, his paid housekeepers—a scheme enthusiastically promoted, for their own ends, by his children. He bought the house and met the bills; they looked after all his needs from the basement. As he said, with relish, it was like the plot of an Iris Murdoch novel. Julian Barnes, invited round to Amis's ground-floor flat for supper, was astonished to see the meal brought in on a tray by Kilmarnock. "Not bad for a boy from Norbury, eh?" said Amis, the moment Kilmarnock was out of the room. "Get your dinner from a peer of the realm." The Norbury boy got to be a knight; the peer in turn became his unofficial butler, and was so referred to outside his hearing. Royalties trumped everything in the end except royalty itself: Amis was duly impressed by the Queen. Jim Dixon would have farted.

IN THE LONG RUN, OF COURSE, WHAT REALLY MATTERS is the quality of Amis's published work; and here, over a decade after his death, it is abundantly clear that his great and undeniable talent suffered from three crippling handicaps. First, he had the bad luck to form his ideas in the mid-twentieth century, and then never changed them, so that the huge wave of social revolution that followed, embodying everything from feminism to post-colonialism and gay lib, left him stranded on the beach, a mere angry historical relic. In 1988, in *Difficulties with Girls,* he had a character mutter, "The bloody world's moved on without consulting us." He was right. Far from defining his age, he ended up as a characteristic product of it. Second, and a corollary of this, though he often attacked other novelists for borrowing characters and situations from real life rather than inventing them, critical research, in particular that by Richard Bradford in *Lucky Him: The Life of Kingsley Amis* (2001), has demonstrated—what not a few of us had guessed from the novels themselves—that his own fiction was heavily autobiographical. Finally, his obsessive drinking not only caused a sizable midlife crisis by leaving "his erotic programme torn in two" (Louis MacNeice's crisp summation), but, worse, also encouraged quarrelsomeness and pompous punditry.

One odd result of all this is that it has become impossible to read Amis's novels, especially the later ones, without a recurrent sense of uncomfortable embarrassment, the prickly awareness of social (and in particular gender-based) assumptions belonging to not only another era but another world. Chauvinism hardly begins to describe it. This may well be one reason why his fiction (*Lucky Jim* always excepted) has largely vanished from American bookstores. For the new, presentist generation, it is hopelessly out of date.

The more we learn about his life, too, the closer fact and fiction become intertwined. There are clearly defined periods. From *That Uncertain Feeling* (1955) to *One Fat Englishman* (1963)—that is, from Swansea through Cambridge, with a bacchanalian entr'acte in Princeton—each novel offers an anchoring bass line of marriage overwritten with the arpeggios of irresistible adultery, plus twinges of puritan guilt, pizzicato, which Amis assuaged by displacing all his own nastiest characteristics onto his antiheroes, especially the appalling Roger Micheldene of *One Fat Englishman.* As Dickens's Mrs. Micawber said, "Experientia does it": when it came to the battle of the sexes, Amis knew whereof he wrote. But in 1963, Hilly wrote on her philandering husband's bare back, in lipstick, as he slept on a Yugoslav beach, ONE FAT ENGLISHMAN I FUCK ANYTHING (thus nicely fusing life and literature) and left him, taking the children with her.

This flummoxed Amis, who had carefully set up a creatively productive scenario (marriage plus ongoing infidelities) and saw no reason why it should change. Neither of them had perhaps bargained on the unprecedented impact of Elizabeth Jane Howard. Sex alone, as Amis's Don Juanism had shown, lacked staying power; but Jane's erotic charms had two formidable winners to back them up. She hit Amis's romantic streak (hinted at in early poems such as "A Bookshop Idyll" and "A Song of Experience"), and she was a much-praised fellow novelist. The combination was irresistible, and Amis, uniquely, fell head over heels in love with her. He had already resigned his Cambridge lectureship. Idyllic freedom beckoned. The marriage of true minds was to brook no impediments.

For a few years—during which, significantly, Amis's friendship with Larkin went into temporary limbo—it worked. Both *The Anti-Death League* (1966) and *I Want It Now* (1968) contain powerful fictional versions of his involvement with Jane. The poem "Waking Beauty" sees Jane as the Sleeping Beauty to Kingsley's post-Freudian Prince. They read and commented on each other's work in progress. During this period, Amis made a serious attempt at monogamy, which necessitated a fundamental rethinking of his well-tried plot line. It all sounds too good to last, and of course it didn't. There were various reasons for this. The initial magic of passionate sex wore off. Amis, the spoiled only child, had been used to Hilly running the household full-time and expected Jane to do the same on top of writing her own books. It took Jane eight years to teach her husband how to use even a washing machine, and he never learned to drive, so that she was also the family chauffeur. He had solipsism and writing, she did the cooking and chores. Her fiction suffered. So did the marriage of true minds.

But the real secret enemy was Amis's nonstop and ever-increasing intake of alcohol. This had worried Jane from the start of their marriage. By 1969, he was putting away at least a bottle of whisky a day in addition to drinks with meals (he kept a keg of single malt in his study) and had begun to suffer mild hallucinations. All this, which duly went into the character of Maurice Allingham in *The Green Man,* was too reminiscent of Waugh's crack-up in *Pinfold* for comfort. Increasingly from then on—something Amis never fully faced in his fiction—his heavy drinking played havoc with his sexual urge, till by about 1975, though not much more than fifty, he seems to have become more or less permanently impotent.

Predictably, his marriage suffered: Jane persisted heroically for another decade, but left him in 1980 after he flatly refused to go on the wagon. ("Look, I'm Kingsley Amis, you see, and I can drink whenever I want," he told her.) Equally predictably, he laid the blame for this contretemps not on his own lifestyle, but on women in general and Jane in particular. With screwing no longer a viable option, the latent streak of misogyny in his nature rose, seething, to the surface, and his later fiction presents a disconcerting parade of harridans, psychotic freaks, and manipulative bitches. The zanier aspects of fashionable psychotherapy, in both *Jake's Thing* (1978) and *Stanley and the Women* (1984), evoked some of his most lethal satirical portraits. He became a red-faced, overweight, choleric clubman. In his later years, he was spending over £1,000 a month on drink alone. The undergraduate whose "Evelyn Waugh face" had been one of the funniest in his repertoire ended up as a bad copy of the real thing, an uncomfortable reminder of Orwell's comment that by fifty every man has the face he deserves.

What remains truly extraordinary, given all this, is the way he went on writing and the standard he kept up till the very end. Patches of flat prose, repetitive situations—these are the worst charges that can be brought against his late novels. As Jane conceded, he was the most disciplined writer she had ever met. It was as though life, for him, was the world he created when he sat down at his typewriter: nothing else really mattered. And that world was not only narrow and largely plotless, in the narrative sense, but formulaic. The circumscribed domestic ambience of homes, pubs, and clubs; sex (and, latterly, its absence); marital and familial spats couched in minimalist staccato dialogue; the witty sniping at pretentiousness, the inspired metaphors and similes—it was as brilliant, and in ways as artificial, as the world of P. G. Wodehouse, for whose work (as one eternal schoolboy to another?) Amis always expressed the greatest admiration and whom in ways he oddly resembled.

Whereas Wodehouse evoked a fantastic parody of pre-1914, Amis's stock in trade remained, throughout his career, a pseudo-realistic version of the 1950s, with its heroes only occasionally taken to task after the sixties for their outdated habits (for example, the three-martini lunch or its equivalent, habitual use of four-letter words in public discourse, troglodytic assumptions about women). In both cases, the society created was total and self-sufficient. Amis on occasion reads as one imagines Wodehouse might have written after a crash course on sex, something singularly absent from his own fiction. And Amis's images, scattered with prodigal abandon through his novels, are pure Wodehouse to the end: the "very serious-looking municipal block" in *The Folks That Live on the Hill* (1990) "made of a material resembling petrified porridge," or the "girl of about thirty" in his last novel, *The Biographer's Moustache* (1995)—written while Eric Jacobs was researching his biography and containing one of his most lethal self-portraits—who "answered his ring apparently clad in an excerpt from the Bayeux Tapestry." Even the famous drunk lecture in *Lucky Jim* owes something to Gussie Fink-Nottle's prize-giving speech at the Market Snodsbury grammar school in *Right Ho, Jeeves*.

"Importance isn't important," Amis once said, "only good writing is." If he saw the improbable irony of his thus aligning himself with Oscar Wilde, he kept it to himself. But there were multifarious and contradictory elements that went to make up this mischievous, self-destructive chameleon of a novelist: the aggressive energy, the obsession with craftsmanship, the refusal to distinguish between "high" and "low" culture except in degree of quality, the sense of the world outside as both hostile and alien, the sardonic eye for self-important cliché, the sparklingly witty aphorisms. The cumulative effect is to make us actually *like* Amis, despite the considerable reasons why we shouldn't. Jacobs may give us more of his subject's embarrassing outbursts, and Bradford remains unsurpassed at working out the subtle exploitation of real life in the novels, but Leader's vast, insightful, and very well-written *biographia literaria* will long remain the benchmark by which all future studies of Amis will necessarily be judged.

Oddly, though, neither Leader nor any other critic pays serious attention to what is perhaps Amis's most memorable feat: his ability, again and again, to hit the reader's funny bone with precise, hilarious, and often outrageous observations. His spot-on talent for mimicry extended beyond funny faces to accents, speech-patterns, and conversational gambits. He parroted feminist arguments to perfection. Even the wilder shores of love he could effortlessly reduce to a bad joke. Listen to Joyce Allingham's reaction to her narrator-husband's suggestion that they brighten up their sex life with a threesome:

> "You'd, well, do her, for instance, and then she and I would work each other over for a bit, until you were ready again, and then you'd do me from behind, I don't mean, you know, just *from* behind while she sort of did the front of me, and then she and I would go on together again and perhaps you could do the same thing again only the other way round, or else you and I could divide her up

and take different bits of her, and then you and she could take different bits of me, and so on. Is that the kind of thing?"

"Roughly, yes."

Listening to Joyce's outline had been not altogether unlike having the plot of *Romeo and Juliet* summarized by a plasterer's mate.

In *Stanley and the Women,* one character (clearly speaking for his author) remarks: "The rewards for being sane are not many but knowing what's funny is one of them." As a wry summing-up of Amis's own creative attitude, that would be hard to beat.

Summer Semester 2009

A version of this lecture appeared in the *New Republic,* 7 July 2007.

13

Elegy for an Empire:
Paul Scott's *Raj Quartet*

MARGARET MACMILLAN

Historians too often ignore works of fiction when they examine the past, perhaps out of a belief that works of imagination cannot somehow be authentic. We reserve particular suspicion for historical fiction, partly because there are, it must be admitted, so many bad examples of the genre, but also because such works cannot be judged as we would judge documents in archives. Yet novels, indeed works of art of all sorts, can offer insights into the ways of thinking and feeling of vanished worlds. And the great writers of historical fiction—think of Hilary Mantel on the French Revolution or Robert Harris on Rome—can bring the past to life just as the best historians can.

Paul Scott's great series, the *Raj Quartet*, is both an historical document reflecting the author's own time and a later reflection upon it such as an historian would attempt. During his wartime service in India, Scott saw for himself the last days of that extraordinary community of British expatriates who ruled over British India. Over the generations, they had created their own world, unlike either India or the one back in the British Isles that they struggled so determinedly to replicate. Few came from the aristocracy or the lower classes; most were middle class, established in India because that was where they could make a decent living and enjoy comforts they could not have afforded at home, or because their families had

been there for generations. Their world had its own language, rituals, food, values, and attitudes. When Scott encountered them during the Second World War, "they seemed preserved in some kind
of Edwardian sunlight." He found them fascinating—and doomed.
When he first saw them, in 1943, the British knew that their time
in India was running out fast. The European empires in Asia had
been broken up forever, as it turned out, by the Japanese advances.
Although India itself remained under British control, Indians demanded independence, and the British no longer had the energy or
the will to refuse them. For years after he left India, Scott steeped
himself in its history. As he started on his huge project, he came
back to India for an extended research trip.

I first read the *Raj Quartet* in the early 1970s, when Scott's decision to set his novels in the dying days of the British Raj seemed
an eccentric choice, almost as though he did not want readers. The
British were tired of their imperial past. Who wanted to know the
names of the long-gone empire builders whose statues dotted cities
and towns? Only a few students wanted to study imperial history.
(I was one, perhaps because Canadians were acutely aware of how
being part of a great empire had shaped them.) The Empire to most
people in Britain was an embarrassment, a joke, and a bore. It must
have been galling to Scott that critical recognition of what is an extraordinary contribution to English literature was so slow in coming. It was only in 1977, shortly before he died, that the moving but
lesser postscript to the series, *Staying On,* won the Booker Prize.

He missed most of the huge wave of nostalgia for the British Raj,
fueled in part by the marvelous television series made from the
Quartet, but also by more romantic writers such as M. M. Kaye. In
the public mind, the British presence in India was not about consti-
tutions, law courts, and railways but about rajahs, holy men, tigers,
and the sahibs and memsahibs in their clubs. Scott saw both aspects
and certainly got some of the sheer drama inherent in a small island ruling a huge, complex country. But he also asked awkward
questions. What were the British doing there anyway? Were they, as
several of his characters wondered, doing any good at all? He rightly
insisted on putting power and politics at the center of his novels, not
as some static background for his characters to play against. The
fact of the Raj, of British dominance of India, was a key component
in making the British community in India and in shaping its relations with the Indians.

Whether civil servants, officers commanding the Indian Army,
businessmen, or their wives and children, the British all had parts to
play in upholding British authority and British prestige. And India
provided a very large stage, one where a people from a small cold

northern island could expand. As Scott says in *The Day of the Scorpion,* the British attempted to express in their buildings "their sense of freedom at having space around themselves at last, a land with length and breadth to it that promised ideal conditions for concrete and abstract proof of their extraordinary talent for running things and making them work. And yet here too there is an atmosphere of circumspection, of unexpected limits having been reached and recognized, and quietly, sensibly settled for." The roads and buildings in the British quarters of Indian towns, he feels, have a sense of being turned inward "to withstand a siege."

When the British in India thought about it, which they usually did not, they saw themselves as part of a civilizing mission to bring India and Indians the benefits of Western progress. Most also thought that the Indians were unlikely to change very quickly, if ever, and that in the meantime, their subjects needed to be managed like the children they were. Children perhaps, but ones who might turn nasty. The British were conscious of how few they were and how many their subjects. When the first census was done, in 1881, out of a total population of 250,000,000, only 145,000 were classified as Europeans. And all British remembered the great mutiny of 1857, when British rule might have ended, when Indian soldiers turned their guns on their officers, and when British women and children were hunted down, killed, and, so it was said, raped. The threat to their women was something the British always remembered and always feared.

Scott does not approve of the casual contempt that so many of the British felt toward the Indians. Nor did he find the cozy middle-class confines of British society in India appealing (being himself an intellectual from lower-middle-class, suburban London, he was not likely to). At the same time, he understands and even sympathizes with the British need to cling to their own kind: "Fear of the strange and alien, of losing one's sense of identity, is what causes like to cling to like. We should observe that ritual with sympathy. Unfortunately, such sympathy seems rare." In 1964, after he tried the experiment of living in a village with an Indian family he knew, he described his culture shock, a term he heard for the first time. He saw how it made him intolerant. As he wrote in his essay "Method: The Mystery and the Mechanics," he recognized *"the terrible dependence we have on our own familiar way of doing things if we are to spare thought and expend kindness on people apparently different from ourselves"* (his italics). He understood, he went on, "better therefore the physical and emotional impulses that had always prompted the British in India to sequester themselves in clubs and messes and forts, to preserve, sometimes to the point of absurdity, their own English middle-class way of life."

That understanding was something E. M. Forster conspicuously lacked, which is why so many of his British figures in *A Passage to India* are types—the memsahib, the choleric soldier—rather than people. (One suspects he disliked them so much in part because they were not Bloomsbury intellectuals.)

TWO STORIES THAT LIE AT THE HEART of all four novels show how difficult it was for the British and the Indians to move beyond the relationship between ruler and ruled and how both were so frequently forced to play roles they did not want. "Compulsive harmony" was the way Edwina Crane, an elderly missionary, describes it. "There was in that word compulsive, she knew, the idea of a key to the situation, the idea of there being somewhere in the curious centuries-long association a kind of love with hate on the obverse side, as on a coin." In *The Jewel in the Crown,* which starts the quartet, she is found sitting beside a road, weeping over the body of her Indian assistant, who has been killed by rioters. In the same novel, young Daphne Manners falls in love with a young Indian, Hari Kumar. Both women had in their own ways gone out of bounds: Daphne chose Hari over a suitable English officer, and Edwina came to doubt that she had ever done any good at all in India. Their lives both end in tragedy. Daphne is raped by unknown Indians and loses Hari, who is falsely accused of the crime. She has a child—we never know whose—and dies as she gives birth. Edwina Crane dresses herself in the white sari of an Indian widow and sets herself on fire. Their deaths become part of the fears and rumors among the British community as their day in India draws to its messy end.

Daphne's lover, Hari Kumar, is an equally tragic figure. Taken to England as a boy by his father, who is determined that his son shall be brought up as a sahib. (As an English gentleman, Hari becomes Harry Coomer at his English school.) When his father loses his money and Hari is forced to return to India, he finds himself in no-man's-land, part neither of an India that sees him as a fake Englishman nor of a British community that sees him as a jumped-up native. When he is falsely accused of the rape, he disappears into prison and then obscurity. The policeman Ronald Merrick, who framed him, flourishes in his own sinister and inimitable way, but also, more happily, does the child.

In the later three volumes, Sarah Layton, surely one of Scott's heroines, comes to her own terms with Indians. The daughter of an officer, and brought up to be a memsahib, she lacked, in the words of a sardonic observer who perhaps speaks for Scott himself, that "compound of self-absorption, surface self-confidence and, beneath, a frightening innocence and attendant uncertainty about the nature of the alien world they lived in." She is aware that the world of her childhood is vanishing forever. She sees that the British still play by the rules but harbor a sneaking fear that someone is about to say that the game is over. She is a dutiful daughter to her mother, a masterly drawn bitch, but she slowly goes her own way. Ignoring her community's disapproval, she meets Daphne's aunt, who is bringing up the orphaned baby, and becomes firm friends with Ahmed Kasim, the son of a jailed nationalist politician.

Edwina Crane's life and death fade more rapidly, being kept alive only in the memory of another missionary, Barbie Batchelor, and in an allegorical picture that they both owned. *The Jewel in the Crown* shows a dumpy Queen Victoria as Empress of India. She sits on her throne while angels soar overhead and representative Indians cluster around her feet. One holds out a cushion with a jewel. Edwina was ambivalent about the unreality of the Indians and the "smugly pious" emotions they called up. Barbie, a comic and deeply touching figure who in her own confused way often hits on the truth, forces it into Merrick's crippled hand with the observation that it shows pomp and circumstance but misses one thing: the unknown Indian. In the last novel, *A Division of the Spoils,* Merrick gives it to his little stepson, perhaps the only person who genuinely loved him. It is now 1947. India is falling to pieces as the British withdraw, leaving Hindus and Muslims to kill one another. The picture has spots of mildew. "The Queen's dead now, of course," says the boy briskly.

One of Scott's great virtues, to my mind, is that unlike Forster, he tries to understand how the Raj pressed on the British, forcing them to play roles. There were millions of Indians, so few of them. Not surprisingly, they huddled together, trying to make a huge alien land cozy with their bungalows and neat cantonments. The Laytons and their like in the Muzzafirabad regiment ("the Muzzy Guides") see the hills behind their station as gentle, when, as Sarah Layton knows, they are "unfriendly, vast and dangerous."

The British were trapped by codes and principles formulated in part to keep their own fears and doubts at bay. Sarah Layton's sister, Susan, secretly believes that she has no center at all. Susan's husband, Teddie, once has an uncomfortable moment when he realizes how boring his life has been "because he never did anything, never would do anything, except according to the rules laid down for what a man of his class and calling should do and for how and why he should do it." Teddie dies because he cannot face the fact that his beloved soldiers have turned traitor.

The scorpion is supposed to sting itself to death if it is surrounded by fire, but in fact it dies as a result of a reflexive action to protect itself. It is doomed by the inadequacy of its armor, just as the British community in India was doomed. When old Mabel Layton, the girls' aunt, withdraws from station social life, it causes a frisson of disquiet: "The god had left the temple, no one knew when, how, or why. What one was left with were the rites which had once been propitiated, once been obligatory, but were now meaningless because the god was no longer there to receive them." The Raj collapsed like a house of cards, and the British who had lived and worked on such a grand scale went back to their small island. As Scott puts it, they "came to the end of themselves as they were."

There are times when Scott is so anxious for his readers to understand the politics of those last days that he becomes a bore, grasping you by the lapels and insisting that you listen to yet another lecture on the Indian National Congress or the Viceroy's latest moves. You forgive him much, though, because his characters are so vivid. Clumsy, shy, awkward, and brave Daphne Manners. Heartbreaking Hari Kumar. Barbie Batchelor, who leaves confusion in her wake "like clues to the direction taken by the cheery and indefatigable leader of a paper chase whose ultimate destination was not clear to anybody, including herself." Merrick, of course, who preys on the vulnerable and weaves his plots around them like a brisk spider, is one of the great villains of literature. He is one of the "hollow men" who has built himself an almost perfect casing, says the elegant old White Russian Bronowsky, himself a wonderful creation.

If there is one character who comes closest to Scott himself, or possibly Scott as he would like to have been, it is Guy Perron, introduced late in the series. Perron is educated, clever, original, amusing, and capable of looking beyond the pieties with which the British console themselves in India. Although Perron comes from a family known throughout British India, he wants no part of the Raj. He loathes Merrick, who debases the Raj by upholding it. Like Scott, Perron watches its end with detached sympathy and with horror at the violence and cruelty that accompany the withdrawal of the British and the subsequent partition. (Perron was based on Peter Green, a brilliant and civilized classical scholar from Cambridge whom Scott first met when they both served in India.) In *Staying On,* the postscript to the *Quartet,* we learn that Perron married Sarah Layton, thus bridging the gap between the daughter of the Raj who knew that it was ending and the observer who studied it but did not mourn its passing.

Scott is less good on the Indians, perhaps because he is writing about them as they intersect with the British, but not about them as they are in their own societies. Yet he still creates some memorable characters: Hari Kumar of course; Ahmed Kasim, the son of an Indian nationalist who himself refuses to get involved in politics and chews garlic to keep the British at bay; and old Lady Chatterjee, who talks her own version of British slang of the 1930s and who is both kind and wise to the confused and ultimately heartbroken Daphne Manners.

Scott's characters, British and Indian alike, are buffeted by great events, by what he describes as the "perpetually moving stream of history," and it is that interplay between lives, often of very ordinary people, and the great world of events that make his novels worth reading yet again. Barbie Batchelor carries her precious tin trunk everywhere through the turmoil of wartime India. "At the end of her career the tide of affairs which had involved her was on the ebb, leaving her revealed. And what was revealed did not amount to a great deal, which meant that every bit counted." As Scott says in his essay "After Marabar: Britain and India, a Post-Forsterian View," it was a symbol from him as well, "for the luggage I am conscious of carrying with me everyday of my life—the luggage of my past, of my personal history and of the world's history—luggage crammed with relics of achievement, of failure, of continuing aspirations and optimistic expectations. One is not ruled by the past, one does not rule or re-order it, one simply is it, in the same way that one is as well the present and the part of the future."

Today we may finally have enough perspective to see the long and complicated shared history of Britain and India not so much as a matter of shame or amused nostalgia, but as an episode that left its mark on each, and as an example of the ways in which power affects relationships among peoples of different backgrounds and cultures. Scott uses the luggage metaphor again when old Lady Chatterjee tells a visitor to the independent India of the 1960s (surely he is a stand-in for Scott himself) that for the British, India is like a storage place where they left behind furniture. "You all went," she says, "but left so much behind that you couldn't carry it with you wherever you were going, and these days those of you who come back can more often than not hardly bother to think about it, let along ask for the key to go in and root about among all the old dust sheets to see that everything worthwhile you left is still there and isn't falling to pieces with dry rot." It is Paul Scott's great achievement to have rummaged around in the decaying luggage and made something lasting of what he found.

Spring Semester 2009

A version of this lecture appeared in the *Spectator,* 11 December 2007.

14

Churchill's Zionism

GEOFFREY WHEATCROFT

In *Men at Arms,* the first volume of Evelyn Waugh's great Second World War trilogy, Guy Crouchback is in the officers' mess of the Halbardiers on the day in May 1940 when a new Prime Minister takes office. Major Erskine, the battalion intellectual, startles the mess by saying, "Winston Churchill is about the only man who may save us from losing this war," but Crouchback reacts differently: "Guy knew of Mr Churchill only as a professional politician, a master of sham-Augustan prose, a Zionist, an advocate of the Popular Front in Europe, an associate of the press-lords and of Lloyd George."[1]

Those are most eloquent words, none more potent than "Zionist." Like his creator, Crouchback is a conservative Catholic at a time when the Vatican was still implacably hostile to any idea of a Jewish state in the Holy Land, and for Guy, nothing was more dubious about Churchill than the fact that he was a Zionist—if he was. His commitment to that cause is widely taken for granted—Jacob Heilbrunn was doing no more than expressing a general view when he wrote not long ago in the *New York Times* that Churchill was "laudably eager to establish a Jewish state"[2]—although others have queried that commitment, notably the Israeli historian Michael J. Cohen in *Churchill and the Jews* (1986).

In any case, Cohen says, there is a crucial distinction between gentile and Jewish Zionists. The non-Jews often warmly identify with the cause, but only in the belief that a small part of the Jewish people might return to Palestine to create a "spiritual home." Which is to say, Cohen writes, that they did not share the true creed of Jewish Zionists, that Zionism is "their movement of national liberation, which requires the territorial concentration of the major part of the Jewish people in their ancient homeland."[3]

Churchill certainly did not share any such conviction, and he was not, to say the least, enthusiastic about "national liberation movements." He would have been perplexed by Cohen's words—and still more by those of another writer, who said that the Zionist "decolonization struggle looks very much like other decolonizations, in the Indian subcontinent, for example."[4] So far from sharing the view that "Israel was an anti-imperialist creation," Churchill saw Zionism, in the first place, Cohen correctly says, as "being interwoven either with his own personal political fortunes, or with Britain's imperial interests."[5]

This is highly relevant today. Speaking at the great Churchill colloquy in Austin, Texas, in 1991, Warren Kimball mentioned the "Churchill cult," which was already so strong in America. It has grown only stronger since. Churchill is the subject of countless books and television programs, and he has become not just the honorary American citizen that he was made by Congress, but well-nigh an imaginary president, as it were platonically gazing down from Mount Rushmore. One writer has claimed that President Kennedy's career was deeply influenced by the example of Churchill; another has linked him and President Reagan as two "extraordinary leaders." President Clinton mused, "What if someone had listened to Winston Churchill?" while President George W. Bush was presented by Tony Blair with a bust of Churchill, which he installed in the White House, later saying, "One by one, we are finding and dealing with the terrorists, drawing tight what Winston Churchill called a 'closing net of doom.'"[6]

No Americans revere Churchill more than the neoconservatives, who naturally applaud his Zionism. And yet for Churchill's American admirers, there is a deeper problem. When he did support the Zionist cause, he did so eloquently and trenchantly, and in terms that have long since ceased to be acceptable. They may help explain the difficulties in which Israel finds itself today.

NOT ONLY WAS CHURCHILL AN IMMENSE PERSONALITY, his career was enormously long and saw more twists and turns than might seem humanly possible, or advisable. The only time I saw him in person was in 1963, when I was a schoolboy visiting the House of Commons, and he took his seat amid a hushed calm. Watching him, one realized that this was a man who had fought in battle for the

Queen-Empress Victoria, had first stood for Parliament in the nineteenth century, had become a Cabinet minister in 1908, and had adorned Parliament for more than sixty years. The length of his career, and his protean nature, make it impossible to generalize about him or his beliefs, including his attitude toward the Jews. "Some people like Jews and some do not," he once wrote. "But no thoughtful man can deny the fact that they are beyond question the most formidable and the most remarkable race which has ever appeared in the world."[7] But for all such admiration, his Zionism was in no way ideological. I doubt whether Churchill ever read any of the texts of Zionist doctrine by Theodor Herzl, Ahad Ha'am, or Vladimir Jabotinsky, although he met the last-named.

His involvement with Zionism came about partly by accident. One twist was that Churchill was briefly (1905–08) Member of Parliament for North-West Manchester, one of the numerous constituencies he represented at different times, which had a substantial and thriving Jewish community. It wasn't "predominantly" Jewish, as Cohen thinks, although perhaps a third of its electorate was Jewish, and this stimulated philo-Semitism on Churchill's part much as representing Finchley did with Margaret Thatcher later in the century.

At that time, Chaim Weizmann, already a prominent member of the Zionist organization and destined to become its leader, was living and working in Manchester as an academic scientist. The two men met and began an association that would endure for many years. As early as 1908, Churchill thought that "the establishment of a strong, free Jewish state astride the bridge between Europe and Africa, flanking the roads to the East, would not only be an immense advantage to the British Empire, but a notable step towards the harmonious . . . disposition of its peoples."[8]

For much of Churchill's life, his career resembled Snakes and Ladders, the nursery game in which a shake of the dice lands you either on a ladder for an upward climb or on a snake for a downward slither. In 1915, he trod on a nasty snake when the Gallipoli expedition turned into a bloody disaster. After the Tories vengefully demanded his head, he left the government and London and, in the most quixotic episode of his life, served for several months on the western front as the forty-one-year-old commanding officer of an infantry battalion.

But he was back at Westminster, and in the government, before November 1917, and thus in time for the fateful Balfour Declaration, which promised the Jewish people a national home in Palestine. The declaration sharply divided opinion, though not on party lines. A. J. Balfour, himself a former Tory Prime Minister, was serving in a coalition under a Liberal Prime Minister who shared his increasing romantic enthusiasm for Zionism: David Lloyd George waxed sentimental about small nations—Wales, Greece, Israel—and he said that as a boy in a humble Caernarvonshire Baptist home, he had known far more about the ancient kings of Israel than the kings and queens of England.

On the other hand, the declaration was bitterly opposed by another Liberal. Edwin Montagu was the only Jewish member of the Cabinet at the time, and, like many assimilated Jews then, was appalled by the very idea of Zionism. He was supported by a High Tory. Lord Curzon reminded his colleagues that the British Empire was the greatest Muslim power on earth—something of which Churchill was also conscious—and was dismayed at the effect the declaration would have on those hundreds of millions of Muslim subjects of the Crown. As to the Jews themselves, Curzon told Montagu, "I cannot conceive a worse bondage to which to relegate an advanced and intellectual community than to exile in Palestine."[9]

From 1917, Churchill's whole political outlook was changed by the Russian Revolution, which appalled him and which he believed to be partly Jewish in inspiration. His interest in Zionism became strengthened by the belief that it would rescue Jews from the temptations of Bolshevism. But when he served as Colonial Secretary in 1921–22, he was reminded the hard way how difficult an enterprise had been undertaken in Palestine. In the course of the First World War, the British made mutually incompatible promises to Zionists and Arab nationalists, and the Balfour Declaration itself contained an internal contradiction: it said that while His Majesty's Government viewed "with favour the establishment of a national home for the Jewish people in Palestine," it was "clearly understood that nothing shall be done which may prejudice the civil and religious rights of existing non-Jewish communities in Palestine, or the rights and political status enjoyed by Jews in other countries."

It became immediately and grimly clear that the Arabs, who were still a very large majority, believed that their rights would indeed be prejudiced by Jewish immigration, let alone the establishment of a "national home," let alone the Jewish state that Zionists dreamed of. Not surprisingly, British politicians began to get cold feet. They included Churchill, who was far from consistent in the matter. In 1915, he had suggested that Palestine should be given to "Christian, liberal, noble" Belgium, but in 1920 he conjured up another vision: "In our lifetime by the banks of the Jordan a Jewish State under the protection of the British Crown, which might comprise three or four millions of Jews".[10] At the time he wrote that, the words "Jewish state" were still so inflammatory—though so exhilarating for Zionists—that Weizmann would never speak them, but only murmur *shem hamforas,* the periphrastic allusion to the ineffable name of the Almighty, which the pious must not utter.

Despite his protestations of sympathy for Zionism, and despite the inspiring sight of young Jewish pioneers when he visited Palestine in 1921, Churchill became increasingly exasperated by "the Jews, whom we are pledged to introduce into Palestine and who take it for granted that the local population will be cleared out to suit their convenience." [11] Nothing if not contradictory, he determined at just this time to fashion a country called "Iraq" out of highly disparate elements, but also agreed to partition the original mandatory territory to the west into Trans-Jordan, which is now the kingdom of Jordan, and Palestine, as it remained for more than quarter of a century—which is to say, the land between Jordan and sea that has been ruled by Israel since 1967.

Soon Churchill was toying with other expedients: perhaps reviving the Ottoman Empire in some form to resume the thankless task or, alternatively, coming to terms with Ataturk's new national Turkish state, after which the British should be ready "to resign them both and quit" Palestine and Iraq "at the earliest possible moment." [12] Or, as he told Lloyd George, he was very much taken with the idea that we should "hand over to the charge of the United States either or both of the Middle Eastern Mandates." [13] This supposed that the Americans would have been willing to assume responsibility for Iraq and Palestine, which was most unlikely, though it remains one of the more fascinating ifs of history.

The straits that divide Europe from Asia were not a lucky waterway for Churchill. He had been undone by the Gallipoli expedition, and seven years later, in October 1922, the Lloyd George government was brought down by the Chanak crisis on the other side of the Dardanelles, leaving Churchill stranded, out of office, and, for a time, out of Parliament. After he quietly crept back into the Conservative fold, he became Chancellor of the Exchequer in Baldwin's ministry of 1924–29. After Labour returned to power in 1929, Churchill renewed his prolific and lucrative journalistic career.

After saying little about Palestine for some years, he now wrote, for the *Zionist Record* of New York, an article that was widely syndicated in America. British obligations toward Jews and Arabs were "of equal weight, but they are different in character," he said. "The first obligation is positive and creative, the second obligation is safeguarding and conciliatory," which turn of phrase, whatever quite it meant, was enough to enrage the Ambassador in Washington. [14] The effect of Churchill's words, Sir Ronald Lindsay wrote, "can only be to induce Jews in America who might wish to take a moderate view, to refrain from doing so. They will expect a purely Zionist policy from the Conservatives when they come into office again and will hamper any move towards settlement till then, and then the chickens will come home to roost with Mr Winston Churchill."[15]

They didn't, or not so soon. After the 1931 crisis, the Conservatives returned to power (in a "National" coalition that they dominated). But Churchill was in the process of detaching himself from the Tory leadership—and all respectable opinion—by his intransigent opposition to any form of self-government for India, and thus ruled himself out of any immediate prospect of office. It is very difficult indeed for the Churchill cultists, his noisy American claque, or anyone at all today to defend his record here. His views on India notoriously remained those of the cavalry subaltern in Bangalore; after sailing home in 1897, he never again set foot in India, and his attitude toward the Indians was simply contemptuous. "Racism" and "racist" are such loaded and tendentious words that they are best avoided, and historians should also eschew the cardinal error of judging the past by the standards of later ages. Nonetheless, Churchill's imperial and racial attitudes were retrograde not in comparison with those of a present-day campus liberal or a *New York Times* editorialist but with those of his own time.

And this is highly germane to his view of Zionism and the conflict in Palestine. When the question of Churchill's racism was being discussed some years ago, the late Lord Deedes, the Tory politician who became editor of the *Daily Telegraph* (and something of a national treasure), said that Churchill's admiration for the Jews must surely disprove the charge. But this was a dangerous argument, replied Robert Harris, the political journalist turned popular novelist: "Churchill's particular veneration for the Jews" might to the contrary have been "simply another facet of his racism."[16] At the very least, Churchill's philo-Semitism was highly problematic.

When violence turned into the full-scale Arab Revolt of 1936–39, the British ruefully contemplated an insoluble problem, and a Royal Commission on Palestine was formed in 1937. Its chairman was Lord Peel, an eminent statesman who had been a Tory MP, Secretary of State for India in 1922–24, and a member of the Indian Round Table Conference in 1930–31, at the very time that Churchill's opposition to self-government had hardened into defiance. Although its practical effect was small, the commission's report was very widely read and would later be called by Isaiah Berlin the best and fullest examination of the question there has been.

On 12 March 1937, Churchill appeared as a witness before the commission. He prudently asked that his evidence should be kept confidential, recognizing how frank, and controversial, it was. And the full implication of his words deserves close examination.[17] He strongly defended the Balfour Declaration, in accordance with which "we are trying to bring in as many [Jewish immigrants] as we possibly can," although that was not in fact the official position of the government at the time. He reiterated his view that, thanks to the declaration, "we gained great advantages in the War. We did not adopt Zionism entirely out of altruistic love of starting a Zionist colony: it was a matter of great importance to this country. It was a potent factor upon public opinion in America."

While Churchill was equivocal about a Jewish state as such, he thought there might a be "a State in which there was a great majority of Jews." Even in putting it like that, Churchill was well aware how sensitive the subject was, which may have been why he thought it wise to speak in private. He also continued to see Palestine above all in imperial terms: "If British mastery disappears you had better be quit of the whole show . . . clear out." And he had no time for the Palestinian Arabs, who had fought for the Ottomans in the last war. "They were beaten out of place" and should be grateful for any mercy shown.

On his return from Palestine in 1921, Churchill had waxed eloquent about the Zionists, "splendid open air men, beautiful women; and they have made the desert blossom like the rose," thus creating "a standard of living far superior to that of the indigenous Arabs." It would be quite shocking if the British were to "cast it all aside and leave it to be rudely and brutally overturned by the incursion of a fanatical attack by Arab population."[18] At the same time, he praised the "civilising action" of the settlers, a phrase echoed by Michael Makovsky in his recent book *Churchill's Promised Land*—"the Zionists' civilisational achievement"—without perhaps stopping to reflect that this was exactly how the French described their intentions—a *mission civilatrice*—in Indo-China, Senegal, and Algeria.[19]

Sixteen years after that inspiring visit to Palestine, Churchill reiterated the same themes for Peel. "When the Mohammedan upset occurred in world history," the Muslim hordes "broke it all up, smashed it all up." The Zionists were today cultivating lands that under Arab rule had remained a desert . . . It is for the good of the world that the place should be cultivated and it will never be cultivated by the Arabs." Asked if the Muslims hadn't created a fine civilization in medieval Spain, Churchill replied briskly, "I am glad they were thrown out." Then, in one more Churchillian flourish, he said that although "we are a very gentle and kindly power," we had "every right to strike hard in support of our authority." When the British had acquired Palestine, "it was understood that it was not all going to be done by kindness."

Two specific questions about Palestine by then preoccupied the British: the possibility both of a further partition into Arab and Jewish parts, and of self-government. Churchill emphasized that he was not endorsing partition, although he was not fundamentally opposed: "I have not thought sufficiently about it." But he suggested that one answer might be to "divid[e] up the country and so on, keeping them in groups as the Turks and Greeks have been sorted out in Asia Minor." This was another revealing comparison: the way that Turks and Greeks had "been sorted out" was by bloodshed and "transfer of population," or ethnic cleansing.

It was no surprise that Churchill dismissed talk of self-government for Palestine for any foreseeable future—"It was bound to be delayed; I have said so"—nor that he was disdainful about the Mandates Commission of the League of Nations in Geneva. But he once again expressed his disdain in terms that were both pungent and revealing. Geneva "wanted to have it both ways," whereas the British had an inescapable choice, either *"to facilitate the establishment of the Jewish National Home, or we are to hand over the government of the country to the people who happen to live there at the moment. You cannot do both"* (emphasis added).

And then came the final rhetorical touch. Should we not have some compunction, Peel asked, about "downing the Arabs" merely because they wanted to remain in their own country? Churchill would have none of that. The Palestinian Arabs could not be allowed to dictate the future of the country simply because they had been there so long. "I do not admit that right. I do not admit, for instance, that a great wrong has been done to the Red Indians of America, or the black people of Australia. *I do not admit that a wrong has been done to these people by the fact that a stronger race, a higher grade race, or, at any rate, a more worldly-wise race, to put it that way, has come in and taken their place"* (emphasis added again).

A month earlier, the commission had heard evidence from another extraordinary figure, a few years younger than Churchill and perhaps the one man of genius the Zionist movement has produced. Vladimir Jabotinsky had been formed by anti-Semitic violence in his native Odessa under the tsars, become a brilliant journalist and orator in the Zionist cause, helped create the Jewish Legion—which, with great symbolic importance for the Zionists, served under that name in the First World War—and had then in the 1920s broken away from the mainstream body to found the New Zionist Organisation, the uniformed youth group Betar, and more broadly what was known as Revisionism. It intended, that is, to "revise" or rescind the first partition, which had created a separate Trans-Jordan. And its simple, compelling slogan was "A Jewish state with a Jewish majority on both banks of the Jordan."

Although "Jabo" (as both his followers and the British knew him) gave evidence to Peel, it had to be in London rather than Jerusalem, where the commission traveled to hear other witnesses, since the authorities had excluded him from Palestine as a dangerous agitator some years earlier and did not readmit him then or before his death in American exile in 1940. He gave a bravura performance before the commission. Both Weizmann and David Ben-Gurion, the leader of the Labour Zionists in Palestine and Jabo's most bitter antagonist, had appeared as witnesses, and both had evasively denied that their foreseeable object was a Jewish state.

But Jabo insisted on this. The Balfour Declaration had always meant a Jewish home in the whole of Palestine, he maintained, and a Jewish state was the immediate goal. He demanded the right to unlimited immigration until a Jewish majority was created, while "confessing," as he put it, that "our demand for a Jewish majority is not our maximum—it is our minimum: it is just an inevitable stage, if we are allowed to go on salvaging our people." And in two peculiarly haunting phrases, he added that what faced European Jews was "not the antisemitism of men: it is, above all, the antisemitism of things," the hopeless position of the Jews as an anomalous minority; and that when the Arab claim to Palestine was compared with "the Jewish demand to be saved, it is like the claims of appetite versus the claims of starvation." [20]

When the report was published on 7 July, it recommended partition between the two communities, with a smaller Jewish portion than the United Nations would propose ten years later, let alone than the division brought about by force of arms in 1948. While the report was rejected out of hand by the Arabs, it was tentatively accepted by Weizmann and his colleagues, albeit in pragmatic terms and faute de mieux. But it was passionately opposed by Jabotinsky, whose path Churchill now crossed.

In July, Jabo approached Churchill through the good offices of Lady Violet Bonham Carter. She was the daughter of H. H. Asquith, the Prime Minister under whom Churchill had served a quarter century earlier, although her flirtatious lifelong friendship with "Dearest Winston" had begun even before that. She had become one of that fascinating group of more patrician Zionists and, more unusually, an associate of Jabotinsky's. He wrote to Churchill, with a covering note from Lady Violet begging him to examine Jabotinsky's letter and detailed memorandum. Now that the Peel report had been published, there was to be a parliamentary debate on it, and Jabo implored Churchill to intervene, while offering to meet him: "I would come to Chartwell if necessary." [21]

Five days later, they did meet for an hour's conversation at Westminster shortly before the debate; "and the results were excellent," Jabotinsky's devout biographer writes. [22] Churchill duly spoke in the Commons: having now made up his mind, he contradicted his earlier evidence by opposing partition. More than that, Churchill wrote for the *Evening Standard* an article that, like his speech, was unmistakably influenced by Jabotinsky. Partition was a counsel of despair, Churchill wrote: "One wonders whether, in reality, the difficulties of carrying out the Zionist scheme are so great as they are portrayed."

Nevertheless, while holding himself "free to study the whole situation anew," Churchill recommended perseverance and suggested that "the genius of a man like Lawrence of Arabia" would be able to make peace, "persuade one side to concede and the other to forebear, and lead both races to bathe their hands together in the ever-growing prosperity and culture of their native land." [23] Even by Churchill's standards, this was a little flowery and far-fetched, although it could perhaps be said that those concluding words are what we still hope for to this day.

Whether or not because of Churchill's advocacy, Parliament shelved the report with its partition scheme, and in 1939 the government published yet another despairing White Paper, which proposed strict limits on Jewish immigration, to the rage of the Zionists. It seems doubtful that Churchill had been convinced by a short conversation with his formidable new acquaintance of all the tenets of Revisionist Zionism, and despite his romantic and impulsive nature, he did not take up the cause of a Jewish state on both banks of the Jordan.

IN MAY 1940, CHURCHILL BECAME PRIME MINISTER and rallied his country in the moment of supreme crisis. The story of the war years need not be traced here, important and terrible though it was, as the Jewish tragedy in Europe escalated into unimaginable horror. Churchill has been accused of indifference to that catastrophe and also of ignoring Palestine. But the British were still in the same cleft stick there, of not knowing how to help the Jews without further inflaming the Arabs, a problem more acute than ever now that the Middle East had become a great war theater as well as a vital source of oil. Writing to Eden, his Foreign Secretary, in May 1941, Churchill admitted the obvious fact that "our Zionist policy is an impediment to our good relations with the Arabs," and yet he was also "quite certain that we should lose in America far more than we should gain in the East" if that policy were changed.[24]

A few months later, relations with Washington in regard to Palestine took a different turn. Churchill and President Roosevelt met at Placentia Bay in Newfoundland in August 1941 and discussed what became known as the Atlantic Charter. This mostly vague and lofty statement of eight war aims—in a war that Roosevelt had still not entered as a combatant power, and as yet showed no very lively enthusiasm for entering—was not really a new version of Woodrow Wilson's Fourteen Points from the previous war, but it was still open to contention. Although the British quibbled over "access on equal terms to the trade and raw materials of the world," what really provoked Churchill were the words "the rights of all peoples to choose the form of government under which they will live."

This was nodded through in the end, but Churchill assured Parliament on his return that it referred only to Europe. As he noted privately and grimly, the possible application of this sentence to Asia and Africa "requires much thought."[25] He had no intention of allowing the charter to be cited by enemies of British imperial rule. More revealingly still, he observed that if this principle of democratic self-government were taken literally in the Middle East, "the Arabs might claim by majority they could expel the Jews from Palestine, or at any rate forbid all further immigration. I am wedded to the Zionist policy, of which I was one of the authors."[26] In other words, he recognized a fundamental contradiction between the claims of "Zionist policy" and the principles of democracy.

There was a poignant personal twist to the story. Churchill and Weizmann had been on friendly though not intimate terms for nearly forty years. In the summer of 1937, Weizmann had dined in London with Archibald Sinclair, the Liberal leader, to meet a group of dissident politicians. They included "Winston in his most brilliant style, but very drunk," as Blanche Dugdale, Balfour's niece and another gentile Zionist, recorded in her diary, while he "inveighed against Partition."[27] During the war, the two men kept in touch, although Churchill avoided meeting Zionist leaders. They did meet after a long interval in November 1944, by which time Weizmann could not contain his horror at the fate of the Jews in Europe, but the two agreed sadly that they could do no more than hope for better times.

A day after this meeting, Lord Moyne was assassinated in Cairo by Zionist extremists. Churchill was always emotional and susceptible. He had been moved by the Zionist dream, he had been moved by those handsome pioneers in Palestine, he had been moved by the death in action of Weizmann's son as an RAF pilot in 1941, he was moved by the "most terrible crime in history" committed against the Jews—and now he was moved to outrage by the death of his old friend Walter Guinness, as Moyne had been, whom he had personally chosen to be the senior British representative in the Middle East. Churchill never saw Weizmann again. Nor did he feel again quite as he had about his movement. "If our dreams for Zionism are to end in the smoke of assassins' pistols and our labours for its future to produce only a new set of gangsters worthy of Nazi Germany," he told Parliament, "many like myself will have to consider the position we have maintained so long and so consistently in the past." [28]

At the general election held in the summer of 1945, Labour won a landslide victory, which surprised Attlee, who won, almost as much as Churchill, who lost. This may not have made much difference to the future of Palestine, since the problem was the same for either party, and it continued to divide opinion across the lines of Left and Right. Although Labour had its own Zionist lobby, Ernest Bevin, the new Foreign Secretary, became something of an ogre to Zionists because of his lack of enthusiasm for their cause; but then Churchill acknowledged in the Commons that "many Hon. friends"—fellow Conservative MPs—had never shared his Zionist sympathies.

In January 1947, he warned Parliament about the "great difficulties in conducting squalid warfare with terrorists . . . Every effort should be made to avoid getting into warfare with terrorists." [29] Some of his neoconservative admirers today might be taken aback by the way he put that—and even more so to realize that the squalid terrorists he so detested were the Irgun, the ultras of armed Zionism. Jabotinsky had died in 1940, but the Irgun claimed his inheritance under the leadership of Menachem Begin and were now conducting an angry campaign of violence against the British and the Arabs. Its ranks at the time included the fathers of both Ehud Olmert and Tzipi Livni, not to mention Rahm Emanuel's father.

When the new state was born, Churchill welcomed it, and received an Israeli representative to his house in 1950, sitting in bed of a morning and smoking a cigar and sipping whisky as he spoke warmly of the new state, although he may have been secretly relieved not to have to bear the burden of office in the years as the new state emerged. After he returned to Downing Street for the three and a half years of his peacetime premiership, his fondness for Israel was increased by his loathing of resurgent nationalist Egypt. Sir Anthony Eden was once again Foreign Secretary, and Sir Evelyn Shuckburgh of the Foreign Office recorded a bibulous evening late in 1951 when Churchill told Eden how to deal with the troublesome Egyptians: "Rising from his chair, the old man advanced on Anthony with clenched fists, saying with the inimitable Churchill growl, 'Tell them that if we have any more of their cheek we will set the Jews on them and drive them into the gutter, from which they should never have emerged.'" [30]

That was pretty much the line Eden did follow five years later when he embarked on the ill-considered and ill-fated Suez enterprise. In April 1955, Eden had at last succeeded Churchill, who warned from offstage of the dangers of appeasing Colonel Nasser—"I never knew Munich was a city on the Nile" [31]—but who privately despaired of the escapade when it took place, saying that it had been a mistake not to let Washington in on the plot. But he had no more to offer in his last ten years of sad decline.

LIKE ANY SUCH CREED, ZIONISM has developed over the years, and different national movements have evolved doctrines that can be misleading or contradictory, sometimes in the distinction between ethnic and "civic" nationalism that historians like to make. Irish "republicanism" pretended to be nonsectarian, embracing "Protestant, Catholic, and Dissenter," when it was actually a coarse and regressive Catholic-Gaelic brand of ethnic nationalism, a contradiction that has not surprisingly produced many psychic traumas.

Although Zionism never pretended to be a civic nationalism, but always honestly said it was a Jewish movement for the Jewish people, it acquired another kind of contradiction: a colonial movement claiming to be anticolonial. The words quoted earlier—"Israel was an anti-imperialist creation," and the Zionists "were not colonialists"—were written on the occasion of the fiftieth anniversary of the founding of Israel by Martin Peretz, the former owner of the *New Republic.* They would have mystified Herzl, who dreamed his dream in the 1890s, the heyday of European colonialism and nationalism, and they would have baffled Jabotinsky, who continually used the language of colonization, who spoke of the need for "a decent European administration" [32] to foster the Zionist settlement, and who observed that it was "utterly impossible to obtain the voluntary consent of the Palestine Arabs" to the Zionist project, since "the native population, civilised or uncivilised, have always stubbornly resisted the colonists . . . and it made no difference whatever whether the colonists behaved decently or not." [33]

As to Peretz's words that the Zionist "decolonization struggle looks very much like other decolonizations, in the Indian subcontinent, for example," they would startle most Indians—and would have shocked Churchill.[34] He despised "decolonization struggles" in what would later be called the Third World, and if he retained all his life a strong affection for the Jews and their state, it was just because Zionism was *not* anticolonial, but the opposite.

Here is the problem for those who now revere Churchill, especially those who would invoke him in support of Western civilization in general and in particular of Israel—not to say the greatest irony of his career, or even one of the greatest ironies of the past century. In the early years of the twentieth century, Churchill became captivated by the idea of Zionism; in 1920, he hoped to see a Jewish state as an extension of British imperial might; in 1931, he opposed self-government for the backward and benighted Indians; in 1937, he expressed ardent support for Zionism on the grounds that the Jews were a stronger and "higher grade" race than those they were supplanting in Palestine. Then he became Prime Minister at the moment of his country's supreme crisis, and led it to victory in a great war against the most evil racial tyranny that ever existed, whose wickedness was inflicted above all on the Jews. And in 1948, a Jewish state was born.

By that point, precisely thanks to the crimes, and then the defeat, of Hitler and the Third Reich, a defeat in which Churchill had played such a central part, the very language he had used to justify the Zionist enterprise less than ten years earlier had become entirely unpalatable. How many Israelis today, how many American friends of Israel, want to be told that Zionism was a European colonial movement, part of a larger imperial scheme in which Zionists were carrying out a civilizing mission among primitive peoples? How many would choose to justify the existence of Israel by saying that the Jews were quite rightly replacing the indigenous inhabitants of the Holy Land, as other settlers had rightly replaced the Red Indians in America and the Aborigines in Australia? How many would care to boast that the Jews deserved to take over the land because they were a stronger or a "more worldly-wise" race than its existing inhabitants?

Whether we like it or not, Churchill once told Parliament, "The coming into being of a Jewish state in Palestine is an event in world history to be viewed in the perspective, not of a generation or a century, but in the perspective of a thousand, two thousand or even three thousand years. That is a standard of temporal values or time values which seems very much out of accord with the perpetual click-clack of our rapidly-changing moods and of the age in which we live."[35] That was well put, by a truly extraordinary man. All the same, as it says on bottles of dangerous liquids, Winston Churchill must be handled with care.

Fall Semester 2008

1. Evelyn Waugh, *Men At Arms* (Boston, 1952), p. 243.

2. Jacob Heilbrunn, "Winston Churchill, Neocon?" *New York Times,* 27 Feb. 2005.

3. Michael J. Cohen, *Churchill and the Jews* (London, 1985), p. 327.

4. Martin Peretz, "The God That Did Not Fail," *New Republic,* 15 Sep. 1997.

5. Cohen, *Churchill and the Jews,* p. xvi.

6. For Bush's comments, see 108th Cong., 2nd. sess., *Congressional Record* 150 (4 Feb. 2004): S 5080.

7. Quoted in Norman Rose, "Churchill and Zionism," in *Churchill,* ed. Robert Blake and Wm. Roger Louis (Oxford, 1993), p. 147.

8. Quoted in Ronald Hyam, "Churchill and the British Empire," in Blake and Louis, *Churchill,* p. 171.

9. Quoted in David Gilmour, *Curzon* (London, 1994) p. 481.

10. Quoted in Paul Addison, *Churchill the Unexpected Hero* (Oxford, 2005) p. 99.

11. Quoted in Gilbert, *Churchill and the Jews: A Lifelong Friendship* (London, 2007), p. 35.

12. Cohen, *Churchill and the Jews,* p. 96.

13. Ibid.

14. Quoted in ibid., p. 171.

15. Quoted in ibid.

16. Robert Harris, "Diary," *Spectator,* 16 Apr. 1994.

17. All quotations from Churchill's evidence to the Peel Commission are found in the full text printed in Martin Gilbert, *Winston S. Churchill,* Vol. V: *The Coming of War; Companion,* pt. 3 (London, 1982), pp. 596–617.

18. Michael Makovsky, *Churchill's Promised Land* (New Haven, 2007), p. 122.

19. Ibid., p. 120.

20. Shmuel Katz, *Lone Wolf: A Biography of Vladimir (Ze'ev) Jabotinsky* (New York, 1996), Vol. II, pp. 1520–21, 1523.

21. Ibid., p. 1554.

22. Ibid.

23. Winston S. Churchill, "Partition Perils in Palestine," *Evening Standard,* 23 July 1937; reprinted in Churchill, *Step by Step, 1936–1939* (London, 1939), p. 64.

24. Churchill to Eden, 30 May 1941, reprinted in Martin Gilbert, ed., *The Churchill War Papers: The Ever-Widening War,* Vol. III: *1941* (New York, 2001), p. 737.

25. Churchill to Franklin Roosevelt, 9 Aug. 1942, reprinted in Churchill, *The Second World War,* Vol. IV: *The Hinge of Fate* (London, 1950), p. 786.

26. Ibid.

27. *Baffy: The Diaries of Blanche Dugdale,* ed. Norman Rose (London, 1973), entry for 9 June 1937, p. 45.

28. Churchill, speech to the House of Commons, 17 Nov. 1944, *Parliamentary Debates,* Commons, 5th ser., Vol. 404, col. 2242.

29. Churchill, speech to the House of Commons, 31 Jan. 1947, *Parliamentary Debates,* Commons, 5th ser., Vol. 432, col. 1343.

30. Evelyn Shuckburgh, diary (unpublished), 16 Dec. 1951; quoted in Wm. Roger Louis, "Churchill and Egypt," in *Ends of British Imperialism* (London and New York, 2006), p. 612.

31. Quoted in Evelyn Shuckburgh, *Descent to Suez: Diaries, 1951–1956* (London, 1986), p. 75.

32. Testimony of Jabotinsky in the *Report of the Commission on the Palestine Disturbances of August 1929* (London, 1930), p. 109.

33. Vladimir Jabotinsky, "The Iron Wall," *South Africa Jewish Herald,* 26 Nov. 1937.

34. Peretz, "The God That Did Not Fail," *New Republic,* 15 Sep. 1997.

35. Churchill, speech to the House of Commons, 22 Jan. 1949, *Parliamentary Debates,* Commons, 5th ser., Vol. 460; quoted in Gilbert, *Churchill and the Jews,* p. 275.

15

Julian Amery: The Ultimate Imperial Adventurer

SUE ONSLOW

Julian Amery is woven through the narrative of the unraveling of Britain's imperial skein. As an active and long-standing Conservative MP, he played a leading role in Conservative Party politics: the private and public Tory debates on Britain's role in the post-war world. In particular, the issues of European integration and Britain's place in the wider world, particularly in the Middle East, loomed large. And I was consistently told, when interviewing former Conservative MPs from this era about the extent to which pressure groups formed and shaped British foreign policy, "Julian Amery is your man." Indeed, even though on the backbenches until 1957, Amery played an important part during a formative period of European integration and in London's response to the challenge of Arab nationalism in its informal empire from the 1940s to the mid-1960s.

The uniform conclusion of his political peers was that Julian Amery was an extraordinary, larger-than-life political character. At one level, Amery reflects the romanticism of the British public-school boy of the inter-war period, an exemplar of a male culture and education that stressed enterprise, patriotism, and adventure and that found full expression in the genre literature of Rudyard Kipling and John Buchan. And his wartime experiences had ingrained these principles and practices. In another sense, he was an example of a highly intelligent, gifted British politician who never achieved high office nor quite fulfilled his intellectual promise. Amery had been expected to get a First in Greats at Balliol College, Oxford, but his studies were interrupted by the outbreak of the Second World War. In 1948, he was elected a Fellow of All Souls in Oxford, a fiercely competitive and much admired imprimatur of intellectual ability. He thought deeply and could argue cogently on an impressively wide range of foreign-policy, industrial, and social-policy issues—indeed, his principal speeches in the House were devoted to foreign and defense policy. The material in his copious private papers at the Churchill College Archive Centre reflects the enduring importance of these issues to his worldview.

A brief biography of this ultimate adventurer: Amery was born in 1919. The younger of Leo Amery's two sons, he was educated at Eton (where he was a contemporary of Lord Carrington, later his successful rival as Margaret Thatcher's first Foreign Secretary) and Balliol (an exact contemporary of the Conservative Prime Minister Edward Heath). On his own initiative, he covered the Spanish Civil War as a war correspondent during the university vacations of 1938–39. This conflict has been described as "the culmination of the European civil war between right and left," and Amery's reporting reflected his passionate engagement with the supreme political issue of the day, namely, the challenge posed by fascism, National Socialism, and their allies among other aggressive European nationalist movements, to the forces of liberal democratic capitalism. (Incidentally, it seems possible Amery himself, briefly flirting with fascism as a teenager, joined the British Union of Fascists in 1934. However, the Amery in question could have been his elder brother John, since the BUF party card in his papers reads "J Amery.")

When war broke out in September 1939, Amery was on the Dalmatian coast, where his father had friends from First World War days, preparing for his final university exams. Swiftly abandoning his studies, Amery volunteered his services to the British Legation in Belgrade. He was immediately appointed as a "press secretary," a nominal position that provided diplomatic cover. He rapidly became involved in British covert activities in the Balkans to counter Axis influence and activity: these ranged from funding a pro-British press agency and sympathetic Yugoslav newspaper editors, to supporting covert efforts by Section D (of the Secret Intelligence Service) to aid Yugoslav political parties opposed to German and Italian influence, to arming a variety of dissident groups. Indeed, Amery's networks were credited with laying the foundations for Special Operations Executive (SOE) activities undertaken after the occupation and partition of Yugoslavia in 1941. He himself had been sent back to Britain, largely in disgrace, in late 1940 for trying to foment parallel British-sponsored coups in Belgrade and Sofia. (Amery was not yet twenty-one at this point.) One of the kinder descriptions of him from the irate British Minister was "a bomb happy parvenu." He joined the RAF in 1940 and transferred to the army in 1941, again in the SOE. It has been said he had "a good war": in 1944, he served as liaison officer with Albanian resistance movement and in 1945 on the staff of General Carton de Wiart, Churchill's personal representative to Generalissimo Chiang Kai-shek.

At the end of the war in Europe, Amery immediately tried to get into politics: he contested Preston North in the July 1945 election, but he and his father were both defeated. He succeeded in February 1950, one of the younger Tories whose different generational experiences and backgrounds represented a changing of the guard from the pre-war party. He married Catherine Macmillan, Harold Macmillan's daughter, the same year. An ardent Francophile, a fluent French speaker, and a passionate advocate of British leadership of European integration (on confederal lines), he served as a parliamentary delegate to the Council of Europe from 1950 to 1953 and again in 1956. In the aftermath of the Suez crisis, during which he had been one of the principal Tory backbench hawks and one of Eden's sternest critics, Macmillan appointed him a junior minister at the War Office (1957–58). This was an astute move by Macmillan to appease the "wounded warriors" on the Conservative backbenches, and effectively silenced an able and articulate critic as Macmillan set about repairing the damage to Britain's international reputation. After a short stint as Parliamentary Under Secretary of State at the Colonial Office between 1958 and 1960, Amery moved to Aviation (1960–64). When the Tories were returned to power in 1970, he was, surprisingly, appointed Minister for Housing, then moved to his "natural" home in the Foreign Office between 1972 and 1974. I say "natural" because Amery's great strengths were his detailed knowledge of defense and foreign affairs. But this was the last time he held political office. Heath was defeated in 1974, and when Thatcher was elected Prime Minister in May 1979, despite Amery's (and his supporters') hopes, he was not appointed her Foreign Secretary. Instead, Carrington got the job. In 1992, he was elevated to the House of Lords, but ill health prevented him from playing an active role there. He died in 1996.

AMERY WAS A FASCINATING, BUT ALSO A COMPLEX and paradoxical personality and political thinker. To a very large degree, his political life and views, and particularly his early career in Parliament, were shaped by his father's political outlook and beliefs. Leo Amery was Churchill's Secretary of State for India during the Second World War—and had clashed significantly with Churchill over whether India should be granted Dominion status. A profound political thinker, Leo Amery has been described as "the high priest of Imperial Preference."[1] His close relationship with his younger son, and the similarity of their political outlooks, is striking—and comes through clearly in their personal diaries. Julian benefited enormously from others' high regard for his father and the personal contacts secured therefrom. He was certainly "born to the habit of power," and his entrée into the world of Westminster as a young MP in 1950 occurred during what was still the magic-circle era of British politics. He also benefited from political connections made through his father-in-law, Harold Macmillan.

As a politician, Amery was highly articulate and able, as well as descended from an impeccable "imperial stable." However, he was not widely liked or trusted by older members of the Conservative Party. He and his father were widely admired for how they sought to come to terms with the tragedy of his brother: John Amery had been hung for treason in Wandsworth jail in December 1945. It was one of the reasons that Amery was not put forward for a constituency by-election in 1946 or 1947. John's execution helps explain his brother's particularly fervent brand of British patriotism. Also, older Tories regarded him as a youthful adventurer—stories of his exploits among Albanian partisans were legion—who manipulated his father's connections to his own advantage and glory. "Born with a silver grenade in his mouth" was one contemporary quip. Amery himself was quite open in admitting he had learned his politics in the Balkans and the Middle East.

It is fair to say that his experiences in British military intelligence and resistance made him a natural plotter—an arch plotter, in some people's book—with an innate passion for intrigue. Amery and his long-standing friend and fellow resistance fighter Colonel "Billy" McLean had been involved in MI6's attempts to overthrow the Hoxha regime in Albania in 1949. (King Zog of Albania remained a close friend of the Amery family.) In his passionate advocacy of Britain's sustained position in the Middle East, Amery consistently pursued both the overt route and covert means. He supported at least three coup attempts against Nasser between 1952 and 1954; and in the Suez venture in 1956, his networks among Egyptian dissidents came to form the basis of MI6 plans to overthrow Nasser. His intriguing in Muscat and Oman in 1958 and 1959 with David Smiley (another of his wartime resistance colleagues) helped ensure continued British influence in the Gulf States. His clandestine activities, in combination with parallel MI6 operations, in Yemen served to stimulate opposition to pro-Nasser forces in South West Arabia in the early 1960s. And finally, he joined the pro-Rhodesia lobby in the 1960s and 1970s to counteract what he saw as a betrayal of the values and benefits of benevolent imperialism.

On the surface, it seems that the resourceful and venturesome Amery was an archetypal Conservative imperialist (albeit an apparent throwback to the era of the Great Game in Central Asia) and firmly in the die-hard wing of the Tory party. In fact, this is a profound misrepresentation of the man and his views. Amery was certainly a passionate advocate of the benefits and the enduring validity of the British Empire in the post-war world. In this he was very much a man of his time: Britain had fought and won a world war. Certainly, the country was on its knees immediately after the war, but Europe was "a basket case."[2] Once accused of being a pessimist, Amery retorted, "No one who lived through 1940 can be called a pessimist."[3] British politicians, both Conservative and Labour, recognized that Britain's fortunes were in eclipse immediately after the war, but believed this could be remedied. In Amery's view, the Empire was more than "the natural order of things." He regarded it as a stabilizing force in international relations and a vital counterweight to the emergence of a bipolar world. It also fitted firmly within his conception of the need to maintain Britain's great-power status and global presence to offset American hegemony. (Like other imperially minded Conservative MPs, Amery harbored a deep-seated distrust and dislike of America and its policies. He did, however, count many Americans among his friends, giving them the backhanded compliment that he "did not think of them as Americans.")[4] Although Amery and his father accepted the logic—indeed, the necessity and desirability—of the independence of the Asian subcontinent from British rule, they retained a belief in the continued importance of a London-Delhi axis. They also felt that Britain had to keep its paramount position in the Middle East, which was increasingly under threat from Arab nationalism, American universalism, and perceived Soviet encroachment. So, to use the words of Enoch Powell, Amery did not subscribe to the logic of abandoning the "Empire of positions."[5]

Any analysis of Amery's imperial thinking requires a consideration of the varying components of the origins and practice of British imperialism in the mid to late nineteenth century: just as there is no mono-causal explanation for the emergence of the

second British empire (the one after 1784), so there is no mono-
causal explanation for a continued attachment to the Empire among
the British political classes in the post-war era. The drive for empire
had emerged from an eclectic mixture of great-power politics, socioeconomic and psychological forces, economic and philosophical
theories, and social-economic theories of national efficiency. Amery
declared that "the Conservative party is the party of Empire, or it is
nothing."[6] By this he meant that support and maintenance of the
Empire should be the creed and religion of all right-thinking Tories.
This set him firmly against the brand of progressive Conservatism
that was emerging by the end of the 1950s. This growing schism
within the Tory party, exacerbated by the drive for accelerated decolonization in Africa during the second Macmillan government,
represented, at the start of the 1960s, a struggle for the identity, philosophy, and future direction of the Conservative Party.

But Amery was not a knee-jerk imperialist. Rather, he had been
"born into the Church of the Chamberlains"[7]—that is, into a particular trend within Conservative and Unionist political thought that
dated back to another high priest of empire, Joseph Chamberlain.
Chamberlain, himself originally a Liberal Unionist, had jumped
ship to join the Conservatives after Gladstone's decision to push for
home rule in Ireland. To Chamberlain, this was disaster. He was
convinced that such a move would stimulate centrifugal forces elsewhere within the Empire and would lead to the breakup of the British nation itself. Julian Amery wholeheartedly subscribed to this
view. So, in the broader sense, Amery represented the endurance
of views that British imperialism was a serious and responsible political movement and not simply a manifestation of its occasional
ally, jingoism. Amery's attitude toward the creative role of political power, including the belief that it could shape the future, together with his willingness to use force, harked back to that other
great Liberal imperialist, Lord Milner. Like Joseph Chamberlain,
Milner, and his father, Leo, Julian Amery was a Big Englander—not
a rabid expansionist, but someone convinced that the Empire was a
force for stability abroad and at home. Like Chamberlain's thought,
Amery's "Social Imperialism" melded elements of Liberalism and
Conservatism together.[8] Through the creation of an Empire Customs Union, the Empire would act as a progressive all-embracing
project, cementing the benefits of British rule, national efficiency,
and the welfare of the British people. Revenue raised through imperial preference would fund domestic social reform and remove the
dangers of democracy—government profligacy through high rates
of income tax and through progressive taxation, the burden of tax-

ation falling on one class in particular. Social Imperialism would also ensure the loyalty and satisfy the interests of the British working class, which represented the majority of the British electorate.

Julian Amery wholeheartedly supported a socioeconomic-developmental view of Britain and its Empire, and his writings and speeches show a remarkable consistency from the late 1930s to the 1950s. He firmly opposed free trade and the convertibility of sterling, policies typified by the Bretton Woods system and the General Agreement on Tariffs and Trade. His arguments were founded upon the need for colonial development. He called for the establishment of a Commonwealth bank and for greater independence of the Bank of England from the British Treasury, but also for the efficient allocation of resources and the differentiation of production within the Commonwealth and Empire. After the war, he passionately believed that using a system of imperial preference would enable the reconstruction of British industry, ensure markets, maintain domestic employment, and fund the welfare state, all without increasing direct domestic taxation. Diffusing the burden of indirect taxation across the population would act as an incentive (rather than a deterrent) to productivity and consumption while also funding social reform. But as Max Beaverbrook warned him in 1945, "You are very wrong if you think what Leo Amery, Max Beaverbrook or Bob Boothby believe has anything to do with what the Tory party believes!"[9]

Amery's socially progressive views did not stop there: he was a lifelong and passionate opponent of the death penalty (the scars of his personal experience ran very deep). He consistently argued for the establishment of worker directorships, that is, the appointment of workers to management boards as a way to overcome the dichotomy of interests between management and the industrial working classes. This idea of co-partnerships again harked back to an earlier tradition within Tory thinking and echoed Continental corporatist ideas of the 1930s. Thus, Amery was a critic of Robert Carr's Industrial Relations Act of 1970, which he felt was divisive. And consistently from the late 1940s through to his time as Minister of Housing in the early 1970s, Amery supported the expansion of working-class property ownership through the sale of council housing. This is often labeled a flagship Thatcherite enterprise of the 1980s. Instead, it can be traced to Amery's time at the Ministry of Housing. While a minister, Amery spoke in favor of selling housing stock at a reduced rate to council tenants after ten years and of having residences revert to owner occupation after thirty years. This was a forerunner to the massive sell-off of council housing—to promote "property owning democracy"—of the Thatcher governments.

YET IF HE WAS SUCH A PROGRESSIVE AND IMPRESSIVE thinker, why did Amery not achieve higher office? He certainly thought he was a political failure. Writing in his diary on his seventieth birthday, in 1989, he noted bitterly that every political cause he had supported had come to nothing. Imperial preference as a policy had been defeated at the Tory party conference in 1954, while the growing extra-Commonwealth and, particularly, European trade further undermined the economic structures of the Empire. Suez had been a disaster, thanks to a failure of British will. Amery resolutely refused to apologize for British collusion with the French and Israelis or for the use of military force. Decolonization in Africa had been pushed through rapidly; Amery did not support Macmillan's view of an expanded Commonwealth under British leadership as either the ideal progressive force in international politics or a natural magnet for attracting newly independent African states away from communist influence. The TSR-2 missile system had been canceled. His vision for a multiracial Rhodesia had failed; and the devolution of Northern Ireland had been introduced by the Thatcher government in 1986. Like Joseph Chamberlain a century earlier, Amery felt that this would be the death knell of the United Kingdom, since only in the wider political context of Westminster would the passions of Northern Irish politics be diluted.

Similarly, his vision of British leadership of a united Europe had not been realized. It is interesting that his autobiography *Approach March,* written in 1966–70, when he was out of Parliament, is a triumphant story. The next volume, which he was planning once he left Parliament and for which there are outline notes in his private papers, would have had to address the failure of the causes he had championed. Amery's own aspirations for Cabinet rank hadn't been realized, and his early bid for the Conservative Party leadership in 1975 had come to nothing.

One of the explanations for his failure to make a more public political mark is that his political style was ill suited to an increasingly image-conscious age. His appearance and style of dress—the swept back hair and the liberal use of brilliantine—looked old-fashioned even at the start of the 1960s. He had a pompous exterior, and his pronunciation ("More Balliol than Balliol," "plummy") was the butt of many political jokes. Even simple words were mangled: political commentators mocked his maiden speech as a minister, in which action became "aircshun" and concerned, "consyearned." In the early days of his political career, there was the shadow of his brother. There was possibly also some latent anti-Semitism within the Conservative establishment, although no one would have dared articulate this in the aftermath of the Holocaust. And after 1963, there was his close connection with Macmillan and his particular brand of progressive Conservativism (although this is not an accurate identification in Amery's case). Amery's open and long-standing support for the Smith regime in Rhodesia certainly boosted his reputation of being a right-winger. But Amery was no racist: he proved actively sympathetic to Seretse Kharma in Botswana when the British government banned his return in the 1940s and 1950s as paramount chief following his marriage to Ruth Williams, out of undue sensitivity to the apartheid government in South Africa. His support for the Smith regime was founded on paternalistic elitism toward African nationalist aspirations.

And Amery was outspoken. For example, in a BBC interview in June 1982 following the Remembrance service for the Falklands campaign at St. Paul's Cathedral, he was trenchant in his criticism of what he regarded as the apologetic and neutralist tone of the Archbishop of Canterbury and the Dean of St. Paul's. His old friend and political colleague Lord Salisbury certainly attributed his failure to go further to this refusal to water down his views.[10]

Another explanation is the shift in British politics. Amery, who concentrated on the world of Westminster, mourned the loss of the collegiate environment of Parliament of 1950s, when lack of facilities meant that MPs congregated in the Tea Room or smoking room. He was also not an assiduous constituency MP: Preston North was a marginal seat, so while representing it, he had to pay more attention to nursing his majority. But once he was elected to the safe Conservative stronghold of Brighton Pavilion in 1969, his visits were much more along the lines of one or two a year. Amery was a "man of the salon" and an inveterate participant in Conservative Party pressure groups—the Monday Club, the Watching Committee, the Sudan Group, the Suez Group, the Aden Group, Friends of Rhodesia, One Flag—all of which had a firmly right-wing stamp. But there is no sign in his papers that he was a member of the key Conservative backbench cabal, Progress Trust (a mark of acceptability within the Tory party establishment on the backbenches). His attempt to create a Conservative SOE by drawing on his wartime links with the intelligence services had fizzled by the 1960s.

However, he remained extraordinarily well connected and incurably hospitable. He was, from the late 1940s, a passionate supporter of European integration. This issue became increasingly divisive in Conservative Party politics in the 1970s, flaring again in the late 1980s. To Amery, a united Europe and a Britain with a united Empire were entirely complementary. It fitted within the prevailing ideas of the post-war period of economic blocs as the solution to reconstruction. But this support for Europe did not chime in with the imperial diehards in the Tory party, who felt that Britain had become entangled with Europe far too closely twice in the twentieth century, with very disagreeable results.

But principally, Amery's failure to achieve political prominence was due to shifts in British society and its attitudes: Amery was a man of empire. Despite his impassioned advocacy for Britain and its Empire-Commonwealth as a progressive and viable entity in the post-war world, the writing was on the wall. Following the Suez crisis, Macmillan's drive for decolonization, and Britain's declining great-power status, he was associated with a bygone era. By the mid-1950s, he and his ideas were swimming against the tide of opinion, economic developments, and political forces.

WHAT IS AMERY'S LEGACY? As a politician, he was important in ways that can be seen with the benefit of hindsight. It was not just his representation of a particular trend of intellectual thought in twentieth-century British politics. He contributed to the downfall of Anthony Eden in 1956–57. Amery supported Duncan Sandys as Eden's successor, but his vision of restored British dominance of the Middle East was wrecked by his father-in-law's deal with the Eisenhower administration. Thanks to his efforts, Britain maintained an extraordinary degree of influence in the sheikdoms of the Persian Gulf. Third, he signed the treaty that initiated the Anglo-French Concorde project, although opinion is sharply divided on whether this was actually a success, since it was marred by budget overruns and technical difficulties.

Amery also left his mark, although not as he necessarily intended, as a political observer. Given the longevity and range of his political activity, and his personal contacts and experiences, he had unique insights and knowledge of leading Conservative politicians of the day. His private papers contain a wealth of material about contemporary political issues. They underline the importance of personal connections, together with the often-overlooked fact that personal likes and dislikes are woven into the very fabric of political discourse. Amery enjoyed intimate friendships and had connections with five British Conservative Prime Ministers: Churchill, Eden, Heath, Thatcher, and, above all, Macmillan.

He clearly had enormous admiration and respect for Churchill, whose titanic political presence as one of "the Big Three" meant that in the decade after the war, Churchill constituted "a one-man pressure group." As Amery once put it, "To go against Churchill, was to lose sleep."[11] In the late 1930s, the young Amery, together with his father, had supported Churchill's opposition to Chamberlain's pursuit of appeasement of Nazi Germany. After the war, Amery believed he had been instrumental in encouraging Churchill's interest in a united Europe. Amery used to tell of being invited to lunch with Richard Coudenhove Kalergi, President of the pre-war Pan European Movement, in Switzerland. After his return to England, Julian was invited with his father down to lunch at Chartwell in Kent; from this meeting emerged the United Europe Movement under Churchill's leadership.

Amery's relationship with Eden, which was much more ambivalent, hardened into active opposition during his premiership. His diary also contains interesting reflections on R. A. B. Butler, whom Amery regarded as "lacking in political sex appeal." In May 1948, he noted, "[Butler] regards Eden as extremely sensitive and astute but doubts whether he can always be relied upon to take the first advice. [Butler] was also pretty critical of Harold. At first he even called him a crook, but then took back the word explaining that what he meant was that he was an unreliable Celt." This was prescient, considering Macmillan's subsequent behavior during the Suez crisis. Amery concluded that Butler was "much more reactionary on social questions than I would have thought and much more the representative of the industrial propertied class."[12]

Amery of course had an unparalleled insight into Harold Macmillan. Macmillan was his publisher for *Sons of the Eagle* and had commissioned Amery to complete the remaining volumes of the life of Joseph Chamberlain in the late 1940s, after James Garvin's death. After Macmillan's funeral, in 1987, Amery wrote a long memoir in his diary, recalling his friendship with his father-in-law, whom he had first met as an undergraduate friend of Maurice Macmillan.

> Then there was the by election at Oxford at the time of Munich when Harold came and spoke against Quintin Hogg, who was backing Neville Chamberlain. I remember being struck by the contrast between his rather dashing rather romantic character in public and his rather staid almost elderly manner in private.

Amery saw Macmillan several times during the war.

> Like my father and myself, he was beaten in the General Election of 1945 and went back to publishing although it was clear he would soon be back in the House of Commons. . . . I saw quite a lot of him in connection with both books, as well as articles I wrote on Greece, Albania and Yugoslavia. I remember in particular a dinner he organised in the House of Commons to which my father

went. It must have been 1948 just after Tito had broken with the Cominform. We all disliked Tito, but were unanimous in asking that the official opposition should tell Attlee that if he stood by Tito, we would stand by him in doing so.

Amery also recalled Macmillan's reaction to the wedding list:

My father had been a colleague in the Coalition Government, as indeed had Harold at a lower level, with all the by this time leaders of the Labour party. He suggested inviting Attlee, Dalton and I think, Cripps. Harold, oddly enough, vetoed them all in spite of my father's protests. I remember my father saying, "I've never been quite sure the fellow was a gentleman."

This passage goes on to comment thoughtfully on Macmillan and Dorothy's marriage, and the impact of her long-lasting relationship with Bob Boothby. He developed this into a comment on Macmillan's pattern of behavior at Birchgrove:

After dinner she would do jigsaw puzzles or play cards with the family. He would say, if you don't like these games, come and read your book, or do your work in the Library with me. This was a new experience. I had been on very intimate terms with my father but would never have presumed to go and sit in the library when he was working or reading. [Macmillan] would invariably offer a glass of port after dinner to give me the opportunity of talking if there was something to say, but then we would separate. This was another story. I would go to the library with a book and sit down. There would be no conversation for quite a time. Then suddenly he would put down his book, or whatever official papers he was reading and ask some question or make some comment. We would talk for anything for five minutes to three quarters of an hour, and then, just as suddenly as he had begun talking, he would pick up his book or his papers again and resume reading. I found this at first rather unnerving. He was a night owl by nature so the process went on for quite a long time. But usually about one o'clock in the morning, he would say, "Dear boy, bring me a glass of whisky". So I would go out and bring back the necessary refreshment for him and myself. We would then embark on a rather longer conversation usually ending by going to bed at about two.

This explains how Amery had an inside view of Britain's foreign policy when Macmillan was Foreign Secretary in 1955 and particularly during the Suez crisis: he spent much time at Birchgrove in the summer recess of 1956, since Catherine Macmillan was expecting twins. As Amery appreciated acutely, "though still quite a junior in Ministerial rank, it gave me the opportunity to share his views on some of the important political decisions of the day. I then came to be very much more in the inner circle than the actual office I held would have normally justified."

Amery clearly admired his father-in-law's "all-embracing" conversation and intellectual curiosity. He learned much from him about the art of speaking, especially the importance of making his most difficult points in the interrogative rather than the declarative. And the importance of diluting a speech—for example, not making more than ten points, no matter how each point was dressed up and returned to.

What is particularly striking in this long diary entry is Amery's affectionate admiration for Macmillan in retirement. After he finished his memoirs—"very long, rather discreet and rather boring," in Amery's view—Macmillan entered a new phase of life.

> His speaking performances were better than anything he had done in office. Like some great wines, he only fully matured in old age. By that time he was very relaxed and cared nothing for discretion.

Although Amery respected and admired Macmillan's mastery of domestic politics, he not unnaturally pronounced his foreign policy a failure.

> In foreign affairs he had one great chance. And missed it. Had he stood firm, Britain and France, would in all probability, have prevailed. The united Europe in which he believed so passionately would have gone ahead, and with Eden's health shaken as much as it already was, he would have succeeded to the Premiership in a day or two. Suez led to the loss of Algeria for France, and so to de Gaulle's rise to power. He and de Gaulle in many ways were rather alike. But de Gaulle was, if anything, tougher and had a stronger domestic base. It was really de Gaulle more than health or the Opposition who defeated him.

In contrast, Amery's relationship with Edward Heath was somewhat strained. Amery had supported Quintin Hogg's candidacy for the party leadership in November 1964, but served in Heath's shadow Cabinet. There were tensions over Amery's highly vocal criticism of the Labour government on Rhodesia. By then, Amery had been sacked from Heath's shadow Cabinet; Amery felt that this division of portfolios among the Conservative front bench was far too prescriptive, and that the technocrat Heath should return to Churchill's more relaxed approach. Rhodesia was an important point of issue between the two men, which eventually culminated in the Conservative Party being split in three pieces on the Unilateral

Declaration of Independence crisis: anti-sanctions; pro-sanctions, but not oil; and wholehearted condemnation. This substantially damaged Conservative prospects in the March 1966 election, when Amery lost his seat. Interestingly, Heath was at pains to court Amery in March 1969 with the promise of a return to the shadow front bench. And it was Heath who sent Amery to the Ministry of Housing, his one domestic ministerial position.

Again, Amery's relationship with Margaret Thatcher was complicated by his own leadership ambitions in 1975. The material in his diary and papers on Thatcher is very guarded about his relationship with her, but he came out in support of her during the 1990 leadership challenge. However, by then he had secured the support of both Heseltine and Thatcher for his elevation to the House of Lords at the next election.

Amery is intriguing as a case study of an Englishman of a particular type and generation: their outlooks strongly affected by the Second World War, they extended wartime social networks into peacetime and, if in politics, kept their secrets. He was "a great adventurer," in the view of his former SOE colleagues from Belgrade days, in the style of Sandy Arbuthnot from John Buchan's *Greenmantle*. Amery reflected the dictum that the Tory party is a "broad church." In letters of condolence to his son, Leo, after his death, his friends and colleagues referred to him as "a great mandarin of politics"; he "linked people to great events, and great men of long ago (Churchill and the War; Macmillan and the recovery)." Margaret Thatcher regarded him as symptomatic of a tradition of talented and able men who thought it their duty to enter public service, and for whom the impact of the war added urgency to everything they did. It must be said that for all his intellectual qualities, and the consistency of his social-imperialist views, Amery was not a great social reformer. His overriding passion, and interest, was defense and foreign policy. But he continued to have a detailed and considered understanding of the importance of industrial policy and the challenges of the energy crisis and inflation to social stability in 1970s and 1980s. Most of all, he epitomized the enduring importance of the Empire and Commonwealth to Conservatism into the later part of the twentieth century.

Fall Semester 2008

1. Enoch Powell interview with author, London, 1992.

2. Sir Peter Smithers, correspondence with author, 1991.

3. Lord Amery, interview with author, London, 1992.

4. Ibid.

5. Powell interview.

6. Quoted in Sue Onslow, "The Conservative Party and Rhodesian UDI," Witness Seminar, Centre for Contemporary British History, September 2000.

7. Powell interview.

8. In 1902, Chamberlain firmly rejected free trade, arguing instead for imperial preference. Branded "Social Imperialism," this represented the ideology of permanence of empire, combined with the cult of good conduct and economic development of the colonies, fused with a program of social reform and economic development at home.

9. Amery diary entry, 2 Nov. 1945, Papers of Julian Amery, Churchill Archives Centre (hereafter cited as AMEJ).

10. Salisbury to Leo Amery, 1996, letters of condolence, AMEJ.

11. Interview with author, London, 1992.

12. Amery diary, May 1948, AMEJ.

16

Colonial Independence

DAVID CANNADINE

When I was growing up in Birmingham during the 1960s, there were two unforgettable images that repeatedly appeared on the evening news bulletins on our recently acquired television. They were from distant places, to none of which I had yet traveled, but they intruded themselves so regularly and so insistently into our living room that they were formative influences on my youth, as I suspect they were for many members of the immediate post-war generation, to which I belong. From one perspective, these pictures were as different in their frequency as they were dissimilar in the stories they made so vividly visible. Night after night, or so it seemed, there were horrifying images of B-52 bombers dropping napalm on the cities and rice fields and peoples of Vietnam in a violent, brutal, and ultimately vain projection of American military might and global reach into a far-off land of which most of us knew nothing. Less often, but at least once, and sometimes twice or three or even four times, a year, there was a very different item on the television news, a report that the Union Jack had been pulled down at midnight in a former British colony, in the presence of a member of the royal family, and in a newly built stadium located in the capital city.[1] Thus was power transferred from the old empire to a new nation, and from a proconsular elite to a popularly elected government, on what would thereafter become known in the newly begotten country, following the American precedent of the Fourth of July, as its independence day.

At the time, these different and discrepant images seemed to be depicting two distinct and disparate worlds, and as such, they were particularly reassuring to those in Britain who believed (as many did then and as some still do now) that *we* were much better than the Americans at dealing with non-Western parts of the globe. The British understood empire, so this argument ran, which meant we were able to end our own dominion over palm and pine relatively amicably and successfully, with the result that many former colonies, on achieving their independence, immediately joined the Commonwealth; the Americans, by contrast, never comprehended or appreciated empire, and so it was scarcely surprising that they botched their neo-imperialistic intervention in the former colonies of French Indo-China. Yet for all these contrasts and dissimilarities, the traumas of Vietnam (and of neighboring Laos and Cambodia) and the ceremonial obsequies of the British Empire were parallel and simultaneous manifestations of the same contemporary trend: they were both part of that process whereby relations between the West and those large areas of the rest of the world that had previously been European colonies were being renegotiated and reconfigured. And the decade in which those relations were most significantly altered and fundamentally adjusted was the 1960s: at the beginning of it, as Harold Macmillan made plain in his "winds of change" speech, delivered in the South African parliament in Cape Town in February 1960, the British Empire had become unsustainable; by the end of it, the American intrusion into Indo-China was doomed to failure.[2]

Such were the mood and the mores of that decade, so it was scarcely surprising that when Bernard Levin produced his coruscating contemporary history of Britain during the 1960s, which was published in London as *The Pendulum Years,* it was repackaged in the United States, more resonantly and more imaginatively, as *Run Down the Flagpole.*[3] It was a good alternative title, for while it took the British half a century to wind up their global imperium, from the independence (and partition) of India and Pakistan in 1947 to the Hong Kong handover precisely fifty years later, it was during the 1960s that that process of imperial withdrawal was at its most intense, and there were more independence celebrations across that decade than during the 1950s (when the momentum of African decolonization was only beginning to gather) or the 1970s (by which time most of the British Empire was truly one with Nineveh and Tyre). Indeed, so frequent were these imperial departures and goodbyes between the years 1960 and 1970 that a retired British army officer named Colonel Eric Hefford embarked on a new (but essentially time-limited) career as a sort of late-imperial, transoceanic, globe-trotting Earl

Marshal, organizing the events that declared and proclaimed "freedom at midnight": in one guise, he was the undertaker of the British Empire, orchestrating valedictory colonial observances; in another, he was the impresario of freedom, planning the independence-day celebrations by which new nations came to birth.

To take a longer view across the half century from 1947 to 1997: there were more than fifty such occasions in as many years, and they form an extraordinary and unique sequence of hybrid spectaculars—collectively for the British Empire, whose end they signified and symbolized, and individually for the post-imperial successor states, whose birth they marked and memorialized. To those who regard such state-sponsored flummery as nothing more (or better) than insubstantial pageants and tinsel ephemera, such occasions are of no scholarly interest or historical significance; but since the British Empire had (among other things) existed and endured as a pageant, it was at least consistent with that element of caparisoned theatricality that it ended and expired in a succession of valedictory rituals, which were not so much, as Colonel Hefford claimed, "plucked from the book of ancient British traditions," but were deliberately made up and self-consciously invented.[4] It has been more than ten years since the Hong Kong handover, it has been nearly forty years since the peak decade of independence ceremonials by which I was so struck when I was growing up, and it has been more than sixty years since the initial celebrations took place in New Delhi and (less enthusiastically) in Karachi; and this means there is now sufficient distance from these episodes and events to see and study them in an historical perspective that, as so often in imperial and post-imperial matters, is simultaneously global and general, yet also place-bound and particular.

THE INDEPENDENCE CEREMONIALS THAT TOOK PLACE in Britain's former colonies between 1947 and 1997 form, in all conscience, a large enough topic, encompassing substantial parts of the globe across half a century; but like many aspects of the history of empire and of decolonization, they also need to be de-parochialized and set in a longer historical time frame and a broader geographical perspective. Before 1776, the very notion of a former colony becoming "independent" of its conquering colonizer was scarcely conceivable, and in the early modern period (and in certain instances thereafter), the great European powers regarded their overseas territories as possessions, which might be won or lost or (occasionally) exchanged, but which never gained or were granted something called "freedom." The Mediterranean island of Menorca, for instance, was traded back and forth across the eighteenth century between Britain, Spain and France, and was eventually ceded by Britain to Spain in 1802. In the same way, the Ionian Islands were given to Greece in 1864, Heligoland was returned to Germany in 1890, and Wei Hai Wei went back to China in 1930. Indeed, it is in this venerable category of territorial transfer and exchange between great powers, rather than that of colonial liberation from a European empire, that the handover of Hong Kong to the Chinese government ought to be set. For no one seriously believed that Britain's last great colony was becoming a free and independent nation-state in 1997.

There were also three instances of colonial separation from the British Empire well before 1947, and none of them was marked by the sort of celebrations and fireworks and transient expressions of mutual admiration that subsequently became so familiar. The first "British experience of decolonization" was the rejection of imperial authority by the thirteen colonies from the mid-1770s: royal statues and coats of arms were torn down by rebellious Americans; the Declaration of Independence denounced George III as an evil and wicked tyrant; and after the British defeat at Yorktown in 1782, there was nothing for it but for the King's troops to cut and run and scuttle.[5] The second was the creation of the Irish Free State in the aftermath of the Anglo-Irish Treaty of 1921. Unlike the thirteen former colonies, this new nation did not initially repudiate the British connection, but instead became a dominion within the Empire. Yet once again, there were no independence celebrations: the last British Lord Lieutenant, Viscount Fitzalan, departed from Dublin Castle in 1922 in a private car; the low-key successor post of governor-general was abolished in 1937; and Eire eventually became a fully independent republic outside the British Commonwealth on Easter Monday 1949, the anniversary of the 1916 Rising. The third was the ostensible "independence" of Egypt, which the British proclaimed in March 1922, when they formally relinquished their protectorate. But unlike the case of the United States or the Irish Free State, Egyptian independence was more nominal than real, the ensuing ceremonials were concerned with the establishment of an Egyptian monarchy rather than with the celebration of Egyptian freedom, and there were widespread protests by nationalists against the continuing British presence.

This was not the way in which colonial ties would be severed across the half century after 1947, in those "ceremonies of goodwill and fraternity" that reached their climax during the 1960s.[6] Yet even during the era of "freedoms at midnight," the "old" imperial dominions of Canada, Australia, New Zealand, and South Africa took another nonceremonial path to independence, which was less complete than the case of the United States or the Irish Republic, but was more so than in the case of inter-war Egypt. In 1914, Britain had declared war on behalf of the whole Empire, but after 1918, and increasingly after 1945, the four dominions gradually moved toward autonomy, which nonetheless did not involve the complete rejection or belligerent repudiation of the British imperial connection. In all four instances, the process that has infelicitously but accurately been described as "de-dominionization" involved some or all of the following: the acceptance of the Statute of Westminster, the appointment of home-grown governors-general, the replacement of the Union Jack by a new national flag, the repudiation of the imperial honors system, the composing of a new national anthem, and the end of constitutional subordination to London (South Africa went the furthest of the four, declaring itself a republic in 1961, although it rejoined the Commonwealth in 1990). As a result of this long, gradual, yet incremental sequence, there was no single date on which dominion "independence" from the British Empire could be publicly proclaimed and ceremonially recognized in the presence of a member of the royal family.

Equally nonceremonial, albeit for very different reasons, were Britain's departures from its territories in the Middle East, which took place at much the same time as this process of "de-dominionization." In May 1948, less than a year after the celebrations in Delhi and Karachi, the British withdrew from Palestine, where they had failed to broker a peace deal between Jews and Arabs, and the last High Commissioner, General Sir Alan Cunningham, retreated to the docks at Haifa in a bulletproof car that had been built to protect King George VI from German bombs in wartime London. In Egypt, real independence came suddenly and acrimoniously in the mid-1950s: the monarchy was overthrown and a republic established; British troops withdrew from their bases; the Suez Canal was nationalized; and Nasser was the hero of the hour. Meanwhile, to the south, in what had previously been the Anglo-Egyptian condominium of the Sudan, a new radical government proclaimed itself independent in January 1956, and no member of the British royal family was invited to be present. Farther east, Iraq and Jordan had ostensibly become independent in 1932 and 1946 respectively, when the League of Nations mandates expired; but in the aftermath of Suez, the pro-British monarchy in Iraq was brutally overthrown in 1958, and King Hussein survived in Jordan only by publicly repudiating the British connection, dismissing General Sir John Glubb from his command of the Arab Legion in March 1956. But the greatest humiliation came in Aden in November 1967: as in Palestine, the British failed to broker a deal between local notables, and they took flight in their helicopters. "We left without glory but without disaster," the last High Commissioner, Sir Humphrey Trevelyan, later recalled; yet others described the episode more brutally as "the worst shambles of the end of Empire."[7]

Nowhere in these once-wide dominions of the British Middle East were there the sort of ceremonial farewells, signifying the "orderly transfer of power," that were taking place at the same time elsewhere in the Empire; and none of these successor states, having repudiated the British and having rejected the staging of "ceremonies of goodwill and fraternity," subsequently joined the Commonwealth: the separation, when it finally (and often brutally) came, was absolute and complete. There are many reasons for this. With the exception of Egypt and the Sudan, British dominion across the Middle East was "shallowly rooted" and of relatively short duration, in some cases lasting scarcely a generation. Many of the mandates, protectorates, and bases were never colonies in a formal sense, which meant that even when the separation was amicable, ceremonials of independence were scarcely appropriate. But often there was a deeper failure, deriving from a lack of mutual sympathy or regard: in part because many Arabs loathed the British as unwelcome invaders and unwanted (and pro-Jewish) infidels; and in part because the British made no serious attempt to accommodate to the forces and leaders of Arab nationalism (Anthony Eden famously likened Nasser to Mussolini and wanted him "destroyed"). From the unhappy and disordered perspective of the Middle East, and also from the gradualist viewpoint of the old dominions, the independence celebrations taking place elsewhere in the British Empire in the half century from 1947 were the exception rather than the norm.

TO BE SURE, THEY WERE THE MOST SIGNIFICANT sequence and symbols of the "end of empire"; but even in the case of the "freedom at midnight" ceremonials, there were more variations to the pattern than has generally been recognized or recollected. For although, from the British perspective, these events formed a recognizable and interconnected series, they were very much one-off happenings in each colony, which meant that no two independence observances were ever wholly alike. Depending on the size, population, and wealth of the new nation to be, the cost and scale of the ceremonials varied markedly: in Colonel Hefford's experience, they ranged from £180,000 in Malta to £2,250,000 in Nigeria, with most of them averaging between £300,000 and £400,000. The joyous crowds did not always behave as they were expected to: in New Delhi, Lord Mountbatten had planned a solemn moment when he and his staff would salute the new Indian flag, but large crowds "surged into the specially prepared arena and threw the display into turmoil."[8] Individual participants could not always be relied upon to perform as required: at the inauguration of Malaysia in September 1963, the new governor of Sarawak collapsed under the strain. The weather was not always cooperative: on Kenya's day of independence in December 1963, heavy rain caused such chaos on the route to the stadium in Nairobi that the British Secretary of State missed the entire ceremony; and at the Hong Kong handover, despite a torrential downpour, the last British Governor, Chris Patten, not only refused to wear the customary proconsular uniform and plumed hat, but also visibly shed a tear when receiving the British flag after it had been hauled down for the last time.

Despite these local variations, it is often supposed that all these independence celebrations were graced by a member of the British royal family; but on a quarter of these occasions, no member of the House of Windsor was present. As with Palestine and Aden, the British were sometimes unable to manage decolonization in the orderly, dignified, and consensual manner that was deemed the essential precondition for the presence of a royal representative. In the case of Burma, the country had been occupied by the Japanese during the Second World War; the return of the British administration in late 1945 was a provocation to the Burmese nationalists; and General Aung San, to whom they hoped to transfer power, was murdered. Accordingly, it was the last Governor, Sir Hubert Rance, who acted as the sovereign's representative in January 1948, when Burma became an independent republic; and unlike India, Pakistan, and (subsequently) Ceylon, it did not join the Commonwealth. A decade later, independence was only slightly better handled on the island of Cyprus, where thousands of British troops had been tied down in the mid-1950s while dealing with the "state of emergency," where they had been unable to hold the balance between Greek and Turkish Cypriots, and where they had seriously misjudged and underestimated the politician-prelate Archbishop Makarios. In August 1960, the Governor, Sir Hugh Foot, left the island after saying goodbye to (by then) President Makarios and making a final troop inspection, but there were no speeches, no sentimental songs, and no royal presence (although Cyprus, unlike Burma, did elect to join the Commonwealth).

Elsewhere in the dissolving Empire, members of the royal family were sometimes scheduled to appear at independence celebrations, but for reasons ranging from the political to the personal, their visits were canceled at the last minute. Although the circumstances were rarely as fraught as in Palestine or Aden or Burma or Cyprus, there were occasions when a sudden and unexpected deterioration in public order meant that a planned royal visit was aborted. In Mauritius, the ceremonials had been arranged along customary lines in March 1968, and Princes Alexandra had agreed to represent the sovereign; but the security situation subsequently worsened, her visit was canceled, and her place was taken instead by Lord Greenwood. Likewise, when Grenada was scheduled to become independent, early in 1974, Prince Richard of Gloucester was deputed to attend, but violent clashes between the government and the opposition meant that the visit was aborted. There were also family and health reasons for occasional royal no-shows. In September 1968, the Duke of Kent had to withdraw from attending the independence celebrations of Swaziland because of the sudden death of his mother, Princess Marina, and his place was taken by George Thomson, the last British Secretary of State for Commonwealth Relations. In the case of the Ellice Islands in the Pacific, Princess Margaret was scheduled to be present in October 1978, but she was unable to do so after being stricken with pneumonia, so she was represented by her private secretary, Lord Napier and Errick.

These were the most commonplace variations on the standard "freedom at midnight" ceremonial as the British Empire decolonized, but there were also others. One very unusual case was that of Southern Rhodesia, which had unilaterally (and illegally) declared its independence in 1965; but this was from the British government rather than from the British Crown, and the colony became officially free only in 1980, when Prince Charles attended the celebrations. There were also former League of Nations mandates that had been assigned to the imperial dominions after the First World War, and that in their turn became independent: Western Samoa from New Zealand; Papua New Guinea and Nauru from Australia; and Namibia from South Africa. But only in the case of Papua New Guinea was the British Crown represented, and once again by the Prince of Wales. Finally, there were nations that became independent twice, once from the British Empire and once again as members of the Commonwealth. East Pakistan had participated in the freedom celebrations of August 1947, but it subsequently declared its independence from West Pakistan and became Bangladesh in December 1971. But this was very much a post-imperial development, and neither the British government nor the British monarchy was in any way involved.

SET IN THIS BROADER PERSPECTIVE and longer time frame, the ceremonials of independence turn out to have been much less central to the wider processes of British decolonization and de-dominionization than it is often commonplace to suppose; and even when the "freedom at midnight" rituals did occur, there were more local variations than is often appreciated. But these end-of-empire observances also shared common characteristics, and it is well worth trying to tease out some general themes. Many of them emerge from a brief examination of the first such occasions, in India and Pakistan, although it is only in retrospect that they may be seen as initiating a trend, for in 1947, few people (and even fewer policy makers) believed that most of the British Empire would be gone in the next twenty years. As the central figure in both independence pageants, the last Viceroy, Lord Mountbatten, was determined to ensure that the transfer of power was well stage-managed: he wanted the new nations of India and Pakistan to begin with peace and order and with feelings of goodwill toward the former imperial power; he wanted the British to leave with dignity and prestige and with as much residual influence as they could retain; he sought to present independence as the triumphant realization, in his hands, of Britain's long-cherished wish to make India free; and he insisted that the accelerated timetable for independence had concentrated minds and resulted in many fewer deaths than would otherwise have been the case.

Yet despite the impression of order and amity that these ceremonials gave, there was much that was at variance with what was in many ways a carefully crafted and deliberately contrived image. The partition of the subcontinent was regarded by many, including Field Marshall Sir Claude Auchinleck, who was the head of the Indian Army, not so much as a triumph, but as the negation and betrayal of Britain's imperial mission. Mountbatten himself had hoped to limit the effects of partition by acting as Governor-General of both new nations and by chairing a common defense council, but in this ambition he was defeated. The rulers of the princely states, who had looked upon the King-Emperor and the Viceroy as their guardians and guarantors, felt a deep sense of betrayal when the British government abandoned its treaty obligations and when Mountbatten gave them no choice but to throw in their lot with the two new successor nations. Many critics felt that the move to independence was too rushed, which meant that, pace Mountbatten, the violence was intensified rather than contained and that, far from being the fulfillment of Britain's imperial designs, the result was (in Churchill's words) a policy of "general surrender and scuttle."[9] (The Viceroy

was also accused of delaying the detailed announcements of partition until after independence so that he would not be held responsible for the bloodshed that ensued.) Although the three nations
had parted on amicable terms, subsequent relations between Britain and India and Britain and Pakistan were nothing like as cordial
as had been hoped, and the residual influence of the former imperial power soon dwindled.

No historian (or anthropologist or sociologist) of state-sponsored
rituals would be surprised at such contradictions, ambiguities, and
paradoxes: from the triumphs of Roman emperors and command-
ers, via the rituals of Renaissance Venice, to the imperial and local spectacles associated with the British monarchy and Communist
Russia, real and deep conflicts have often been concealed beneath
a ceremonial consensus that was simultaneously manufactured yet
also spontaneous. Thus it was for what became, in retrospect, the
prototypical independence observances that took place in South
Asia, and so it was for those that were subsequently played out in
other parts of the British Empire, albeit with their own marked and
particular local variations, and also with fewer people involved. As
in India and Pakistan, the aim of the "freedom at midnight" ceremonials was to give the impression that independence had always been
the intention of the British imperial mission; that power was being
transferred voluntarily, with dignity, and with mutual expressions
of esteem and good will; that a member of the British royal family
would appear to set a regal seal of approval on the proceedings; that
Britain and its former colony would remain on good terms thereafter, with the former still wielding some benevolent influence over
the latter; and that the new nation, happy and secure in the annual
observance of its independence day, would go on to enjoy freedom,
democracy, prosperity, unity, and consensus. From the Gold Coast
to Kenya to Southern Rhodesia, this was the public rhetoric of independence, and the expression of high hopes for the future, that was
articulated by such enemies-turned-friends of Britain and its empire
as Kwame Nkrumah, Jomo Kenyatta, and Robert Mugabe.

But as had been the case with the independence celebrations
in India and Pakistan, the reality was at best more complex and at
worst very different. However much delight there was in the prospect
of freedom at midnight from British imperial rule, the consensus
that characterized such independence celebrations was often little
more than superficial, temporarily papering over significant dis-
agreements and deep-rooted tensions and briefly erasing unhappy
memories and bitter resentments. In Malaya, freedom came after a
tumultuous decade and a half that left many scars: the Japanese in-

vasion, the British surrender and return, the communist insurgency, racial strife between Malays and Chinese, and the still-continuing state of emergency, all of which invested the independence celebrations of August 1957 with varied and contradictory meanings. In Kenya, freedom followed the decade-long Mau Mau emergency, the detention of thousands of Africans, the imprisonment and release of Jomo Kenyatta, and the constant complaints of British settlers that they were being betrayed: at independence, Kenyatta was determined to "forget" Mau Mau, though many of his fellow countrymen were not.[10] In the Gold Coast, the politics of independence meant the traditional tribal chiefs of the north had been outmaneuvered by the urban-based middle-class nationalists of the south, led by Kwame Nkrumah, to whom the British transferred power: like the ruling princes in India ten years before, they found little at which to rejoice in their nation's freedom. And in Southern Rhodesia, the official independence from Britain took place after more than a decade of international sanctions, civil war, settler bitterness, and economic deterioration, which cast its shadow over the "freedom at midnight" observances: Margaret Thatcher conspicuously refused to attend, many white Rhodesians felt betrayed, and so did Joshua Nkomo, who had expected to be the new leader of the new nation, but who had been defeated by Robert Mugabe.

Thus regarded, the independence celebrations of these colonies-becoming-countries afforded only a brief, temporary respite in the nationalist struggle against Britain, and they also intensified the internal battle between parties and tribes and personalities for control of the post-colonial state. Despite their fulsome expressions of gratitude and friendship, and (in most cases) their decision to join the Commonwealth, the new leaders of new nations soon distanced themselves from Britain, and they rebranded their countries in further repudiation of their imperial past: the Gold Coast became Ghana, Nyasaland became Malawi, Basutoland became Lesotho, British Honduras became Belize, and so on. In capital cities across Asia and Africa, statues of British monarchs and proconsuls were toppled and banished, and streets and roads with royal or imperial appellations were renamed. Most former colonies soon became republics and instituted their own systems of indigenous honors, thereby rejecting the monarchical and hierarchical aspects of the British Empire that had last been asserted in the royal presence at the independence-day celebrations. As for parliamentary democracy, which the British were so eager to bequeath to the successor states of the Empire: this was the first and greatest casualty of the post-independence struggles for power. Often the result was one-party rule, military dictatorship, tribal conflict, civil war, the abuse of human rights, and economic ruin (as is all too apparent today in Zimbabwe). This in turn means that the subsequent annual observance of independence day in many former colonies has become a celebration of indigenous culture, of an adored (and feared) charismatic leader, and of a long and glorious history into which the British Empire often seems little more than a relatively brief and now unlamented intrusion.

In retrospect, the midnight celebrations in India and Pakistan in August 1947 had portended this de-imperializing half century of ceremonial contradictions and ambiguities, of high hopes and false dawns; and the Hong Kong handover on 30 June 1997, completed the cycle in a no less paradoxical and multilayered way. Since the colony was being returned to China, rather than given its independence, the sinologists in the Foreign Office believed that the most important priority for Chris Patten, the last British Governor, appointed by John Major in 1992, was to keep on good terms with the Chinese authorities, for the sake of the future of Sino-British relations. But Patten regretted that Hong Kong had not become a more democratic colony while it had been under British rule; he was determined to make significant advances in that direction, however hostile the government might be in Beijing; and he was equally determined to seek guarantees from the Chinese that once Hong Kong reverted to them, they would respect such reforms as he was able to implement. These very significant differences of policy were fought out in public, in London and Beijing as well as in Hong Kong itself, and Patten's record remains controversial to this day, just as Hong Kong's future remains unclear. But although Chinese officials were itching to move in and reclaim it, they did allow the British to make a dignified exit from their last great colony. The Prince of Wales represented the queen, John Major and Tony Blair were both present, and after the ceremonials, the British dignitaries departed in the royal yacht *Britannia,* which was subsequently laid up in Scotland, on the Firth of Forth at Leith, and not replaced. And so Britain's seaborne empire and its maritime monarchy both came to an end in 1997—the year that was also, by agreeable coincidence, the one hundredth anniversary of the Diamond Jubilee of Queen Victoria, which may not have witnessed the climax of the British Empire in its territorial extent, but which certainly did so in imperial consciousness on the streets of London.

So much for independence celebrations in the British Empire, the pomp and the partying and the paradoxes of imperial closure:

yet what, meanwhile, of the imperial metropolis itself? For as John Darwin has rightly written, the United Kingdom was no less "a successor state of the old imperial system" than India or Pakistan, or Sudan or Malaya, or Nigeria or Ghana, or Barbados or Antigua.[11] In other European nations that were the epicenters of empires, post-war decolonization was marked not so much by celebration or ceremonial as by bitter, divisive, and sometimes extreme domestic politics: witness the struggles in France over Algeria in the 1950s and 1960s, and in Portugal over Mozambique and Angola in the 1970s. This was not true in Britain: partly because Clement Attlee and Harold Macmillan handled the crucial phases of South Asian and African decolonization with considerable political skill; partly because the far-right section of the Conservative Party, which opposed such policies of "scuttle," never gained serious traction in Parliament or in the country; partly because, as with the case of the old dominions, Britain de-imperialized incrementally rather than instantaneously; and partly because the peak years of decolonization were also the time when applying to join what was then called Europe seemed to offer an attractive and appealing alternative whereby Britain might continue to exert influence in what was rapidly becoming a post-imperial world, but through a neighboring continent rather than a distant empire.

But there were also some grand, one-off ceremonials that took place in the former imperial capital and that carried with them an unmistakable sense of recessional and retreat. There was the long-delayed dedication of the Chapel of the Order of the British Empire in the crypt of St. Paul's Cathedral in 1960, ironically in the very same year that Macmillan's "wind of change" speech portended that empire's end. There were Winston Churchill's magnificent obsequies on a grey January day in 1965: not only the last rites of the great man himself, but also, as it seemed to many, a requiem for Britain as a great imperial power. There was Lord Mountbatten's ceremonial funeral in August 1980: mourning the passing of the last of the great captains and the last Viceroy of India. There was the service held in Westminster Abbey in June 1998, in the presence of the Queen, to mark the formal end, after the Hong Kong handover, of what had once been known as the Colonial Service. And there was Queen Mother's state funeral in March 2000: the last British queen consort who had also been Empress of India. But that metropolitan sequence of imperial valedictions is not yet over, for when the reign of Queen Elizabeth II ends, it will surely be recalled that on her twenty-first birthday, which she celebrated in South Africa in April 1947, she had pledged herself "to the service of our great imperial family to which we all belong."[12] In the course of her reign, that great imperial family has dispersed and dissolved, the imperial children have grown up and left home, and it was the "freedom at midnight" ceremonials of independence that set them on their way.

Spring Semester 2009

Appendix: Independence Dates and Royal Participation, 1947–97

1. BRITISH EMPIRE

Dependency	Date	Royal participant
India	August 1947	Lord Mountbatten
Pakistan	August 1947	Lord Mountbatten
Burma	January 1948	none
Ceylon	February 1948	Duke of Gloucester
Palestine	May 1948	none
Libya	December 1951	none
Sudan	January 1956	none
Gold Coast	March 1957	Princess Marina
Malaya	August 1957	Duke of Gloucester
British Somaliland	July 1960	none
Cyprus	August 1960	none
Nigeria	October 1960	Princess Alexandra
Sierra Leone	April 1961	Duke of Kent
Kuwait	June 1961	none
Southern Cameroons	October 1961	none
Tanganyika	December 1961	Prince Philip
Trinidad	August 1962	Princess Royal
Jamaica	August 1962	Princess Margaret
Uganda	December 1962	Duke of Kent
Sarawak	September 1963	none
Singapore	September 1963	none
British North Borneo	September 1963	none
Kenya	December 1963	Prince Philip
Zanzibar	December 1963	Prince Philip
Nyasaland	July 1964	Prince Philip
Malta	September 1964	Prince Philip
Northern Rhodesia	October 1964	Princess Royal
The Gambia	February 1965	Duke of Kent
Maldive Islands	July 1965	none
British Guiana	May 1966	Duke of Kent
Bechuanaland	September 1966	Princess Marina
Basutoland	October 1966	Princess Marina
Barbados	November 1966	Duke of Kent
Aden	November 1967	none

Mauritius	March 1968	none
Swaziland	September 1968	none
Tonga	June 1970	Prince William of Gloucester
Fiji	October 1970	Prince Charles
Bahrain	August 1971	none
Qatar	September 1971	none
Bahamas	July 1973	Prince Charles
Grenada	February 1974	none
Seychelles	June 1976	Prince Richard of Gloucester
Solomon Islands	July 1978	Prince Richard of Gloucester
Ellice Islands	October 1978	none
Dominica	November 1978	Princess Margaret
St. Lucia	February 1979	Princess Alexander
Gilbert Islands	July 1979	Princess Anne
St. Vincent and the Grenadines	October 1979	Prince Richard of Gloucester
Southern Rhodesia	April 1980	Prince Charles
New Hebrides	June 1980	Prince Richard of Gloucester
British Honduras	September 1981	Prince Michael of Kent
Antigua and Barbuda	November 1981	Princess Margaret
St. Kitts-Nevis	September 1983	Princess Margaret
Brunei	January 1984	Prince Charles
Hong Kong	June 1997	Prince Charles

2. DOMINIONS

Dependency	Date	Royal participant
Western Samoa (New Zealand)	January 1962	none
Nauru (Australia)	February 1968	none
Papua New Guinea (Australia)	September 1975	Prince Charles
Namibia (South Africa)	March 1990	none

Sources: Brian Lapping, *End of Empire* (London, 1985), rear endpaper; Anthony Kirk-Greene, *On Crown Service: A History of HM Colonial and Overseas Civil Services, 1837–1997* (London, 1999), p. 81; Ronald Hyam, *Britain's Declining Empire: The Road to Decolonisation, 1918–1968* (Cambridge, 2006), pp. 411–12.

1.   The peak years for the granting of independence within the British Empire were 1960–66, when it happened twenty-four times; only in 1969 were there no such celebrations.

2.   Alistair Horne, *Harold Macmillan,* Vol. II: *1957–1986* (London, 1989), pp. 193–98.

3.   Bernard Levin, *The Pendulum Years: Britain and the Sixties* (London, 1970); *Run Down the Flagpole: Britain in the Sixties* (New York, 1971). In both editions, chapter 8 was entitled "Run Down the Flagpole."

4.   Quoted in David Cannadine, *Ornamentalism: How the British Saw Their Empire* (London, 2001), p. 161.

5.   David George Boyce, *Decolonisation and the British Empire, 1775–1997* (Basingstoke, 1999), pp. 12, 27.

6.   James Morris, *Farewell the Trumpets: An Imperial Retreat* (London, 1978), p. 519.

7.   Brian Lapping, *End of Empire* (London, 1985), pp. 309–10.

8.   Christopher Bayly and Timothy Harper, *Forgotten Wars: The End of Britain's Asian Empire* (London, 2007), p. 292.

9.   Quoted in Boyce, *Decolonisation and the British Empire,* p. 157.

10.   David Anderson, *Histories of the Hanged: Britain's Dirty War in Kenya and the End of Empire* (London, 2005), pp. 335–37.

11.   John Darwin, *Britain and Decolonisation: The Retreat from Empire in the Post-War World* (London, 1988), pp. 324, 327–28.

12.   Sarah Bradford, *Elizabeth: A Biography of Her Majesty the Queen* (London, 1996), p. 120.

17

The Failure of the West Indies Federation

JASON PARKER

The story of the rise and fall of the West Indies Federation (WIF) sheds light on a number of important issues that played out in the Third World during the Cold War, including what Stephen Howe, in a previous *Britannia* essay, called "the distinctive modernity of Caribbean peoples."[1] Fidel Castro's shadow gave the "attempted country" of the WIF a unique Cold War weight. The federation's passive sponsor in Washington intended it to make a Cold War statement; its active sponsor in London, to cure the headache of imperial rule while sustaining British regional influence; its members, to showcase a regional-cum-racial solidarity that would prove the imperial era was over. This attempted country collapsed at the worst possible moment in the Cold War Caribbean. It left all parties scrambling to salvage some good out of a process that would shortly bring into existence perhaps a dozen new, majority-black, independent nations, many of them vulnerable to falling under Castro's sway.

The background of the federation idea in the Caribbean was the longest of any of the dozen-odd federations attempted after 1945. The concept had recurred periodically in the islands and in the Colonial Office for centuries. It had never gotten further than the drawing board, and usually not even that far, before being filed away in the face of metropolitan or colonial hesitation. By the early 1900s, the West Indies were a backwater of the British Empire, which was then reaching its apogee in Africa, and administrative reform in the islands was far down the list of Whitehall's priorities. The rebirth of the federation idea after the First World War had a varied parentage. West Indians' military service in Europe fired a sense of nationalism among returning veterans, some of whom became vocal advocates for reform of the colonial regime. The migration of more than a hundred thousand West Indians to the United States further enlivened the discussion. Many expatriates took up residence in Harlem, where insular identities dissolved into an embryonic pan-Caribbean one, and indeed into one encompassing the larger African diaspora as the migrants found themselves neighbors with African Americans recently arrived from the Jim Crow South. Marcus Garvey is the best known of the expatriates to stoke black radicalism in Harlem and beyond, but he was hardly alone. His significance, and that of inter-war black-consciousness movements, regarding the eventual WIF was indirect. By cultivating the conclusion that black peoples had a destiny other than as imperial subjects, and a common one to boot, Garvey and his fellow West Indians imagined the black future along racial and "nationalist" lines of unity and independence.

These connections ensured that Harlem quaked when the 1930s saw a wave of labor unrest sweep the West Indian colonies. The disorder, brought on by the poverty, suffering, and brutal labor conditions in the Depression-era Caribbean, called the future of the colonial regime into question—and not just in that region. During the labor disturbances, leaders such as Jamaica's Norman Manley and Alexander Bustamante came to prominence in colonial politics. Officials in London became convinced that effective proprietorship in the islands had been wanting. The Crown's neglect of health, nutrition, education, and labor there was undeniable. In 1938–39, the Moyne Commission studied the conditions that had led to the unrest, in hopes of avoiding further explosions. Its report was so explosive that publication was withheld for five years for fear of handing the Nazis a propaganda bonanza. A summary of the findings circulated in the Chamberlain government, though, and painted a picture shocking enough to prompt a twofold change in British thinking. The first was a shift from essentially malign neglect to stewardship, in which the metropole accepted responsibility for colonial welfare and development. The second was a determination to find ways to reduce costs by reorganizing colonial governance, with an eye to creating a viable state apparatus for the day (however distant) when full self-government would come. A federation of some form was the obvious means of doing all of the above. Though the war prevented much progress to this end—not least by draining the

Exchequer of monies—it laid the groundwork for, and elicited British blessing of, eventual federation.

British officials were not the only ones among whom the federal idea was gaining ground. It did so as well within two crucial constituencies in the United States, both connected to New York City. There, in the cultural capital of the black diaspora, West Indian expatriates and their African American neighbors saw the prospect of federation as the chance to express a common destiny grounded in racial solidarity. Especially on the Left, where most West Indian and African American intellectuals made their home, this "pan-African" dimension only enhanced the appeal of an envisioned federal entity that would make a statement of trans-island class solidarity as well. In addition, a federal entity would prevent the possible consequence that West Indians most feared: a transfer of the islands to American custody. Federation, either in promise or in progress, could block such an outcome.[2]

The other constituency was grounded in New York but housed in Washington: the Franklin D. Roosevelt administration. Some of FDR's top lieutenants, including Sumner Welles, Rexford Tugwell, and Charles Taussig, were long familiar with the Caribbean. Taussig especially was well versed in regional conditions and intellectual currents through Harlem connections such as Walter White of the National Association of Colored People (NAACP). As a ranking New Dealer, Taussig was also by disposition inclined toward centralized solutions. He perceived that regional sufferings were not confined by national flags; that is, the gravest Caribbean problems were regionally endemic. He successfully lobbied Roosevelt for the creation of what became a precedent for federal design: the Anglo-American Caribbean Commission (AACC). Though the British were far less enthusiastic than the Americans, the commission began its work in 1941 as a joint body charged with studying long-term regional problems. Though its original writ was quite small, the commission soon found itself, thanks to the supply shortages brought on by German U-boats, pressed into short-term crisis management. Its success in that endeavor gave credibility to the notion of cooperative region-wide activity. Both Washington and London knew that the Caribbean was, in this and other ways, a template for the post-war world and a testing-ground for Anglo-American initiatives in decolonization and development. The commission, in particular its American side, saw federation as the next logical step once peace returned.

After the Second World War, the Labour government made federation the interim goal of British policy in a number of colonial areas marked for self-rule. At a meeting in Montego Bay, Jamaica, in September 1947, Colonial Secretary Arthur Creech-Jones announced just such a plan for the West Indies. The NAACP followed suit immediately after by organizing a Harlem meeting on the prospective federation. During the 1950s, the WIF took rough shape. Its British and West Indian designers sought to congregate as many of the British West Indian territories as possible under one semi-independent roof. This, so the plan went, would endure for a few years as a kind of regionwide halfway house, a chance to practice internal self-government en route to full, collective independence, external self-government, and Commonwealth membership. The idea had the support of most West Indian leaders, including those of a more romantic stripe, who saw in it the poetry of race unity rather than the prose of state machinery. They, along with London and Washington, believed federation would exemplify the benefits of Western-guided decolonization, enhance hemispheric security, and, for Britain, be a vehicle for the sort of "imperialism of decolonization" capable of sustaining British influence in the area.[3]

The project faced problems from the start. Geography, economics, and politics undergirded a pan-Caribbean nation in theory but condemned it in practice. For example, devising a federal constitution is a difficult task in the best of times, but was made no easier in the WIF's case by a welter of strategic and political factors. The Standing Closer Association Committee (SCAC), formed in 1953, set about drawing up a blueprint. In 1956, Parliament validated its efforts and planned the establishment of the WIF for two years later, but did so with some trepidation. The committee had found that even seemingly simple matters could prove unmanageably complicated, and some of these lingered on unresolved. Among these was the question of where to site the new state's capital. The proposed union lacked an obvious first-choice city. Insular jealousies prevented any one territory from emerging as a consensus favorite. (Indeed, to the extent the Caribbean can be said to have had a regional capital, its most obvious site would be the place where intellectuals nurtured a common West Indian identity: New York City!) The two most populous islands—Jamaica and Trinidad—made logical candidates.[4] But neither wished to see the other get the honor, and the smaller islands had mixed feelings about seeing either one get it. Caribbean geography precluded the "Brasilia" option, and the islands' poverty put a premium on using existing infrastructure rather than building a capital city from scratch.

Of greater importance, though, was that the capital-site controversy led to a large, nigh-insurmountable new one: it brought the embryonic nation-state into direct conflict with the United States. In outline, what became known as the Chaguaramas crisis went some-thing like this: After heated internal battles among West Indians and between islanders and British officials, the SCAC selected Cha-guaramas, on Trinidad's northwest peninsula, as the best site for the WIF capital. This, alas, was at the time the largest U.S. military base in the Caribbean, other than Guantánamo Bay, Cuba. Chaguaramas was one of the last active areas Washington still held from the 1940 "destroyers for bases" deal; most had been deactivated, returned to colonial custody, or both. But Chaguaramas held a prominent place in U.S. military planning during the Cold War, as it had during the world war. It also boasted infrastructure that weighed on the col-lective mind of the SCAC, which hoped that the facilities might be given to the WIF to house the capital complex. For the Americans, it made strategic and financial sense to retain Chaguaramas. For the West Indian leadership, it was logical to claim the base. For the British, the outcome was less important in its details than in the possibility of its damaging either British or West Indian relations with Washington. All sides knew, in any event, that a strong WIF was in all parties' interest, and so it seemed that the clash need not become an impasse.

Chaguaramas became exactly that, thanks to the initiative of Trinidadian Chief Minister Eric Williams. Williams was the progen-itor of a multiracial Trinidadian nationalism, having risen to power quite unexpectedly in 1956 on the strength of a genuinely popu-lar movement. He was also an Oxford-trained historian who took the burdens of the Caribbean past more seriously than most. At a meeting in London in July 1957, Williams surprised his allies and counterparts alike by going on the attack. He denounced the U.S. base as an injustice foisted upon the Trinidadian people without their consent and demanded that the Americans leave. His stance marked the beginning of what would become a nearly four-year-long, on-again-off-again crusade to evict the United States from Cha-guaramas. The symbolism of the dispute was plain: a soon-to-be-sovereign nation demanding that a foreign military presence depart to make way for the new nation's capital. But the principle at stake was complicated by practical details and personality clashes. The crusade Williams launched in the summer of 1957 was in full swing when the WIF came into being the following April. The federation's inauguration thus took place in a kind of limbo: in temporary quar-ters, in a state of impassioned impasse with the new country's most important ally, and with internal disputes in full fester.

For Washington, a particularly disturbing aspect of the Cha-guaramas crisis was its timing. April 1958 was one month after Fidel

Castro's call to revolution in Cuba, and one month before Vice President Richard Nixon was attacked by a mob in Caracas, Venezuela. The Eisenhower administration wondered whether all these events signaled a burgeoning anti-Americanism in the hemisphere. The Cold War in the Americas had seemed well in Washington's hand after its intervention in Guatemala in 1954, but the apparent rise of anti-Americanism—even if Eisenhower and his team did not necessarily equate this with a rise in pro-communism—called for a rethinking. During the remainder of Eisenhower's term and especially after Castro's triumph in January 1959, Washington abandoned its post-Guatemala hands-off policy in Latin America. Eisenhower and Kennedy set in motion an array of initiatives against Castro himself in Cuba and against Castroism in the hemisphere. These included the familiar, such as the Operation Mongoose plots to depose or kill Castro, the hilarity of which in retrospect was matched by their futility at the time, and the Alliance for Progress, whose effectiveness was far more promised than real.

Less familiar, though, was the U.S. determination to bolster the WIF as, in a sense, an anti-Castro bulwark. Washington believed—egged on by London, which hoped to elicit more aid monies for the new country—that the federation could be a showcase of decolonization and development "done right," under Western auspices and eschewing the Castro-revolutionary path. The United States was more spectator than actor, more able to cheer on London and the West Indians (other than Williams) than to affect the course of events on the ground. But the Chaguaramas crisis showed that the United States was not without a role to play. As a consequence, the last eighteen months of the Eisenhower administration saw the country give up on hopes of solving the Williams problem by waiting him out, supporting his political rivals, buying him off, or strong-arming the British into acting. Instead, Washington resolved to solve Chaguaramas on favorable-enough terms for all parties and to support West Indian development directly and indirectly through greater aid payments and a commitment to purchase regional resources such as bauxite. These efforts would complement the more dastardly U.S. activities in Cuba and would firm up a Caribbean area now on the front lines of the Cold War.

WITHIN THE FEDERATION, TROUBLES MOUNTED. Williams, Jamaican Chief Minister Manley, and the federal Prime Minister, the Barbadian Grantley Adams, found themselves at odds more often than not. Chaguaramas and other questions pitted the new country against outside powers, and member units against one another.

Each of the leaders, moreover, faced savvy domestic opposition. Though usually confined to individual islands, political turmoil at times coalesced into a regionwide counterforce to the ascendancy of the federation and its leadership triumvirate. The internal battles and deepening fissures that marked the first three years of the WIF were exacerbated by the Chaguaramas crisis. Luck and timing, along with Adams's clever tongue, gave Washington an opening to solve the matter, at least temporarily. A settlement was struck, tabling the Chaguaramas issue for seven years—and thus guaranteeing that an incensed Williams, who denounced the settlement, would continue his crusade.

The dispute over Chaguaramas alienated Washington just as the United States was revamping its hemispheric policy, leading Americans to wonder whether the WIF might harbor a second Castro. The likeliest candidates, as seen from the White House, were Williams and British Guiana's Cheddi Jagan. The latter flirted with communism in ways both Britain and the United States found unacceptable. The former had seemingly staked his new government and nationalist movement on a confrontation with the Yankee hegemon. But Williams was correct about the questions at stake in Chaguaramas and their meaning for the WIF, even if he was impolitic in his presentation. He made the crisis a microcosm of the thorny issues that inevitably attended decolonization, though these would undoubtedly have surfaced in one form or another even without the capital-site demand. Williams argued correctly that the destroyers-for-bases deal had been concluded by the British without local consent. The agreement was thus with London, not with the sovereign West Indian Federation, which had the right to decide for itself whether it wanted foreign troops on its soil. But in making this case, Williams claimed to be speaking for the new West Indian nation—an action that exceeded his official capacity and that caused him to eclipse Adams's elected federal government. Moreover, neither Williams nor Adams had responsibility for the federation's external relations. That power still lay with Whitehall. As Williams took his "eviction" crusade to new heights in the summer of 1959, whatever its considerable merits, it came with costs. It rent the West Indian leadership, raised legitimate questions of sovereignty and responsibility, and made the transition to full independence more difficult.

As far as Washington was concerned, though, the larger Caribbean context made the WIF critically important. Especially after Fidel Castro "came out" on the communist side in the spring of 1960, the United States made it a top priority to settle the Chaguaramas question. The first National Security Council document to deal exclusively with the West Indies, NSC-6002, underlined the significance of resolving the crisis and of granting aid (military and otherwise) to the new country forthwith.[5] Williams, for his part, continued his intermittent crusade, even after aid talks began in the later months of 1960. Offers of generous aid mollified Williams, and the new Kennedy administration announced with great relief in February 1961 that the matter was settled. The relief intensified two months later when Manley met with JFK in Washington and reassured him that the federation would stand strong with the U.S. against the Castro challenge. One can imagine the comfort that Kennedy and his team took from the meeting, which concluded within twenty-four hours of the fiasco unfolding just ninety miles from Jamaica at the Bay of Pigs.

Along with an avowal of the federation's pro-Western Cold War stance, however, Manley brought words of warning. He apprised Kennedy of the challenge to the federation from Manley's nemesis, Bustamante, who had launched a campaign to force Jamaica to secede from the union. Bustamante had never been much more than lukewarm on the federation idea. He had supported it earlier on when it seemed the best, and perhaps only viable, path to independence. But he now considered it an obstacle: Jamaicans had got out from under British rule, only to find themselves under the "imperial" rule of their poorer cousins around the archipelago. As the richest and most populous island, Jamaica would, Bustamante warned his countrymen, find itself footing the aid-and-development bill that the British had once paid. Bustamante successfully maneuvered Manley into an island-wide referendum on Jamaica's continued membership in the federation, set for the coming September. Manley warned Kennedy that he and the federation he championed were in for a fight, but he assured Kennedy that Jamaicans would ultimately vote to stay in. Despite this and other occasional warning signs as the referendum drew near, most of the players, including the Kennedy administration, continued placing their chips on a yes vote.

The outcome, alas, was a no as decisive as it was surprising to most informed observers around the Atlantic. By a margin of 54%–46%, Jamaicans voted to withdraw from the WIF. At a stroke, they brought British, West Indian, and American designs to naught. Other than Jamaica's certain departure, nothing was clear. London had planned on the WIF being a way out, especially of financial obligations to the islands; those commitments now promised to continue for years more. The West Indies had planned on the WIF being the vehicle to independence and development; its now-reduced size now seemed to leave it too small, frail, and poor to have a viable future. The United States had planned on the WIF being its bulwark against Castroism and its showcase of decolonization done right, which is to say peaceably, cooperatively, gradually; the implosion of the federation left even believers wondering whether such a happy outcome was possible anywhere.

Beyond these real-world and realpolitik implications, moreover, the collapse of the WIF disappointed those focused on its symbolic dimension, who found their confidence in solidarity badly shaken. Watching from Ghana, Pan-African avatar Kwame Nkrumah begged Manley, Williams, and the Caribbean leadership to reconsider: "I hold the sincere conviction that success in the establishment of a powerful West Indian nation would substantially assist the efforts we are making in Africa to redeem Africa's reputation in world affairs and to re-establish the personality of the African and people of African descent everywhere."[6] Nkrumah's plea was to no avail. Bustamante rode the referendum victory to power in 1962, having made Jamaica's solo independence his cause. Trinidad, the next largest and richest, withdrew from the federation soon after. Both islands achieved independence in August and became the foci of a quickly improvised "twin pillars" U.S. strategy to hold the Caribbean line. As the smaller islands and Britain set about picking up the pieces, they drifted into an uncertain limbo.

Upon their independence in August 1962, Jamaica and Trinidad ended an era that had begun with Columbus. The lowering of the Union Jack after three centuries was epochal in its own right. But even on a shorter time line, the event was not much less momentous. Consider again the above dates. The Jamaican referendum in September 1961 came a mere five months after the Bay of Pigs disaster. The island's accession to independence in August 1962 was a mere two months before the Cuban missile crisis, which came closer than any other Cold War moment to leaving the earth in cinders. During that crisis, Jamaica and Trinidad stood firmly with the United States, to the Kennedy team's untold relief. From the American point of view, the dissolution of the WIF was, at the last, both a happy ending and a near miss. Less happy, of course, was the fate of the rest of the British West Indies, which drifted into independence over the next decade—and in the case of British Guiana, suffered, in the early 1960s, the only U.S. intervention of the pre-independence era.

One cannot tell the story of decolonization without accounting for the short, unhappy lives of federations like the WIF. They were attempted all over the post-war globe, and all followed more or less the same arc. Almost all were launched during the first half of the Cold War, and almost all collapsed within a decade of launch, but their disintegration had practically nothing to do with the super-power conflict, which in most cases had a nonspeaking, background part in the local drama. Rather, the unions fractured along eth-nolinguistic lines that long predated the U.S.-Soviet conflict. The federations thus pose deeper questions about what it takes, and what it means, to make a nation. From 1945 to 1980, more than one hundred new countries joined the United Nations, most of them constructed from former European colonies. The idea of federat-ing marked many of these nation-building projects, but it failed time and again in the face of "single-nationalist," as opposed to "pan-nationalist," sentiment by Third World peoples. Even those whose leaders had promoted "pan" passions—pan-Caribbean, Pan-African, pan-Arab, pan-Asian—in the end rejected such roman-tic formulations in favor of insular identities. If the British were practicing the "imperialism of decolonization," many Third World proponents of pan-racial solidarity were practicing an idealism of decolonization, only to have their visions dashed by their erstwhile followers' older attachments and animosities.

Spring Semester 2008

1. Stephen Howe, "Empire in the Twenty-First Century English Imagination," in Wm. Roger Louis, ed., *Penultimate Adventures with Britannia: Personalities, Politics, and Culture in Britain* (New York, 2008), p. 284.

2. See Norman Manley, "Selling the British West Indian Islands?" *Public Opinion,* 22 June 1940, folder: 4/60/2A/2, Norman Manley Papers, Jamaica Archives, Spanish Town, Jamaica.

3. Wm. Roger Louis and Ronald Robinson, "The Imperialism of Decolonisation," *Journal of Imperial and Commonwealth History,* 22 (September 1994), pp. 462–511.

4. A note on style: this essay uses the term "Trinidad" rather than "Trinidad and Tobago," since the events described took place on the big island. No disrespect to Tobago is thereby intended.

5. "Statement of U.S. Policy Toward the West Indies," NSC 6002/1, 21 Mar. 1960, in *Foreign Relations of the United States, 1958–1960,* Vol. V, pp. 433–43; "Semi-Annual Appraisal of Policy Towards the West Indies (NSC-6002/1)," 16 Sep. 1960, folder: West Indies, Box 8, OSANSAP: OCB Series - Subject Subseries, White House Office Files, Dwight D. Eisenhower Library, Abilene, Kansas.

6. Nkrumah to Manley et al., 8 June 1962, folder: 4/60/2B/27, Manley Papers.

18

W. K. Hancock and the Question of Race

SAUL DUBOW

As an historian of the British Empire and Commonwealth—indeed, as a British historian—William Keith Hancock (1898–1988) does not always receive the recognition he deserves. In addition to his enduring contribution to Australian history writing, Hancock's major works include the highly original and widely influential three-volume *Survey of British Commonwealth Affairs* (1937–42), the *British War Economy* (1949, with Margaret Gowing), and a magisterial double volume biography of the South African political leader and commonwealth statesman Jan Smuts (1962, 1968). While there are plenty of historians who recognize the contribution Hancock made to their own specialist fields, the themes that link his conception of history are seldom considered as a whole.

Keith Hancock was probably the most original and authoritative historian of the British Empire from the 1930s, when the subject underwent academic professionalization, through the post-war era, when it came to be thoroughly reshaped by scholars such as Ronald Robinson and Jack Gallagher. Unlike many of his contemporaries, Hancock appreciated the significance of the Empire and Commonwealth from the metropolitan as well as the colonial perspective, and he was fully alert to the broader international environment shaping the emerging Commonwealth. In the considered judgment of Wm. Roger Louis, Hancock "transformed the subject of Imperial history by integrating its component parts—especially the constitutional, economic, demographic, and religious—into a single, coherent and comprehensive interpretation."[1]

Among the qualities that stand out in Hancock's work are his enormous intellectual range and points of reference (he called this "span"), his compelling gifts as a stylist, and his ability to convey a sense of refined moral purpose while exemplifying the high standards of the historian's craft: technical precision, fidelity to evidence, and the ability to strike a balance between emotional attachment and austere intellectual detachment.

Hancock's overriding view of the Commonwealth, especially as this concerned the relationship between the British metropole and its white dominions, is captured by the tension between *imperium* and *libertas,* namely, the challenge "of reconciling the equal freedom of the parts of an association with the unity of the whole."[2] This defining theme in the *Survey of British Commonwealth Affairs* recurs over and again in Hancock's writings, whether in relation to questions of sovereignty, state power, or nationalism. A proud Australian as well as a staunch Anglophile, Hancock envisioned the Commonwealth as a mutual association in which local patriotisms could cohere within a wider sense of belonging and freedom.

Following the example of Richard Jebb and others, Hancock pursued and significantly developed the idea that national loyalties with the dominions, "so far from being disruptive of the Empire, were the stuff out of which it must be re-created."[3] Greater Britain was not for Hancock, as it was for Seeley or Dilke, England writ large; nor was it Anglo-Saxonist, as in the racialized idiom of E. A. Freeman. Instead, Hancock anticipated contemporary understandings of a transnational "British world" constituted by shared history, cultural identity, and institutional formation; he would surely have found common cause with J. G. A. Pocock's eloquent call to write Greater British history as the "intercultural" story of "conflict and cross-breeding between societies differently based."[4]

For all Hancock's range and insight, his discussion of race and race relations—at least to a modern audience—is glaringly inadequate. This point has been variously made by the pioneering African historian Roland Oliver, who elides Smuts's "blind spot" about Africans with Hancock's own, and by Roger Louis, who states that the Smuts biography is flawed because it "stops short of exploring the African dimension of the subject."[5] It should be noted that comments on Hancock's view on race, such as those noted above, have all been made by way of retrospective assessment. In gauging Hancock's views, we should therefore consider whether, judged by his own stated intentions and given the state of debate at the time, Hancock ought to have been expected to be more forthcoming on race. Was his blindness a sin of omission or commission? In Hancock's life work, how consistent a feature is this caesura? And to what extent was it conscious or deliberate? These questions are not easy to address in the case of an historian of consummate subtlety who chose to adopt a coolly dispassionate approach to the difficult problems he nevertheless found so compelling.

At the outset, we might distinguish between two aspects of Hancock's perspective on race and empire. First and foremost, there is the view of the colonial nationalist who takes whiteness for granted while remaining deeply aware of the divisions of class, religion, and nationality within the imperial family. Second, and more at a remove, there is the historian who is aware of the growing challenge posed by the color question to the primary Commonwealth family and who therefore acts to preserve the geographical integrity of a fragmenting imperial domain. Hancock is pragmatic and at times far seeing about the nature of this challenge; his perspective remains that of the aloof and knowing observer, acting independently but in broad concert with establishment opinion.

In *Australia* (1930), Hancock exemplifies his interest in the first aspect of race, the familial. The book begins with a breezy assertion: "Many nations adventured for the discovery of Australia, but the British peoples have alone possessed her."[6] The thematic approach adopted by Hancock, coupled with his droll, epigrammatic style, allows ample space for a distinctive interpretation of the Australian condition and national character. *Australia* is replete with conventional references to British "stock," "race," "type," and "blend." Yet rather than being argumentatively load bearing, such terminology is used with a casual indulgence that reflects the idiom of the day. He describes the White Australia policy and immigration restriction as the "negative condition of a positive policy." Rooted in colonial "idealism," it was a means of guarding against the "demoralization" and "degradation" of Australian civilization rather than signaling an aggressive dislike or fear of foreigners. Although temperamentally supportive of its insistent Anglo-Saxonism, Hancock is not blind to the "hypocrisy and cant" associated with White Australia policies; he is skeptical, for example, of eugenic arguments purporting to prove that the tropical areas of the white man's country are in fact unsuitable for European settlement.

More interesting and original is Hancock's espousal of the "independent Australian Briton," whose composite British nationality is forged through the introduction of civilization to an alien, and largely empty, continent. As Stuart Macintyre points out, the novelty of this formulation lies in its effort to bridge the assumed contradiction between assertive colonial nativism on the one hand, and

imperial loyalism on the other—the point being to show how colonial patriotism can coexist with a more capacious sense of imperial
belonging. For Hancock, it is thus "quite possible to be pro-British
without being anti-English." The "Australian type" he describes is a
composite "product of the blending of all the stocks and regional
types which exist within the British Isles, nourished by a generous
sufficiency of food and breathing-space and sunshine." If there is
such a thing as an "average Briton," we are assured, he will be found
in Australia.[7] It is the formation of this demotic Australian type
that helps explain the country's distinctive egalitarian ethos and its
political culture, wherein rugged individualism coexists with state
socialism. In Hancock's usage, the phrase "independent Australian
Briton" may also have been intended to orient the Australian commonwealth back to the mother country and away from the republican but increasingly powerful United States.

Hancock was not oblivious of the implications of conquest and
civilization. In *Australia,* and even more in his later writings on the
country, Hancock demonstrates sensitivity to the negative effects of
colonization, especially its environmental costs. He describes the
process of settlement as an "invasion" (the title of chapter 1), but the
weight of this word is spread, since the costs of invasion are borne as
much by the fragile land as its vulnerable aboriginal peoples (who
are dismissed in a summary, academic, ground-clearing paragraph).
In playing down the tendency to narrate in triumphalist terms the
spread of white civilization, and by affirming that the invasion of
plants, animals, and men did more to enrich than to impoverish the
soil, Hancock thus deftly avoids the consequences of land dispossession for those indigenous Australians who survived the conquest.

This avoidance touches on Hancock's allegiance to the land, a
relationship that is as much about aesthetics and contemplation as
it is about ownership and productivity. His approach reinforces his
strong preference for expansive forms of civic patriotism and his
disavowal of narrow or exclusive expressions of romantic nationalism allied to notions of race or *volk*. Personal identification with
landscape and soil is thus key to Hancock's understanding of the capacious commonwealth connection, and it is exemplified in his own
enlarged sense of self. This enduring theme is powerfully signaled
in *Australia* and reinforced in many of his later writings: "A country
is a jealous mistress and patriotism is commonly an exclusive passion; but it is not impossible for Australians, nourished by a glorious literature and haunted by old memories, to be in love with two
soils."[8] The capacity, indeed the desirability, of being in love with
two soils is powerfully elaborated in Hancock's biography of Smuts

and also in his autobiographical ruminations on his ties to the Australian, English, and Tuscan landscapes.

Hancock's next major work, the *Survey of British Commonwealth Affairs,* essays this approach on a much larger scale. In this unparalleled interpretive study of commonwealth political economy, Hancock skillfully combines economic history with a comparative treatment of problems of nationality and power. The invitation to write the *Survey* came from Arnold Toynbee (then at Chatham House) in 1934, and it was intended to serve as a companion to Toynbee's own *Survey of International Affairs.* In the inter-war years, Chatham House's self-selecting community of intellectuals and opinion makers became absorbed by the maintenance of international order, and they promoted a conservative form of enlightened imperialism that, in the recent assessment of Paul Williams, was apt to ignore growing struggles for racial equality, "other than when they had repercussions that threatened to impinge directly on issues of imperial order."[9]

Although Toynbee helped shape the Commonwealth Survey project, he did not seek to direct Hancock. Hancock was skeptical of those who regarded the Empire with patrician complacency (in 1936, Hancock left the Round Table, frustrated by its mood of appeasement toward Hitler). Hancock records that at this time there was a tendency among politicians and professors to underemphasize the Commonwealth's external dangers and to exaggerate its "inward tranquilities": "They took it too much for granted, as Sir Alfred Zimmern had done in his stimulating [1925] lectures on *The Third British Empire,* that all the territories marked red on the map were keeping their appointed places in a triumphant procession to the finishing post of self-government."[10]

While Hancock might have wished this to be true, he could not help noticing that the "procession was getting rather ragged here and there" as constituent elements from Newfoundlanders and Maltese to Irish and South Africans variously grunted, jeered, shrieked, or mixed catcalls with cheers. And yet these "overseas communities of European stock" were the easy cases. If the Commonwealth were genuinely to fulfill its aspirations, it would have to make itself acceptable also to "Indians, Burmese and Africans—not to mention the Irish."[11] It was with the Irish that he elected to begin.

We should bear in mind that Hancock wrote these words in the 1950s, when the momentum of decolonization was becoming unstoppable. This was also a time when the language of multiracialism was becoming pervasive in policy circles. Hancock was in tune with these events, and perhaps in advance of them too. Thus, there is good reason to accept his claim that the *Survey* anticipated the disruptions to the cozy commonwealth relations that suffused the inter-war and wartime eras. Hancock was often prescient, seldom complacent, and always alive to deep historical problems and contradictions. In respect of his treatment of race, worth noting are his comments on Gunnar Myrdal's contemporaneous *The American Dilemma* (1944), which he liked to think was similar in approach and subject matter to his own *Survey*, the South African sections in particular. Like Myrdal, Hancock viewed his task as one of distinguishing between "*what is*" and "*what ought to be.*"[12] He too wanted to distinguish between the ideological claims of the dominant racial group and the realities on the ground.

But Hancock was no Myrdal. His trenchant analysis differs markedly from Myrdal's bold prescriptiveness. Hancock did not collaborate with or consult black opinion, as Myrdal did. And whereas Myrdal's report anticipated and helped give succor to the optimistic forces of democratic internationalism and liberal progressivism that flowered in the post-war period, Hancock's survey may instead be seen as mounting a cautious defense of a commonwealth whose identity was coming under increasing strain. This was strongly evident in his Penguin paperback *Argument of Empire* (1943), intended for an American audience, wherein he defended the British Empire and argued in overly insistent language that the purpose of the Commonwealth was to enlarge human freedom. In his writings on South Africa especially, Hancock showed very little comprehension of, or interest in, blacks' aspirations, nor was he attuned to the consequences of the ever more stringent imposition of white supremacy.

HANCOCK'S *SURVEY* CAN USEFULLY BE SEEN as part of a much longer survey tradition within imperial history, one that bears the conspicuous imprimatur of establishment opinion in London, Oxford, and Cambridge. The lineage of this tradition can be traced through the writings of Anthony Trollope, J. A. Froude, J. R. Seeley, and Charles Dilke. They all attempt to take account of Britain's overseas possessions, to map out their interconnections, and to sketch out the challenges and opportunities for neo-Britons expanding into territories overseas. Except in the case of Seeley, travel to distant parts formed the basis of the imperial reckoning in such surveys. A striking but sometimes overlooked feature of these works is the broad assumption that Greater Britain comprises its colonies of settlement and (future) dominions, but that the dependent Empire, India in particular, is categorically different and poses its own distinctive problems.

By the 1930s, the survey approach was everywhere in vogue. It had become far more systematic, not to say encyclopedic, and was acquiring a developed sense of method, not least in sociology; it is in this context that we should place Lord Hailey's *African Survey* (1938) and related works by S. H. Frankel and E. B. Worthington. For historians, the multivolume *Cambridge History of the British Empire* (1929–59) was a landmark. Although diverse in character (not least because it was thirty years in the making) and touched by the insecurities of the inter-war era, the ethos of the *Cambridge History* remained firmly rooted in the notion of the "Empire-Commonwealth as a benevolent and progressive force in human history."[13]

For Hailey and Hancock, the survey method was a way to audit Britain's possessions and to create a suitable knowledge base and intellectual framework for the guidance of policy decisions. But whereas Hailey's work exemplifies the descriptive and narrative approach in its most exhaustive (and positivistic) form, Hancock's *Survey* is strongly interpretive. Rather than aiming at encyclopedic comprehensiveness, it is built around illuminating case studies. There is nevertheless an overriding unity of conception linking Hancock's with other examples of the survey tradition, including Nicholas Mansergh's later *Survey of British Commonwealth Affairs* (1952–58): namely, the tendency to reify the Commonwealth as a force for good. This is suggested by the survey method's style, the magisterial tone adopted by the surveyor, and his central location in British intellectual and policy-making culture. Such accounts are, moreover, held together by a restrained, albeit palpable, moral teleology that is played out in the progression from empire to loose federation or self-government. Hancock is acutely aware of the disjunctures and peculiarities of the Commonwealth, yet he is also clear that the objects of his study are linked not only by common allegiance to the Crown, but also "in the unity of an historical idea."[14]

The semi-official British survey tradition may usefully be contrasted with the large-scale enquiries sponsored by internationalist-minded American institutions at this time. Not only were these flush with resources, they also came free of imperial baggage. The Carnegie Corporation of New York initiated Myrdal's *American Dilemma* and provided funding for Hailey's *Survey* as well as the five-volume *Poor White Commission* (1927–32), a pioneering analysis of the sociology of white poverty in South Africa, with implicit American parallels. Raymond Buell's two-volume *Native Problem in Africa* (1928) was another noteworthy American initiative that reflected a growing awareness of U.S. global influence—and its questioning, even suspicious, attitude toward British imperialism. The Anglophile Hancock was keen to allay such skepticism. Wm. Roger Louis has shown that Hancock saw the rise of Pax Americana ("Yank-land," as he privately described it to A. L. Rowse in 1926) as a threat to the British Commonwealth.[15] Toward the end of his life, Hancock actively resisted the presence of American communication bases on Australian soil.

In the first volume of the Commonwealth *Survey*, Hancock announces that race and nationality are recurring themes (though, interestingly, he takes care to distance himself from the "racialist idealizers of the British Empire").[16] Race pertains mostly to different variants of British and non-British nationality, especially in respect of Hancock's treatment of Ireland, South Africa, and Canada. By contrast, color is introduced in—and confined to—the chapter on "India and Race Equality." The point of the exercise is to explore how the treatment of India and Indians posed a fundamental challenge to the unity of the Commonwealth after 1917. He seems more amenable to the wish that India be accorded parity as a dominion within the Commonwealth than to the notion that India's diasporic and emigrant population ought to be granted equality within the white-settler dominions. To think otherwise would be to interfere in the internal politics of the white dominions and to highlight manifest inconsistencies in concepts of imperial citizenship.

Hancock is illuminating on the amorphous meanings of imperial citizenship, drawing on Roman and French republican theories to illustrate different connotations attaching to the notion of equal rights. In his view, India's demands for equality were not synonymous with nineteenth-century "abstract individualism," that is, as these pertained to "isolated individuals in a cosmopolis." Instead, such freedoms concerned the "equality of historically diverse communities living together in a wider community of rights and duties." Foreshadowing the language of cultural pluralism and multiculturalism, Hancock glosses this theory in the phrase "equal rights for diverse communities."[17]

Having dispensed with the question of color in the discussion of India, Hancock devotes the remainder of the *Survey* (volume one) to politics, nationality, and constitutionalism. Africa is introduced only in volume II, part 2 of the *Survey*, the focus of which is largely economic. In *Country and Calling*, Hancock attests to his reluctance to deal with race: "In my imaginative map-making I had marked Africa with the legend, 'Here be Dragons'. For a year and more I had been protesting to myself in my notebooks that I would never, never implicate myself in that continent."[18] But realizing that the central themes of his work were intricately intertwined with that continent, Hancock did indeed "implicate" himself in matters African: first in the *Survey,* and even more fully in his biography of Smuts, which occupied seventeen years of his career. He also served as a mediator in the affairs of the Buganda chiefdom during the 1950s as moves were made to devolve power to a federated East Africa.

Part two of the *Survey* is organized around the notion of "frontiers" (missionaries', traders', planters', etc.), a heuristic device chosen by Hancock in preference to abstractions like imperialism or capitalism. "Imperialism," he announced, "is no word for scholars."[19] The specter of Marxist theories looms darkly over Hancock's neoclassical view of the commonwealth political economy (a great commercial republic), and he includes an appendix, "Communist Doctrines of Empire," by his Birmingham colleague W. H. B. Court as a refutation. Hancock is also keen to sidestep the question of "exploitation," partly because he does not think exploitation is an appropriate category for understanding noncapitalist forms of social organization, but also in recognition of the fundamental liberal antisegregationist tenet of the day, namely, that South Africa was already a unitary society economically—from which it followed that segregation was not practicable. Hence, Hancock's advice that South Africa's white rulers should bring their policies into accordance with "the basic fact of economic co-operation."[20] "Cooperation" is a deliberately anodyne choice of word, but it suits Hancock's purpose well. He is opposed to racial segregation not so much because of injustice or inhumanity as because it distorts the labor market, with negative consequences for the welfare of whites as well as blacks.

Hancock's views on race are distilled in his discussion of the "settlers' frontier" of South Africa. Writing just after the enactment of Prime Minister Hertzog's package of segregationist measures, he was well placed to comment, but he fails to condemn racial rule and seeks instead to inject a note of realism into the discussion. Later, Hancock registered profound distaste for the terrific "emotional heat" he found in South Africa. He considered it his "business as an historian to look for light" and set himself the task of assembling "the salient economic facts with which the protagonists of rival doctrines would have to reckon. It was not for me to prophesy whether or not their reckoning would be honest or adequate."[21]

If Hancock professed a disinclination to debate the merits of competing ethical dilemmas in the present, he was more than happy to take on those of the past. Indeed, one of the more original aspects of his treatment of South Africa in the *Survey* is its challenge to the self-serving liberal interpretation of South African history, in which British idealism and respect for human rights were contrasted with insular Afrikaner racial bigotry. In characteristic Hancockian style, the *Survey* railed against the philosophy of nineteenth-century liberalism and its "unconscious philistinism which ignored all values except those of bourgeois European society, which it assumed to be of universal validity."[22]

The point of such remarks was to cut through moral pretence and to get to the unadulterated facts. For Hancock, it was the "South African situation which is abnormal, and not the South Africans. The racial-economic system of South Africa is an extraordinary one, but the impulses which have created it are 'natural'. There is quite good reason for believing that the Australians, or for that matter the English, if their situation had been a similar one, might have adopted very similar policies."[23] This dose of realism allowed Hancock to spread the blame for racism more widely. In a caustic comment designed to subvert commonplace and complacent British assumptions, Hancock credited the adoption of racial discrimination not only to Afrikaners but also to "those sturdy British workmen who made themselves at home on South African soil": it was their Labour Party, he noted, that first "appealed to the white voters of South Africa with a full-blooded programme of racial segregation."[24] In Hancock's view, the critical question was whether such policies were "valid," and he argued they were not. Protectionist policies, while understandable and even acceptable in the short term, were ultimately doomed to failure: they merely exacerbated the problems they attempted to solve. Economic efficiency was both the key to poverty and "no respecter of races."[25]

HANCOCK'S ECONOMIC LIBERALISM COEXISTED WITH a more conservative political view with respect to racial segregation. Taking into account the manifold constraints on policy, he argued that the segregationist land legislation of 1936 honestly fulfilled the belated promise of the 1913 Land Act to provide additional land for Africans—and more: the new policy amounted to "something far more positive than the belated honouring of a pledge." Admittedly, the amount of land released for African occupation might not be enough to relieve congestion and to solve the wider "native question." But this disappointing conclusion did not invalidate the positive merits of the Native Land and Trust Act.[26] In *Argument of Empire*, Hancock smugly asserted that the loss of the African franchise represented a "defeat for my own side," adding that the "new franchise which took its place gave to the Bantu people a more effective representation in parliament than they had possessed before."[27] The extent to which Hancock was prepared to concede a spirit of good faith in the 1936 segregation legislation is striking. Also revealing, not least in its condescension, is the way he turns a loss for his "own side" into a gain for "the Bantu." For one thing, Hancock overestimated the preparedness of whites to honor even the promises of 1936.

In the absence of a developed theoretical or ethical perspective, Hancock was forced to explain the South African predicament by reference to "the minds of the white men who had made and were making and would for some time continue to make the political-economic pattern of the Union."[28] He blithely ignored African resistance to the Hertzog legislation of 1936 (such opposition, it must be said, was badly divided and demoralized). More generally, Hancock clearly did not think it necessary to discuss South African policies with those outside the paternalistic academic and social-work liberal circles associated with the Institute of Race Relations. Although he is disposed, in much of his work, to moralize and demonstrate "attachment," in his South African writings, Hancock elects to criticize segregation on the grounds that it does not fit with "the facts," a phrase that recurs over and again in the concluding pages of the chapter on the evolution of the settlers' frontier. In the face of becoming voteless, Africans remain faceless and voiceless.

If this approach is not altogether surprising in the *Survey,* whose analysis is rooted in classical political economy and which was written at a time when militant black opposition to segregation was muted and fragmented, the effacement of black political organization in Hancock's two-volume biography of Smuts is a more serious weakness; we should recall that the Smuts biography was written in the post-Sharpeville era, when the claims of African nationalism and the inequities of apartheid were shifting the national debate away from intra-white politics. Like Smuts, Hancock appreciated abstractly that race was the most intractable political problem in South Africa, yet he displayed little interest in it, and no originality in analyzing it, except as race influenced white South Africa and the country's place in the Commonwealth. Hancock was invariably inclined to forgive or explain away Smuts's contribution to racial rule in South Africa because he considered that it was outweighed by the South African statesman's contribution to the fight against fascism, the creation of international institutions, and the modern commonwealth idea. Hancock's personal correspondence indicates that he was privately troubled by the question whether Smuts believed in white supremacy, yet he proved unable—or unwilling—to pronounce decisively on the matter.

In his chapter on "native policy" in volume one of the Smuts biography, which is revealingly titled "The Stranger within the Gates,"

Hancock defined the problem of nationalism as follows: how to rec-
oncile the joint freedom of Boers and Britons in South Africa with
the interests of blacks. This might seem a defensible description of
the problem facing the creators of the Union in the first two decades of the century, yet Hancock provides far too sympathetic an
account of how Smuts dealt with the issue. He concedes that Smuts
may have been responsible for squandering opportunities to resolve
this "intractable" problem and observes what "appears to be a glar-
ing discrepancy" between Smuts's philosophy of holism and the "jar-
ring racial discords of South Africa."[29] But Hancock is throughout
willing to accept Smuts's good intentions, and he portrays his subject as caught between political extremes not of his making. He also
displays a very limited understanding of African nationalist politics,
typically doing little more than trotting out the overrated liberal
black figurehead D. D. T. Jabavu as the most acceptable mouthpiece
of black political aspirations.

Whereas black Africans are almost invisible as active agents in
South African history, Indians, Gandhi in particular, are afforded a
disproportionate amount of attention in the Smuts biography, just
as in the South African sections of the *Survey*. Hancock's fascination
with the epic battle between Smuts and Gandhi helps explain this
authorial decision. For Hancock, the struggle between Gandhi and
Smuts over the Asiatic Registration Act of 1907 epitomized the conflict between South Africa and India within the Commonwealth.
Their encounter is presented as a titanic battle between two great
men who have a surprising amount in common (belief in the collective human soul, for instance). Hancock reads great significance
into this relationship, stressing both the antagonism and the respect
that Gandhi and Smuts subsequently declared for each other. He
was also struck by the irony that it was Mrs. Vijaya Lakshmi Pan-
dit who denounced South Africa so vigorously at the first meeting
of the United Nations General Assembly, the very institution that
Smuts had worked so hard to create and whose preamble he helped
write, including the crucial reference to "human rights."

Hancock's treatment of Smuts's racial attitudes therefore amounts
to an apologia. For all the sophistication of Smuts's high-minded
prognostications, Hancock overlooks the simple fact that Smuts remained a supporter of white supremacy throughout his life. He also
glides over the undercurrent of virulent racism that sometimes surfaced in Smuts's views. Admittedly, this aspect of Smuts's manifold
hypocrisy was not much discussed at the time Hancock was writing,
but given the insight with which Hancock addresses other aspects

of Smuts's personality and intellectual outlook, such an elision suggests a degree of collusion with his subject.

Two examples must suffice. Consider first the passage wherein Hancock contrasts the daily grind of politics and elections with the cosmological time span within which Smuts thought about the human condition. Here he remarks that Smuts's absorption in the study of paleontology and prehistory "excluded the crude doctrine of the inequality of races" and that it pleased Smuts "to place European Man and the South African Bushman upon the same branch of humanity's family tree."[30] Here Hancock is mistaken. That Smuts was quick to endorse new findings about hominid evolution in support of the (then) highly contested theory that Africa was the cradle of humanity did not mean that he saw all its inhabitants as equal. On the contrary, evolution might show that divergence from a common stock was the defining pattern. This indeed was the tenor of Smuts's views as he expressed them to the South African Association for the Advancement of Science in 1925: "Our Bushmen" are "nothing but living fossils whose 'contemporaries' disappeared from Europe many thousands of years ago." As such, Bushmen could be compared to the cycads of the botanical world, which were also survivors from prehistory.[31]

Another instance in which Hancock smooths over Smuts's racism appears toward the end of the biography, when Hancock explain how South Africa was condemned for its racial policies at the first meeting of the United Nations General Assembly, in 1946. Smuts was tortured by the cruel irony that he, a symbol of world freedom and a much-vaunted wartime political leader, was being assailed for his country's policies at the international organization whose founding philosophy he had helped define—and by India at that. Ruefully, he wrote to his confidante Lady Daphne Moore: "I continue to swim in my sea of troubles, and may yet drown in it. On one side I am a human and a humanist, and the author of the preamble to the Charter. On the other I am a South African European, proud of our heritage and proud of the clean European society we have built up in South Africa, and which I am determined not to see lost in the black pool of Africa."[32] While these quotations appear in the printed collection of Smuts's letters, which Hancock edited jointly with Jean van der Poel, this revealing passage is glossed very differently in Hancock's biography.

Hancock was absorbed by Smuts's dual (and contradictory) roles as colonial nationalist and internationalist; as anti-imperialist patriot and as champion of the Commonwealth; as war leader and man of peace; as scientist and man of faith. He was also fascinated by aspects of Smuts's life story that in several respects paralleled his own. In a telling phrase, Hancock attributed to Smuts a patriotism that "at the deepest levels of feeling, was a patriotism more of place than of race." By this, he meant that Smuts's sense of national sentiment was rooted in an appreciation and love for the "the soil of South Africa" and its countryside.[33] Hancock's espousal of the "patriotism of place" helps us understand his own identity as an Australian whose strong attachment to the countryside of Gippsland, Canberra, and the Snowy Mountains coexisted with a wider sense of belonging. In this, he evidently considered himself different from Australian compatriots for whom "pride of race counted for more than love of country."[34]

Like Smuts, Hancock was disposed toward a lonely kind of patriotism: cerebral, austere, and disdainful of the irrational enthusiasms of crowds. It was a lofty, high-minded sense of affinity that prized citizenship and liberty above narrow national sovereignty, that recognized that nationalism could as likely destroy as advance these values, and that found its ultimate expression in the shared political culture of the white Commonwealth. In short, Hancock expressed his race patriotism through assumption and presumption rather than by crude assertion.

ALL THIS MAKES IT DIFFICULT TO FORMULATE a conclusive statement about Hancock's attitudes toward race. Should Hancock have been expected to be more aware of race and clearer in his views? The fairest way of doing this is to map his subtle evasiveness against broader historical trends. In his early writings—*Australia* (1930), for example—Hancock's kith-and-kin race patriotism may be deemed unremarkable, given the assumptions of the time. By the time of the *Survey* (1937–42), Hancock was clearly aware of the depth of the challenge that race and nationality posed to the future of the Commonwealth. This was a time when anthropologists were actively criticizing the scientific concept of race and defining the post-war anti-racist consensus. Hancock was now more deliberate in his circumspection. This is evident not only in his treatment of India and Africa, but also in the concluding section of the *Survey,* wherein he refers obliquely to debates about the scientific basis of the race idea, only to prevaricate about the question of biologically determined superior and inferior races: "For the present the historian is justified in maintaining an attitude of sceptical reserve."[35]

With the same skeptical reserve, Hancock reassures himself that his study does not cast light on the racial interpretation of history, and he wisely reminds his readers that there are many other salient factors in the story of the British Commonwealth. Among these are civic British values and traditions and the territorial integrity of the enterprise. Again, this strategy of avoidance might just be defensible. However, by the time of the double-volume *Smuts* biography (1962, 1968), Hancock's strategy of avoidance had become creakily untenable: his treatment of Smuts, written at the height of the apartheid era, reads at times like a refined apology for an exhausted form of white liberal paternalism. Hancock projects his own personality so fully into the subject of his biography, whose emulatory qualities render it a disguised form of autobiography, that *Smuts* might be read as fully revelatory of the author's own inner convictions and attitudes.

Spring Semester 2009

This is a shortened version of a paper presented at the Neale Colloquium, University College, London, April 2008; it will be published in Catherine Hall and Keith McClelland, eds., *Race, Nation, and Empire: Making Histories, 1750 to the Present* (Manchester University Press, forthcoming).

1. Wm. Roger Louis, "Introduction," in Robin Winks, ed., *The Oxford History of the British Empire*, Vol. V: *Historiography* (Oxford, 1999), pp. 28–29.

2. W. K. Hancock, *Survey of Commonwealth Affairs* (London, 1937), Vol. I, p. 22.

3. Ibid., p. 41.

4. J. G. A. Pocock, "British History: A Plea for a New Subject," *Journal of Modern History*, 47 (1975), pp. 604–05.

5. R. Oliver, "Blinkered Genius," review of Hancock's *Smuts*, Vol. II, *Journal of African History*, 9, 3 (1968), pp. 491–94; Louis, "Introduction," p. 29.

6. W. K. Hancock, *Australia* (London, 1930), p. 11.

7. Ibid., pp. 50, 38; S. Macintyre, "'Full of Hits and Misses': A Reappraisal of Hancock's *Australia*," in D. A. Low, ed., *Keith Hancock: The Legacies of an Historian* (Melbourne, 2001), pp. 37, 50–51.

8. Hancock, *Australia*, p. 68.

9. P. Williams, "A Commonwealth of Knowledge: Empire, Intellectuals and the Chatham House Project, 1919–1939," *International Relations*, 17, 1 (2003), p. 52.

10. W. K. Hancock, *Country and Calling* (London, 1954), pp. 150–51, 180–81.

11. Ibid., p. 151.

12. Ibid., p. 173; W. K. Hancock, *Professing History* (Sydney, 1976), pp. 8–9.

13. Louis, "Introduction," p. 11.

14. Hancock, *Survey*, Vol. I, p. 486.

15. Quoted in Wm. Roger Louis, "Sir Keith Hancock and the British Empire," *English Historical Review*, 120 (2005), pp. 940–41.

16. Hancock, *Survey*, Vol. I, pp. 20, 22, 83, 497.

17. Ibid., p. 182.

18. Hancock, *Country and Calling*, pp. 169–70.

19. W. K. Hancock, *Survey of British Commonwealth Affairs*, Vol. II, part 1 (London, 1942), pp. 1–2.

20. Hancock, *Survey*, Vol. II, part 2, p. 152.

21. Hancock, *Country and Calling*, pp. 172, 174.

22. Hancock, *Survey*, Vol. I, pp. 177–78.

23. Hancock, *Survey*, Vol. II, part 2, p. 64.

24. Ibid., p. 42.

25. Ibid., pp. 66, 152; Hancock, *Argument of Empire* (Harmondsworth, 1943), p. 114.

26. Hancock, *Survey*, Vol. II, part 2, pp. 87, 88.

27. Hancock, *Argument of Empire*, p. 45.

28. Hancock, *Country and Calling*, p. 172.

29. W. K. Hancock, *Smuts*, Vol. I: *The Sanguine Years* (Cambridge, 1962), p. 311.

30. Ibid., pp. 311–12.

31. J. C. Smuts, "South Africa in Science," *South African Journal of Science*, 22 (1925), p. 17.

32. W. K. Hancock and J. van der Poel, eds., *Smuts Papers*, Vol. VII, doc. 743, Smuts to Daphne Moore, 3 Feb. 1947.

33. Hancock, *Smuts*, Vol. I, p. 148.

34. Hancock, *Australia* (1961 edn.), p. 49.

35. Hancock, *Survey*, Vol. II, part 2, pp. 299–300.

19

Historians of the British Empire, plus 100 Top Hits of Imperial History

JOHN DARWIN

I suppose it is probably true that historians are not intrinsically very interesting. But it also is true, perhaps, that historians can perform three functions that do make them interesting in a vicarious way. They can reflect, to some extent, the society in which they live; they can act in some ways as the amplifiers of the ideas, prejudices, and beliefs of that society; and third, they can on occasion actually exert an influence perhaps over the mentalities, the thinking, the values and outlook of that society. If they are clever enough or, to put it more accurately, lucky enough, they can find themselves chiming with a particular mood and exert an influence upon a wider circle of opinion.

If we look at the historians of the British Empire, I think what their collective experience suggests is really three things. The first is that within Britain itself, certainly toward empire and the project of empire, there was always really quite a high degree of intellectual ambivalence—was it really a good thing, was it really a respectable thing, was it really a reputable thing, was it really a moral thing, was it really something that was actually going to benefit Britain itself rather than waste its substance in the outer reaches of a faraway world of which the British knew nothing and preferred to know little? Second, of course, there is the extent to which what the writings of even historians of Empire suggest for the most part is that they are really preoccupied not so much with the faraway places as with the effects of those faraway places upon the motherland. It is the fate of Britain and British society, the effects on British society of possessing an empire, and the kind of reflux or backwash of empire upon domestic society that tend, on the whole, to interest them most. And third, I think there has also been a reluctance or perhaps an inability to grasp the full complexity of the British world empire, of the British global system. Perhaps that is reflected in the prominence in the vocabulary of empire of that portmanteau phrase "Pax Britannica." "Pax Britannica," oddly enough, despite what many historians think and say, does not seem to have been coined as an expression until the very end of the 1870s, perhaps even the 1880s, and doesn't seem to have been widely used perhaps until the Edwardian period or after the First World War. But we can see its utility because it enabled historians as well as the man in the street and the politician in Westminster to capture—but without really investigating—the sense of Britain's global position extending beyond those spheres where British rule and sovereignty obtained. But the very popularity of that vague and ill-defined term suggests the extent to which historians found it hard to grapple with the full complexity of the pattern of imperial expansion.

Let's begin somewhere near the beginning. I am tempted to say that the beginning of a British world empire is really to be found in the 1830s and 1840s. Now you may say before that the British won the Battle of Plassey in 1757. There had been an ill-fated attempt to colonize North America, and the British, indeed, before 1800 had begun to colonize Australasia as well. And by 1795, they had even captured the Cape, and kept it for good after 1806. So why 1830–40? I think the answer would be that although there certainly existed an empire of dispersed possessions and an empire organized around the principle of mercantilism, that is to say, to control trade through political means, the notion that Britain could act as a world empire, free to move around the world where, by and large, she wished in pursuit of trade, in pursuit of influence, in pursuit of souls, that kind of empire does not really take off until the 1830s and 1840s, and the reason for that is to be found first of all in economics and second in geopolitics. In economics because although there had been an industrial revolution in Britain from (historians debate this endlessly) the 1760s onward, it was not really until 1810–30 that there was the capacity to penetrate into faraway markets with attractive consumer goods, above all cotton textiles, that really were priced at a level that made them enormously attractive everywhere. One historian has calculated that British textiles could be manufactured at prices between 14 and 200 times cheaper than those made by those not using machinery elsewhere in the world. Britain became the China, if you like, of the early nineteenth-century world.

So it was not until steam-powered weaving, which happened in the 1830s, that the British were really equipped to break into markets all over the world. Second, the capacity to conduct global imperialism really had to wait upon the completion of a set of geopolitical changes that came in the 1820s and 1830s. It was not until the 1820s that the British really had (almost) full command of India; it was not until the 1820s that the fall of the Spanish American empire opened up the Western Hemisphere fully to British trade; it was not until the 1830s that, as a consequence of their control of India and the exploitation of the resources of India for trade, the British were able to push their way into what until then had been the largely closed economy of China. During the years 1839–42, China's trade doors were kicked open, not least by the deployment of Indian manpower and the steamships of the East India Company sent from India. And last, perhaps as a footnote to all this, it was again in the 1830s that you see the moving out in Australasia from the original bridgeheads of British colonization—convict colonization—into the interior of Australia and the beginning of Australia's transformation into the greatest wool producer in the world, the greatest provider of raw wool to the British textile industry. So I think that was really the moment when Britain began to become a world empire rather than an old-fashioned mercantilist empire. It was then that the British could take advantage of the fact that the way the Napoleonic wars ended had smashed open forever, as it turned out—well, almost forever, because we might say a hundred years ahead it swung back again— that old world in which the globe was cut up into exclusive zones of trade controlled by a number of great European colonizing powers: Spain, Portugal, France, and Britain.

But when you look at the way in which British historians responded to this moment of hugely enhanced British power in the world, their reactions seem to have been very ambivalent, tentative, and perhaps really rather uninterested. Maybe to some extent they were conscious of the shadow of Gibbon. After all, it was Gibbon who warned that the greatest danger that lay in wait for a power—he was writing about Rome, but in an era of imperial crisis for Britain— was to become overmighty, overlarge. Remember Gibbon's famous statement that the single greatest cause of the collapse of the Roman Empire was that it became overextended. There, you might say, is the origin of the great overextension thesis popularized in the 1980s by a number of very distinguished historians. Then think about Macaulay. After all, no historian had more influence in Victorian England, certainly from the 1840s through the 1860s and later, and his books were sold by the tens of thousands. Macaulay is very interesting because, of course, he did go to India. He went there to make money as an employee of the East India Company, as a lawyer. And he did, indeed, write two very well-known essays about Clive and Hastings, in which he emphasized that they had had a role as dramatic and exciting, he said, as that of Cortés and Pizarro. But of course if you ask what did Macaulay himself write about when he wrote his *History of England,* he ignored all that completely and instead presented English history as being above all about the attainment not of democracy but of parliamentary freedom, the classic statement of the Whig history of England.

And then, of course, there was also to be found in this period a strong tendency among a very influential class of writers and, indeed, politicians to regard England's destiny, Britain's destiny—the words of course were used interchangeably then—as lying in its ability to exploit all the advantages of free trade. And that by comparison with this commercial expansion, other kinds of expansion were really not all that significant. Indeed, the colonies as such, like the Cape, like the Canadas (as they still were), like Australia, and like the infant New Zealand, annexed in 1840, were, as a famous politician once remarked, millstones round Britain's neck because they cost a great deal of money for garrisons and they seemed constantly troublesome in terms of rebellions in Canada, frontier wars in South Africa, rather smaller frontier struggles in Australia, and a very expensive frontier war, indeed, in the 1860s in New Zealand. So the colonies had, you might say, rather limited appeal as a subject on which you might wish to write a history of Britain's destiny in the world; and then there was India.

Macaulay had been to India, Macaulay had written about India, but in general, the feeling about India was that it was in some ways a rather bizarre anomaly. After all, it did not fit very well with the classic notion of English history as being about the rights of freeborn Englishmen. And there was a long surviving suspicion that India's role in British life was to corrupt it. Whether it was from the Oriental habits brought back by returning nabobs from India, laden with loot and able to buy their way into British social life; or from the fear that mere contact with the Oriental world would expose Britain to the emasculating, corrupting, luxury-loving tendencies attributed by Enlightenment writers to Oriental civilizations, India seemed a threat to English masculinity and muscularity. All of these things made India a rather strange and suspect place. It was still governed, after all, by a monopoly company that recruited its servants, as its officials were called, by methods that were regarded as being rather too enclosed and private, and that was also suspected of engaging not so much in trade, which would have profited England, as in a continual cycle of wars of conquest whose principal aim was to enrich those who worked for the company rather than to enrich Britain at home.

For all these reasons, up until maybe the 1860s and 1870s it is very hard to find (other than some compendia that celebrate the success of British trade) accounts of Britain's empire that present it as being a natural or desirable or even particularly important aspect of Britain's history. All this begins to change in the 1860s and 1870s. One of the early signs of change, although he was not writing a history, is the famous book by Charles Dilke, then a young, aspiring radical politician springing from a gentry family in Warwickshire. The book was *Greater Britain,* and its opening line, a very famous opening line, is "In 1866 and 1867, I followed England round the world." Here is the idea that—again he uses "England" for what we might call Britain—England had populated great tracts of the world and would, indeed, go on to populate even more. Dilke speculated, for example, that whereas the Chinese would gradually die out, the English would grow increasingly in numbers and eventually start to colonize China. Well, you can't be right all the time, I suppose. Dilke certainly emphasized the extent to which England's destiny had been to expand around the world. And, of course, he famously made no real distinction between England and the United States. He made one rather charming remark: "Through America, England is speaking to the world." I don't know if you still feel like that, but that was Dilke's view in 1868.

So here is somebody who is beginning to celebrate England's colonization by demographic expansion. Second, of course, in the 1870s you get the famous attempt by Disraeli, a great romancer, as many leaders of the Conservative Party have been, to present the role of Britain—or England, as he would have said—in the East as being that of a natural ruler. Of course, it was Disraeli who famously decided to repackage the British Queen as the Empress of India and to turn India into a great feudal appendage to Britain through the personality of the monarch. So here are some straws in the wind to suggest that now there were attempts to see ways in which the two forms of British world expansion, the colonization mode and the mode of rule, were being brought more directly into the center of English intellectual as well as political life, and were being presented fundamentally in very positive terms. But the real breakthrough in this process came in the 1880s, and it came through the influence and impact of an historian, John Robert Seeley, Regius Professor of History at Cambridge.

SEELEY WROTE A SERIES OF LECTURES that he published in 1883 at the instigation of Macmillan, which was very keen to print them. And once published, they became known, rather famously, as *The Expansion of England,* although, of course, really Seeley is talking about the expansion of Britain, and, indeed, he takes up and uses without acknowledgment the term that Dilke had coined fifteen years earlier, "Greater Britain." *The Expansion of England* was a book that had an enormous influence—I'll say a bit more about that in a minute. It sold in the course of two years more than 80,000 copies, and even in 1919 it sold 11,000 copies. In 1931, not a good year to be wasting your money on books, it sold 3,000 copies, and it stayed in print from 1883 to 1956 (it was reprinted in 1971 by the University of Chicago Press, with an introduction by John Gross). It was published in innumerable translations. Seeley himself was supposed to have been delighted that there was a Hindi translation. Interestingly, there was a Japanese translation, which appeared in 1942, quite a good year in the expansion of Japan. So Seeley's book had a very wide readership. In other times, he might have become a pundit on television, but then again, he was, like all Cambridge historians, self-effacing and modest.

What did Seeley say in this book? Seeley's most famous remark was that the English had acquired an empire "in a fit of absence of mind." Another term he used was that they had done it "in a trance of insularity." In other words, they had acquired this empire without really noticing. So it is true, I think, that part of Seeley's purpose was to remind an audience, a readership, a public in Britain of what it had acquired in the course of fifty or sixty years or so in the nineteenth century. It is not true, of course, that Seeley was recommending more expansion—I think rather the reverse. He was really saying that this is what has happened, and I think his book contains the suggestion that it would be unwise to go any further: enough is enough. His real concern, it has been argued, was to educate public opinion, or that part of it that he saw as the new ruling class in British society. Seeley was a Liberal. He was a meritocratic Liberal. He was somebody who certainly had no time for the old aristocracy. So he certainly did not equate empire with conservatism or Toryism. But what he was conscious of from his earlier studies (Seeley's earlier interests had lain very largely in the history of Prussia and of Germany, and he had written a very famous biography of the great awakener of Prussia against Napoleonic tyranny, Baron von Stein) was the need to enlighten the new ruling class (who had to replace the old, jaded, worn-out aristocracy that he wanted to bundle into the graveyard of history) about the realities of the world, the realities of power, the realities of security and insecurity, the realities of commercial prosperity and what it depended upon. In the book, therefore, you find almost a diatribe against the folly and ignorance of those who imagined that because there was free trade at the time he was writing, in the 1880s, that somehow it was a natural condition that was always there and whose continuation could be safely assumed. Instead, says Seeley, you have to look back into the eighteenth century and see what a struggle there had been for Britain to acquire the basis for its commercial prosperity against the relentless hostility of the French, the Spanish, and the Dutch.

Seeley was anxious to enlighten this new Liberal elite about what he saw as the realities of global history and against the foolishness of assuming that the world was a safe, cosmopolitan place where you didn't need armies or navies and you didn't need to worry about protecting your interests by forceful means. He said two other things of great importance. One of them was that Britain was different from the rest of Europe because it was what he calls a world state. Unlike the rest of Europe, it was engaged much more deeply with the world beyond Europe, not least because of its position as an offshore island facing westward into the Atlantic and reaching out all round the world. Indeed, simply in terms of its colonial empire, Britain enjoyed a phenomenal preponderance over its European neighbors. A recent book has calculated that in 1880 the British occupied 8 percent of the land area of the world's colonial empires and ruled over 90 percent of colonial subject peoples. So here is a vision of British exceptionalism; America is not the only country to have doctrines of exceptionalism. And second, of course, Seeley urged that there should be a new concept of England. England, he said, was wherever there are English people. In other words, wherever there had been British settlement, those populations and those communities formed part of a greater British nation, a "Greater Britain." Their loyalty and attachment to Britain at home, England at home, was something to be treasured, not least, of course, as a way of enabling Britain to remain on terms with the other great territorial states of the world, including Russia and, of course, by this time, the United States, which unfortunately he never visited.

These were the core ideas of Seeley. I have suggested already that we can to some degree measure their influence in terms of the publication and republication of his book. But, of course, his influence is not simply to be measured in that way. He had a profound influence upon the thinking of a whole generation, perhaps three generations, of British politicians, of British public figures, and perhaps of British educated people in general. This was surely because of the way in which he presented Britain as having a version of manifest destiny, one that was primarily about the expansion of the British people. Now nobody, I think, among those British politicians and opinion formers absorbed Seeley's message more fully than Lord Milner. Milner is best known today as the proconsul who by most accounts single-handedly created the Boer War of 1899–1902—a not entirely fair reputation. Milner, like Seeley, was a Liberal. And like Seeley, of course, he accepted the idea that Britain lived in a dangerous world in which realpolitik had to be the doctrine of British leaders and governments, and that cosmopolitanism was a false and perilous doctrine. And like Seeley, again, he emphasized right through his life how critical it was to gather in the scattered communities of British people overseas to form them ideally into a great imperial federation, certainly into a conscious group of what he called "British nations" or "British peoples," united by common allegiance, common attachment, and common values to form a great bloc in the world.

But Milner was simply the most outstanding example. If you think of Joseph Chamberlain, if you think, indeed, of Joseph Chamberlain's sons, Austen and the more famous Neville, if you think of Stanley Baldwin—and there are two Prime Ministers in that group of four—they accepted, I think, almost completely the account that Seeley gave of the nature of Britain's place in the world, even if they didn't necessarily meet to the full his requirement to think in harsh realpolitik terms. Certainly, Baldwin and Neville Chamberlain fell a little short in that respect. Nevertheless, there were certain limitations to Seeley's analysis. First of all, there was no real examination of the economic foundations of British power in the world. Second, of course, in his account of these colonizing populations there was little real recognition that they might have feelings of their own, attitudes of their own, aspirations of their own, which wouldn't necessarily mean that they would be at all times and in all circumstances devoted to their connection with Britain.

Yet against what you might call the dominant Seeleyesque discourse, other sorts of imperial history really had a hard struggle to make their claim. India languished, despite Disraeli and despite the fact that the later nineteenth century seemed to be the moment when the British were reaping the full reward of their rule over India and it was becoming much more important both economically and militarily. Historians of India, or the Indo-British connection, found it uphill work to persuade the British public that India really was as important as they thought it should be. A whole generation of British officials, the scholar-mandarins of the Raj, wrote books to celebrate or emphasize the importance of India to Britain with on the whole rather little success.

So the great Lord Curzon, Viceroy of India between 1899 and 1905, was to give a lecture in which he lamented how little India's importance to Britain was grasped by the British at home. Little did they realize, so he meant to say, that without India, Britain would be a rather minor country off the coast of Europe. India was essential to Britain's claim to greatness, and the voice of its Viceroy had to be heard, at least when that Viceroy was Curzon. "I stand at the head of a constituency made up of 300 million people," he once wrote to the British minister in London responsible for Indian affairs, neglecting of course to mention that none of those 300 million had the vote. It was also true that those concerned with British expansion into Africa found it hard, by and large, to make their mark on British opinion. It was really Livingstone and the missionary ideal that allowed Africa to be packaged up for British comprehension as somewhere where the path of duty if not of profit might lead. South Africa, despite the Boer War and despite the influence of Rhodes, made surprisingly little impact upon British opinion, and what impact it did make was marked by ambivalence and unease from very early days about whether it really was a respectable expansion of British influence.

The one (partial) exception to this generalization, and it is a rather curious one, was Egypt, whose British connection was celebrated very effectively in the writings of both Milner and Lord Cromer, the great Proconsul in Egypt from 1883 through to 1907. Cromer wrote two huge volumes that he called *Modern Egypt* but that, as a rather rude critic observed, was really an *apologia pro sua vita*. But the success of his volumes and of Milner's *England in Egypt* were very significant because Egypt had been a very delicate point in Liberal thinking about empire. The Liberals (under Gladstone) had gone into Egypt in 1882: they had occupied it, but they hadn't dared annex it. Even so, many Liberals felt that this was a bridge too far, and a canal too far as well. It would expose Britain to a whole range of geostrategic risks, and what, after all, were the British doing there? Milner and Cromer provided an answer that satisfied a large tract of Liberal opinion. They were there for the uplift of the Egyptian fellahin. They were there to bring order where there had been disorder, to bring solvency where there had been bankruptcy, to lead the Egyptians into a lighter, brighter future. This was, I think, a surprisingly effective set of propaganda arguments, and it soothed Liberal opinion in the late nineteenth century. But it was still the case that very few people in Britain knew (or cared) much about Egypt. My former mentor, Jack Gallagher, once complained that very few British historians wanted to write about Egypt. He said, "It must be because it's too important."

And last, of course, in this collection of people struggling against the dominant discourse there were also those who attacked the global expansion of British power from a rather different angle. They made the claim that it was really all about the pursuit of profit for a small number of people. This was an argument that was particularly associated with the writer and radical Liberal journalist J. A. Hobson, and that was later incorporated into accounts of empire by people like Leonard Woolf, husband of the more famous Virginia. This school of writers expressed the radical suspicion that the whole grand apparatus of empire and all the expenditure on the navy and, to some extent, on the army and the colossal expenditure, of course, on the Boer War, were all a consequence of a conspiracy of the few who were profiting from empire. One radical wisecrack was "The more the empire expands the more the Chamberlains contract," a reference to Joseph Chamberlain's steelmaking firm. But despite the success of this sort of critique among a circle of radical opinion, I think it can't be said right up until the Second World War that it made enormous inroads upon broader British opinion, not least because even these radical critics themselves were ultimately reconciled to British expansion, provided, they said, it was done in the right and decent way, through the application of trusteeship in dealing with native peoples, looking after them as long as (as Hobson put it) "they remained in their non-adult state." So, many of the fundamental ideas of empire and imperialism were just as prevalent among these "anti-imperial" critics. What they were really concerned about, as I suggested at the beginning, was the effect of empire upon Britain. As long as the Empire didn't damage what they saw as the real values and strengths of British society or set back the prospects of its progressive reform, they were happy to keep it.

IN MANY WAYS, I THINK, THIS PATTERN I have been describing held good up until the Second World War. It was the Second World War that was really the great moment of transition in thinking historically about empire in Britain. Because, of course, in so many obvious ways it delivered an enormous shock both to the belief that the Empire—even if adapted to meet the aspirations of different sorts of colonial subjects, even if it had to respond to different kinds of economic environments—would in one way or another go on indefinitely. The Second World War dealt an appalling shock to that kind of complacency, that kind of assumption about the permanence of the imperial system. Second, of course, by exposing the acute dependence of Britain upon the United States and the extent to which Britain itself had been impoverished by war in a way that was unimaginable even in the late 1930s, it enforced a kind of rethinking about the nature of empire. And the real fruit of this great rethink comes (although they drew upon ideas that had been floating around in the 1930s) in the early 1950s with two historians, Jack Gallagher and Ronald Robinson. It was their famous article "The Imperialism of Free Trade" that marked, I think, a great shift away from the pre-war tradition in several ways that I'll try briefly to capture.

The first thing to say is that they wrote about empire totally unsentimentally. Most previous writers of empire wrote about it as something that was to be treasured, to be discussed, to be debated, or as a subject on which they wanted to exert their influence, perhaps on the way it was governed. Gallagher and Robinson were totally indifferent to all those considerations. As far as they were concerned, it was something to be viewed as if it lay on an historical slab, something to be dissected. And, indeed, you might say the whole premise of their writing was that the British Empire was going to be over quite soon, if it wasn't already. Second, what is very fascinating is the way in which to a far greater extent than any previous writer, they presented it as a system of power, indeed, a global system of power, extending right around the world but operating, of course, in different modes in different parts of the world to take account of the different circumstances, different distributions of power, different kinds of elites, different sorts of cultures with which the British came into contact. Third, they met that gap that I mentioned a minute ago that exists in Seeley's account. The weakness of Seeley had been not to spend much time thinking about (or certainly not writing about) the economic foundations of British world power, whereas this has center stage in that first great essay by Gallagher and Robinson, in which they say explicitly that empire was all about the pursuit of trade, the breaking into what they called the "new countries," creating new economies, bringing them into contact with Britain and the industrial world.

And last, in a way at which Seeley had hinted when he talked about India (and half of *The Expansion of England* is about India), they emphasized the extent to which empire depended upon a pattern of cooperation, what they called, famously, "collaboration." So in all these ways, you might say, they plugged some of the largest gaps in the Seeleyesque structure while at the same time emphasizing that they rejected Seeley's view of empire as a great constitutional political structure. For them, it was much more than that, what we might call in our language a geopolitical and "geo-economic" structure. Like many great historical orthodoxies, and one might think in the American context of Frederick Jackson Turner's frontier thesis, this orthodoxy carried all before it in the 1960s and, perhaps, even into the 1970s. It seemed to supply a kind of all-purpose explanation for almost every aspect of British imperial expansion. Indeed, people were very quick to apply some of its ideas to the expansion of other empires as well. The use of some of its key concepts proliferated far beyond academic history into many other branches of the social sciences. Nevertheless, by the mid-1970s, you begin to see that orthodoxy breaking down, and what begins to happen is an outbreak of what might be called a series of history wars, which were really wars of academic succession. And what were these about? I think they reflected the fact that for many new sorts of concerns and interests, for many new sets of people concerned with the role of history in their lives and in the lives of their societies, there were many things missing in the Robinson and Gallagher account, which they wanted to put in.

Now the first and perhaps most obvious of these—the first wave in these history wars—was the need felt, particularly with the end of empires and the emergence of a hundred and fifty new countries out of the colonial empires of Europe, to construct histories that explained and preferably celebrated the emergence of new nation-states. So these were histories that had to present the reader with heroes, with struggle, with ultimate triumph over the forces of darkness, over the evil empires that had long prevented those nations from coming into being. And that wave of nationalist historiography is to be found right across Asia and Africa and also, of course, in the countries of the so-called White Commonwealth: Australia, New Zealand, Canada, and, in a somewhat different way, perhaps, South Africa. The second wave was what is often described as the subalternity movement, "subaltern studies," history from below. Although there were some intimations in Robinson and Gallagher's account of the fact that there might be elements of struggle going on inside colonized societies, by and large their preoccupation was with the dealings between imperialism and its agents, on the one hand, and local elites on the other. What the subaltern historians wanted to bring out was the extent to which within colonized societies there were enormous differences and conflicts around class, around race, and (increasingly emphasized by the 1980s) around gender. So these three elements of identity, which, by and large, Gallagher and Robinson didn't seem to be particularly interested in, were now being brought onto the historical agenda in a major way.

Third, there was what might broadly be called "post-coloniality," that is to say, the ideas deriving much of their force from the writings of Edward Said, the claim that the real oppression that empire had brought had been the disparagement, subjugation, or destruction of indigenous or non-European cultures. By inflicting "epistemic violence" upon colonial societies, the empire builders had robbed them of their thought systems, value systems, and belief systems, destroying their sense of a cultural self and imposing instead a hybrid, artificial, and derivative culture. I think it would be wrong to suggest for a minute that the contributions made by historians along these three lines were not in many ways of great interest, importance, and value, and there is no doubt that they spoke to very important constituencies of interest and feeling both in societies that once formed parts of empire and, indeed, by an indirect route, to opinion back in the countries of the former colonial powers themselves. For example, part of the reason why an interest in imperial history was revived in Britain was because of the growing belief that Britain itself had been a deeply imperialized country, enjoying the satisfactions of rule over subject peoples, and that this, in turn, had corrupted British society in important ways, above all in the matter of race. Empire was being reinterpreted as the source of racism in British society. To those who believed this, it was only by stripping away empire's false veil of respectability that the British public could be taught the origins of those unacceptable prejudices apparently still rife in British society, taught to reject the false values that empire had brought.

There is no question, I think, that in various ways these different sorts of writing about empire reflected demands, needs, feelings, and senses of urgency in societies abroad as well as back in Britain (and the same phenomenon can be seen in other former imperial countries, especially France). What was sometimes lost in these accounts was three things. To some extent, they tended to lose a sense of the context of empire—the fact that the places described were once part of a larger imperial system, not simply isolated "national" units. Second, they lost a sense of the subtleties of collaboration, on which Gallagher and Robinson had laid such emphasis, by insisting that there was a kind of dichotomy, a clash, a total clash, between the agents of empire and the subject peoples of the colonies. In reality, there had often been a great deal of collaboration not only in political and economic terms but in cultural terms as well. By squeezing this out of the picture, some historians tended to construct far too simple an account of the nature of cultural change inside colonial societies. And third, much of this writing tended to obliterate a larger set of reciprocities and exchanges going on between societies in different parts of the world, especially their reciprocities and exchanges with Europe—not just in terms of the movements of peoples, goods and ideas but also of values as well. And to some extent, part of the contemporary vogue for global history, part of its attraction for historians of empire, is that it allows a bringing back into the picture of some of those missing elements that I have just tried to list. Above all, I suppose, global history is concerned with reciprocities and exchanges, a sense of the mutual influence of different "sites" upon one another. This is not just a matter of one dominating the other or exploiting the other. Global history also allows us, at least if it is done properly, to bring back into the picture some of the critical geopolitical elements that more recent accounts have tended rather to sideline.

Perhaps I have done enough to suggest, I hope I have, that the history market is rather like the stock market. Stocks have gone up and they have also come down. We might be tempted to say that in some periods of the writing of imperial history there have even been a number of "structured historical products" that have not contained quite as much value as appeared at first sight, and perhaps even a few you might call definitely toxic. But all things considered, an intellectual investment in the history of empire has turned out, in the long term and on the whole, to be quite a profitable one.

Spring Semester 2009

As noted in the introduction, John Darwin's lecture stimulated a vigorous discussion about seminal or significant articles, which sometimes, though not often, can have just as much influence as books. To continue with the stock market analogy used by Darwin, on the following pages is a list, compiled by graduate students in history at the University of Texas, of more than 100 blue-chip essays.

W.R.L.

*100 Top Hits of Imperial History**

Adas, Michael, 'Contested Hegemony: The Great War and the Afro-Asian Assault on the Civilizing Mission Ideology,' *Journal of World History,* 15 (2004).

Amin, Shahid, 'Gandhi as Mahatma: Gorakhpur District, Eastern UP, 1921–1922,' *Subaltern Studies,* 3 (1984).

Ball, S. J., 'Banquo's Ghost: Lord Salisbury, Harold Macmillan, and the High Politics of Decolonisation, 1957–1963', *Twentieth Century British History,* 16 (2005).

Bayly, C. A., 'Patrons and Politics in Northern India,' in John Gallagher, Gordon Johnson, and Anil Seal, eds., *Locality, Province, and Nation* (1973).

———, 'Eric Thomas Stokes,' in *Oxford Dictionary of National Biography* (2004).

Bickers, Robert, 'Shanghailanders: The Formation and Identity of the British Settler Community in Shanghai, 1843–1937,' *Past and Present,* 159 (1998).

Brown, Judith, 'War and the Colonial Relationship: Britain, India, and the War of 1914–1918,' in M. R. D. Foot, ed., *War and Society* (1973).

———, 'Gandhi—A Victorian Gentleman,' in Robert D. King and Robin W. Kilson, eds., *The Statecraft of British Imperialism* (1999).

Buckner, Phillip, 'Canada and the British Empire,' introductory essay in *Canada and the British Empire* in *Oxford History of the British Empire* Companion Series (2008).

Cell, J. W., 'On the Eve of Decolonization: The Colonial Office's Plans for the Transfer of Power in Africa, 1947,' *Journal of Imperial and Commonwealth History,* 8 (1980).

Chakrabarty, Dipesh, 'A Small History of Subaltern Studies,' in Dipesh Chakrabarty, *Habitations of Modernity: Essays in the Wake of Subaltern Studies* (2002).

Cole, Juan R. I., 'Of Crowds and Empires: Afro-Asian Riots and European Expansion, 1857–1882,' *Comparative Studies in Society and History,* 31 (1989).

Cooper, Frederick, introductory chapter in Frederick Cooper and Ann Laura Stoler, eds., *Tensions of Empire* (1997).

Daly, M. W., 'Egypt,' in *Cambridge History of Africa,* 7 (1986).

Darwin, John, 'Imperialism in Decline? Tendencies in British Imperial Policy between the Wars,' *Historical Journal,* 23 (1980).

———, 'Imperialism and the Victorians. The Dynamics of Territorial Expansion,' *English Historical Review,* 112 (1997).

———, 'Gallagher's Empire,' *Yet More Adventures with Britannia* (2005).

Davidson, J. W., 'Problems of Pacific History,' *Journal of Pacific History,* 1 (1966).

Devine, T. M. 'The Break-Up of Britain? Scotland and the End of Empire,' *Penultimate Adventures with Britannia* (2008).

Dubow, Saul, 'Colonial Nationalism, the Milner Kindergarten, and the Rise of "South Africanism," 1902–10,' *History Workshop,* 43 (1997).

Falola, Toyin, 'West Africa,' *Oxford History of the British Empire,* 5 (1999).

Falola, Toyin, and A. D. Roberts, 'West Africa,' *Oxford History of the British Empire,* 4 (1999).

Ferns, H. S., 'Britain's Informal Empire in Argentina, 1806–1914,' *Past and Present,* 4 (1953).

Fieldhouse, D. K., '"Imperialism": An Historiographical Revision,' *Economic History Review,* 14 (1961).

———, 'The Official History of Colonial Development,' *English Historical Review,* 97 (1982).

Fisher, Michael H., 'Indirect Rule in the British Empire: The Foundation of the Residency System in India, 1764–1858,' *Modern Asian Studies,* 18 (1984).

* plus a few more for good measure

Flint, John E., 'Britain and the Scramble for Africa', *Oxford History of the British Empire*, 5 (1999).

———, 'The Failure of Planned Decolonization in British Africa,' *African Affairs*, 82, (1983).

———, 'Managing Nationalism,' in Robert D. King and Robin W. Wilson, eds., *The Statecraft of British Imperialism* (1999).

Gallagher, John, 'Nationalisms and the Crisis of Empire, 1919–1922,' *Modern Asian Studies*, 15 (1981).

Gopal, Sarvepalli, 'Churchill and India,' in Robert Blake and W. R. Louis, eds., *Churchill* (1993).

———, 'All Souls and India,' in Robert D. King and Robin W. Kilson, eds., *The Statecraft of British Imperialism* (1999).

Harlow, Vincent, 'The New Imperial System, 1783–1815,' *Cambridge History of the British Empire*, 2 (1940).

Harper, T. N., 'Diaspora and the Languages of Globalization,' in A. G. Hopkins, ed., *Globalization in World History* (2000).

Holland, R. F., 'The Imperial Factor in British Strategies from Atlee to Macmillan, 1945–1963,' *Journal of Imperial and Commonwealth History*, 12 (1984).

———, 'Never Never Land: British Colonial Policy and the Roots of Violence in Cyprus, 1950–1954,' *Journal of Imperial and Commonwealth History*, 21 (1993).

Hopkins, A. G., 'The Victorians and Africa: A Reconsideration of the Occupation of Egypt, 1882,' *Journal of African History*, 27 (1986).

———, 'Rethinking Decolonization,' *Past and Present*, 200 (2008).

Hourani, Albert, 'The Myth of T. E. Lawrence,' *Adventures with Britannia* (1995).

Howe, Stephen, 'When If Ever Did Empire End? "Internal Decolonization" in British Culture since the 1950s,' in Martin Lynn, ed., *The British Empire in the 1950s: Retreat or Revival?* (2006).

———, 'The Slow Death and Strange Rebirths of Imperial History,' *Journal of Imperial and Commonwealth History*, 29 (2001).

Hyam, Ronald, 'The British Empire in the Edwardian Era,' *Oxford History of the British Empire*, 4 (1999).

———, 'The Primacy of Geopolitics: The Dynamics of British Imperial Policy, 1763–1963,' in Robert D. King and Robin W. Kilson, eds., *The Statecraft of British Imperialism* (1999).

———, 'Perspectives, Policies, and Peoples,' in Ronald Hyam, ed., *Understanding the British Empire* (in press). 'If I am to be remembered by one thing, it will be this essay.'

Jeffery, Keith, 'Sir Henry Wilson and the Defence of the British Empire, 1918–1922,' *Journal of Imperial and Commonwealth History*, 5 (1982).

Kamtekar, Indivar, 'England and India, 1939–1945,' *Penultimate Adventures with Britannia* (2008).

Kedourie, Elie, 'The Chatham House Version,' chapter 12 in *The Chatham House Version and Other Middle Eastern Studies* (1984).

Kendle, J. E., 'The Round Table Movement and "Home Rule All Round,"' *Historical Journal*, 11 (1968).

Kennedy, Dane, 'Imperial History and Post-Colonial Theory,' *Journal of Imperial and Commonwealth History*, 24 (1996).

———, 'The Boundaries of Oxford's Empire,' *International History Review*, 23 (2001).

Kent, John, 'Anglo-French Colonial Cooperation, 1939–1949,' *Journal of Imperial and Commonwealth History*, 17 (1988).

Langer, W. L., 'The Triumph of Imperialism,' chapter 3 in *The Diplomacy of Imperialism* (1956 edition).

Lavin, D. M., 'Margery Perham's Initiation into African Affairs,' *Journal of Imperial and Commonwealth History,* 19 (1991).

Levine, Philippa, 'Why Gender and Empire?' in Philippa Levine, ed., *Gender and Empire* in *Oxford History of the British Empire* Companion Series (2004).

———, 'States of Undress: Nakedness and the Colonial Imagination,' *Victorian Studies,* 50 (2008).

Lonsdale, John, 'Britannia's Mau Mau,' *Penultimate Adventures with Britannia* (2007).

———, 'East Africa,' *Oxford History of the British Empire,* 4 (1999).

Louis, W. R., 'The Historiography of the British Empire,' introductory chapter, *Oxford History of the British Empire,* 5 (1999).

———, 'The Dissolution of the British Empire in the Era of Vietnam,' *American Historical Review,* 107 (2002).

Louis, W. R., and R. E. Robinson, 'The Imperialism of Decolonization,' *Journal of Imperial and Commonwealth History,* 22 (1994).

Low, D. A., 'The End of the British Empire in Africa,' in Prosser Gifford and W. R. Louis, eds., *Decolonization and African Independence: The Transfer of Power, 1960–1980* (1988).

———, 'Rule Britannia—Subjects and Empire in the *Oxford History of the British Empire*,' *Modern Asian Studies,* 36 (2002).

Lynn, Martin, 'The "Imperialism of Free Trade" and the Case of West Africa, c. 1830–c. 1870,' *Journal of Imperial and Commonwealth History,* 15 (1986).

Lyon, Peter, 'The Commonwealth and the Suez Crisis,' in W. R. Louis and Roger Owen, eds., *Suez 1956: The Crisis and its Consequences* (1989).

Mackenzie, John, 'On Scotland and the Empire,' *International History Review,* 15 (1993).

———, 'Empire and National Identities,' *Transactions of the Royal Historical Society,* 8 (1998).

Mackinder, H. J., 'The Geographical Pivot of History,' *Geographical Journal,* 20 (1904).

McIntyre, W. D., 'The Strange Death of Dominion Status,' *Journal of Imperial and Commonwealth History,* 27 (1999).

———, 'Clio and Britannia's Lost Dream: Historians and the British Commonwealth of Nations in the First Half of the Twentieth Century,' *Round Table,* 93 (2004).

Madden, A. F., 'Changing Attitudes and Widening Responsibilities, 1895–1914,' chapter 10 in *Cambridge History of the British Empire,* 3 (1959).

———, '1066, 1776 and All That: The Relevance of English Medieval Experience of "Empire" to Later Imperial Constitutional Issues,' in John E. Flint and Glyndwr Williams, eds., *Perspectives of Empire* (1973).

Marks, Shula, 'Jan Smuts, Race, and the South African War,' *Still More Adventures with Britannia* (2003).

Marks, Shula, and Stanley Trapido, 'Lord Milner and the South African State,' *History Workshop,* 8 (1979).

Marshall, P. J., 'Britain and the World in the Eighteenth Century,' four presidential addresses, *Transactions of the Royal Historical Society,* 8–11 (1998–2001).

Morris-Jones, W. H., '36 Years Later: The Mixed Legacies of Mountbatten's Transfer of Power,' *International Affairs,* 59 (1983).

Newbury, C. W., 'Patrons, Clients, and Empire: The Subordination of Indigenous Hierarchies in Asia and Africa,' *Journal of World History,* 11 (2000).

O'Brien, Patrick, 'The Costs and Benefits of British Imperialism, 1846–1914,' *Past and Present*, 120 (1988).

Offer, Avner, 'The British Empire, 1870–1914: A Waste of Money?' *Economic History Review*, 46 (1993).

Osterhammel, Jürgen, 'Semi-Colonialism and Informal Empire in Twentieth-Century China,' in Wolfgang J. Mommsen and Jürgen Osterhammel, eds., *Imperialism and After* (1986).

Owen, Nicholas, introductory chapter, in Nicholas Owen, *The British Left and India* (2007).

Pares, Richard, 'The Economic Factors in the History of the Empire,' *Economic History Review*, 7 (1937).

Perham, Margery, 'A Re-Statement of Indirect Rule,' *Africa*, 7 (1934).

Pham, Julie, 'J. S. Furnivall and Fabiansim: Representing the "Plural Society" in Burma,' *Modern Asian Studies*, 39 (2005).

Platt, D. C. M., 'Further Objections to an "Imperialism of Free Trade," 1830–1860', *Economic History Review*, 26 (1973).

Porter, Andrew, 'Religion, Missionary Enthusiasm, and Empire,' *Oxford History of the British Empire*, 3 (1999).

Porter, Bernard, 'Introduction to the Second Edition,' in *Critics of Empire: British Radicals and the Imperial Challenge* (2008).

Prakash, Gyan, 'Subaltern Studies as Postcolonial Criticism,' *American Historical Review*, 99 (1994).

Ranger, T. O., 'Connexions between Primary Resistance Movements and Modern Mass Nationalism in East and Central Africa,' *Journal of African History*, 9 (1968).

Rathbone, Richard, 'Things Fall Apart: The Erosion of Local Government, Local Justice and Civil Rights in Ghana, 1955–60,' in Martin Lynn, ed., *The British Empire in the 1950s: Retreat or Revival?* (2006).

Raychaurdhuri, Tapan, 'India, 1858 to the 1930s,' *Oxford History of the British Empire*, 5 (1999).

Roberts, A. D., 'The Imperial Mind,' in *Cambridge History of Africa*, 7 (1986).

Robinson, Francis, 'The British Empire and the Muslim World,' *Oxford History of the British Empire*, 4 (1999).

Robinson, Ronald, 'Non-European Foundations of European Imperialism,' in Roger Owen and Bob Sutcliffe, eds., *Studies in the Theory of Imperialism* (1972).

———, 'Oxford in Imperial Historiography,' in Frederick Madden and D. K. Fieldhouse, eds., *Oxford and the Idea of Commonwealth* (1982).

Robinson, Ronald, and John Gallagher, 'The Imperialism of Free Trade,' *Economic History Review*, 6 (1953).

Sanderson, G. N., 'Sudanese Nationalism and the Independence of Sudan,' in Michael Brett, ed., *Northern Africa, Islam, and Modernisation* (1973).

———, 'The European Partition of Africa,' *Journal of Imperial and Commonwealth History*, 3 (1974).

Schölch, Alexander, 'The "Men on the Spot" and the English Occupation of Egypt in 1882,' *Historical Journal*, 19 (1976).

Seal, Anil, 'Imperialism and Nationalism in India,' *Modern Asian Studies*, 7 (1973).

Shlaim, Avi, 'The Protocol of Sèvres, 1956: Anatomy of a War Plot,' *International Affairs*, 73 (1997).

———'The Balfour Declaration and Its Consequences,' *Yet More Adventures with Britannia* (2005).

Sluglett, Peter, 'Formal and Informal Empire in the Middle East,' *Oxford History of the British Empire*, 5 (1999).

Stockwell, A. J., 'British Imperial Policy and Decolonization in Malaya, 1942–1952', *Journal of Imperial and Commonwealth History,* 13 (1984).

———, 'British Expansion and Rule in South-East Asia,' *Oxford History of the British Empire,* 3 (1999).

Stokes, Eric, 'The First Century of British Colonial Rule in India: Social Revolution or Social Stagnation?' *Past and Present,* 58 (1973).

———, 'Traditional Resistance Movements and Afro-Asian Nationalism: The Context of the 1857 Mutiny Rebellion in India,' *Past and Present,* 48 (1970).

Supple, Barry, 'Fear of Falling: Economic History and the Decline of Britain,' in Peter Clarke and Clive Trebilcock, eds., *Understanding Decline* (1997).

Thompson, A. S., 'The Language of Imperialism and the Meanings of Empire: Imperial Discourse in British Politics, 1895–1914,' *Journal of British Studies* (1997).

———, 'Is Humpty-Dumpty Together Again? Imperial History and the *Oxford History of the British Empire,' Twentieth Century British History,* 12 (2001).

Tinker, Hugh, introduction to Hugh Tinker, ed., *Burma: The Struggle for Independence, 1944–1948* (1983).

Tomlinson, B. R., 'The Contraction of England: National Decline and the Loss of Empire,' *Journal of Imperial and Commonwealth History,* 11 (1982).

Vereté, Mayir, 'The Balfour Declaration and Its Makers,' *Middle Eastern Studies,* 6 (1970).

Washbrook, David, 'Orients and Occidents: Colonial Discourse Theory and the Historiography of the British Empire,' *Oxford History of the British Empire,* 5 (1999).

Watt, David, 'The Foundations of the "Round Table,"' *Round Table,* 60 (1970).

Winn, Peter, 'British Informal Empire in Uruguay in the Nineteenth Century,' *Past and Present,* 73 (1976).

Wolfe, Patrick, 'History and Imperialism: A Century of Theory, from Marx to Postcolonialism,' *American Historical Review,* 102 (1997).

Young, Crawford, 'The Colonial State and Post-Colonial Crisis,' in Prosser Gifford and W. R. Louis, eds., *Decolonization and African Independence* (1988)

20

Gertrude Bell and the Creation of Iraq

SHAREEN BRYSAC

From Trebizond to Tripoli
She rolls the Pashas flat
And tells them what to think of this
And what to think of that.
Anonymous

Mesopotamia, 17 October 1920. Baghdad is adorned with flags, palms, and triumphal arches celebrating Sir Percy Cox's return as Britain's High Commissioner. Gertrude Bell, his Oriental Secretary, dressed in her new Paris frock, welcomes him on the railway platform, where he is greeted by a cheering crowd, a seventeen-gun salute, and a military band playing "God Save the King." A week later, Bell is invited to join two military colleagues, Captain Clayton and Major Murray, to meet Ja'far al-'Askari, a military commander who served as an adviser to Faisal, Syria's former king, who has recently been expelled from Damascus by the French. "It was an amazing evening, Ja'far opened out like a flower, told us the whole Syrian story," Bell wrote to her father, Sir Hugh Bell. Ja'far Pasha then described how "he found the extreme Nationalists here as impossible to bring to reason as they had been in Syria. 'I say to them, you want complete independence? So do I. Do we not each and all of us dream of a beautiful maiden, her age 14, her hair touching her waist? She does not exist! so complete independence under existing conditions is impossible.'" Bell countered by saying complete independence was what we the British ultimately wished to give. "Khatun," the Pasha answered (they were speaking Arabic, one of Ja'far's eight languages) "complete independence is never given; it is always taken." But believing in their "honesty of purpose," he was ready to work with the British for the salvation of his country, despite a disability that would continue to haunt him. "When I go to my brothers to persuade them to help they turn aside and say 'You're English.'" [1]

Bell thought the Pasha a remarkable man, and she approved when he accepted Britain's offer the next day to join the country's first cabinet as Minister for Defense. He agreed, eventually to be joined by his brother-in-law, Nuri al-Said (also Pasha), the future Prime Minister. Ex-Ottoman officers, both men had been close associates of Faisal in Damascus, having fought beside him during the Arab Revolt. Ja'far would serve two terms as Prime Minister; between 1930 and 1958; Nuri would serve a record fourteen times in the same office. Bell would often dine, as she wrote, "en famille" with the two pashas and their wives.

Gertrude Margaret Lowthian Bell, CBE, was a distinctive hybrid, part new woman, part proper Victorian. She might have emanated from a play by George Bernard Shaw or a middle-period novel by Henry James. With her "Paris frocks and Mayfair manners," Miss Bell strode with masculine self-assurance into the tents of tribal sheiks.[2] Nicknames are subsurface signatures, like watermarks: Sir Percy Cox became "Kokus," the local pronunciation of Cox. Writing home from Baghdad in 1917, Gertrude took amused note of these sobriquets: "The word Kokus is rapidly passing into the Arabic language, not as a name but as a title. You are a Kokus, just as once upon a time you were a Chosroes or a Pharaoh. I'm currently described as Kokusah, i.e., a female Chosroes. Isn't it delicious!"[3] (Later, her authority established, she was known "al-Khatun," an Important Lady, one of the few representatives of his majesty's government remembered by the Arabs with anything resembling affection.)

Kokusah was born in 1868, the green-eyed, ginger-haired daughter of a wealthy and cultivated ironmaster, Sir Hugh Bell, and his wife, Margaret, the offspring of a well-to-do Newcastle family (who died when Gertrude was three). As incisively rendered by Jan Morris, the Bells of County Durham typified their Liberal caste and kind: "They lived lavishly, they read widely, they became baronets and Fellows of the Royal Society, they had their homes built by Philip Webb and their drawing-rooms decorated by William Morris."[4] Young Gertrude's intellectual promise was evident from childhood. At twenty, Miss Bell became the first woman at Oxford to qualify for a coveted First in Modern History, telling her examiner, S. R. Gardiner, the great authority on the early Stuarts, that she differed "from his estimate of Charles I."[5] (Degrees, however, were not conferred upon women at Oxford until 1920.)

With focused intrepidity, she next undertook an exhausting grand tour, her itinerary ranging from the cultural and natural wonders of continental Europe (where she scaled the Matterhorn from the Italian side) to the dusty byways of the Ottoman Middle East and Persia. In Egypt, she left her card with Lord Cromer. It was the beginning of her lifelong friendships with the powerful and influential lords—Cromer, Curzon, and Robert Cecil. She would share their antisuffrage views and would dedicate one of her books, *Amurath to Amurath,* to Lord Cromer. Exhibiting her considerable linguistic gifts—Arabic, Persian, and Turkish as well French, German, and Italian—she ventured through the Syrian Desert to visit the Druze and penetrated Arabia as far as Hail.

With her firsthand knowledge of local sheiks and tribes, and her mapping skills, Bell was poised, when the First World War broke out, and after a hesitant Ottoman Turkey unwisely chose to side with the Central Powers, to serve her country in the Middle East. In November 1915, she traveled to Egypt to join the newly formed Arab Bureau in Cairo. Under the supervision of General Gilbert Clayton, the bureau's mission was to gather intelligence, make maps, generate propaganda, and promote an Arab uprising against the Turks. Bell set to work compiling a handbook on the Bedouin tribes of northern Arabia and their complex lineage.

Over dinner at the elegant Savoy Hotel, where the bureau had its three-room office, complete with whirling ceiling fans and staff officers sporting desert boots and swagger sticks, Bell found herself chain-smoking and agreeing with her colleagues on what would come to be known as the Cairo consensus. In broad terms, Cairo believed that France's post-war ambitions in Syria were insupportable and to be strongly resisted, and that the likeliest candidate to lead a British-backed Arab revolt was Hussein, the Sharif of Mecca and King of the Hejaz, and not his blood rival, Abdul Aziz Ibn Saud, the warrior ruler of eastern Arabia, the husband of sixty-five wives, and the champion of the otherwise puritanical Wahhabi doctrine.

Although Bell continued to be in the thrall of her Savoy colleagues, her stint in Cairo was brief. After a mere two months, she was aboard the troop transport SS *Euripides,* journeying to India at the invitation of the Viceroy, Lord Hardinge, a family friend. Relations between Cairo and Delhi had deteriorated to the extent, wrote Bell, that "there is no kind of touch between us except rather bad tempered telegrams!" Bell was dispatched to "establish more direct and friendly relations, so that each side might cease to regard the other as composed mostly of knaves."[6]

In the early spring of 1916, Lord Hardinge dispatched Bell to Basra, still without a salary but with a positive recommendation to Sir Percy Cox, now serving as Chief Political Officer in Mesopotamia: "She is a remarkably clever woman with the brains of a man."[7] The generals of the Indian Expeditionary Force moved her to a pleasant veranda with a cool room behind it, where she helped draw maps and recommended guides to aid the army now struggling toward Baghdad. She needed all her contacts to win over the local tribes and their sheiks in order to obtain their help in defeating the Turks, and make converts she did. One sheik spoke to his followers, "Now we all know that Allah has made all women inferior to men. If the women of the Angiliz are like her, the men must be like lions, in strength and valour. We had better make peace with them."[8]

Yet Sir Percy's political staff treated Bell with the utmost suspicion. They ignored her at the officers' mess, called her conceited, lectured her on the Official Secrets Act, and censored her letters, but she persevered. The Foreign Office commended her after complaining that no important information had reached either Cairo or London before her arrival. During the protracted missions of Sir Percy in London and Tehran, Captain (later Colonel) Arnold T. Wilson was seconded to the expeditionary army's headquarters at Basra to serve as deputy to his old chief, becoming in Cox's absence Mesopotamia's chief administrator. As Bell's sympathetic friend Harry St. John ("Jack") Philby, the father of the infamous Kim, noted, Wilson never took her into his confidence on policy issues: "These were bandied about between Whitehall and Simla and Basra in code telegrams and secret dispatches, to which she was denied access and for knowledge of whole contents she had to depend, *faute de mieux,* on the *obiter dicta* of the great man, flung casually across the tea-table of the political mess."[9] In spite of her difficulties with Wilson, Cairo and Delhi agreed that Bell would stay on for the time being with the title of Oriental Secretary and a salary of three hundred rupees— one-fifth of the salary of her male colleagues—making her the only female political officer in the British forces.

ON 11 MARCH 1917, ANGLO-INDIAN FORCES CAPTURED BAGHDAD. Gertrude Bell, her hair, as she remarked, now turned white, resettled in Baghdad in a riverbank bungalow, hidden Arab-style behind a high wall on a narrow street (called Chastity Close by her mimicking juniors). Here she gave her Sunday teas, known as PSAs (pleasant Sunday afternoons). At the suggestion of Cox, on Tuesdays she served tea from her perfectly appointed table to the wives of Arab notables. They met in her large garden, where she cultivated roses and imposed English garden staples—daffodils, hollyhocks and chrysanthemums—on Baghdad's arid landscape with the same fierceness she would apply as imperial taskmaster to the "few really first class shaikhs who will assume responsibility and preserve order." [10]

In 1914, A. T. Wilson had written, "I should like to see it announced that Mesopotamia was to be annexed to India as a colony for India and Indians"—its desert wastes peopled "with martial races from the Punjab." [11] He believed that under direct rule, it would become "a shining jewel in the British crown." [12] The defense of its territory would require the incorporation of all the former Ottoman provinces of Baghdad, Basra, and Mosul. True, Mosul had been promised to France, but it already looked as if it might turn out to be oil-rich (drilling would begin in 1927), and its revenues could be used to finance the emerging country. But the publication in November 1918 of the Anglo-French Declaration, which spoke of a "complete and final liberation" of former parts of the Ottoman Empire, including Syria and Mesopotamia, encouraged the belief that local populations would have a voice in choosing their governments. Wilson, now Acting Civil Commissioner, was horrified, while Bell noted that the declaration threw things into a "ferment."

Bell, writing to her father, opined, "It doesn't happen often that people are told that their future as a State is in their hands and asked what they would like." But on two points practically everyone agreed: "They want us to control their affairs and they want Sir Percy as High Commissioner. Beyond that all is divergence. Most of the town people want an Arab Amir but they can't fix upon the individual. My belief is (but I don't yet know) that the tribal people in the rural districts will not want any Amir so long as they can have Sir Percy—he has an immense name among them—and personally I think that would be best. It's an immense business setting up a court and a power." [13]

Her relations with her chief began to deteriorate as their views on Iraq's future diverged further. Wilson delegated her to represent British interests at the Paris Peace Conference. Once there, she came under the influence of T. E. Lawrence and met with his protégé, the Emir Faisal. Always susceptible to crushes, she was impressed by Faisal's hawk-like visage, intelligence, and sly humor, his simplicity and sincerity sometimes articulated in the pleasing French he had acquired at school in Constantinople.

On her way back from Paris she visited Damascus, where she admitted that "the Arab Govt. is all round perceptibly worse than that of the Turks."[14] In her report *Syria in October 1919*, she reiterated that the local government left much to be desired, but if the Arabs failed, it would be due to "British indifference and French ambition." She concluded that the British had no other choice than to support Arab self-government in Mesopotamia.

The mandates for former Ottoman lands were parceled out at San Remo in April 1920: Arabia would remain independent, Syria would go to France, Mesopotamia and Palestine to the British. There was a misunderstanding about the translation of the word *mandate* into Arabic. It produced the same effect as the word *protectorate* did in Egypt. Even A. T. Wilson thought the word most unfortunate, and when news reached Iraq, the nationalists were encouraged to claim immediate and complete independence without a mandate. Winston Churchill's "ungrateful volcano" erupted. Nationalists sought complete independence, and in May, during the month of Ramadan, there were demonstrations in Baghdad; clerics in both Sunni and Shia mosques preached jihad. The revolt spread down the Euphrates. Shiite leaders incited their followers in Najaf, Karbala, and Kadhimain; Faisal's agents crossed over from Syria. Only Baghdad remained calm, partly from the efforts of Sayyid Talib, son of the Naqib (Governor) of Basra, recently returned to Iraq after years of British-enforced exile in India. About the situation in the capital, a chastened Bell remarked, "It's very significant that there should be so few 'wise' people in Baghdad—i.e. people who want a British mandate. No one knows exactly what they do want, least of all themselves, except that they don't want us."[15]

At the height of the revolt, in late July, Faisal was dispatched from Syria at bayonet point by the French, and relations between the acting commissioner and his deputy irretrievably soured when Gertrude Bell became the ousted Syrian king's indispensable champion in Baghdad. But this volte-face would bring her directly into conflict with Wilson, who blamed Lawrence and Faisal for Iraq-Syria border problems. But on one point she agreed with her chief: more troops were needed. Wilson could not expect to govern 150,000 square miles with seventy police officers, but withdrawal was the worst option: "If we leave this country to go to the dogs it will mean that we shall have to reconsider our whole position in Asia. If Mesopotamia goes, Persia goes inevitably, and then India. And the place which we leave empty will be occupied by seven devils a good deal worse than any which existed before we came."[16]

Churchill, undoubtedly egged on by Lawrence's articles critical of Wilson in *The Times*, vented his own frustration with Wilson in an unsent letter to Prime Minister David Lloyd George: "It is an extraordinary thing that the British civil administration should have succeeded in such a short time in alienating the whole country to such an extent that the Arabs have laid aside the blood feuds that they have nursed for centuries and that the Suni and Shiah tribes are working together. We have even been advised locally that the best way to get our supplies up the river would be to fly the Turkish flag, which would be respected by tribesmen." [17] Bell commented further, "I suppose we have underestimated the fact that this country is really an inchoate mass of tribes which can't as yet be reduced to any system. The Turks didn't govern and we have tried to govern . . . and failed." [18]

The insurgency in "Mess-pot" lasted several months. It was finally quelled when Wilson forbade meetings in mosques and imposed a general curfew. The cost was ten thousand Arabs dead, an estimated nine thousand from RAF bombs, many on civilian targets, several hundred British and Indian casualties, and a bill of £50 million. "The wild drive of discontented nationalism from Syria and of discontented Islam from Turkey might have proved too much for us however farseeing we may have been," wrote Bell "but that doesn't excuse us for having been so blind." [19]

The end of the revolt marked the end of Wilson and his attempt to Indianize Mesopotamia, the end of the military regime, and the beginning of an Arab provisional government. Expectations in England ran high, from Bell's reading of the papers: "It would appear that Sir Percy has only to say 'Hey Presto' for an Arab Govt to leap onto the stage, like another Athene springing from the forehead of Zeus. You may say, if you like, that Sir Percy will play the role of Zeus but his Athene will find the stage encumbered by such trifles as the Shi'ah problem, the tribal problem and other matters, over which even a goddess might easily stumble. But if he's not a Zeus he is a very skilful physician and one in whom his patient has implicit confidence." [20]

Elections had been promised but not held. Instead, Percy Cox asked Bell and Philby to assemble a provisional government. This included choosing a cabinet, most of whose ministers, following Ottoman practice, would come from the minority Sunnis. The Naqib of Baghdad became Prime Minister, and as Bell noted in February, the Mesopotamian officers who had been in Syria with Faisal began to return, the first to come being Nuri Pasha, Ja'far's brother-in-law:

It's true that Ja'far himself is one of them, but good fellow as he is and animated by the highest ideals, he lacks force. He is naturally very easy going, colossally fat, with a beaming smile; he responds at once to friendliness and sympathy and at once gives you his confidence. The wonder is that a man of his mental and physical characteristics should be so ardent in his political convictions. But he doesn't carry over the footlights. He has not succeeded, though he has tried, in getting hold of the young extremists of Baghdad and convincing them of our integrity, as he is convinced of it. They say "Oh you've become an Englishman" and though they regard him kindly, they don't listen to him. Very different is his brother in law Nuri. . . . The moment I saw him, exceedingly slender and lithe, with a small pointed face and grey eyes that gradually awoke as he talked, I realized that we had before us a strong and supple force with which we must either work or engage in difficult combat—too difficult for victory.[21]

Nuri concurred with Bell that no one but Faisal could be the ruler of Iraq, as the British were now calling Mesopotamia.

EVERYONE WHO WAS ANYONE IN THE MIDDLE EAST king-making business gathered in Cairo for a two-week conference that began on Saturday, 12 March 1921. Before the conference began, Britain's economy had collapsed, yet the British taxpayer continued to bear the costs of invading Russia; occupying Constantinople, Palestine, and Egypt; keeping open the routes to India; and, nearer home, policing Ireland. Even *The Times,* normally the house organ of imperialism, urged, "We must evacuate Mesopotamia while we can, and now is the moment," in a series of articles, reasoning that "so long as we stay there will ever be a fresh reason for staying, and a fresh reason for spending. Let us arise and go."[22]

The Empire was overstretched. There was little enthusiasm for further imperial adventures. But if Mesopotamia was not to be abandoned, there was a need for some kind of military force, even though Churchill had confessed that the army was "extremely weak and maintained with great difficulty and expense and we have not secured a single friend among the local powers."[23]

Middle East policy had been consolidated under Churchill as the new Colonial Secretary. He believed that the cost of maintaining Mesopotamia was excessive: "Apart from its importance as a link in the aerial route to India and the air defense of the Middle East, and apart from the military significance of the oil deposits," Churchill had written when submitting his Army Estimates for 1920, "the General Staff are not pressing for the retention of Mesopotamia, or any part of it, on strategic grounds of Imperial security."[24] Commenting further to Lloyd George, he felt it "gratuitous" to squander slender military resources and pour "armies and treasure into these thankless deserts."[25]

Among the topics for discussion at the Cairo Conference were the future of the new entities of Palestine and Transjordan; how to protect British oil interests in Persia; how to cobble the three Ottoman provinces of Mesopotamia—Basra, Baghdad and Mosul—together on the cheap, utilizing airpower instead of ground forces; and how to maneuver a malleable monarch onto the throne of Iraq, against the wishes of an intransigent indigenous population.[26] The conference would mark the apogee of the formulation of post-war British Middle Eastern policy.

Cairo's "forty thieves," as Churchill dubbed the delegates, were split between two committees: one political, with the Colonial Secretary presiding, and one military. From the outset, it appeared to the politicos that Lawrence, who was assisting Churchill, had trumped the ousted A. T. Wilson, and that the notion of Arab self-government had triumphed over outright annexation. The unanimous conclusion at Cairo would be to offer the throne to Faisal, who promised "the best and cheapest solution." Furthermore, in exchange for giving up his claim to Iraq, his older brother, Abdullah—plump, affable, and so Westernized that a copy of the Paris daily *Figaro* arrived on his doorstep most weekdays—was being auditioned by the British for the crown in neighboring Transjordan.

Before the Military Committee, Air Marshal Sir Hugh Trenchard outlined his proposals for the control of Mesopotamia: eight Royal Air Force squadrons, including two bombing units, would be backed up by three British armored-car companies. Airplanes were a more discreet method of intimidation than ground forces, as one RAF officer explained: "One objective must be selected—preferably the most inaccessible village of the most prominent tribe which it is desired to punish . . . The attack with bombs and machine-guns must be relentless and unremitting and carried on continuously by day and night, on houses, inhabitants, crops, and cattle. No news travels like bad news. The news would travel like wildfire." Threats would prove efficacious "if the lesson is properly learnt."[27] The goal was to bring down the staggering costs of garrisoning the country by employing local Arab forces and reducing the number of British troops from nearly ninety thousand to fifteen thousand.

The Political Committee also discussed the possibility of a separate Kurdistan, which would act as a buffer state between Turkey and Iraq. Churchill did express some concerns—rightly so—about how the Kurds would fare under a Hashemite ruler backed by an Arab army, but the committee decided that a viable Iraq would need to be composed of all three provinces. After the conference concluded, Churchill sent a cable informing Prime Minister Lloyd George: "Prospects Mesopotamia promising."[28] He felt able to assure the House of Commons that his basic goals had been attained: in Iraq, occupation forces would be substantially reduced; strategic air routes had been secured; and costs to taxpayers would fall by £5 million in the first year, £12 million in the second. "The ungrateful volcano" might yet become a model of constitutional Arab rule and a friendly ally. Describing the mandate as "all this obsolescent rigmarole," he accepted it pragmatically.

"It has been wonderful," Bell confided to a friend. "Mr Churchill was admirable, most ready to meet everyone half way and masterly alike in guiding a big meeting and in conducting the small political committees into which we broke up. Not the least favorable circumstance," she claimed, "was that Sir Percy and I, coming out with a definite programme, found when we came to open our packets that it coincided exactly with that which the S[ecretary] of S[tate] had brought with him. The general line adopted is, I am convinced, the only right one, the only line which gives real hope of success."[29]

Bell returned from the Cairo Conference in a "fever pitch of excitement," primed to begin her new career as kingmaker.[30] But despite Churchill's energy and eloquence, despite the admirable hopes expressed by Lawrence and Gertrude Bell, and despite Sir Percy Cox's evident popularity as Iraq's inaugural High Commissioner, the British failed. The fault lay not in the stars, but in the British assumption of gratitude on the part of a new, barely cohering Iraqi nation. Bell admitted that the imposition of Faisal came not from strength but from weakness. "The tribes of the Euphrates," she wrote to Cornelius Van H. Engert, an American diplomat stationed in Tehran, "discouraged by the failure of the rising which they now regard as a relapse into madness, are also bewildered to find that the sharif's house which last year (so they were told) was anxious to turn us out, is now regarded by us as a suitable source from which an amir might spring."[31]

Bell was willing to overlook the part that Faisal, the Pashas, and their agents had played in stirring up the recent revolutionary fever. In the same letter, she describes Faisal as "a man of high principles and high ideals."[32] She believed, as Lawrence did, that once Iraqi chiefs met the charismatic claimant to the new throne, they would be impressed. After all, Emir Faisal was a direct descendent of the Prophet, a leader of the Arab Revolt, and a son of the Sharif of Mecca. It was the nearest the British could come to establishing a dynasty whose sons could be sent to Harrow and Sandhurst like proper English royals (and like Sir Percy Cox). Still, the Hashemites were Sunnis, from the dominant branch of Islam. The underclass Shiites, who constituted a majority in Iraq, plausibly suspected that the British had promoted Faisal to empower a favored minority.

Gertrude Bell orchestrated Faisal's coronation on 23 August 1921 in the courtyard of the Baghdad Serai, where, wearing her CBE star and three war ribbons, she caught his eye and gave him a "tiny salute."[33] With the help of her father, she was busy inventing traditions: Bell designed a new flag, a heraldically accurate coat of arms, and a national anthem, although the band played "God Save the King" at the coronation. For a few years after this, Elizabeth Monroe wrote, "Gertrude retained her close relationship with Faisal, rode with him, furnished his houses, fixed protocol for the royal ladies, advised him on ladies-in-waiting for his queen, or on who to see next. She valued his friendship so much that she felt profoundly disturbed when she reckoned that he was temporizing with factions, and behaving in a way she thought unworthy."[34]

To Bell's surprise and dismay, once enthroned, Faisal opposed ratifying a treaty that would establish Britain as Iraq's mandatory master and entrench British rights. For the new King, a foreigner with no real following in the country, quickly discovered that attacking the British was the theme most likely to unite his subjects in foot-stamping cheers. A frustrated Cox was now describing his protégé as "crooked and insincere."[35] In a tea-time interview with the King in June 1922, Bell deplored his support for the "most ignoble extremists" and candidly described to her parents his purported lack of character: "With the highest ideals, he will trip every moment over the meanest obstacle—he has hitched his wagon to the stars, but with such a long rope that it gets entangled in every thicket."[36] An unhappy Bell told the King, "I had formed a beautiful and gracious image and I saw it melting before my eyes. Before every noble outline had been obliterated, I preferred to go; in spite of my love for the Arab nation and my sense of responsibility for its future, I did not think I could bear to see the evaporation of the dream which had guided me."[37] She had played her last card.

Finally, having obtained face-saving assurances that Britain favored Iraq's prompt accession as a sovereign member of the League of Nations, Faisal prevailed on his parliament to ratify the unpopular treaty. But the British held the trump cards: the High Commissioner would still exercise the right of veto, and Britain would control Iraq's foreign affairs and finance and defense policies.

Churchill continued to view Faisal as a British vassal: "We cannot accept the position of Feisal having a free hand & sending in the bill to us," he had written to Cox in 1921, "but while we have to pay the piper we must be effectively consulted as to the tune."[38] Two years later, Churchill could conclude that the Cairo gambit had paid off: "Our difficulties and our expenses have diminished with every month that has passed. Our influence has grown, while our armies have departed."[39] Departing also was the all-important Sir Percy, who retired in 1923.

BELL HAD A COMFORTABLE HOUSE ADORNED WITH CHINTZES, Persian carpets, Sumerian shards, servants, two saluki dogs, a white pony, the occasional pet gazelle, and a life devoted to rounds of picnics, swims in the Tigris, gymkhanas, shooting parties, balls, teas, and bridge—all of which defined British expatriate life. But with less to do officially, Bell assumed a new role as Honorary Director of Antiquities of the Baghdad Museum, housed within the royal palace. She supervised digs and portioned out finds among Baghdad, London, and Philadelphia. While flattered by her title, she knew that her position was temporary—the director should be a trained museum official and know cuneiform.

Increasingly, Bell felt lonely and depressed, her letters home alternating between sanguine hope and bitter despair. Faisal no longer consulted her. "Except for the museum, I am not enjoying life at all," she wrote to a friend. "One has the sharp sense of being near the end of things with no certainty as to what, if anything, one will do next. It is also very dull, but for the work. . . . It is a very lonely business living here now."[40] She was frequently ill, and on her last visit home, in 1925, her London doctors counseled her to avoid the taxing climate of Iraq. But returning to England seemed out of the question: "I don't care to be in London much . . . I like Baghdad, and I like Iraq. It's the real East, and it's stirring; things are happening here, and the romance of it all touches me and absorbs me.[41]

On the evening of 11 July 1926, three days before her fifty-eighth birthday, leaving no note but known to be depressed, she swallowed a lethal dose of pills and died in her sleep. Bell was given the honor of a military funeral, and thousands of Arabs followed her coffin to the British cemetery in Baghdad as it was borne by her British colleagues. In London, a memorial service was held at St. Margaret's Church, Westminster.

IN 1932, A SOVEREIGN IRAQ BECAME THE FIRST Arab member of the League of Nations. But this occurred only after Nuri Pasha had negotiated a treaty that gave the British air bases, granted them the exclusive right to supply weapons and train the Iraqi army, and exempted British military personnel from Iraqi taxes and laws. Secured by British bayonets, Iraq was at best a pseudo-democracy.[42] In 1936, Ghazi, Faisal's son and successor, supported a military coup led by General Bakr Sidqi, which replaced the civilian government with the military. When Ja'far, the outgoing Minister of Defense, tried to head off the coup by driving out north of Baghdad to find Bakr, four army officers stopped the car and shot the Pasha dead. The coup was the first in a long series that were to take place in the Arab world (Ghazi died in a mysterious car accident in 1939, local rumors said on the orders of Nuri Pasha at the behest of the British, who feared that the King entertained Nazi sympathies). The government proved equally fragile: between Faisal's accession to the throne, in 1921, and the murder of his grandson in 1958, fifty-seven ministries took office

In 1954, the Baghdad Pact, which included Iraq, Turkey, Iran, Pakistan, and Great Britain, was established, its aim being to counter Egyptian President Gamal Nasser's influence as well as Syria's. In 1955, the British withdrew their last forces from Iraq. Belatedly, Prime Minister Nuri al-Said served notice on the British that they could not interfere in pact affairs, and he offered help to Nasser. When anti-Hashemite, pro-Nasser violence erupted in Mosul, Najaf, Kut, and Baghdad, Nuri instituted martial law, suspended parliament, and threw hundreds of his opponents into jail. A bloody climax occurred on 14 July 1958, when troops loyal to Brigadier Abd al-Karim Qassem surrounded the villa that served as the royal palace and set fire to it. The royal family fled to the basement. Ordered out at gunpoint, the Regent—Faisal II—and other members of the family were machine-gunned to death. Nuri crept out of his house disguised as a woman, but someone in the mob spotted his pajamas under his dress. He was stripped, killed, castrated, and dismembered, his legless trunk dragged through the streets behind a truck. According to Baghdad reports, all members of Nuri's family, including his Egyptian wife and their two children, were also killed.[43]

Mercifully, Gertrude Bell herself was spared the grisly epilogue that claimed the Iraqi leadership she had striven so steadfastly to empower. Still, one suspects she would not have been surprised by the coup. And her hopes for Iraq were to be grievously mocked by the rise of Saddam Hussein and, in the knife's final twist, by the trashing and sacking in 2003 of the Baghdad Museum she had founded, even as triumphant U.S. occupation forces passively looked on.

Spring Semester 2009

1. Gertrude Bell to Hugh Bell, 1 Nov. 1920, available online at http://www. gerty.ncl.ac.uk. Except as otherwise noted, all citations to Gertrude Bell's correspondence are to this source.

2. Marguerite Harrison, "Gertrude Bell: A Desert Power," *New York Times,* 18 July 1926.

3. Gertrude Bell to Hugh Bell, 8 June 1917.

4. Jan (neé James) Morris, introduction to *The Letters of Gertrude Bell,* (Harmondsworth, 1987), p. vi.

5. Janet (Hogarth) Courtney, quoted in Elizabeth Monroe, "Gertrude Bell (1868–1926)," *Bulletin (British Society for Middle Eastern Studies),* 7, 1 (1980), p. 4.

6. Gertrude Bell to Hugh Bell, 16 Jan. 1916.

7. Quoted in Janet Wallach, *Desert Queen: The Extraordinary Life of Gertrude Bell, Adventurer, Adviser to Kings, Ally of Lawrence of Arabia* (New York, 1996), p. 160.

8. Monroe, "Gertrude Bell," p. 19.

9. H. S. J. Philby, *Arabian Days* (London, 1948), p. 103.

10. Gertrude Bell to Hugh Bell, 8 Feb. 1918.

11. A. T. Wilson, Nov. 1914, quoted in Wallach, *Desert Queen,* p. 159.

12. Quoted in Philby, *Arabian Days,* p. 188.

13. Gertrude Bell to Hugh Bell, 28 Nov. 1918.

14. Gertrude Bell, 12 Oct. 1919.

15. Gertrude Bell to Hugh Bell, 30 Aug. 1920.

16. Gertrude Bell to Florence Bell, 10 Apr. 1920.

17. Winston Churchill, 31 Aug. 1920 (Chartwell 16/48), quoted in Christopher Catherwood, *Churchill's Folly: How Winston Churchill Created Modern Iraq* (New York, 2004), p. 88.

18. Gertrude Bell, 20 Aug. 1920.

19. Gertrude Bell to Florence Bell, 5 Sep. 1920.

20. Gertrude Bell to her parents, 10 Oct. 1920.

21. Gertrude Bell to Hugh Bell, 24 Feb. 1921.

22. *The Times,* 27, 28, and 29 Dec. 1921, quoted in Aaron Kleiman, *Foundations of British Policy in the Arab World: The Cairo Conference* (Baltimore, 1970), p. 240.

23. Churchill, Cabinet Memorandum, 16 Dec. 1920 (Chartwell 16/53), quoted in Catherwood, *Churchill's Folly,* p. 93.

24. Quoted in Catherwood, *Churchill's Folly,* pp. 74–75.

25. Ibid., p. 87.

26. Cairo Conference Folder 3 FO 371/6350—Cairo Conference No. 1, Mr. Churchill to Colonial Office, received 15 Mar. 1921, copy in St. Antony's Middle East Archives, Oxford.

27. A. N. Wilson, *After the Victorians: The Decline of Britain in the World* (New York, 2005), p. 219.

28. Quoted in Kleiman, *Foundations of British Policy,* chap. 3.

29. Gertrude Bell to Frank Balfour, 25 Mar. 1921.

30. Ibid.

31. Gertrude Bell to Cornelius Engert, 3 Mar. 1921, quoted in Elie Kedourie, *The Chatham House Version* (London, 1970), p. 262.

32. Ibid., p. 263.

33. Gertrude Bell to Hugh Bell, 28 Aug. 1921.

34. Monroe, "Gertrude Bell," pp. 20–21.

35. Quoted in Catherwood, *Churchill's Folly,* p. 197.

36. Gertrude Bell, 4 June 1922.

37. Ibid.

38. Churchill to Cox, 15 Aug. 1921, quoted in Catherwood, *Churchill's Folly*, p. 172.

39. Churchill, "Mesopotamia and the New Government," pp. 696–97, quoted in Kleiman, *Foundations of British Policy*, p. 238.

40. Gertrude Bell to J. M. Wilson, quoted in Susan Goodman, *Gertrude Bell* (Dover, N.H., 1985), p. 114.

41. Quoted in Kerry Ellis, "Queen of the Sands," *History Today*, Jan. 2004, p. 36.

42. Quoted in Kedourie, *Chatham House Rules*, p. 250.

43. James Morris, *The Hashemite Kings* (New York, 1959), p. 178.

21

The Aftermath of
the 1958 Revolution in Iraq

ROBY BARRETT

F rom its inception as a British colonial creation, in 1920, Iraq, then called Mesopotamia, presented an ongoing foreign-policy challenge. Early on, the British government avoided an all-out civil war by only the narrowest of margins, and the out-lays for troops and other support drained British resources. In the 1930s, the extent of Iraq's petroleum resources became apparent, yet sustained political stability eluded the grasp of the British and the Hashemite government in Baghdad. Iraq remained a simmering kettle of ethnic, sectarian, and political factions. Only the specter of British military intervention kept it from boiling over.

The rebellion instigated by Colonel Rashid Ali al-Gaylani in 1941 provides a case in point. With Rommel at the gates of Cairo and the German army marching from one victory to the next, officers in the Iraqi army revolted, assuming that the British government was far too preoccupied to do anything about it. They miscalculated. To recoup their position, the British cobbled together an invasion force, removed the plotters—who received direct support from the Germans and Italians—placed the Hashemite monarch back on the throne, and installed a friendly government. Whether Britain's position in Iraq was critical to either its national survival or its overall position in the Middle East was a moot point; London had decided that that Rashid Ali rebellion would not be allowed to succeed and then had made good on that decision. The crushing of the revolt reinforced the perception that the British were the ultimate arbiters in Iraq.

On 14 July 1958, Iraq dispelled this perception, transforming itself from a British client into an enduring challenge for American foreign policy. Two years earlier, the Suez crisis had shaken U.S. confidence in Britain's conduct of its foreign affairs, and the July coup seemed to further emphasize Britain's inability to protect its own interests in the region, much less those of the Western alliance. British policy toward Qasim's Iraq undermined U.S. confidence even more. Britain's attempts to protect its oil and commercial investments in Iraq placed policy makers in London at loggerheads with Washington. The threat posed by the Communist Party of Iraq (CPI) was the primary issue. From the U.S. perspective, the British appeared willing to tolerate an Arab Soviet satellite on the Persian Gulf in return for short-term economic and commercial gain. For many in the Eisenhower administration, particularly Vice President Nixon, it bordered on lunacy for the British to support the Qasim regime as the best available alternative in Iraq and a customer for continued trade and arms shipments. Those holding Nixon's views believed that unless something was done quickly about the revolutionary regime, it would be only a matter of time until the CPI took complete control. Interestingly, Moscow agreed and shifted its regional focus from the United Arab Republic (UAR) to Iraq, much to the aggravation of UAR President Gamal Abdel Nasser.

The U.S. government knew very little about how Qasim's Iraq actually functioned. The coup had resulted from a highly complex interaction of political, economic, and social forces: it was, in fact, a social revolution carried out by a military and political coup. The Eisenhower administration had to learn the internal dynamics of Iraqi society and politics on the fly. The British, with four decades' experience in the region, sought to use its better understanding to prevent their principal ally from plunging over a cliff and dragging Her Majesty's government along with it. Harold Macmillan and his Foreign Office had to manage not only what was left of British interests in Iraq, but also the United States and its problematic Arab ally Nasser—a challenge by any standard.

The Iraqi drama of 1958 should have been a cautionary tale about intervention in Iraq, but for the willful ignorance of British and American policy makers in 2003. Like the events of 2003, those of 1958 and 1959 occurred during a period of global instability, acute national insecurity, and strident debate over strategies for influencing the developing world. With the launch of *Sputnik* in the late 1950s, the United States first faced an immediate, imminent threat to its existence. Understood in the context of the times, this threat equaled, even exceeded, the insecurity and the fears of Islamic extremism that resulted from the attacks of 11 September 2001. Americans had to come to grips with "duck and cover" reality, in which geography and the strongest navy and air force in the world could not protect them. *Sputnik* meant that American cities were defenseless against an attack by nuclear ballistic missiles. The Soviet Union openly promised to "bury" not only U.S. power and influence but also, based on the rhetoric of its leaders, the nation itself. It appeared that Moscow and its blustering leader, Premier Nikita Khrushchev, had gained the upper hand in the missile race, and, with its powerful allies, was supplanting U.S. influence in the developing world.

Soviet gains in the Middle East were particularly threatening. Moscow had leveraged the 1955 Czech arms deal with Nasser into a rapidly expanding influence across the region, at a time when Middle East petroleum resources were becoming increasingly critical to the West. Against the backdrop of *Sputnik,* the destruction of the Hungarian revolution, the Suez crisis, and the influx of Soviet arms and advisers into the region, President Eisenhower's commitment to defend the Middle East from Soviet aggression, the so-called Eisenhower Doctrine, rang hollow. Suez and its aftermath created a strong sense that the region would succumb to Soviet-backed radical secular nationalism and that Egypt's Nasser was the wave of the future. In the United States, right-wing hand-wringing surged, along with Democrats' criticism of U.S. foreign policy. Political pressure grew to "do something" about the Middle East. It was in this environment that Iraq, the namesake of the pro-Western Baghdad Pact, fell under the sway of a radical nationalist leftist army whose officers' best-organized support came from the powerful CPI. The coup led directly to Anglo-American intervention in Lebanon and Jordan and brought calls from elements within the British and U.S. governments to remove Qasim's government.

THE CORE ISSUE OF ANGLO-AMERICAN RELATIONS WITH IRAQ centered on influence and control or, as has often been the case, the lack of either. Iraq constitutes a crucial pivot between the non-Arab Muslim world and the rest of the Arab world. Geopolitical tension in the Mesopotamian valley, fueled by oil and the competition for political dominance, steadily intensified over the first half of the twentieth century. In the mid-1950s, nationalist and pan-Arab fervor drained what little support had existed for Hashemite Iraq. Nasser was far more popular in Baghdad than the Iraqi government or the British, to whom he was single-mindedly hostile.

After the Suez crisis, the preeminent questions for U.S. and British policy in the Middle East were how to deal with Nasser and, in a broader sense, what secular Arab nationalism actually represented. In the early 1950s, Washington's attempts to co-opt Nasser had failed. After Suez, Nasser emerged as the most influential political figure in the Arab world. Attempts to marginalize or isolate him failed. In early 1958, he engineered the creation of the United Arab Republic, a union of Egypt and Syria led by himself. Unable to isolate Nasser, the Eisenhower administration embarked on a policy of limited, cautious cooperation with the UAR. Secretly, various low-key attempts to foment Arab opposition to the Egyptian leader continued, including the formation of a union between Iraq, Saudi Arabia, and Jordan. Bitter about U.S. Secretary of State John Foster Dulles's perceived "betrayal" at Suez, the British repeatedly warned the Iraqis and Prime Minister Nuri Sa'id to avoid entanglement in any U.S.-sponsored schemes. London believed that the Iraqis were no match for the Egyptians in either propaganda or subversion, and the British had no interest in seeing its political or petroleum investments go up in a conflagration ignited by Dulles.

In addition, the British were nervous about Iraq's efforts to enlist Kuwait into its Arab Union with Hashemite Jordan. London feared that any close alignment between Iraq and Kuwait could become an Iraqi pretext for undermining the latter's sovereignty. Iraqi Prime Minister Nuri Sa'id, a former Ottoman official and army officer, viewed Kuwait, as would his successors, as part of Iraq. Thus, the British had well-founded reasons for opposing any Iraqi cooperation in U.S. schemes that might leave Baghdad out on a limb in a confrontation with Nasser or that might stoke Iraqi ambitions or that might enhance its influence in the Gulf vis-à-vis Kuwait.

Ironically, it was the British, not the Americans, who made the key contribution to the undoing of the Hashemite regime in Baghdad. During the first half of 1958, facing mounting UAR pressure on Lebanon and more specifically on Hashemite Jordan, London acquiesced in Nuri Sa'id's desire to confront Nasser. London indicated to Sa'id that an Iraqi military demonstration near the Syrian border might inhibit the efforts of Colonel Abd-al-Hamid al-Sarraj, who was Nasser's lieutenant and the director of Syrian intelligence, to subvert the governments of Jordan and Lebanon. With this nod from London, Nuri Pasha ordered several Iraqi military units to the Syrian border. This move included stationing a brigade east of Baghdad under the command of Brigadier Qasim. Ignoring normal security precautions, the unit was issued ammunition and routed through rather than around the capital. Longtime plotters against the government, Qasim and his deputy, Colonel Abd-al-Salam al-Aref, made the most of the opportunity. They made an unscheduled stop in Baghdad and overthrew the government. Later governments took heed. Not even Saddam Hussein, with his pervasive, ruthless internal security apparatus, would allow army units to enter Baghdad.

Initially, the United States and Britain assumed that the UAR had orchestrated the coup. This was a logical conclusion. The UAR was actively attempting to subvert Iraq, Lebanon, and Jordan. This perception drove U.S. intervention in Lebanon and British support of Jordan. While Nasser and the Syrians may have inadvertently caused the coup, in point of fact Cairo was as much in the dark as Washington and London. Within a matter of days, the British realized that Nasser, who was in Moscow lobbying for Soviet support to combat "Western aggression," was probably not pulling the strings behind the Iraqi enterprise. London determined that Iraqi nationalists, many of whom were as hostile to Nasser and his vision for the UAR as they were to the old Hashemite regime, dominated the Qasim government. Although the new government included Nasserists and Ba'thists, the communists and Qasim were opposed to any real union or, for that matter, cooperation with Nasser.

IN BAGHDAD, DURING THE EARLY HOURS OF COUP, rebel army units rounded up and executed all the members of the royal family that they could find. Rioting and looting broke out, some of it orchestrated by the coup plotters themselves, but much of it spontaneous. British and Western installations and expatriates became targets of Iraqi mobs, which attacked and burned the British Embassy, killing the British defense attaché in the process. The chaos endangered the new regime in its infancy because it threatened to spark British intervention. Qasim understood this. Not wanting to repeat the experience of Rashid Ali's rebel government of 1941, Qasim issued shoot-on-sight orders against rioters and looters and ruthlessly imposed order. He quickly apologized for the destruction of the British Embassy and shrewdly promised to honor Anglo-Iraqi oil agreements. The new Iraqi leadership also guaranteed the safety of foreigners.

The restoration of order and the promise to recognize oil agreements had the desired effect in London. The British preferred to work something out with Qasim in order to avoid the risks and expense of an invasion. However, the burned embassy, the dead defense attaché, and the slaughter of the Hashemite family and Prime Minister Nuri Sa'id, a loyal supporter of Britain, put London in an awkward position. Intervention was risky, particularly with the old leadership dead, so a more practical course was chosen. The British shed a few tears for past supporters, awarded a posthumous medal to the dead attaché, and set about making friends with the new government. In a strategy memo, the Foreign Office summed up the cold pragmatism of the Macmillan government: "It looks as if the new regime is in firm control. The sooner we can get on to proper terms with it the better. Its present intentions seem respectable, particularly as regards the oil and direct Anglo-Iraqi relations. Of course we cannot immediately condone the murders and the burning of the Embassy, but soon after the Baghdad Pact meeting we ought to extend recognition of the regime."[1]

British Iraq had been effectively eliminated, but the new government under Qasim appeared to be a surprisingly acceptable alternative. The British not only received assurances from Qasim about the Iraqi Petroleum Company (IPC), but also concluded that Qasim would pursue a policy line independent of Nasser. Despite later comments by Macmillan that Britain had had no ability to intervene, a Nasserist takeover in Baghdad might have brought a very different reaction from London. For the British, the strong support of the CPI for Qasim was problematic, but preferable to Iraq's alignment with Nasser. London checked the economic bottom line, swallowed its pride, and moved to support the new leader.

Macmillan and his advisers began to devise strategies that would enhance Qasim's ability to act independently of his communist, Nasserist, and Ba'thist supporters. Early on, the British pressed for U.S. concurrence in the resumption of weapons shipments to Iraq. The new British Ambassador in Baghdad, Sir Humphrey Trevelyan, summed up the benefits of supporting Qasim; "Conversely a refusal [to ship weapons] would be profoundly depressing and demoralizing to Qasim's anti-communist supporters who want to retain links with the West. It might indeed have the effect of just pushing Qasim himself over the communist brink. Her Majesty's government therefore believes that the action they are taking is in the best interests of the Middle East as a whole."[2] The alternative—namely, a reconquest—was not impossible but rather impractical. In addition, London, well aware of the fractious nature of Iraq and the elimination of key members of the old regime, had no stomach for trying to build a nation from scratch and again risking the near disaster of 1920.

Despite assertions by Colonial Office officials that the credibility of the British government required the immediate removal of the Qasim regime, London took a remarkably pragmatic position. In August, the Foreign Office summarized London's new strategy for the region: "We hold on to the Gulf. We establish the best relations we can with the new regime in Iraq. We try to 'neutralize' the Lebanon and Jordan in such a way as to permit the withdrawal of United States and United Kingdom forces as soon as possible. We improve our relations with Israel. Our relations with Egypt are not affected, i.e. we work for a return to cool normality. We try to reconstitute the Baghdad Pact as a Northern Tier without Iraqi participation." The Foreign Office went on to say,

> It is essential in the interests of the maintenance of our economy and standard of living to maintain our control of British oil interests in the Gulf, more particularly Kuwait. . . . Hold the Gulf States. It is militarily feasible. It is expected of us by the Americans, who will probably take parallel action themselves as regards Dhahran if need arises. It is perhaps even desirable to hold Kuwait in the interests of our relations with the new regime in Iraq; if the Arab nations control completely all the sources of Arab oil they can hold us to ransom, but so long as the Iraqis know that we can do without Iraqi oil if necessary, by relying on Kuwait, they have a strong inducement to come to terms with us."[3]

The British understood that, geopolitically and economically, Kuwait was their best leverage on Iraq—the cork in the Iraqi bottle.

British policy also included a blunt statement of what London was willing to do to protect its interests, that is, to intervene if necessary:

> If say, the Ruler of Kuwait returns from Damascus and announces his intention of breaking off his association with us and joining the U.A.R., we are faced with the dilemma of either deposing him and more or less occupying and running Kuwait as a colony, or acquiescing in the loss of the remaining most important source of Middle Eastern oil. We should presumably choose the former alternative, but to do so would run us into serious difficulties with the rest of the Arab world and make our task of returning to normal relations with Iraq more difficult. Nevertheless these difficulties would have to be faced.[4]

Intervention was an acceptable alternative, but only as a last option.

INITIALLY, THE EISENHOWER ADMINISTRATION BELIEVED that the British would topple the new Iraqi regime. Secretary of State

John Foster Dulles fully expected the British to intervene. Initial discussions with British Foreign Secretary Selwyn-Lloyd contributed to this expectation. Eisenhower and Dulles concluded that the Iraqi coup was obviously another Nasserist enterprise and that both Lebanon and Jordan would undoubtedly be next. To prevent this, the United States began deploying troops in Lebanon and pushed the British to support Jordan. As the *Nation* accurately pointed out in an editorial: "The news from Baghdad sent us barging into Lebanon before we had received a second report from the observers— before, indeed, we even knew exactly what was happening in Iraq."[5] London's decision to work with Qasim alarmed Washington. Vice President Nixon summed up the concern, questioning whether the British "considered Nasser a greater danger than the Communists to the Near East."[6]

Congress launched closed-door hearings into the "intelligence failure." The Director of the Central Intelligence Agency (CIA), Allen Dulles, blamed the British, but when he could not offer insight into the Qasim government, Senator J. William Fulbright accused him of "fumbling in the dark."[7] The coup, the criticism, and the communist threat pushed Iraq to the top of the intelligence agenda. It placed enormous pressure on Allen Dulles. In addition, Foster Dulles's close relationship with Eisenhower provided the CIA Director with an unprecedented level of political protection. In the winter of 1959, the Secretary of State's colon cancer became terminal. This personal loss aside, this meant that the CIA Director no longer had the political cover that he had historically enjoyed. Not wanting to be accused of another failure, the CIA began reporting on Iraq in a steadily more ominous tone. If the communists were to take over, no one would be able to say that the CIA had not predicted it.

On 22 December 1958, William Rountree, of the State Department's Bureau of Near Eastern Affairs (NEA), wrote, "The growth of Communist influence in the Qassim government has been of such rapidity and extensiveness as to cause serious alarm both to non-Communist nationalists in Iraq and to the United Arab Republic." Rountree then raised the question of "mutual accommodation with Nasser regarding Iraq."[8] On 17 February 1959, a Special National Intelligence Estimate (SNIE) concluded that Qasim lacked the "ability to stem the movement toward a Communist takeover."[9] In Baghdad, U.S. Ambassador John D. Jernegan reported a "grave danger" that in "the short run" Iraq would "come under predominantly Communist control."[10]

In the fall of 1958, Washington began to realize that Nasser had not been the hidden hand behind the July coup. Nasserists and

Ba'thists found themselves under attack by Qasim and his CPI supporters. Aggravating as Nasser was, the Egyptian leader had established his anticommunist credentials with a merciless assault on
communists in both Syria and Egypt. Unhappy with Soviet support
for Iraq, Nasser now engaged in a heated war of words with both
Qasim and Khrushchev. Nasser had concluded that Qasim was the
most immediate threat to his leadership of the pan-Arab movement.
In discussions with Rountree, Nasser offered "a scarcely-veiled invitation to collaborate on Iraq."[11] Washington quickly shifted from
alarm over Nasserist plots in the region to encouraging Nasser's
propaganda war against, and subversion of, the Qasim regime.
Eisenhower likened it to an unappealing choice between "John Dill-
inger and Al Capone."[12]

THIS SITUATION CREATED A STRAIN in Anglo-American relations.
Intent on protecting their oil investment, the British preferred to
gamble on Qasim. Vice President Nixon complained, "The British
thought they could make a deal with the Iraqi Communists."[13] In
Baghdad, British Ambassador Trevelyan stated, "One of our main
problems is how to improve relations between the Americans and
Qasim."[14] The Macmillan government pressed Washington to rein
in Nasser's attempts to destabilize the Qasim regime. For its part,
the Eisenhower administration ignored British requests and encouraged Nasser's anti-Qasim efforts. As the State Department explained, "While we have not directly linked with Nasser's present
campaign against communism the steps we have recently taken to
aid Egypt, there is no doubt that Nasser knows that we have taken
these steps as a sign of approval of his current campaign and that
they have emboldened him in his anti-Communist efforts."[15]

Using the February National Intelligence Estimate for support,
CIA Director Dulles told the National Security Council on 5 March
1959 that "events seem to be moving in the direction of ultimate
Communist control."[16] Then, on 6 March, a planned communist
rally in Mosul brought events in Iraq to a head. With the support
of Nasser's henchman in Syria, Colonel Abd-al-Hamid al-Sarraj, pro-Nasser elements in Mosul under Colonel Abd-al-Wahhab
al-Shawwaf launched a premature coup. It failed, and Qasim allowed the communists to run amok, hanging regime opponents
from lampposts. Nationalists and pan-Arabists were eliminated from
the government, and the communists began to pressure Qasim for
more cabinet positions, including key roles in the military and security services, and for the creation of peoples' militias.

The propaganda war escalated. Baghdad Radio labeled Nasser
the "foster son of American imperialism" and Washington's "chosen

instrument." Nasser countered by declaring that Qasim had delivered Iraq into the "hands of the Communists." In a typical tirade, Nasser declared, "If a Communist State is established, the Communists will smite down all patriotic and nationalist elements—or eliminate them, as we say—by inventing incidents until they get rid of all these elements and will then establish a Red terrorist dictatorship in which subservience prevails."[17] For once, Washington and its "chosen instrument" on the Nile absolutely agreed.

The failure of the Mosul coup shook Washington. The Eisenhower administration had pegged its hopes in Iraq on a successful pro-Nasserist coup. Dying of cancer, Foster Dulles resigned as Secretary of State. Vice President Nixon, the presumed Republican nominee in 1960, took on an expanded foreign-policy role. Believing that the foreign-policy apparatus, and the State Department in particular, was being too cautious in the face of communist gains, he pressed for a more aggressive approach to Iraq. Nixon chaired an NSC meeting on 17 April 1959. Nixon questioned Rountree for stating that although "the U.S. could not tolerate a Communist take-over in Iraq," he refused to support intervention. Nixon pointedly commented that if the State Department analysis were taken at face value, "there was really nothing that the U.S. could do to prevent the worst from happening." Some wanted to be "invited" into Iraq, but Nixon observed that after a communist takeover, there would be "no one left to invite us or anyone else to intervene."[18]

Rountree responded, "The revulsion against any government set up under [U.S.] aegis would be so great that it would probably be swept away and its replacement would in all likelihood be a Communist government. Thus for this reason alone we cannot advocate this course, apart from the long standing United States principles which would be violated by what would in effect be unprovoked United States aggression and apart from the catastrophic psychological reaction throughout Africa and Asia which would inevitably portray us as being worse aggressors than the Communists."[19] Trying to appease the Vice President, Rountree offered the alternative of encouraging the UAR, stating "military action would consist of infiltration of U.A.R. military forces into Iraq to work hand in hand with dissident forces." After additional discussion, the meeting adjourned with a decision to examine options and "courses of action."[20]

At the next NSC meeting, predictions about Iraq were dire, but the limits of U.S. action remained tightly drawn. When asked what happened following the Nixon-led NSC meeting on 17 April, General Andrew Goodpaster, the President's chief of staff, stated that he had informed Eisenhower by telephone of the thrust of Nixon's apparent position and that Eisenhower had absolutely rejected immediate overt or covert intervention. Eisenhower's innate conservatism and experience triumphed over any possibility of precipitous, ideologically driven activism.

Eisenhower pushed for, and London welcomed, a joint working group on Iraq. London saw it as a means of influencing U.S. policy. In June 1959, a Cabinet paper entitled "The Status Quo" outlined London's position: "We should avoid appearing to push them (the US) into a decision one way or the other."[21] If U.S. intervention appeared imminent, London would then decide whether to try to discourage it. The paper concluded: "It has always been our appreciation that our interests are best likely to be served by Qasim's maintaining himself in a position dependent neither on the Communists nor on the pro-Nasserites and able to pursue a central and neutralist line of policy. . . . So long as Qasim remains in power and continues to give evidence of his intention to maintain the independence of Iraq we should not countenance, still less encourage, any designs against him from any quarter."[22] The British intended to avoid intervention.

In June, Eisenhower and Macmillan were rewarded. In direct contradiction of the 17 February SNIE, a 30 June SNIE concluded: "We now feel that our recent SNIE's have been too gloomy. . . . We now think Communist control of Iraq is less likely."[23] What had happened? The communists overplayed their hand. In the immediate aftermath of the Mosul coup, Qasim appointed more communists to the government but resisted key communist demands. Qasim turned his attention to the CPI. In May and June 1959, the communists found their power being steadily curtailed. In the summer of 1959, when CPI-sponsored demonstrations and mob violence against nationalists broke out, Qasim dismissed several communists in the government and arrested their leaders in a show of strength. Then in a deft political maneuver, Qasim acknowledged a splinter group as the "legitimate" Iraqi communist party. By the fall of 1959, the British policy of supporting Qasim against the CPI had paid off, as had Eisenhower's rejection of intervention.

By its second anniversary, the Iraqi revolution had ground to a halt. Qasim complained to the British that the Americans were organizing a Muslim league to overthrow him. Increasingly unpopular, Qasim tried to distract Iraqis' attention from the moribund economy and political stagnation. He began an anti-imperialist campaign in the Gulf, and then resurrected the Iraqi claim to Kuwait. On 1 May 1961, British Ambassador Trevelyan reported, "We would not read anything immediately sinister" into Qasim's comments about "blood ties" and "no frontier" between Iraq and Kuwait, treating it instead as "a typically unconsidered outburst."[24] In late June, Qasim began to move tanks and troops to the Kuwaiti border. British reaction was swift and decisive. After a request from the Sabah, the Kuwaiti ruling family, the British deployed marine and air units from Bahrain to Kuwait. Ambassador Trevelyan stated that he attached "overriding importance" to the ability to deal effectively with an Iraqi attack, but warned that "the fallout from a military confrontation with Iraq would once again excite anti-British sentiment throughout the Middle East."[25]

The Iraqis backed down, and Arab League forces ultimately replaced the British in Kuwait. In the Egyptian newspaper *Al-Ahram,* Muhammad Heikal wrote, "The original Suez symbolized the victorious struggle for Arab rights but Qasim had, by threatening a small Arab country which had just become independent, produced the incredible situation wherein Saudi and Kuwaiti troops were standing shoulder to shoulder with British Imperialists who had returned with no bloodshed and no shots fired facing an Arab army."[26] As a bonus, Kuwaitis obtained UAR recognition and membership in the Arab League. In Cairo, U.S. Ambassador John Badeau speculated to Nasser that the lack of financial success from Qasim's nationalization of the Iraq Petroleum Company drove the decision. Nasser said, "Yes, you are right, that is what people say, but I don't think that is ultimately what the reason was. I think that one morning Qasim was in the men's room and he met his Chief of Staff and one man said to the other, 'Why don't we take Kuwait?' Then the other man said, '*Wallahi, billahi, tallahi*' [By God that's a good idea, let's do it]. That's the way we sometimes reach decisions."[27]

As for Qasim, Nasserist and Ba'thist plotters caught up with him in February 1963. He was summarily executed, along with his closest supporters. In a bloodbath, the plotters utterly destroyed the Communist Party of Iraq. As Hanna Batatu stated, "The Communists fought as only men could fight who knew that no mercy was to be looked for in defeat." King Hussein of Jordan stated that he knew "for a certainty" that the coup had the support of U.S. intelligence. The King also claimed that a "secret radio" provided information on communists so that they could be "arrested and executed." Although an overstatement, it contains a grain of truth. Washington certainly encouraged Qasim's opponents, particularly Nasser. In the end, Eisenhower and even Nixon got exactly what they wanted, and without having to resort to overt intervention.[28]

One can only speculate about what might have ensued in 1959 if a president, inexperienced in foreign and military affairs and unduly influenced by an ideologically driven vice president, had intervened in Iraq. Luckily, Eisenhower knew more than a little about the military, about invasions, about occupations, about choosing and listening to good advisers, and about balancing the interests of the United States. The President also represented the best in an American conservative tradition that favored a pragmatic, risk-adverse foreign policy as well as fiscal responsibility. Knowing what London had created in Iraq, Macmillan saw the situation between Qasim and the communists for what it really was and backed Qasim while shrewdly influencing Eisenhower and contributing to the "wait and see" approach that paid off so handsomely. In 1922, Churchill had told Lloyd George, "We are paying eight millions a year for the privilege of living on an ungrateful volcano out of which we are in no circumstances to get anything worth having."[29] In 1959, an American President at a political low point decided that intervention in Iraq had to truly be a last resort. For forty-five years, Eisenhower's judgment stood as policy. Even after Iraq's invasion of Kuwait in 1990, the United States avoided overt intervention in Iraq. It was frustrating, particularly given the American urge to do something and to fix things, but what was Eisenhower's real alternative? We now have an idea.

Fall Semester 2008

1. "Policy in the Middle East," Shuckburgh to FO, 24 Aug. 1958, PRO, FO 371/132545, p. 7.

2. Telegram, Baghdad to FO, 28 Apr. 1959, No. 429 (Eq1071/21), PRO, FO 371/140957, p. 1.

3. "Policy in the Middle East," 24 Aug. 1958, PRO, FO 371/132545, p. 2.

4. Ibid., p. 5.

5. "What Now?" *Nation,* 2 Aug. 1958, pp. 42–43.

6. Discussion, 404th NSC Meeting, 30 Apr. 1959, Dwight D. Eisenhower Library (DDEL), box 11, pp. 9–10.

7. Allen Dulles, "Briefing on the Middle East Situation," 22 July 1958, *Executive Sessions of the Senate Foreign Relations Committee,* Vol. X, p. 572.

8. Rountree to Dillon, 2 Dec. 1958, *Foreign Relations of the United States, 1958–1960,* Vol. XII, p. 368.

9. SNIE, 17 Feb. 1959, ibid., pp. 381–83.

10. Baghdad to WDC, 26 Mar. 1959, no. 2758, Part 1, DDEL, staff secretary, box 8, pp. 1–2.

11. Memo, Rountree to Dillon, 22 Dec. 1958, *FRUS, 1958–1960,* Vol. XII, p. 370.

12. Remembrance of General Andrew Goodpaster, 8 Aug. 2003.

13. Discussion, 404th NSC Meeting, 30 Apr. 1959, DDEL, box 11, pp. 9–10.

14. Baghdad to FO, 19 July 1959, PRO, FO371/140948, p. 1.

15. Memorandum, Calhoun to Goodpaster, 15 Apr. 1959, DDEL, staff secretary, box 8, pp. 4–5.

16. Discussion, 398th NSC Meeting, 5 Mar. 1959, DDEL, NSC Series, box 11, p. 2.

17. Quoted in Robert Stephens, *Nasser: A Political Biography* (New York, 1971), p. 309.

18. Discussion, 402nd NSC Meeting, 17 Apr. 1959, *FRUS, 1958–1960,* Vol. XII, pp. 423–37.

19. Memorandum, Calhoun to Goodpaster, 15 Apr. 1959, DDEL, staff secretary, box 8, pp. 2–3.

20. Discussion, 402nd NSC Meeting, 17 Apr. 1959, DDEL, NSC Series, box 11, pp. 1, 8–11.

21. Cabinet Paper, "Policy Towards Iraq," 25 June 1959, PRO, CAB 21/5595, pp. 1–4, 5, 13.

22. Ibid.

23. SNIE, 30 June 1959, *FRUS, 1958–1960,* Vol. XII, p. 471.

24. Baghdad to FO, 1 May 1961, PRO, FO371/156833, p. 2.

25. Cairo to FO, 2 July 1961, PRO, FO371/156875, p. 1

26. Ibid.

27. Quoted in John S. Badeau, *The Middle East Remembered* (Washington, D.C., 1983), pp. 205–06.

28. Hanna Batatu, *The Old Social Classes and the Revolutionary Movement of Iraq* (Princeton, 1978), pp. 982–87.

29. Quoted in A. N. Wilson, *After the Victorians: The Decline of Britain in the World* (New York, 2005), p. 204.

22

Comparing British and American "Empires"

A. G. HOPKINS

T he third week of March 2008 marked the fifth anniversary of the invasion of Iraq. The event itself has already galvanized commentators and participants into producing a substantial library of polemics, memoirs, and analyses covering military, political, and international aspects of the war and its aftermath. As yet, however, there have been few attempts to place the episode in its larger historical context. My aim is to outline an interpretation of the last two centuries that, if correct, will provide grounds for believing that the Iraq venture was doomed from the outset. I shall not suggest that this knowledge, had it been considered, would have prevented war, gratifying though such a conclusion would be. It seems to me unlikely that the "lessons of history," even if agreed on by historians, would have been learned—for reasons that I shall touch on later. Nevertheless, if on this occasion a mixture of collective forgetfulness and selective perception trumped historical experience, there is all the more reason for historians to expand their efforts to inform policy makers of their findings. The odds of success may be long, but the consequences of failure are momentous.

The difficulty of re-creating the historical context for understanding the invasion of Iraq stems not so much from the absence of history from the debate over the Iraq war as from the way in which the problem has been conceived. Most commentators have drawn analogies with the past in a random, or at least a highly selective, way, without pausing to reflect on the serious problems of comparing like with like across many centuries. Since the use of history in this connection depends on how the comparative "method" is deployed, I must begin by commenting on some of the numerous pitfalls that can engulf historical generalizations of this kind.

The loftiest level of comparison is characterized by eye-catching selective analogies, which the commentariat has drawn on to suit its varying purposes. The use made of Rome illustrates the infinite malleability of the classical analogy. After the terrorist attacks of 11 September 2001, commentators of various persuasions compared the United States to the Rome of steel and purpose (the Pentagon's Rome), the Rome of the strong state (Roosevelt's or Bush's Rome, according to taste), the Rome of privatization (Reagan's Rome), the Rome of introspective myopia addled by corruption (the Rome of a Congress enamored of earmarks and add-ons) and, inevitably, the Rome of pride, followed by the Rome of imperial overstretch, ruin, and retribution.

These very general allusions have been complemented by references to what appears to be the most relevant detailed comparison: Britain's invasion of Iraq in 1915. This inglorious episode, long known to specialists and Iraqis, was rediscovered by commentators after March 2003. In April 1915, a British force attempted to take control of Mesopotamia, thus striking a blow at Germany's ally, Turkey. General Maude's proclamation following the eventual capture of Baghdad in 1917 has been much cited for its declaration that the British army, like its American successors, had come not as conquerors but as liberators. However, the comparison extends beyond similarities of stated intentions. The episode shows that Britain, like the United States, had an unreflective belief in the justice of its cause, failed to anticipate or understand the opposition its invasion provoked, was ill-equipped to deal with insurgents, was unable to establish a legitimate basis for its presence, lacked an exit strategy, and found itself in a quagmire of its own making.

The similarities, both general and detailed, are striking because they seem so exact. They are also reassuring, even when the news they convey is unwelcome, because they offer guidance at a time when events appear to have slipped their moorings. If our ancestors, however distant, were in a similar mess, then at least we are not alone, in the dark and without a compass; we can consider historical outcomes and steer our course accordingly.

On reflection, however, the "lessons of history" turn out to be more ambiguous than we would like them to be. It is one thing to draw a general moral that advises great leaders not to be too ambitious, not to underestimate their adversaries, and so on, though it is also unlikely that they will take any notice. But the most eminent commentators have higher aspirations: they want to use history to predict the future and to shape policies to control it. At this point, applying history to the present becomes a serious business; it is also accompanied by the considerable risk of misreading the past.

The danger of random selection to suit different political purposes is evident from the use made of analogies to Rome. An even greater hazard takes the form of a fallacy of composition whereby what is true of a part is held also to be true of the whole. The best-known example claims that because Britain, by general agreement, was an empire, the United States, which has some features in common with Britain in terms of its worldwide reach, economic dominance, cultural influence, and so on, is also an empire. This claim appears most prominently in the much publicized and influential work of Niall Ferguson. In Ferguson's view, the United States is the successor to Britain: it is an empire in reality, though not yet in name because it has yet to recognize and accept its role. Since the world has always needed a dominant state, the United States should become the new Rome; global stability could then be guaranteed and the barbarians thrown back from the gates, taking their anarchic purposes with them.

The aggregation of shared features makes it possible to claim that the two units are similar, thus justifying a common label: empire. This is where semantics really does matter. If it can be established that the United States is an empire, it becomes possible to draw comparisons that are relevant for policy making. Britain's decline can then be studied to see how, for example, the United States can avoid the fate of its predecessor. On the other hand, if the United States is not an empire, no comparison is possible beyond the generalities I have referred to that apply eternally to all great powers.

The argument that the United States is an empire rests on two unpersuasive propositions. The first presents a definition of the term that is so broad that it covers virtually all states that have spread beyond their homelands (and therefore includes Venice and the Omani empire). The precision suggested by applying a common term, "empire," is therefore spurious, and the polities so described are too diverse to support policy recommendations designed for the present day. Historically, empires have been hierarchical, territorial organizations that sought to integrate subordinate states and influence their domestic as well as their foreign policies. The United States qualified in a minor way after 1898, but not after 1945, when it became a world power and cast off or incorporated its few colonial possessions. Thereafter, its influence was felt in a more limited and almost entirely informal manner, whereas Britain's informal influence was exercised in association with its huge territorial empire. If the United States is, as has been claimed, "an empire like no other," perhaps it would be better to describe it by another term. All holistic terms have their frailties, but the term "hegemon" more accurately describes the aspirations of the United States to the role of global leader in a world in which, after 1945, empires were being dissolved.

The second proposition is even more dubious. It purports to discern a selection of similarities without reference to the historical context that produced them. This procedure places empires side by side and compares their various capabilities and experiences on the assumption that the passage of time has no significant effect on the validity of the comparison. But Rome and the United States occupied wholly different eras, as did General Maude and General Franks. Britain's era of world dominance is much closer to that of the United States than either power is to the age of Rome. Nevertheless, as I shall try to show, the singularities of context that shaped the world roles of Britain and the United States outweighed the similarities in crucial respects.

This changing context can be thought of as covering two phases of globalization, each characterized by a different type of global polity. The first phase of modern globalization, which ran from around 1800 to around 1950, favored the creation and expansion of empires, and was dominated by Britain. The second phase, which began in the mid-twentieth century and is still with us today, is that of post-colonial globalization, which has witnessed the end of the empires inherited from the nineteenth century and has been dominated by the United States. Different conditions were marked by different motives. Britain's interest as a global power lay primarily in controlling the means of production. The interest of the United States lies primarily in controlling the means of destruction.

BRITAIN WAS A SMALL OFFSHORE ISLAND with an uncertain Irish adjunct. Two considerations long determined its foreign policy: the potential threat from larger Continental neighbors, and a marked dependence on foreign trade. An active foreign policy was mandatory: isolationism was never a serious political proposition. Moreover, Britain was well organized to promote the overseas expansion that was vital to its security and prosperity. It developed a unitary state with a strong central government controlled by a majority party whose leader was also Prime Minister. The political elite that ran the system was a cohesive and outward-looking group, and worked closely with a permanent civil service that guaranteed the continuity needed for long-term projects, such as empire building. The monarch, who was placed permanently at the apex of the structure, was a symbol of imperial as well as national unity. If structure reflects size, as Montesquieu held, the unitary state can be seen as a particular response to the need to mobilize limited resources of manpower against more powerful neighbors and to augment the strength and wealth of the country by expansion overseas.

Britain's economic development was the single most important influence on the world economy during the first phase of modern globalization. The double transformation brought about by the financial and industrial revolutions created a pattern of global specialization that lasted well into the twentieth century: manufactures produced in the metropolis were exchanged for raw materials drawn largely from outside Europe; the two were brought together by British finance and commercial services. By the close of the nineteenth century, Britain stood at the center of an economic, political, and social network that spanned the world. The result was the extension of formal empire and informal influence in the nineteenth century and the installation of a system of imperial management that held the Empire together until the middle of the twentieth century. The sprawling imperial system required considerable start-up and protection costs, but these were necessary investments in a set of global economic relations that were vital to Britain's welfare.

Empire, however, not only molded Britain's economic development; it also helped form the emerging nation-state by shaping the ethos and perpetuating the dominance of the ruling elite, and by creating a broad sense of national identity that fashioned a bond of unity between social classes during the period of unprecedented economic and social change that followed the world's first industrial revolution. Today, globalization presents a challenge to the sovereignty of the nation-state; in the nineteenth century, the relationship was mutually supportive. Luminaries of the time, such as John Stuart Mill, saw the Empire as an extension of the nation, which it both consolidated and reflected. Their view was exemplified by the colonies of white settlement, the Greater Britains overseas, which were intended to replicate Britain's own sociopolitical order. Britain's imprint was found elsewhere in the formal and informal empire, too, where systematic efforts were made to create clusters of like-minded elites who would be standard-bearers of British values.

It used to be customary to suppose that Britain's world position, and hence its imperial system too, began to decline in the late nineteenth century, and was hastened by the effects of the First World War. Revisionist research has challenged this view by attaching new importance to finance and commercial services, which were expanding when manufacturing was losing its share of world production and trade. One consequence of this work has been to reappraise the influence these interests exerted on foreign policy; another has been to doubt the use of industrial performance either as an index of Britain's economic strength or as a proxy for the timing of its decline as a world power. Measured in absolute terms, Britain was less powerful after the First World War than before (depending on what indices are selected), but in relative terms, she remained ahead of her rivals, and by the close of the 1930s was still the only truly world power. Some concessions were made to nationalist aspirations, but Britain safeguarded her key interests and drew the Empire together even more closely during the slump of the 1930s and the world war that followed.

Accordingly, the imperial age remained vibrant at least down to the Second World War and arguably into the 1950s. Empires were familiar occupants of the international terrain, and their presence was legitimated by time, even if not always by consent. But consent had yet to become a cardinal principle of the international order, notwithstanding the cautious advertisement given to the notion of self-determination by President Wilson. Aspiring powers, like Germany and Japan, were keen to join the imperial set: the "haves" and "have-nots," which featured so prominently in the debates of the 1930s, referred not to rich and poor countries but to those that possessed colonies and those that did not. Spokesmen for the haves remained unquestioningly imperial in their attitudes. Their instinctive response to the disaffected powers was to appease them by giving away other people's territory. The diplomacy of the day assumed proprietary rights that were inherited directly from the 1880s, when the map of Africa was redrawn in the corridors of power in Europe. The doctrine of *terra nullius* (land belonging to no one), like the doctrine of racial supremacy, remained a largely unchallenged orthodoxy among the political leaders of the world.

THE SECOND PHASE OF GLOBALIZATION, which began after the Second World War, marked the transition from conditions that favored the creation of empires to those that ensured their downfall. Two world wars and the world slump checked the globalizing impulses that had acquired momentum before 1914. When the process resumed, its character altered. The most important economic change was the growth of trade and financial flows among advanced economies and the corresponding weakening of ties between developed countries and their colonies. The triad of North America, Western Europe, and East Asia became more integrated; the old, imperial lines of connection were reduced or realigned. Countries in the triad of developed states had neither the ambition nor the capacity to colonize one another. Small, poor ex-colonial states could still be recolonized, but, special interests aside, economic motives for doing so were significantly diluted because the ex-colonial world had ceased to be central to the development of advanced countries.

The imprint of post-war globalization extended far beyond the international economy. Winning the war called for a commitment to a set of ideals that, on this occasion, survived the peace. Declarations of support for self-determination, racial equality, and human rights, though rarely implemented with alacrity, could not be set aside easily. The onset of the Cold War elevated the ideological battle for hearts and minds to global status. The foundation of a cluster of international organizations, headed by the United Nations, provided a novel means of advertising these ideals and created agencies for monitoring them.

Ultimately, the colonial powers were forced to concede the principle of self-determination. The United States was obliged, in complementary fashion, to implement civil rights for all its citizens. The principle of racial equality made it impossible to maintain empires founded on the notion of ethnic hierarchies and white supremacy. Violations of human rights in the colonies and in the United States generated adverse publicity at home and abroad. The resumption of international migration after the war contributed to these developments by increasing ethnic diversity in Britain and the white dominions and by adding to the multi-ethnic complexion of the United States. The ideology that had underpinned white supremacy in both the Empire and the republic could no longer be sustained.

These novel ideological prescriptions were not freestanding determinants but were linked to economic and political goals. The growth of the international economy would have been retarded without the free and efficient movement of labor, which depended in turn on the abolition of racial discrimination. Without radical political reform, the prospect of losing the Cold War greatly increased. The outcome, in both cases, would have been the comprehensive defeat of the economic and humanitarian principles that the United States and its allies, generalized as the free world, claimed to uphold.

The altered geopolitical context within which the two great powers operated is the key to understanding the position of the United

States today. The shift in the character of globalization after the Second World War was inconsistent with the perpetuation of empires of the type established by the Western powers in the nineteenth century and, if recent history is any guide, of empires of any type, including those advertised today as being "benign" or "cooperative." The interests of the United States were undoubtedly global and expanding after 1945: evidence of the desire to influence and, if necessary, intervene appeared as soon as the Cold War superseded the world war. After the Second World War, however, the United States acquired no new colonies and reordered or shed the few it still possessed. The aim was to achieve hegemony by controlling the foreign policies of key states rather than by attempting to incorporate them in an unattainable dream of empire.

This strategy reflected changing realities; it also fit the historical inheritance of the United States. Even if conditions had not changed after the Second World War in the way I have suggested, the United States would have faced much greater difficulty than Britain in creating an imperial order. The United States, unlike Great Britain, occupied the better part of a vast continent, was separated from foreign powers by two oceans, and was largely self-sufficient economically until the late twentieth century. Isolationism was not just a possibility espoused by a tiny minority, as it was with the Little Englanders; it was an important principle of policy. Advocates of an assertive foreign policy had to contend with the view that the best defense of the republic was to distance it from a world that was likely to contaminate it. Moreover, the anticolonial sentiment that had led to the creation of the United States was inscribed both in its philosophy and its Constitution, which made it hard to acquire territories unless they were to be incorporated into the Union. Britain's constitution contained no such impediment, and indeed permitted the devolution of power within the wider empire.

Whereas Britain's political system was designed to facilitate imperial expansion, the federal structure of the United States was devised, again following Montesquieu's law, to prevent it. Federalism was adopted for the very different purpose of maintaining order in a rapidly developing continental society without at the same time enabling an authoritarian central government to take root. Fear of tyranny and the need to preserve a particular conception of liberty restrained presidential power and curtailed the development of an overmighty bureaucracy. Even though foreign policy was the preserve of the federal government, the president could be checked in the exercise of power either by an uncooperative Congress or by the undertow of devolved authority, which followed the principle that "all politics is local." The orientation of elites was also different. Elites in the United States, unlike those in Britain, tended to look inward, were divided among several centers, and often pulled in different directions. Those who formulated foreign policy in Washington worked through a civil service that was politicized to a greater degree than in Britain. Elections brought changes of personnel that, arguably, were not conducive to the continuity needed for running an empire.

When the United States planned the reconstruction of Europe and took charge of some of the decolonizing parts of the British and French colonial empires, its primary aim was security and its principal inspiration was ideological. When the threat to security appeared to end after the collapse of the Soviet Union, the United States reduced its commitment to states in the Third World instead of seeking to dominate them, and allowed regionalism to flourish in new states that were struggling to implement the principle of self-determination. The ex-colonial world was not vital to the economic interests of the United States, as it had been to Britain's welfare; U.S. investments there were influenced heavily by political and strategic considerations.

The paramount importance attached to security does not mean that strategy was purely defensive. On the contrary, the search for security developed into an endless quest for control that led to the creation of a multiplicity of military bases throughout the world. Security became expansive (and expensive) beyond state borders because military technology had put an end to the historic defense by distance provided by the oceans. The invention of first airplanes and then nuclear weapons meant that the home state could be attacked from afar. These developments, which can be summarized as the globalization of violence, presented a challenge to American foreign policy that the British had not been obliged to confront. The response of the United States was to redefine the concept of security and to add the doctrine of pre-emption. At this point, foreign policy acquired an assertiveness that was characteristic of imperialism (albeit without empire).

This argument does not mean that economic considerations were unimportant. It is rather that the course of economic development after 1945 took a turn away from the imperial option. An industrial-military complex had grown up after the war, and in Eisenhower's view it had become sufficiently powerful to threaten the balance of the Constitution. Yet, as its name implies, the military-industrial complex was itself a product of security needs and the increasingly costly means of meeting them. It is hard to portray this interest, influential though it was, as representing U.S. capitalism as a whole: the large civilian sector of the economy still concentrated overwhelmingly on the home market; overseas trade and finance were oriented mainly toward the developed world and not toward the ex-colonial territories. Globalization began to alter these relationships in the last quarter of the twentieth century by increasing the share of finance, services, and high-tech manufactures in the economy and raising the ratio of external trade to total trade. The result reinforced established ties between the United States and the triad of advanced regions, which (it will be recalled) were not candidates for colonization. At the same time, the United States acquired immigrants at a growing rate rather than sending settlers into the wider world. This trend enabled the periphery, though not formally an empire, to "strike back" as Mexican immigrants effectively reclaimed territory taken from them in the nineteenth century. By the end of the twentieth century, the contrast with the conditions that drew Britain and other European powers into empire was greater than it had ever been.

Nationalism provides a more convincing explanation of the expansion of the security state than does capitalism, though there is a subtle link between the two. The externally oriented sectors of the U.S. economy generally favor free trade without imperialism. Most voters are uninterested in foreign adventures and dislike the expense they incur. Support for substantial overseas commitments can be won only by claiming that the national interest—to the point of national survival—is at stake. The success of this appeal depends on the ability of politicians to mobilize public opinion at times of crisis, as was the case during the Second World War and the Cold War. Toward the close of the century, globalization contributed a new, though generalized, fear of the unknown, especially the unknown foreigner, and laid the ground for a nationalist reaction in the United States, as elsewhere. Rapid socioeconomic change produced tensions and uncertainties that could be seen in the displacement of jobs caused by outsourcing, the loss of security and benefits for those who remained in employment, the inflow of migrants from Mexico and Central America, and the alarm raised by foreign purchases of national assets.

The traumatic events of 11 September 2001 increased these fears and simultaneously concentrated them. The invasion of Iraq that followed in 2003 was the product of a galvanized and fearful nationalism responding to a presumed threat to the overriding national interest in self-preservation. What was different about the case of Iraq was that established security priorities were harnessed to an ambitious scheme of social engineering designed to reconstruct the political order in the Middle East. The scheme implied, and has now involved, a commitment of a colonial kind, even if some of the schemers failed to think the implications of their project through. The attempt to revive a defunct tradition of empire building, however, is an anachronism and an anomaly. Events have now confirmed what was self-evident to many observers and ought to have been seen even by policy makers: namely, that today we live in a post-colonial world and one, moreover, that the United States itself has helped bring about.

THE TRANSFORMATION OF THE HISTORICAL CONTEXT, which I have portrayed as a transition from one phase of globalization to another, can be summarized as a shift from vertical to horizontal integration. Imperial integration was vertical: economic links joined production and consumption by means of a single, dominant center; social relations reflected racial hierarchies; political ties were based on the dominance of monarch and metropole and the ranked subordination of the constituents of empire. Post-colonial integration was horizontal: economies became specialized in a narrow range of intermediate goods and services that were traded among multiple regional centers; social relations were founded on a belief in equality that was the necessary counterpart to the creation of multicultural societies; political systems were correspondingly open and, in principle, increasingly democratic. The first set of conditions favored the creation of empires; the second guaranteed their demise.

Although this analysis strikes me as being wholly persuasive, it is unlikely that a future administration will decide to take history seriously. It is hard to imagine a president in the twenty-first century sitting down with a famous historian, as Tamerlane sat down for seven weeks with Ibn Khaldun to discuss the affairs of the world during the siege of Damascus in 1401. If change occurs, it will be brought about by the same brute forces that move economies and give vent to nationalism. For all its many merits, the United States is a society that remains largely uninformed about the outside world, believes in technological solutions to complex sociopolitical problems, and requires instant and preferably simple answers to long-term, complex questions. Moreover, academics today have a smaller role in the public domain than in the past because their place has been taken by think tanks that have different agendas and a better hold on the ear of government.

For these and many other reasons, the United States is not especially well placed to relate to the globalized world it has done so much to promote. On the contrary, it continues to express symptoms of a condition known to specialists as the Great Power Syndrome, which ensures that only congenial analogies are carried forward from the past, that rulers continue to believe their own ideology, and that the problems of today are fought with the weapons of yesteryear.

But at this point I am myself in danger of drawing on a Greek moral—something, as I recall, about hubris and nemesis.

Spring Semester 2008

British Studies at
the University of Texas, 1975–2009

Fall Semester 1975

Paul Scott (Novelist, London), 'The *Raj Quartet*'

Ian Donaldson (Director, Humanities Research Center, Australian National University), 'Humanistic Studies in Australia'

Fritz Fellner (Professor of History, Salzburg University), 'Britain and the Origins of the First World War'

Roger Louis (UT History), 'Churchill, Roosevelt, and the Future of Dependent Peoples during the Second World War'

Michael Holroyd (Biographer, Dublin), 'Two Biographies: Lytton Strachey and Augustus John'

Max Beloff (former Gladstone Professor of Government, Oxford University, present Principal of Buckingham College), 'Imperial Sunset'

Robin Winks (Professor of History, Yale University), 'British Empire-Commonwealth Studies'

Warren Roberts (Director, HRC), and David Farmer (Assistant Director, HRC), 'The D. H. Lawrence Editorial Project'

Harvey C. Webster (Professor of English, University of Louisville), 'C. P. Snow as Novelist and Philosopher'

Anthony Kirk-Greene (Fellow of St. Antony's College, Oxford), 'The Origins and Aftermath of the Nigerian Civil War'

Spring Semester 1976

Joseph Jones (UT Professor of English), 'World English'

William S. Livingston (UT Professor of Government), 'The British Legacy in Contemporary Indian Politics'

John Higley (UT Associate Professor of Sociology), 'The Recent Political Crisis in Australia'

Elspeth Rostow (UT Dean of General and Comparative Studies), Standish

Meacham (UT Professor of History), and Alain Blayac (Professor of English, University of Paris), 'Reassessments of Evelyn Waugh'

Jo Grimond (former Leader of the Liberal Party), 'Liberal Democracy in Britain'

Gaines Post (UT Associate Professor of History), Malcolm Macdonald (UT Government), and Roger Louis (UT History), 'The Impact of Hitler on British Politics'

Robert Hardgrave (UT Professor of Government), Gail Minault (UT Assistant Professor of History), and Chihiro Hosoya (Professor of History, University of Tokyo), 'Kipling and India'

Kenneth Kirkwood (Rhodes Professor of Race Relations, Oxford University), 'The Future of Southern Africa'

C. P. Snow, 'Elite Education in England'

Hans-Peter Schwarz (Director of the Political Science Institute, Cologne University, and Visiting Fellow, Woodrow Wilson International Center for Scholars), 'The Impact of Britain on German Politics and Society since the Second World War'

B. K. Nehru (Indian High Commissioner, London, and former Ambassador to the United States), 'The Political Crisis in India'

Robert A. Divine (UT Professor of History), Harry J. Middleton (Director, LBJ Library), and Roger Louis (UT History), 'Declassification of Secret Documents: The British and American Experiences Compared'

Fall Semester 1976

John Farrell (UT Associate Professor of English), 'Revolution and Tragedy in Victorian England'

Anthony Honoré (Regius Professor of Civil Law, Oxford University), 'British Attitudes to Legal Regulation of Sex'

Alan Hill (UT Professor of English), 'Wordsworth and America'

Ian Nish (Professor of Japanese History, London School of Economics), 'Anglo-American Naval Rivalry and the End of the Anglo-Japanese Alliance'

Norman Sherry (Professor of English, University of Lancaster), 'Joseph Conrad and the British Empire'

Peter Edwards (Lecturer, Australian National University), 'Australia through American Eyes: The Second World War and the Rise of Australia as a Regional Power'

David Edwards (UT Professor of Government), Steven Baker (UT Assistant Professor of Government), Malcolm Macdonald (UT Government), Bill Livingston (UT Government), and Roger Louis (UT History), 'Britain and the Future of Europe'

Michael Hurst (Fellow of St. John's College, Oxford), 'The British Empire in Historical Perspective: The Case of Joseph Chamberlain'

Ronald Grierson (English Banker and former Public Official), 'The Evolution of the British Economy since 1945'

Marian Kent (Lecturer in History, University of New South Wales), 'British Oil Policy between the World Wars'

Constance Babington-Smith (Fellow of Churchill College, Cambridge), 'The World of Rose Macaulay'

William Todd (UT Kerr Professor of English History and Culture), Walt Rostow (UT Professor of History and Economics), and James McKie (UT Dean of Social and Behavioral Sciences), 'Adam Smith after 200 Years'

Spring Semester 1977

Carin Green (Novelist), and Elspeth Rostow (UT American Studies), 'The Achievement of Virginia Woolf'

Samuel H. Beer (Professor of Government, Harvard University), 'Reflections on British Politics'

David Fieldhouse (Fellow of Nuffield College, Oxford), 'Decolonization and the Multinational Corporations'

Gordon Craig (Wallace Professor of Humanities, Stanford University), 'England and Europe on the Eve of the Second World War'

John Lehmann (British Publisher and Writer), 'Publishing under the Bombs— The Hogarth Press during World War II'

Philip Jones (Director, University of Texas Press), William S. Livingston (UT Christian Professor of British Studies), Michael Mewshaw (UT Assistant Professor of English), David Farmer (Assistant Director, HRC), Roger Louis (UT History), and William Todd (UT History), 'The Author, his Editor and Publisher'

Dick Taverne (former M.P), 'The Mood of Britain: Misplaced Gloom or Blind Complacency?'

James B. Crowley (Professor of History, Yale University), Lloyd C. Gardner (Professor of History, Rutgers University), Akira Iriye (Professor of History, University of Chicago), and Roger Louis (UT History), 'The Origins of World War II in the Pacific'

Rosemary Murray (Vice-Chancellor of Cambridge University), 'Higher Education in England'

Burke Judd (UT Professor of Zoology), and Robert Wagner (UT Professor of Zoology), 'Sir Cyril Burt and the Controversy over the Heritability of IQ'

Alessandra Lippucci (UT Government), Roger Louis (UT History), Bill Livingston (UT Government), and Walt Rostow (UT Economics), 'The Wartime Reputations of Churchill and Roosevelt: Overrated or Underrated?'

Fall Semester 1977

Donald L. Weismann (UT University Professor in the Arts), 'British Art in the Nineteenth Century: Turner and Constable—Precursors of French Impressionism'

Standish Meacham (UT Professor of History), 'Social Reform in England'

Joseph Jones, 'Recent Commonwealth Literature'

Lewis Hoffacker (former US Ambassador), 'The Katanga Crisis: British and other Connections'

James M. Treece (UT Professor of Law), Roger Louis (UT History), Warren Roberts, and Bill Todd, (UT History) 'The Copyright Law of 1976'

Charles Heimsath (Visiting Professor of Indian History), Bob Hardgrave (UT Government), Thomasson Jannuzi, (Director, UT Center for Asian Studies), C. P. Andrade (UT Professor of Comparative Studies), and Bill Livingston (UT Government), 'Freedom at Midnight: A Reassessment of Britain and the Partition of India Thirty Years After'

Lord Fraser of Kilmorack (Chairman of the Conservative Party Organization), 'The Tory Tradition of British Politics'

Bernth Lindfors (UT Professor of English), 'Charles Dickens and the Hottentots and Zulus'

Albert Hourani (Director, Middle East Centre, Oxford University), 'The Myth of T. E. Lawrence'

Mark Kinkead-Weekes (Professor of English, University of Kent) and Mara Kalnins (British Writer), 'D. H. Lawrence: Censorship and the Expression of Ideas'

J. D. B. Miller (Professor of International Relations, Australian National University), 'The Collapse of the British Empire'

Peter Green (UT Professor of Classics), Robert King (UT Dean of Social and Behavioral Sciences), Bill Livingston (UT Government), Bob Hardgrave (UT Government), Roger Louis (UT History), and Warren Roberts (Director, HRC), 'The Best and Worst Books of 1977'

Spring Semester 1978

Peter Green (UT Classics), Malcolm Macdonald (UT Government), and Robert Crunden (UT Professor of American Studies), 'British Decadence in the Interwar Years'

Terry Quist (UT Undergraduate), Steve Baker (UT Government), and Roger Louis (UT History), 'R. Emmet Tyrrell's *Social Democracy's Failure in Britain*'

Stephen Koss (Professor of History, Columbia University), 'The British Press: Press Lords, Politicians, and Principles'

John House (Professor of Geography, Oxford University), 'The Rhodesian Crisis'

T. S. Dorsch (Professor of English, Durham University), 'Oxford in the 1930s'

Stephen Spender (English Poet and Writer), 'Britain and the Spanish Civil War'

Okot p'Bitek (Ugandan Poet), 'Idi Amin's Uganda'

David C. Goss (Australian Consul General), 'Wombats and Wivveroos'

Leon Epstein (Professor of Political Science, University of Wisconsin), 'Britain and the Suez Crisis of 1956'

David Schoonover (UT School of Library Science), 'British and American Expatriates in Paris in the 1920s'

Peter Stansky (Professor of History, Stanford University), 'George Orwell and the Spanish Civil War'

Alexander Parker (UT Professor of Spanish), 'Reflections on the Spanish Civil War'

Norman Sherry (Professor of English, Lancaster University), 'Graham Greene and Latin America'

Martin Blumenson (Office of the Chief of Military History, Department of the Army), 'The Ultra Secret'

Fall Semester 1978

W. H. Morris-Jones (Director, Commonwealth Studies Institute, University of London), 'Power and Inequality in Southeast Asia'

Hartley Grattan (UT Emeritus Professor of History), Gilbert Chase (UT Professor of American Studies), Bob Crunden (UT Professor of American Studies), and Roger Louis (UT History), 'The British and the Shaping of the American Critical Mind: A Discussion of *Edmund Wilson's Letters on Literature and Politics*'

James Roach (UT Professor of Government), 'The Indian Emergency and its Aftermath'

Bill Todd, (UT History) 'The Lives of Samuel Johnson'

Lord Hatch (British Labour Politician), 'The Labour Party and Africa'

John Kirkpatrick (HRC Bibliographer), 'Max Beerbohm'

Brian Levack (UT Associate Professor of History), 'Witchcraft in England and Scotland'

M. R. Masani (Indian Writer), 'Gandhi and Gandhism'

A. W. Coates (Economics), 'The Professionalization of the British Civil Service'

John Clive (Professor of History and Literature, Harvard University), 'Great Historians of the Nineteenth Century'

Geoffrey Best (University of Sussex), 'Flightpath to Dresden: British Strategic Bombing in the Second World War'

Kurth Sprague (UT Instructor in English), 'T. H. White's *Once and Future King*'

Gilbert Chase, 'The British Musical Invasion of America'

Spring Semester 1979

Peter Green (UT Professor of Classics), Alessandra Lippucci (UT Instructor in Government), and Elspeth Rostow (UT Dean of the LBJ School of Public Affairs), 'P. N. Furbanks's biography of E. M. Forster'

Roger Louis (UT History), Bob Hardgrave (UT Government), Gail Minault (UT Professor of History), Peter Gran (UT Assistant Professor of History), and Bob King (UT Dean of Liberal Arts), 'E. M. Forster and India'

Paul M. Kennedy (East Anglia University, Visiting Professor of History, Institute of Advanced Study, Princeton), 'The Contradiction between British Strategic Policy and Economic Policy in the Twentieth Century'

Richard Rive (Visiting Fulbright Research Fellow from South Africa), 'Olive Schreiner and the South African Nation'

Charles P. Kindleberger (Professor of Economics, Massachusetts Institute of Technology), 'Lord Zuckerman and the Second World War'

John Press (English Poet), 'English Poets and Postwar Society'

Richard Ellmann (Goldsmiths' Professor of English Literature, Oxford University), 'Writing a Biography of Joyce'

Michael Finlayson (Scottish Dramatist), 'Contemporary British Theater'

Lawrence Stone (Professor of History, Institute of Advanced Study, Princeton), 'Family, Sex, and Marriage in England'

C. P. Snow, 'Reflections on the Two Cultures'

Theodore Zeldin (Oxford University), 'Are the British More or Less European than the French?'

David Edwards (UT Professor of Government), 'How United the Kingdom: Greater or Lesser Britain?'

Michael Holroyd (British Biographer), 'George Bernard Shaw'

John Wickman (Director, Eisenhower Library), 'Eisenhower and the British'

Fall Semester 1979

Robert Palter (Philosophy), 'Reflections on British Philosophers: Locke, Hume, and the Utilitarians'

Alfred Gollin (Professor of History, University of California at Santa Barbara), 'Political Biography as Political History: Garvin, Milner, and Balfour'

Edward Steinhart (History), 'The Consequences of British Rule in Uganda'

Paul Sturges (Loughborough University), and Dolores Donnelly (Toronto University), 'History of the National Library of Canada'

Sir Michael Tippett (British Composer), 'Moving into Aquarius'

Steven Baker (UT Assistant Professor of Government), 'Britain and United Nations Emergency Operations'

Maria Okila Dias (Professor of History, University of São Paulo), 'Intellectual Roots of Informal Imperialism: Britain and Brazil'

Alexander Parker (UT Professor of Spanish), 'Reflections on *Brideshead Revisited*'

Barry C. Higman (Professor of History, University of the West Indies), 'West Indian Emigrés and the British Empire'

Gaines Post (UT Associate Professor of History), 'Britain and the Outbreak of the Second World War'

Karen Gould (UT Lecturer in Art), 'Medieval Manuscript Fragments and English 17th Century Collections: New Perspectives from *Fragmenta Manuscripta*'

John Farrell (UT Associate Professor of English), Eric Poole (HRC) and James Bieri (UT English): Round Table Discussion of Jeanne MacKenzie's new biography, *Dickens: A Life*

Joseph O. Baylen (Regents Professor of History, Georgia State University), 'British Journalism in the Late Victorian and Edwardian Eras'

Peter T. Flawn (President of UT), 'An Appreciation of Charles Dickens'

Spring Semester 1980

Annette Weiner (UT Assistant Professor of Anthropology), 'Anthropologists in New Guinea: British Interpretations and Cultural Relativism'

Bernard Richards (Lecturer in English, Oxford University), 'Conservation in the Nineteenth Century'

Thomas McGann (UT Professor of History), 'Britain and Argentina: An Informal Dominion?'

Mohammad Ali Jazayery (Director, Center for Middle Eastern Studies), 'The Persian Tradition in English Literature'

C. Hartley Grattan (UT Professor of History) 'Twentieth-Century British Novels and the American Critical Mind'

Katherine Whitehorn (London *Observer*), 'An Insider's View of the *Observer*'

Guy Lytle (UT Assistant Professor of History), 'The Oxford University Press' *History of Oxford*'

C. P. Snow, 'Reflections on *The Masters*'

Harvey Webster, '*The Masters* and the Two Cultures'

Brian Blakeley (Associate Professor of History, Texas Tech University), 'Women and the British Empire'

Stephen Koss (Professor of History, Columbia University), 'Asquith, Balfour, Milner, and the First World War'

Tony Smith (Associate Professor of Political Science, Tufts University), 'The Expansion of England: New Ideas on Controversial Themes in British Imperialism'

Stanley Ross (UT Professor of History), 'Britain and the Mexican Revolution'

Rowland Smith (Chairman, Department of English, Dalhousie University), 'The British Intellectual Left and the War 1939–1945'

Richard Ellmann (Goldsmiths' Professor of English, Oxford University), 'Oscar Wilde: A Reconsideration and Problems of the Literary Biographer'

James Bill (UT Professor of Government), 'The United States, Britain, and the Iranian Crisis of 1953'

Fall Semester 1980

Decherd Turner (Director, HRHRC), 'The First 1000 Days'

Roger Louis (UT History), 'Britain and Egypt after the Second World War'

Alistair Horne (Visiting Fellow, Woodrow Wilson Center, Washington, DC), 'Britain and the Fall of France'

Edward Rhodes (UT Associate Professor of History), Peter Green (UT Classics), William Todd (UT History), and Roger Louis (UT History), 'Literary Fraud: H. R. Trevor-Roper and the Hermit of Peking'

Mark Kinkead-Weekes (Professor of English, Kent University), 'D. H. Lawrence's *Rainbow:* Its Sense of History'

Sir John Crawford (Vice-Chancellor, Australian National University), 'Hartley Grattan: In Memoriam'

John Stubbs (Assistant Professor of History, University of Waterloo), 'The Tory View of Politics and Journalism in the Interwar Years'

Donald L. Weismann (UT University Professor in the Arts), 'British Art in the Nineteenth Century'

Fran Hill (UT Assistant Professor of Government), 'The Legacy of British Colonialism in Tanzania'

R. W. B. Lewis (Professor of English, Yale University), 'What's Wrong with the Teaching of English?'

Charlene Gerry (British Publisher), 'The Revival of Fine Printing in Britain'

Peter Gran (UT Assistant Professor of History), 'The Islamic Response to British Capitalism'

Tina Poole (HRHRC) 'Gilbert and Sullivan's Christmas'

Spring Semester 1981

Bernard N. Darbyshire (Visiting Professor of Government and Economics), 'North Sea Oil and the British Future'

Christopher Hill (Master of Balliol College, Oxford), 'The English Civil War'

Elizabeth Heine (Assistant Professor of English, UT San Antonio), and Roger Louis (UT History), 'A Reassessment of Leonard Woolf'

Bernard Richards (Brasenose College, Oxford), 'D. H. Lawrence and Painting'

Miguel Gonzalez-Gerth (UT Professor of Spanish), 'Poetry Once Removed: The Resonance of English as a Second Language'

John Putnam Chalmers (Librarian, HRHRC), 'English Bookbinding from Caedmon to Le Carré'

Peter Coltman (UT Professor of Architecture), 'The Cultural Landscapes of Britain: 2,000 Years of Blood, Sweat, Toil & Tears to Wrest a Living from this Bloody Mud'

Thomas H. Law (former Regent University of Texas), 'The Gold Coins of the English Sovereigns'

Sidney Weintraub (Rusk Professor of International Affairs, LBJ School), James W. McKie (UT Professor of Economics), and Mary Williams (Canadian Consulate, Dallas), 'Canadian-American Economic Relations'

Amedée Turner (Conservative Member of the European Parliament), 'Integrating Britain into the European Community'

Muriel C. Bradbrook (Fellow of Girton College, Cambridge), 'Two Poets: Kathleen Raine and Seamus Heaney'

Ronald Sampson (Chief of the Industrial Development Department, Aberdeen), 'Scotland—Somewhat of a British Texas?'

Fall Semester 1981

Jerome Bump (UT Professor of English), 'From Texas to England: The Ancestry of our Victorian Architecture'

Lord Fraser of Kilmorack, 'Leadership Styles of Tory Prime Ministers since the Second World War'

William Carr (Professor of History, University of Sheffield), 'A British Interpretation of American, German, and Japanese Foreign Policy 1936–1941'

Iqbal Narain (Professor of Political Science and former Vice-Chancellor, Rajasthan University, Jaipur), 'The Ups and Downs of Indian Academic Life'

Don Etherington (Assistant Director, HRHRC), 'The Florence Flood, 1966: The British Effort—or: Up to our Necks in Mud and Books'

E. V. K. Fitzgerald (Visiting Professor of Economics), 'The British University: Crisis, Confusion, and Stagnation'

Robert Crunden (UT Professor of American Studies), 'A Joshua for Historians: Mordecai Richter and Canadian Cultural Identity'

Bernth Lindfors (UT Professor of English), 'The Hottentot Venus and Other African Attractions in Nineteenth-Century England'

Chris Brookeman (Professor of American Studies, London Polytechnic), 'The British Arts and Society'

Nicholas Pickwood (Freelance Book Conservator), 'The Libraries of the National Trust'

Kurth Sprague (UT Instructor), 'John Steinbeck, Chase Horton, and the Matter of Britain'

Martin J. Wiener (Professor of History, Rice University), 'Cultural Values and Socio-Economic Behavior in Britain'

Werner Habicht (Professor of English, University of Würzburg), 'Shakespeare in Nineteenth-Century Germany'

Spring Semester 1982

Stevie Bezencenet (Lecturer in Photography, London College of Printing), 'Contemporary Photography in Britain'

Jane Marcus (UT Assistant Professor of English), 'Shakespeare's Sister, Beethoven's Brother: Dame Ethel Smyth and Virginia Woolf'

Wilson Harris (UT Professor of English), and Raja Rao (UT Professor of Philosophy), 'The Quest for Form: Britain and Commonwealth Perspectives'

Al Crosby (UT Professor of American Studies), 'The British Empire as a Product of Continental Drift'

Lord St. Brides (Visiting Scholar, University of Texas), 'The White House and Whitehall: Washington and Westminster'

Elizabeth Fernea (Senior Lecturer in English and President of the Middle East Studies Association), 'British Colonial Literature of the Middle East'

Maurice Evans (Actor and Producer), 'My Early Years in the Theater'

Joan Bassin (Kansas City Art Institute), 'Art and Industry in Nineteenth-Century England'

Eugene N. Borza (Professor of Ancient History, Pennsylvania State University), 'Sentimental British Philhellenism: Images of Greece'

Ralph Willett (American Studies Department, University of Hull), 'The Style and Structure of British Television News'

Roger Louis (UT History), 'Britain and the Creation of the State of Israel'

Peter Russell (Professor of Spanish, Oxford University), 'A British Historian Looks at Portuguese Historiography of the Fifteenth Century'

Rory Coker (UT Professor of Physics), 'Frauds, Hoaxes and Blunders in Science—a British Tradition?'

Ellen DuBois (Professor of History, SUNY Buffalo), 'Anglo-American Perspectives on the Suffragette Movement'

Donald G. Davis, Jr. (UT Professor of Library Science), 'Great Expectations—and a Few Illusions: Reflections on an Exchange Teaching Year in England'

Anthony Rota (Managing Director, Bertram Rota Ltd.), 'The Changing World of the Bookdealer'

Eisig Silberschlag (former President, Hebrew College, Visiting Gale Professor of Judaic Studies), 'The Bible as the Most Popular Book in English'

Fall Semester 1982

Woodruff Smith (Professor of History, UT San Antonio), 'British Overseas Expansion'

The Rt. Hon. George Thomas (Speaker of the House of Commons), 'Parliamentary Democracy'

Nigel Nicolson (English Historian and Biographer), 'The English Country House as an Historical Document'

Lord St. Brides (Visiting Scholar), 'A Late Leaf of Laurel for Evelyn Waugh'

Lt. Col. Jack McNamara, USMC (Ret.), 'The Libel of Evelyn Waugh by the *Daily Express*'

James Wimsatt (UT Professor of English), 'Chaucer and Medieval French Manuscripts'

Christopher Whelan (Visiting Professor, UT Law School), 'Recent Developments in British Labour Law'

Brian Wearing (Senior Lecturer in American Studies, Christchurch, New Zealand), 'New Zealand: In the Pacific, but of It?'

Robert Hardgrave (UT Professor of Government), 'The United States and India'

James McBath (Professor of Communications, University of Southern California), 'The Evolution of *Hansard*'

Paul Fromm (Professor of Economics, University of Toronto), 'Canadian-United States Relations: Two Solitudes'

John Velz (UT Professor of English), 'When in Disgrace: Ganzel's Attempt to Exculpate John Payne Collier'

Roger Louis (UT History), 'British Origins of the Iranian Revolution'

Spring Semester 1983

Sir Ellis Waterhouse (Slade Professor of Fine Arts, Oxford University), 'A Comparison of British and French Painting in the late Eighteenth Century'

E. J. L. Ride (Australian Consul General), 'Australia's Place in the World and her Relationship with the United States'

Edward Bell (Director of the Royal Botanic Gardens, Kew), 'Kew Gardens in World History'

The Very Rev. Oliver Fiennes (Dean of Lincoln), 'The Care and Feeding of Magna Carta'

C. V. Narasimhan (former Under-Secretary of the United Nations), 'Last Days of the British Raj: A Civil Servant's View'

Warren G. Osmond, 'Sir Frederic Eggleston and the Development of Pacific Consciousness'

Richard Ellmann (Goldsmiths' Professor, Oxford University), 'Henry James among the Aesthetes'

Janet Caulkins (Professor of French, University of Wisconsin at Madison), 'The Poor Reputation of Cornish Knights in Medieval Literature'

Werner Habicht (Professor of English, University of Würzburg), 'Shakespeare and the Third Reich'

Gillian Peele (Fellow of Lady Margaret Hall, Oxford), 'The Changing British Party System'

John Farrell (UT Professor of English), 'Scarlet Ribbons: Memories of Youth and Childhood in Victorian Authors'

Peter Russell (Professor of Spanish, Oxford University), 'A Not So Bashful Stranger: *Don Quixote* in England, 1612–1781'

Sir Zelman Cowen (Provost of Oriel College, Oxford), 'Contemporary Problems in Medicine, Law, and Ethics'

Dennis V. Lindley (Visiting Professor of Mathematics), 'Scientific Thinking in an Unscientific World'

Martin Blumenson (Office of the Chief of Military History, Department of the Army), 'General Mark Clark and the British in the Italian Campaign of World War II'

Fall Semester 1983

Anthony King (Professor of Politics, University of Essex), 'Margaret Thatcher and the Future of British Politics'

Alistair Gillespie (Canadian Minister of Energy, Mines, and Resources), 'Canadian-British Relations: Best and Worst'

Charles A. Owen, Jr. (Professor of English, University of Connecticut), 'The Pre-1400 Manuscripts of the *Canterbury Tales*'

Major-General (Ret.) Richard Clutterbuck (Reader in Political Conflict, University of Exeter), 'Terrorism in Malaya'

Wayne A. Wiegand (Associate Professor of English, University of Kentucky), 'British Propaganda in American Public Libraries during World War I'

Stuart Macintyre (Australian National University, Canberra), 'Australian Trade Unionism between the Wars'

Ram Joshi (Visiting Professor of History, former Vice-Chancellor, University of Bombay), 'Is Gandhi Relevant Today?'

Sir Denis Wright (former British Ambassador in Iran), 'Britain and the Iranian Revolution'

Andrew Horn (Head of the English Department, University of Lesotho), 'Theater and Politics in South Africa'

Philip Davies (Professor of American Government, University of Manchester), 'British Reaction to American Politics: Overt Rejection, Covert Assimilation'

H. K. Singh (Political Secretary, Embassy of India), 'United States-Indian Relations'

Roger Louis (UT Professor of History), Ram Joshi (UT Visiting Professor of History), and J. S. Mehta (UT Professor, LBJ School), 'Two Cheers for Mountbatten: A Reassessment of Lord and Lady Mountbatten and the Partition of India'

Spring Semester 1984

M. S. Venkataramani (Director of International Studies, Jawaharlal Nehru University), 'Winston Churchill and Indian Freedom'

Sir John Thompson (British Ambassador to the United Nations), 'The Falklands and Grenada in the United Nations'

Robert Farrell (Professor of English, Cornell University), 'Medieval Archaelogy'

Allon White (Lecturer in English, University of Sussex), 'The Fiction of Early Modernism'

Peter Green (UT Professor of Classics), Roger Louis (UT Professor of History), Miguel Gonzalez-Gerth (UT Professor of Spanish & Portuguese), Standish Meacham (UT Professor of History), and Sid Monas (UT Professor of Slavic Languages and History): 'Orwell's *1984*'

Uriel Dann (Professor of English History, University of Tel Aviv), 'Hanover and Britain in the Time of George II'

José Ferrater-Mora (Fairbank Professor of Humanities, Bryn Mawr), 'A. M. Turing and his "Universal Turing Machine"'

Rüdiger Ahrens (University of Würzburg), 'Teaching Shakespeare in German Universities'

Michael Brock (Warden of Nuffield College, Oxford), 'H. H. Asquith and Venetia Stanley'

Herbert Spiro (Professor of Political Science, Free University of Berlin), 'What Makes the British and Americans Different from Everybody Else: The Adversary Process of the Common Law'

Nigel Bowles (Lecturer in American Government and Politics, University of Edinburgh), 'Reflections on Recent Developments in British Politics'

Harold Perkin (Mellon Distinguished Visiting Professor, Rice University), 'The Evolution of Citizenship in Modern Britain'

Christopher Heywood (Senior Lecturer, Sheffield University), '*Jane Eyre* and *Wuthering Heights*'

Dave Powers (Curator, Kennedy Library), 'JFK's Trip to Ireland, 1963'

R. W. Coats (Visiting Professor of Economics), 'John Maynard Keynes: The Man and the Economist'

David Evans (UT Professor of Astronomy), 'Astronomy as a British Cultural Export'

Fall Semester 1984

John Henry Faulk, 'Reflections on My Sojourns in the British Middle East'

Lord Fraser of Kilmorack, 'The Thatcher Years—and Beyond'

Michael Phillips (Lecturer in English Literature, University of Edinburgh), 'William Blake and the Rise of the Hot Air Balloon'

Erik Stocker (HRHRC), 'A Bibliographical Detective Story: Reconstructing James Joyce's Library'

Amedée Turner (Member of the European Parliament), 'Recent Developments in the European Parliament'

Michael Hurst (Fellow of St. John's College, Oxford), 'Scholars versus Journalists on the English Social Classes'

Charles Alan Wright (UT William B. Bates Professor of Law), 'Reflections on Cambridge'

J. M. Winter (Fellow of Pembroke College, Cambridge), 'Fear of Decline in Population in Britain after World War I'

Henk Wesseling (Director of the Centre for the History of European Expansion, University of Leiden), 'Dutch Colonialism and the Impact on British Imperialism'

Celia Morris Eckhardt (Biographer and author of *Fannie Wright*), 'Frances Wright and *England as the Civilizer*'

Sir Oliver Wright (British Ambassador to the United States), 'British Foreign Policy—1984'

Leonard Thompson (Professor of African History, Yale University), 'Political Mythology and the Racial Order in South Africa'

Flora Nwapa (Nigerian Novelist), 'Women in Civilian and Military Rule in Nigeria'

Richard Rose (Professor of Political Science, University of Strathclyde), 'The Capacity of the Presidency in Comparative Perspective'

Spring Semester 1985

Bernard Hickey (University of Venice), 'Australian Literary Culture: Short Stories, Novels, and "Literary Journalism"'

Kenneth Hafertepe (UT American Studies), 'The British Foundations of the Smithsonian Castle: The Gothic Revival in Britain and America'

Rajeev Dhavan (Visiting Professor, LBJ School and Center for Asian Studies), 'Race Relations in England: Trapped Minorities and their Future'

Sir John Thompson (British Ambassador to the United Nations), 'British Techniques of Statecraft'

Philip Bobbitt (UT Professor of Law), 'Britain, the United States, and Reduction in Strategic Arms'

David Bevington (Drama Critic and Theater Historian), 'Maimed Rites: Interrupted Ceremony in *Hamlet*'

Standish Meacham (UT Professor of History), 'The Impact of the New Left History on British and American Historiography'

Iris Murdoch (Novelist and Philospher), and John O. Bayley (Thomas Warton Professor of English, Oxford University), 'Themes in English Literature and Philosophy'

John P. Chalmers (Librarian, HRHRC), 'Malory Illustrated'

Thomas Metcalf (Professor of History, University of California at Berkeley), 'The Architecture of Empire: The British Raj in India'

Robert H. Wilson (UT Emeritus Professor of English), 'Malory and His Readers'

Lord St. Brides, '*A Passage to India* Better Film than Novel?'

Derek Pearsall (Medievalist at York University), 'Fire, Flood, and Slaughter: The Tribulations of the Medieval City of York'

E. S. Atieno Odhiambo (University of Nairobi, Visiting Professor, The Johns Hopkins University), 'Britain and Kenya: The Mau Mau, the "Colonial State," and Dependency'

Francis Robinson (Reader in History, University of London), 'Indian Muslim Religious Leadership and Colonial Rule'

Charles B. MacDonald (Deputy Chief Historian, US Army), 'The British in the Battle of the Bulge'

Brian Levack (UT Associate Professor of History), 'The Battle of Bosworth Field'

Kurth Sprague (UT Lecturer in English), 'The Mirrors of Malory'

Fall Semester 1985

A. P. Thornton (Distinguished University Professor, University of Toronto), 'Whatever Happened to the British Commonwealth?'

Michael Garibaldi Hall (UT Professor of History), and Elizabeth Hall (LBJ School), 'Views of Pakistan'

Ronald Steel (Visiting Professor of History), 'Walter Lippmann and the British'

Douglas H. M. Branion (Canadian Consul General), 'Political Controversy and Economic Development in Canada'

Decherd Turner and Dave Oliphant (HRHRC), 'The History of the Publications of the HRHRC'

Robert Fernea (UT Professor of Anthropology), 'The Controversy Over Sex and Orientalism: Charles Doughty's *Arabia Deserta*'

Desley Deacon (Lecturer, UT Department of Government), 'Her Brilliant Career: The Context of Nineteenth-Century Australian Feminism'

John Lamphear (UT Associate Professor of History), 'The British Colonial "Pacification" of Kenya: A View from the Other Side'

Kingsley de Silva (Foundation Professor of Ceylon History at the University of Peradeniya, Sri Lanka), 'British Colonialism and Sri Lankan Independence'

Thomas Hatfield (UT Dean of Continuing Education), 'Colorado on the Cam 1986: From "Ultra" to Archaeology, from Mr. Micawber to Mrs. Thatcher'

Carol Hanbery MacKay (UT Assistant Professor of English), 'The Dickens Theater'

Ronald Brown, Jo Anne Christian, Roger Louis (UT History), Harry Middleton, and Ronald Steel—Panel Discussion: 'The Art of Biography: Philip Ziegler's *Mountbatten*'

Spring Semester 1986

B. J. Fernea (UT English and Middle Eastern Studies), Bernth Lindfors (UT Professor of English), and Roger Louis (UT History), '*Out of Africa:* The Book, the Biography, and the Movie'

Robert Litwak (Woodrow Wilson International Center for Scholars, Washington, DC), 'The Great Game: Russian, British, and American Strategies in Asia'

Gillian Adams Barnes (UT English), and Jane Manaster (UT Geography), 'Humphrey Carpenter's *Secret Gardens* and the Golden Age of Children's Literature'

Laurie Hergenhan (Professor of English, University of Queensland), 'A Yankee in Australia: The Literary and Historical Adventures of C. Hartley Grattan'

Brian Matthews (Flinders University of South Australia), 'Australian Utopianism of the 1880s'

Richard Langhorne (Fellow of St. John's College, Cambridge), 'Apostles and Spies: The Generation of Treason at Cambridge between the Wars'

Ronald Robinson (Beit Professor of the History of the British Empire, Oxford University), 'The Decline and Fall of the British Empire'

William Rodgers (Vice-President, Social Democratic Party), 'Britain's New Three-Party System: A Permanent or Passing Phenomenon?'

John Coetzee (Professor of Literature, University of Cape Town), 'The Farm Novel in South Africa'

Ayesha Jalal, (Fellow, Trinity College, Cambridge), 'Jinnah and the Partition of India'

Andrew Blane (Professor of History, City College of New York), 'Amnesty International: From a British to an International Movement'

Anthony Rota (Antiquarian Bookdealer and Publisher), 'London Pride: 1986'

Elspeth Rostow (Dean, LBJ School), 'The Withering Away of Whose State? Colonel Qaddafi's? Reflections on Nationalism at Home and Abroad, in Britain and in the Middle East'

Ray Daum (Curator, HRHRC), 'Broadway—Piccadilly!'

Fall Semester 1986

Dean Robert King and Members of the '"Unrequired Reading List" Committee—The British Component': Round Table Discussion.

Paul Sturges (Loughborough University), 'Popular Libraries in Eighteenth-Century Britain'

Ian Bickerton (Professor of History, University of Missouri), 'Eisenhower's Middle East Policy and the End of the British Empire'

Marc Ferro (Visiting Professor of History), 'Churchill and Pétain'

David Fitzpatrick (Visiting Professor of History, Queen's University, Kingston, Ontario), 'Religion and Politics in Ireland'

Adam Watson (Center for Advanced Studies, University of Virginia, former British Ambassador to Castro's Cuba), 'Our Man in Havana—or: Britain, Cuba, and the Caribbean'

Norman Rose (Chaim Weizmann Professor of History, Hebrew University), 'Chaim Weizmann, the British, and the Creation of the State of Israel'

Elaine Thompson (Senior Fulbright Scholar, American University), 'Legislatures in Canberra and Washington'

Roger Louis (UT Professor of History), 'Suez Thirty Years After'

Antonia Gransden (Reader in Medieval History, University of Nottingham), 'The Writing of Chronicles in Medieval England'

Hilary Spurling (British Biographer and Critic), 'Paul Scott's *Raj Quartet:* The Novelist as Historian'

J. D. B. Miller (Professor of International Relations, Australian National University), 'A Special and Puzzling Relationship: Australia and the United States'

Janet Meisel (UT Associate Professor of History), 'The Domesday Book'

Spring Semester 1987

Miguel Gonzalez-Gerth (UT Liberal Arts), Robert Fernea (UT Anthropology), Joe Horn (UT Psychology), Bruce Hunt (UT History), and Delbert Thiessen (UT Psychology), 'Contemporary Perspectives on Evolution'

Alistair Campbell-Dick (Chief Executive Officer, Research and Development Strategic Technology), 'Scottish Nationalism'

Anthony Mockler (British Freelance Historian and Biographer), 'Graham Greene: The Interweaving of His Life and Fiction'

Michael Crowder (Visiting Professor of African History, Amherst College), 'The Legacy of British Colonialism in Africa'

Carin Green (UT Lecturer in Classics), 'Lovers and Defectors: Autobiography and *The Perfect Spy*'

Lord St. Brides, 'The Modern British Monarchy'

Victor Szebehely (UT Richard B. Curran Professor of Engineering), 'Sir Isaac Newton'

Patrick McCaughey (Visiting Professor of Australian Studies, Harvard University; Director, National Gallery of Victoria, Melbourne), 'The Persistence of Landscape in Australian Art'

Adolf Wood (Deputy Editor of the *Times Literary Supplement*), 'An Informal History of the *TLS*'

Nissan Oren (Visiting Professor of Political Science, The Johns Hopkins University; Kaplan Professor, Hebrew University, Jerusalem), 'Churchill, Truman, and Stalin: The End of the Second World War'

Sir Michael Howard (Regius Professor of History, Oxford University), 'Britain and the First World War'

Sir John Graham (former British Ambassador to NATO), 'NATO: British Origins, American Security, and the Future Outlook'

Daniel Mosser (Virginia Polytechnic Institute and State University), 'The Chaucer Cardigan Manuscript'

Sir Raymond Carr (Warden of St. Antony's College, Oxford), 'British Intellectuals and the Spanish Civil War'

Michael Wilding (Reader in English, University of Sydney), 'The Fatal Shore? The Convict Period in Australian Literature'

Fall Semester 1987

Peter Green (UT Professor of Classics), Winfred Lehmann (UT Temple Professor of Humanities), Roger Louis (UT Kerr Professor), and Paul Woodruff (UT Professor of Philosophy), 'Anthony Burgess: The Autobiography'

Robert Crunden (UT Professor of History and American Studies), 'Ezra Pound in London'

Carol MacKay (UT Associate Professor of English), and John Henry Faulk, 'J. Frank Dobie and Thackeray's Great-Granddaughter: Another Side of *A Texan in England*'

Sarvepalli Gopal (Professor of Contemporary History, Jawaharlal Nehru University, and Fellow of St. Antony's College, Oxford), 'Nehru and the British'

Robert D. King (UT Dean of Liberal Arts), 'T. S. Eliot'

Lord Blake (Visiting Cline Professor of English History and Literature, former Provost of Queen's College, Oxford), 'Disraeli: Problems of the Biographer'

Alain Blayac (Professor of Comparative Literature, University of Montpellier), 'Art as Revelation: Gerard Manley Hopkins's Poetry and James Joyce's *Portrait of the Artist*'

Mary Bull (Oxford University), 'Margery Perham and Africa'

R. J. Moore (Professor of History, Flinders University), 'Paul Scott: The Novelist as Historian, and the *Raj Quartet* as History'

Ian Willison (Head of the Rare Books Division of the British Library), 'New Trends in Humanities Research: The *History of the Book in Britain* Project'

The Duke of Norfolk, 'The Lion and the Unicorn: Ceremonial and the Crown'

Hans Mark (Chancellor, The University of Texas System), 'The Royal Society, the Royal Observatory, and the Development of Modern Research Laboratories'

Henry Dietz (UT Professor of Government), 'Sherlock Holmes: A Centennial Celebration'

Spring Semester 1988

Lord Jenkins (Chancellor of Oxford University), 'Changing Patterns of British Government from Asquith via Baldwin and Attlee to Mrs. Thatcher'

Lord Thomas (author of *The Spanish Civil War* and *Cuba, or the Pursuit of Freedom*), 'Britain, Spain, and Latin America'

Barbara Harlow (UT English), Bernth Lindfors (UT English), Wahneema Lubiano (UT English), and Robert Wren (University of Houston), 'Chinua Achebe: The Man and His Works'

Charles Townshend (Professor of History, Keele University), 'Britain, Ireland, and Palestine, 1918–1947'

Richard Morse (Program Secretary for Latin America, Woodrow Wilson Center), 'T. S. Eliot and Latin America'

Chinua Achebe (Nigerian Novelist), 'Anthills of the Savannah'

Tapan Raychaudhuri (Reader in Indian History, Oxford University), 'The English in Bengali Eyes in the Nineteenth Century'

Lord Chitnis (Chief Executive of the Rowntree Trust and Chairman of the British Refugee Council), 'British Perceptions of US Policy in Central America'

Kurth Sprague (Senior Lecturer in English), 'Constance White: Sex, Womanhood, and Marriage in British India'

George McGhee (former US Ambassador to Turkey and Germany), 'The Turning Point in the Cold War: Britain, the United States, and Turkey's Entry into NATO'

Robert Palter (Professor of the History of Science, Trinity College), 'New Light on Newton's Natural Philosophy'

J. Kenneth McDonald (Chief Historian, CIA), 'The Decline of British Naval Power 1918–1922'

Yvonne Cripps (UT Visiting Professor of Law), '"Peter and the Boys Who Cry Wolf": *Spycatcher*'

Emmanuel Ngara (Professor of English, University of Zimbabwe), 'African Poetry: Nationalism and Cultural Domination'

Kate Frost (UT Assistant Professor of English), 'Frat Rats of the Invisible College: The Wizard Earl of Northumberland and His Pre-Rosicrucian Pals'

B. Ramesh Babu (UT Visiting Professor of Government), 'American Foreign Policy: An Indian Dissent'

Sir Antony Ackland (British Ambassador to the United States), 'From Dubai to Madrid: Adventures in the British Foreign Service'

In the Spring Semester 1988 British Studies helped to sponsor four lectures by Sir Brian Urquhart (former Under-Secretary of the United Nations) on 'World Order in the Era of Decolonization'

Fall Semester 1988

Peter Green (UT Dougherty Professor of Classics), Diana Hobby (Rice University, Editor of the *Yeats Papers*), Roger Louis (UT Kerr Professor), and Elspeth Rostow (UT Stiles Professor of American Studies), Round Table Discussion on Richard Ellman's *Oscar Wilde*

Hugh Cecil (University of Leeds), 'The British First World War Novel of Experience'

Alan Knight (UT Worsham Professor of Mexican History), 'Britain and the Mexican Revolution'

Prosser Gifford (Former Deputy Director, Woodrow Wilson Center, Washington, DC), and Robert Frykenberg (Professor of Indian History, University of Wisconsin at Madison), 'Stability in Post-Colonial British Africa: The Indian Perspective'

Joseph Dobrinski (Université Paul-Valéry), 'The Symbolism of the Artist Theme in *Lord Jim*'

Martin Stannard (University of Leicester), 'Evelyn Waugh and North America'

Lawrence Cranberg (Consulting Physicist and Fellow of the American Physical Society), 'The Engels-Marx Relationship and the Origins of Marxism'

N. G. L. Hammond (Professor of Greek, Bristol University), 'The British Military Mission to Greece, 1943–1944'

Barbara Harlow (UT English), 'A Legacy of the British Era in Egypt: Women, Writing, and Political Detention'

Sidney Monas (UT Professor of Slavic Languages and History), 'Thanks for the Mummery: *Finnegans Wake*, Rabelais, Bakhtin, and Verbal Carnival'

Robert Bowie (Former Director, Harvard Center of International Affairs and Deputy Director, Central Intelligence Agency), 'Britain's Decision to Join the European Community'

Shirley Williams (Co-Founder, Social Democratic Party), 'Labour Weakness and Tory Strength—or, The Strange Death of Labour England'

Bernard Richards (Fellow of Brasenose College, Oxford), 'Ruskin's View of Turner'

John R. Clarke (Art History), 'Australian Art of the 1960s'

Round Table Discussion on Paul Kennedy's *The Rise and Fall of the Great Powers:* Alessandra Lipucci (UT Government), Roger Louis (UT Kerr Professor), Jagat Mehta (LBJ School), Sidney Monas (UT Professor of Slavic Languages and History), and Walt Rostow (UT Economics and History)

Spring Semester 1989

Brian Levack (UT Professor of History), 'The English Bill of Rights, 1689'

Hilary Spurling (Critic and Biographer), 'Paul Scott as Novelist: His Sense of History and the British Era in India'

Larry Carver (Director of the Humanities Program), 'Lord Rochester: The Profane Wit and the Restoration's Major Minor Poet'

Atieno Odhiambo (Professor of History, Rice University), 'Re-Interpreting Mau Mau'

Trevor Hartley (Reader in Law, London School of Economics, and Visiting Professor, UT Law School), 'The British Constitution and the European Community'

Archie Brown (Fellow of St. Antony's College, Oxford), 'Political Leadership in Britain, the Soviet Union, and the United States'

Lord Blake (Former Provost of Queen's College, Oxford, and Editor of the *Dictionary of National Biography*), 'Churchill as Historian'

Weirui Hou (Professor of English Literature, Shanghai University), 'British Literature in China'

Norman Daniel (British Council), 'Britain and the Iraqi Revolution of 1958'

Alistair Horne (Fellow of St. Antony's College, Oxford), 'The Writing of the Biography of Harold Macmillan'

M. R. D. Foot (former Professor of History, Manchester University, and Editor of the *Gladstone Diaries*), 'The Open and Secret War, 1939–1945'

Ian Willison (former Head of Rare Books Division of the British Library), 'Editorial Theory and Practice in The History of the Book'

Neville Meaney (Professor of History, University of Sydney), 'The "Yellow Peril": Invasion, Scare Novels, and Australian Political Culture'

Round Table Discussion on *The Satanic Verses:* Kurth Sprague (UT Associate Professor of American Studies), Peter Green (UT Dougherty Professor of Classics), Robert A. Fernea (UT Professor of Anthropology), Roger Louis (UT Kerr Professor), and Gail Minault (UT Associate Professor of History and Asian Studies)

Kate Frost (UT Associate Professor of English), 'John Donne, Sunspots, and the British Empire'

Lee Patterson (Professor of English, Duke University), 'Chaucerian Commerce'

Edmund Weiner and John Simpson (Editors of the new *OED*), 'Return to the Web of Words'

Ray Daum (Curator, HRHRC), 'Noel Coward and Cole Porter'

William B. Todd (UT Emeritus Professor of History), 'Edmund Burke on the French Revolution'

Fall Semester 1989

D. Cameron Watt (Stevenson Professor of International History, LSE), 'Britain and the Origins of the Second World War: Personalities and Politics of Appeasement'

Gary Freeman (UT Associate Professor of Government), 'On the Awfulness of the English: The View from Comparative Studies'

Hans Mark (Chancellor, UT System), 'British Naval Tactics in the Second World War: The Japanese Lessons'

T. B. Millar (Director, Menzies Centre for Australian Studies, London), 'Australia, Britain and the United States in Historical Perspective'

Dudley Fishburn (Member of Parliament and former Editor of *The Economist*), '*The Economist*'

Lord Franks (former Ambassador in Washington), 'The "Special Relationship"'

Herbert L. Jacobson (Drama Critic and friend of Orson Wells), 'Three Score Years of Transatlantic Acting and Staging of Shakespeare'

Roy Macleod (Professor of History, University of Sydney) 'The "Practical Man": Myth and Metaphor in Anglo-Australian Science'

David Murray (Professor of Government, the Open University), 'Hong Kong: The Historical Context for the Transfer of Power'

Susan Napier (UT Assistant Professor of Japanese Language and Literature), 'Japanese Intellectuals Discover the British'

Dr. Karan Singh (Ambassador of India to the United States), 'Four Decades of Indian Democracy'

Paul Woodruff (UT Professor of Philosophy), 'George Grote and the Radical Tradition in British Scholarship'

Herbert J. Spiro (UT Professor of Government), 'Britain, the United States, and the Future of Germany'

Robert Lowe (Wine Columnist for the *Austin American-Statesman*), '"God Rest you Merry, Gentlemen": The Curious British Cult of Sherry'

Spring Semester 1990

Thomas F. Staley (Director, HRHRC), 'Harry Ransom, the Humanities Research Center, and the Development of Twentieth-Century Literary Research Collections'

Thomas Cable (UT Blumberg Professor of English), 'The Rise and Decline of the English Language'

D. J. Wenden (Fellow of All Souls College, Oxford), 'Sir Alexander Korda and the British Film Industry'

Roger Owen (Fellow of St. Antony's College, Oxford, and UT Visiting Professor of Middle Eastern History), 'Reflections on the First Ten Years of Thatcherism'

Robert Hardgrave (UT Temple Centennial Professor of Humanities), 'Celebrating Calcutta: The Solvyns Portraits'

Donatus Nwoga (Professor of English, University of Nigeria, Nsukka, and Fulbright Scholar-in-Residence, University of Kansas), 'The Intellectual Legacy of British Decolonization in Africa'

Francis Sitwell (Etonian, Seaman, and Literary Executor), 'Edith Sitwell: A Reappraisal'

Robert Vitalis (UT Assistant Professor of Government), 'The "New Deal" in Egypt: Britain, the United States, and the Egyptian Economy during World War II'

James Coote (UT Professor and Cass Gilbert Teaching Fellow, School of Architecture), 'Prince Charles and Architecture'

Harry Eckstein (Distinguished Professor of Political Science, University of California, Irvine), 'British Politics and the National Health Service'

Alfred David (Professor of English, Indiana University), 'Chaucer and King Arthur'

Ola Rotimi (African Playwright and Theater Director), 'African Literature and the British Tongue'

Derek Brewer (Professor of English and Master of Emmanuel College, Cambridge), 'An Anthropological Study of Literature'

Neil MacCormick (Regius Professor of Public Law and the Law of Nations, University of Edinburgh), 'Stands Scotland Where She Should?'

Janice Rossen (Senior Research Fellow, HRHRC), 'Toads and Melancholy: The Poetry of Philip Larkin'

Ronald Robinson (Beit Professor of the History of the British Commonwealth, Oxford, and Visiting Cline Professor, University of Texas), 'The Decolonization of British Imperialism'

Fall Semester 1990

Round Table Discussion on 'The Crisis in the Persian Gulf': Hafez Farmayan (UT Professor of History), Robert Fernea (UT Professor of Anthropology), Roger Louis (UT Kerr Professor), and Robert Stookey (United States Foreign Service Officer, Retired, now Research Associate, Center for Middle Eastern Studies)

John Velz (UT Professor of English), 'Shakespeare and Some Surrogates: An Account of the Anti-Stratfordian Heresy'

Michael H. Codd (Secretary, Department of the Prime Minister and Cabinet, Government of Australia), 'The Future of the Commonwealth: An Australian View'

John Dawick (Senior Lecturer in English, Massey University, New Zealand), 'The Perils of Paula: Young Women and Older Men in Pinero's Plays'

Gloria Fromm (Professor of English, University of Illinios in Chicago), 'New Windows on Modernism: The Letters of Dorothy Richardson'

David Braybrooke (UT Centennial Commission Professor in the Liberal Arts), 'The Canadian Constitutional Crisis'

Sidney Monas (UT Professor of Slavic Languages and History), 'Paul Fussell and World War II'

James Fishkin (UT Darrell Royal Regents Chair in Ethics and American Society), 'Thought Experiments in Recent Oxford Philosophy'

Joseph Hamburger (Pelatiah Perit Professor of Political and Social Science, Yale University), 'How Liberal Was John Stuart Mill?'

Richard W. Clement (Special Collections Librarian, Kenneth Spencer Research Library, University of Kansas), 'Thomas James and the Bodleian Library: The Foundations of Scholarship'

Michael Yeats (Former Chairman of the Irish Senate and only son of the poet William Butler Yeats), 'Ireland and Europe'

Round Table Discussion on 'William H. McNeill's *Arnold J. Toynbee: A Life*': Standish Meacham (UT Dean of Liberal Arts), Peter Green (UT Dougherty Professor of Classics), Roger Louis (UT Kerr Professor), and Sidney Monas (UT Professor of Slavic Languages and History)

Jeffrey Meyers (Biographer and Professor of English, University of Colorado), 'Conrad and Jane Anderson'

Alan Frost (Professor of History, La Trobe University, Melbourne), 'The Explorations of Captain Cook'

Sarvepalli Gopal (Professor of History, Jawaharlal Nehru University, and Fellow of St. Antony's College, Oxford), 'The First Ten Years of Indian Independence'

Round Table Discussion on 'The Best and Worst Books of 1990': Alessandra Lippucci (UT Lecturer in Government), Roger Louis (UT Kerr Professor), Tom Staley (Director, HRHRC), Steve Weinberg (UT Welch Foundation Chair in Science Theory), and Paul Woodruff (UT Thompson Professor in the Humanities)

Spring Semester 1991

David Hollway (Prime Minister's Office, Government of Australia), 'Australia and the Gulf Crisis'

Diane Kunz (Yale University), 'British Post-War Sterling Crises'

Miguel Gonzalez-Gerth (UT Professor of Spanish Literature and HRHRC), 'T. E. Lawrence, Richard Aldington, and the Death of Heroes'

Robert Twombly (UT Professor of English), 'Religious Encounters with the Flesh in English Literature'

Alan Ryan (Princeton University), 'Bertrand Russell's Politics'

Hugh Kenner (Andrew Mellon Professor of the Humanities, The Johns Hopkins University, and Visiting Harry Ransom Professor), 'The State of English Poetry'

Patricia Burnham (UT American Studies), 'Anglo-American Art and the Struggle for Artistic Independence'

Round Table Discussion on 'The Churchill Tradition': Lord Blake (former Provost of Queen's College, Oxford), Lord Jenkins (Chancellor, Oxford University), Field Marshal Lord Carver (former Chief of the Defence Staff), Sir Michael Howard (former Regius Professor, Oxford, present Lovett Professor of Military and Naval History, Yale University), with a concluding comment by Winston S. Churchill, M.P.

Woodruff Smith (Professor of History, UT San Antonio), 'Why Do the British Put Sugar in their Tea?'

Peter Firchow (Professor of English, University of Minnesota), 'Aldous Huxley: The Poet as Centaur'

Irene Gendzier (Professor of History and Political Science, Boston University), 'British and American Middle Eastern Policies in the 1950s: Lebanon and Kuwait. Reflections on Past Experience and the Postwar Crisis in the Gulf'

John Train (*Harvard* Magazine and *Wall Street Journal*), 'Remarkable Catchwords in the City of London and on Wall Street'

Adam Sisman (Independent Writer, London), 'A. J. P. Taylor'

Roger Louis (UT Kerr Professor), 'The Young Winston'

Adrian Mitchell (Professor of English, Melbourne University, and Visiting Professor of English and Australian Studies), 'Claiming a Voice: Recent Non-Fiction Writing in Australia'

Bruce Hevly (Professor of History, University of Washington), 'Stretching Things Out versus Letting Them Slide: The Natural Philosophy of Ice in Edinburgh and Cambridge in the Nineteenth Century'

Henry Dietz (UT Professor of Government), 'Foibles and Follies in Sherlock's Great Game: Some Excesses of Holmesian Research'

Summer 1991

Roger Louis (UT Kerr Professor), and Ronald Robinson (Beit Professor of the History of the British Commonwealth, Oxford University, and Visiting Cline Professor), 'Harold Macmillan and the Dissolution of the British Empire'

Robert Treu (Professor of English, University of Wisconsin, Lacrosse), 'D. H. Lawrence and Graham Greene in Mexico'

Thomas Pinney (Chairman, Department of English, Pomona College), 'Kipling, India, and Imperialism'

Ronald Heiferman (Professor of History, Quinnipiac College), 'The Odd Couple: Winston Churchill and Chiang Kai-shek'

John Harty (Professor of English, Alice Lloyd College, Kentucky), 'The Movie and the Book: J. G. Ballard's *Empire of the Sun*'

A. B. Assensoh (Ghanaian Journalist and Professor of History, Southern University, Baton Rouge), 'Nkrumah'

Victoria Carchidi (Professor of English, Emory and Henry College), 'Lawrence of Arabia on a Camel, Thank God!'

James Gump (Chairman, Department of History, University of California, San Diego), 'The Zulu and the Sioux: The British and American Comparative Experience with the "Noble Savage"'

Fall Semester 1991

Round Table Discussion on Noel Annan's *Our Age:* Peter Green (UT Dougherty Professor of Classics), Robert D. King (UT Dean of Liberal Arts), Roger Louis (UT Kerr Professor), and Thomas F. Staley (Director, HRHRC)

Christopher Heywood (Okayama University, Japan), 'Slavery, Imagination, and the Brontës'

Harold L. Smith (University of Houston, Victoria), 'Winston Churchill and Women'

Krystyna Kujawinska-Courtney (University of Lodz), 'Shakespeare and Poland'

Ewell E. Murphy, Jr. (Baker & Botts, Houston), 'Cecil Rhodes and the Rhodes Scholarships'

I. N. Kimambo (University of Dar-es-Salaam), 'The District Officer in Tanganyika'

Hans Mark (Chancellor, UT System), 'The Pax Britannica and the Inevitable Comparison: Is There a Pax Americana? Conclusions from the Gulf War'

Richard Clutterbuck (Major-General, British Army, Ret.), 'British and American Hostages in the Middle East: Negotiating with Terrorists'

Elizabeth Hedrick (UT Assistant Professor of English), 'Samuel Johnson and Linguistic Propriety'

The Hon. Denis McLean (New Zealand Ambassador to the United States), 'Australia and New Zealand: The Nuisance of Nationalism'

Elizabeth Richmond (UT Assistant Professor of English), 'Submitting a Trifle for a Degree: Dramatic Productions at Oxford and Cambridge in the Age of Shakespeare'

Kenneth Warren, M.D. (Director for Science, Maxwell Macmillan), 'Tropical Medicine: A British Invention'

Adolf Wood (Deputy Editor of the *TLS*), 'The Golden Age of the *Times Literary Supplement*'

Eugene Walter (Poet and Novelist), 'Unofficial Poetry: Literary London in the 1940s and 1950s'

Sidney Monas (UT Professor of Slavic Languages and History), 'Images of Britain in the Poetry of World War II'

The St. Stephen's Madrigal Choir, 'Celebrating an English Christmas'

Spring Semester 1992

Jeremy Treglown (Critic and Author), 'Wartime Censorship and the Novel'

Toyin Falola (UT Professor of History), 'Nigerian Independence 1960'

Donald S. Lamm (President, W.W. Norton and Company), 'Publishing English History in America'

Colin Franklin (Publisher and Historian of the Book), 'The Pleasures of Eighteenth-Century Shakespeare'

Thomas F. Staley (Director, HRHRC), '*Fin de Siècle* Joyce: A Perspective on One Hundred Years'

Sarvepalli Gopal (Jawaharlal Nehru University), '"Drinking Tea with Treason": Halifax and Gandhi'

Michael Winship (UT Associate Professor of English), 'The History of the Book: Britain's Foreign Trade in Books in the Nineteenth Century'

Richard Lariviere (UT Professor of Sanskrit and Director of the Center for Asian Studies), 'British Law and Lawyers in India'

Round Table Discussion on A. S. Byatt's *Possession:* Janice Rossen (Visiting Scholar, HRHRC), John P. Farrell (UT Professor of English), and Roger Louis (UT Kerr Professor)

William H. McNeill (University of Chicago and former President of the American Historical Association), 'Arnold Toynbee's Vision of World History'

Derek Brewer (Master of Emmanuel College, Cambridge), 'The Interpretation of Fairy Tales: The Implications for English Literature, Anthropology, and History'

David Bradshaw (Fellow of Worcester College, Oxford), 'Aldous Huxley: Eugenics and the Rational State'

Steven Weinberg (Josey Regental Professor of Science), 'The British Style in Physics'

Sir David Williams (Vice-Chancellor, Cambridge University), 'Northern Ireland'

Summer 1992

R. A. C. Parker (Fellow of Queen's College, Oxford), 'Neville Chamberlain and Appeasement'

Adrian Wooldridge (Fellow of All Souls College, Oxford, and Staff Writer for *The Economist*), 'Reforming British Education: How It Happened and What America Can Learn'

Chris Wrigley (Professor of Modern British History, Nottingham University), 'A. J. P. Taylor: An English Radical and Modern Europe'

Fall Semester 1992

Round Table Discussion on E. M. Forster's *Howards End:* The Movie and the Book. Robert D. King (UT Liberal Arts), Roger Louis (UT Kerr Professor), Alessandra Lippucci (UT Government), and Thomas F. Staley (HRHRC)

Lord Skidelsky (Warwick University), 'Keynes and the Origins of the "Special Relationship"'

Sir Samuel Falle (former British Ambassador), 'Britain and the Middle East in the 1950s'

Ian MacKillop (University of Sheffield), 'We Were That Cambridge: F. R. Leavis and *Scrutiny*'

Walter Dean Burnham (Frank G. Erwin Centennial Chair in Government), 'The 1992 British Elections: Four-or-Five-More Tory Years?'

Don Graham (UT Professor of English), 'Modern Australian Literature and the Image of America'

Richard Woolcott (former Secretary of the Australian Department of Foreign Affairs), 'Australia and the Question of Cooperation or Contention in the Pacific'

Ian Willison (1992 Wiggins Lecturer, American Antiquarian Society), 'The History of the Book in Twentieth-Century Britain and America'

Iain Sproat, (Member of Parliament), 'P. G. Wodehouse and the War'

Standish Meacham (UT Sheffield Professor of History), 'The Crystal Palace'

Field Marshal Lord Carver (former Chief of the British Defence Staff), 'Wavell: A Reassessment'

Lesley Hall (Wellcome Institute for the History of Medicine, London), 'For Fear of Frightening the Horses: Sexology in Britain since William Acton'

Michael Fry (Director of International Relations, University of Southern California), 'Britain, the United Nations, and the Lebanon Crisis of 1958'

Brian Holden Reid (King's College, London), 'J. F. C. Fuller and the Revolution in British Military Thought'

Neil Parsons (University of London), '"Clicko" or Franz Taaibosch: A Bushman Entertainer in Britain, Jamaica, and the United States *c.* 1919–40'

John Hargreaves (Burnett-Fletcher Professor of History, Aberdeen University), 'God's Advocate: Lewis Namier and the History of Modern Europe'

Round Table Discussion on Robert Harris's *Fatherland:* Henry Dietz (UT Government), Robert D. King (UT Liberal Arts), Roger Louis (UT Kerr Professor), and Walter Wetzels (UT Germanic Languages)

Kevin Tierney (University of California), 'Robert Graves: An Outsider Looking In, or An Insider Who Escaped?'

Spring Semester 1993

Round Table Discussion on 'The Trollope Mystique': Janice Rossen (author of *Philip Larkin* and *The University in Modern Fiction*), Louise Weinberg (UT Angus G. Wynne Professor of Civil Jurisprudence), and Paul Woodruff (UT Director of the Plan II Honors Program and Thompson Professor of Philosophy)

Bruce Hunt (UT Associate Professor of History), 'To Rule the Waves: Cable Telegraphy and British Physics in the Nineteenth Century'

Martin Wiener (Jones Professor of History, Rice University), 'The Unloved State: Contemporary Political Attitudes in the Writing of Modern British History'

Elizabeth Dunn (HRHRC), 'Ralph Waldo Emerson and Ireland'

Jason Thompson (Western Kentucky University), 'Edward William Lane's "Description of Egypt"'

Sir Michael Howard (former Regius Professor of Modern History, Oxford University, present Lovett Professor of Military and Naval History, Yale University), 'Strategic Deception in the Second World War'

Gordon A. Craig (Sterling Professor of Humanities, Stanford University), 'Churchill'

Round Table Discussion on the Indian Mathematician Ramanujan: Robert D. King (UT Rapoport Professor of Liberal Arts), James W. Vick (Vice-President for Student Affairs and Professor of Mathematics), and Steven Weinberg (UT Regental Professor and Josey Chair in Physics)

Martha Merritt (UT Lecturer in Government), 'From Commonwealth to Commonwealth, and from Vauxhall to *Vokzal:* Russian Borrowing from Britain'

Sidney Monas (UT Professor of Slavic Languages and History), 'James Joyce and Russia'

Peter Marshall (Professor of History, King's College, London), 'Imperial Britain and the Question of National Identity'

Michael Wheeler (Professor of English and Director of the Ruskin Programme, Lancaster University), 'Ruskin and Gladstone'

Anthony Low (Smuts Professor of Commonwealth History and President of Clare College, Cambridge University), 'Britain and India in the Early 1930s: The British, American, French, and Dutch Empires Compared'

Summer 1993

Alexander Pettit (University of North Texas), 'Lord Bolingbroke's *Remarks on the History of England*'

Rose Marie Burwell (Northern Illinois University), 'The British Novel and Ernest Hemingway'

Richard Patteson (Mississippi State University), 'New Writing in the West Indies'

Richard Greene (Memorial University, Newfoundland), 'The Moral Authority of Edith Sitwell'

Fall Semester 1993

Round Table Discussion on 'The British and the Shaping of the American Critical Mind—Edmund Wilson, Part II': Roger Louis (UT Kerr Professor), Elspeth Rostow (UT Stiles Professor in American Studies), Tom Staley (Director, HRHRC), and Robert Crunden (UT Professor of History and American Studies)

Roseanne Camacho (University of Rhode Island), 'Evelyn Scott: Towards an Intellectual Biography'

Christopher Heywood (Okayama University), 'The Brontës and Slavery'

Peter Gay (Sterling Professor of History, Yale University), 'The Cultivation of Hatred in England'

Linda Ferreira-Buckley (UT English) 'England's First English Department: Rhetoric and More Rhetoric'

Janice Rossen (Senior Research Fellow, HRHRC), 'British University Novels'

Ian Hancock (O Yanko Le Redzosko) (UT Professor of Linguistics and English), 'The Gypsy Image in British Literature'

James Davies (University College of Swansea), 'Dylan Thomas'

Jeremy Lewis (London Writer and Editor), 'Who Cares about Cyril Connolly?'

Sam Jamot Brown (British Studies), and Robert D. King (Linguistics), 'Scott and the Antarctic'

Martin Trump (University of South Africa), 'Nadine Gordimer's Social and Political Vision'

Richard Clogg (Professor of Balkan History, University of London), 'Britain and the Origins of the Greek Civil War'

Herbert J. Spiro (United States Ambassador, Ret.), 'The Warburgs: Anglo-American and German-Jewish Bankers'

Colin Franklin (Publisher and Antiquarian Bookseller), 'Lord Chesterfield: Stylist, Connoisseur of Manners, and Specialist in Worldly Advice'

Jeffrey Segall (Charles University, Prague), 'The Making of James Joyce's Reputation'

Rhodri Jeffreys-Jones (University of Edinburgh), 'The Myth of the Iron Lady: Margaret Thatcher and World Stateswomen'

John Rumrich (UT Associate Professor of English), 'Milton and Science: Gravity and the Fall'

J. D. Alsop (McMaster University), 'British Propaganda, Espionage, and Political Intrigue'

Round Table Discussion on 'The Best and the Worst Books of 1993': David Edwards (UT Government), Creekmore Fath (UT Liberal Arts Foundation), Betty Sue Flowers (UT English), and Sidney Monas (UT Professor of Slavic Languages and History)

Spring Semester 1994

Thomas F. Staley (Director, HRHRC), 'John Rodker: Poet and Publisher of Modernism'

Martha Fehsenfeld, and Lois More Overbeck (Emory University), 'The Correspondence of Samuel Beckett'

M. R. D. Foot (Historian and Editor), 'Lessons of War on War: The Influence of 1914–1918 on 1939–1945'

Round Table Discussion on 'Requiem for Canada?' David Braybrooke (UT Centennial Chair in Liberal Arts), Walter Dean Burnham (UT Frank Erwin Chair in Government), and Robert Crunden (UT Professor of American Studies)

Ross Terrill (Harvard University), 'Australia and Asia in Historical Perspective'

Sir Samuel Falle (British Ambassador and High Commissioner), 'The Morning after Independence: The Legacy of the British Empire'

Deborah Lavin (Principal of Trevelyan College, University of Durham), 'Lionel Curtis: Prophet of the British Empire'

Robin W. Doughty (UT Professor of Geography), 'Eucalyptus: And Not a Koala in Sight'

Al Crosby (UT Professor of American Studies and History), 'Captain Cook and the Biological Impact on the Hawaiian Islands'

Gillian Adams (Editor, *Children's Literature Association Quarterly*), 'Beatrix Potter and Her Recent Critics'

Lord Amery, 'Churchill's Legacy'

Christa Jansohn (University of Bonn), and Peter Green (Dougherty Professor of Classics) '*Lady Chatterley's Lover*'

R. A. C. Parker (Fellow of Queen's College, Oxford), 'Neville Chamberlain and the Coming of the Second World War'

John Velz (UT Professor of English), 'King Lear in Iowa: Jane Smiley's *A Thousand Acres*'

Jan Schall (University of Florida), 'British Spirit Photography'

Daniel Woolf (Dalhousie University), 'The Revolution in Historical Consciousness in England'

Fall Semester 1994

Kenneth O. Morgan (Vice-Chancellor, University of Wales), 'Welsh Nationalism'

Round Table Discussion on Michael Shelden's *Graham Greene: The Man Within:* Peter Green (UT Dougherty Professor of Classics), Roger Louis (UT Kerr Professor), and Thomas F. Staley (Director, HRHRC)

Robert D. King (Rapoport Regents Chair in Liberal Arts), 'The Secret War, 1939–1945'

Brian Boyd (Professor of English, University of Auckland), 'The Evolution of Shakespearean Dramatic Structure'

Lord Weatherill (former Speaker of the House of Commons), 'Thirty Years in Parliament'

Hans Mark (UT Professor of Aerospace Engineering), 'Churchill's Scientists'

Steven Weinberg (UT Josey Regental Professor of Science), 'The Test of War: British Strengths and Weaknesses in World War II'

Dennis Welland (Professor of English Literature and American Studies, University of East Anglia), 'Wilfred Owen and the Poetry of War'

Alan Frost (Professor of History, La Trobe University), 'The Bounty Mutiny and the British Romantic Poets'

W. O. S. Sutherland (UT Professor of English), 'Sir Walter Scott'

Hazel Rowley (Lecturer in Literary Studies, Deakin University, Melbourne), 'Christina Stead's "Other Country"'

Herman Bakvis (Professor of Government, Dalhousie University), 'The Future of Democracy in Canada and Australia'

Peter Stansky (Professor of History, Stanford University), 'George Orwell and the Writing of *Nineteen Eighty-Four*'

Henry Dietz (UT Associate Professor of Government), 'Sherlock Homes and Jack the Ripper'

James Coote (UT Professor of Architecture), 'Techniques of Illusion in British Architecture'

Round Table Discussion on 'The Best and Worst Books of 1994': Dean Burnham (UT Government), Alessandra Lippucci (UT Government), Roger Louis (UT Kerr Professor), Sidney Monas (UT Professor of Slavic Languages and History), and Janice Rossen (HRHRC)

Spring Semester 1995

Elizabeth Butler Cullingford (UT Professor of English), 'Anti-Colonial Metaphors in Contemporary Irish Literature'

Thomas M. Hatfield (UT Dean of Continuing Education), 'British and American Deception of the Germans in Normandy'

Gary P. Freeman (UT Associate Professor of Government), 'The Politics of Race and Immigration in Britain'

Donald G. Davis, Jr. (UT Professor in the Graduate School of Library and Information Science), 'The Printed Word in Sunday Schools in Nineteenth-Century England and the United States'

Brian Bremen (UT Assistant Professor of English), "Healing Words: The Literature of Medicine and the Medicine of Literature'

Frances Karttunen (Linguistic Research Center), and Alfred W. Crosby (American Studies and History), 'British Imperialism and Creole Languages'

Paul Lovejoy (Professor of History, York University, Canada), 'British Rule in Africa: A Reassessment of Nineteenth-Century Colonialism'

Carol MacKay (UT Associate Professor of English), 'Creative Negativity in the Life and Work of Elizabeth Robins'

John Brokaw (UT Professor of Drama), 'The Changing Stage in London, 1790–1832'

Linda Colley (Richard M. Colgate Professor of History, Yale University), 'The Frontier in British History'

Iwan Morus (University of California, San Diego), 'Manufacturing Nature: Science, Technology, and Victorian Consumer Culture'

Brian Parker (Professor of English, University of Toronto), 'Jacobean Law: The Dueling Code and "A Faire Quarrel" (1617)'

Kate Frost (UT Professor of English), '"Jack Donne the Rake": Fooling around in the 1590s'

Mark Kinkead-Weekes (Professor of English, University of Kent), 'Beyond Gossip: D. H. Lawrence's Writing Life'

Summer 1995

S. P. Rosenbaum (Professor of English, University of Toronto), 'Leonard and Virginia Woolf at the Hogarth Press'

Maria X. Wells (Curator of Italian Collections, HRHRC), 'A Delicate Balance: Trieste 1945'

Kevin Tierney (Professor of Law, University of California at Berkeley), 'Personae in Twentieth Century British Autobiography'

Fall Semester 1995

Brian Levack (UT Professor of History), 'Witchcraft, Possession, and the Law in Jacobean England'

Janice Rossen (Senior Fellow, HRHRC), 'The Home Front: Anglo-American Women Novelists and World War II'

Dorothy Driver (Professor of English, University of Cape Town), 'Olive Schreiner's Novel *From Man to Man*'

Philip Ziegler (London), 'Mountbatten Revisited'

Joanna Hitchcock (Director, UT Press), 'British and American University Presses'

Samuel H. Beer (Eaton Professor of the Science of Government Emeritus, Harvard University), 'The Rise and Fall of Party Government in Britain and the United States, 1945–1995'

Richard Broinowski (Australian Ambassador to Mexico and Central America), 'Australia and Latin America'

John Grigg (London), 'Myths about the Approach to Indian Independence'

Round Table Discussion on *Measuring the Mind* (Adrian Wooldridge) and *The Bell Curve* (Richard J. Herrnstein and Charles Murray): David Edwards (UT Professor of Government), Sheldon Ekland-Olson (UT Dean of Liberal Arts), Joseph Horn (UT Professor of Psychology), and Robert D. King (UT Rapoport Chair in Liberal Arts)

Paul Addison (Professor of History, University of Edinburgh), 'British Politics in the Second World War'

John Sibley Butler (UT Professor of Sociology), 'Emigrants of the British Empire'

Round Table Discussion on the Movie *Carrington:* Peter Green (UT Dougherty Professor of Classics), Robin Kilson (UT Assistant Professor of History), Roger Louis (UT Kerr Professor), Sidney Monas (UT Professor of Slavic Languages and History), and Elizabeth Richmond-Garza (UT Assistant Professor of English)

Spring Semester 1996

Kevin Kenny (UT Assistant Professor of History), 'Making Sense of the Molly Maguires'

Brigadier Michael Harbottle (British Army), 'British and American Security in the Post-Cold War'

Carol MacKay (UT Professor of English), 'The Singular Double Vision of Photographer Julia Margaret Cameron'

John Ramsden (Professor of History, University of London), '"That Will Depend on Who Writes the History": Winston Churchill as His Own Historian'

Jack P. Greene (Andrew W. Mellon Professor in the Humanities, The Johns Hopkins University), 'The *British* Revolution in America'

Walter D. Wetzels (UT Professor of German), 'The Ideological Fallout in Germany of Two British Expeditions to Test Einstein's General Theory of Relativity'

Thomas Pinney (William M. Keck Distinguished Service Professor of English, Pomona College), 'In Praise of Kipling'

Michael Charlesworth (UT Assistant Professor of Art History), 'The English Landscape Garden'

Stephen Gray (South African Novelist), 'The Dilemma of Colonial Writers with Dual Identities'

Jeremy Black (Professor of History, University of Durham), 'Could the British Have Won the War of American Independence?'

Dagmar Hamilton (UT Professor of Public Affairs, LBJ School), 'Justice William O. Douglas and British Colonialism'

Gordon Peacock and Laura Worthen (UT Theater and Dance), 'Not Always a Green and Pleasant Land: Tom Stoppard's *Arcadia*'

Bernard Crick (Professor of Politics, University of London), 'Orwell and the Business of Biography'

Geoffrey Hartman (Sterling Professor of English, Yale University), 'The Sympathy Paradox: Poetry, Feeling, and Modern Cultural Morality'

Dave Oliphant (HRHRC), 'Jazz and Its British Acolytes'

R. W. B. Lewis (Professor of English and American Studies, Yale University), 'Henry James: The Victorian Scene'

Alan Spencer (Vice-President, Ford Motor Company), 'Balliol, Big Business, and Mad Cows'

Peter Quinn: A Discussion of His Novel, *Banished Children of Eve*

Summer 1996

Martin Stannard (Professor of English, Leicester University), 'Biography and Textual Criticism'

Diane Kunz (Associate Professor of History, Yale University), 'British Withdrawal East of Suez'

John Cell (Professor of History, Duke University), 'Who Ran the British Empire?'

Mark Jacobsen (US Marine Corps Command and Staff College), 'The North-West Frontier'

Theodore Vestal (Professor of Political Science, Oklahoma State University), 'Britain and Ethiopia'

Warren F. Kimball (Robert Treat Professor of History, Rutgers University), 'A Victorian Tory: Churchill, the Americans, and Self-Determination'

Louise B. Williams (Assistant Professor of History, Lehman College, The City University of New York), 'British Modernism and Fascism'

Fall Semester 1996

Elizabeth Richmond-Garza (UT Associate Professor of English and Comparative Literature), 'The New Gothic: Decadents for the 1990s'

Robin Kilson (UT Assistant Professor of History), 'The Politics of Captivity: The British State and Prisoners of War in World War I'

Sir Brian Fall (Principal of Lady Margaret Hall, Oxford), 'What does Britain Expect from the European Community, the United States, and the Commonwealth?'

Roger Louis (UT Kerr Professor), 'Harold Macmillan and the Middle East Crisis of 1958'

Ian Willison (former head of the Rare Books Branch, British Museum, and Editor of *The Cambridge History of the Book in Britain*), 'The History of the Book and the Cultural and Literary History of the English-Speaking World'

Walter L. Arnstein (Jubilee Professor of the Liberal Arts and Sciences, University of Illinois), 'Queen Victoria's Other Island'

Noel Annan (London), '*Our Age* Revisited'

Michael Cohen (Lazarus Philips Professor of History, Bar-Ilan University, Tel Aviv), 'The Middle East and the Cold War: Britain, the United States, and the Soviet Union'

Reba Soffer (Professor of History, California State University, Northridge), 'Catholicism in England: Was it Possible to be a Good Catholic, a Good Englishman, and a Good Historian?'

Wilson Harris (Poet and Novelist), 'The Mystery of Consciousness: Cross-Cultural Influences in the Caribbean, Britain, and the United States'

H. S. Barlow (Singapore), 'British Malaya in the late Nineteenth Century'

Donald G. Davis, Jr. (UT Professor of Library and Information Science), 'British Destruction of Chinese Books in the Peking Siege of 1900'

Round Table Discussion on the Film *Michael Collins:* Elizabeth Cullingford (UT Professor of English), Kevin Kenny (UT Assistant Professor of History), Robin Kilson (UT Assistant Professor of History), and Roger Louis (UT Kerr Professor)

A. G. Hopkins (Smuts Professor of Commonwealth History, University of Cambridge), 'From Africa to Empire'

The Austin Chapter of the Society for the Preservation and Encouragement of Barber Shop Quartet Singing in America

Spring Semester 1997

Round Table Discussion on 'T. S. Eliot and Anti-Semitism': Robert D. King (UT Rapoport Chair in Jewish Studies), Sidney Monas (UT Professor of Slavic Languages and History), and Thomas F. Staley (Director, HRHRC)

Phillip Herring (Professor Emeritus of English, University of Wisconsin-Madison), 'Djuna Barnes and T. S. Eliot: The Story of a Friendship'

Bryan Roberts (UT Smith Chair in United States-Mexican Relations), 'British Sociology and British Society'

Andrew Roberts (London), 'The Captains and the Kings Depart: Lord Salisbury's Skeptical Imperialism'

Colin Franklin (London), 'In a Golden Age of Publishing, 1950–1970'

Susan Pedersen (Professor of History, Harvard University), 'Virginia Woolf, Eleanor Rathbone, and the Problem of Appeasement'

Andrew Seaman (Saint Mary's University, Halifax, Nova Scotia), 'Thomas Raddall: A Novelist's View of Nova Scotia during the American Revolution'

Gordon Peacock (UT Frank C. Erwin Professor of Drama), 'Noel Coward: A Master Playwright, a Talented Actor, a Novelist and Diarist: Or a Peter Pan for the Twentieth Century?'

Roland Oliver (Professor of African History, School of Oriental and African Studies, University of London), 'The Battle for African History, 1947–1966'

Alistair Horne (St. Antony's College, Oxford), 'Harold Macmillan's Fading Reputation'

Richard Begam (Professor of English, University of Wisconsin, Madison), 'Samuel Beckett and the Debate on Humanism'

Christopher Waters (Associate Professor of History, Williams College), 'Delinquents, Perverts, and the State: Psychiatry and the Homosexual Desire in the 1930s'

Sami Zubaida (University of London), 'Ernest Gellner and Islam'

Walter Dean Burnham (UT Frank C. Erwin Chair in Government), 'Britain Votes: The 1997 General Election and Its Implications'

Fall Semester 1997

Judith Brown (Beit Professor of the History of the British Commonwealth, Oxford University), 'Gandhi—A Victorian Gentleman'

Thomas Cable (UT Blumberg Professor of English), 'Hearing and Revising the History of the English Language'

Round Table Discussion on 'The Death of Princess Diana': Judith Brown (Oxford), David Edwards (UT Professor of Government), Elizabeth Richmond-Garza (UT Associate Professor of English), Anne Baade (British Studies), Alessandra Lippucci (UT Government), and Kevin Kenny (UT Associate Professor of History)

David Hunter (Music Librarian, Fine Arts Library), 'Handel and His Patrons'

Anne Kane (UT Assistant Professor of Sociology), 'The Current Situation in Ireland'

James S. Fishkin (UT Darrell K. Royal Regents Chair in Ethics in American Society), 'Power and the People: The Televised Deliberative Poll in the 1997 British General Election'

Howard D. Weinbrot (Vilas Research Professor of English, University of Wisconsin, Madison), 'Jacobitism in Eighteenth-Century Britain'

J. C. Baldwin, M.D. (Houston), 'The Abdication of King Edward VIII'

Kenneth E. Carpenter (Harvard University), 'Library Revolutions Past and Present'

Akira Iriye (Professor of History, Harvard University), 'Britain, Japan, and the International Order after World War I'

Anthony Hobson (London), 'Reminiscences of British Authors and the Collecting of Contemporary Manuscripts'

David Killingray (Professor of History, University of London), 'The British in the West Indies'

Alan Knight (Professor of Latin American History, Oxford University), 'British Imperialism in Latin America'

Round Table Discussion on King Lear in Iowa: The Movie '*A Thousand Acres*': Linda Ferreira-Buckley (UT Associate Professor of English), Elizabeth Richmond-Garza (UT Associate Professor of English), Helena Woodard (UT Assistant Professor of English), and John Velz (UT Professor of English)

Timothy Lovelace (UT Assistant Professor of Music) and the Talisman Trio

Spring Semester 1998

Richard Ollard (Biographer and Publisher), 'A. L. Rowse: Epitome of the Twentieth Century'

Round Table Discussion of Arundhati Roy's *The God of Small Things:* Phillip Herring (HRHRC, Professor Emeritus of English, University of Wisconsin), Brian Trinque (UT Economics), Kamala Visweswaran (UT Anthropology), and Robert Hardgrave (UT Government)

Jonathan Schneer (Professor of History, Georgia Institute of Technology), 'London in 1900: The Imperial Metropolis'

Trevor Burnard (Senior Lecturer in History, University of Canterbury, New Zealand), 'Rioting in Goatish Embraces: Marriage and the Failure of White Settlement in British Jamaica'

Felipe Fernández-Armesto (Oxford University), 'British Traditions in Comparative Perspective'

Michael Mann (Professor of Sociology, University of California, Los Angeles), 'The Broader Significance of Labour's Landslide Victory of 1997'

Dane Kennedy (Professor of History, University of Nebraska at Lincoln), 'White Settlers in Colonial Kenya and Rhodesia'

Round Table Discussion on 'Noel Annan, Keynes, and Bloomsbury': Jamie Galbraith (UT LBJ School), Elspeth Rostow (UT LBJ School), and Walt Rostow (UT Professor of Economics and History)

Lisa Moore (UT Associate Professor of English), 'British Studies—Lesbian Studies: A Dangerous Intimacy?'

James Gibbs (University of the West of England), 'Wole Soyinka: The Making of a Playwright'

Marilyn Butler (Rector of Exeter College, Oxford), 'About the House: Jane Austen's Anthropological Eye'

R. J. Q. Adams (Professor of History, Texas A&M University), 'Britain and Ireland, 1912–1922'

John M. Carroll (UT Asian Studies), 'Nationalism and Identity in pre-1949 Hong Kong'

Round Table Discussion on the Irish Referendum: Anne Kane (UT Sociology), Kevin Kenny (UT History), Roger Louis (UT Kerr Professor), and Jennifer O'Conner (UT History)

Fall Semester 1998

Louise Hodgden Thompson (UT Government), 'Origins of the First World War: The Anglo-German Naval Armaments Race'

John P. Farrell (UT Professor of English), 'Thomas Hardy in Love'

Carol MacKay (UT Professor of English), 'The Multiple Conversions of Annie Besant'

Roy Foster (Carroll Professor of Irish History, Oxford University), 'Yeats and Politics, 1898–1921'

Robert Olwell (UT History), 'British Magic Kingdoms: Imagination, Speculation, and Empire in Florida'

Sara H. Sohmer (Lecturer in History, Texas Christian University), 'The British in the South Seas: Exploitation and Trusteeship in Fiji'

Helena Woodard (UT Associate Professor of English), 'Politics of Race in the Eighteenth Century: Pope and the Humanism of the Enlightenment'

D. A. Smith (Grinnell College), 'Impeachment? Parliamentary Government in Britain and France in the Nineteenth Century'

Round Table Discussion on the Irish Insurrection of 1798: Robert Olwell (UT History), Lisa Moore (UT English), and Kevin Kenny (UT History)

Robert D. King (UT Rapoport Regents Chair of Jewish Studies), 'The Accomplishments of Raja Rao: The Triumph of the English Language in India'

Donald G. Davis, Jr. (UT Professor of Library and Information Science and History), 'Religion and Empire'

A. D. Roberts (Professor of History, School of Oriental and African Studies, University of London), 'The Awkward Squad: African Students in American Universities before 1940'

Chaganti Vijayasree (Professor of English, Osmania University, Hyderabad), 'The Empire and Victorian Poetry'

Martha Deatherage (UT Music), 'Christmas Celebration: Vauxhall Gardens'

Spring Semester 1999

Round Table Discussion on *Regeneration,* Pat Barker's Trilogy on the First World War: Betty Sue Flowers (UT Professor of English), Roger Louis (UT Kerr Professor), and Paul Woodruff (UT Professor in the Humanities)

Alistair Campbell-Dick (Founding Member of British Studies and Director of Cybertime Corporation), 'The Immortal Memory of Robert Burns'

Hugh Macrae Richmond (Professor of English and Drama,, University of California at Berkeley), 'Why Rebuild Shakespeare's Globe Theatre?'

Ralph Austen (Professor of History, University of Chicago), 'Britain and the Global Economy: A Post-Colonial Perspective'

Jerome Meckier (Professor of English, University of Kentucky), 'Aldous Huxley's American Experience'

Peter Marsh (Professor of History, Syracuse University), 'Joseph Chamberlain as an Entrepreneur in Politics: Writing the Life of a Businessman Turned Statesman'

Roger Adelson (Professor of History, Arizona State University), 'Winston Churchill and the Middle East'

Margot Finn (Associate Professor of History, Emory University), 'Law, Debt and Empire: The Calcutta Court of Conscience'

Fred M. Leventhal (Professor of History, Boston University), 'The Projection of Britain in America before the Second World War'

Larry Siedentop (Fellow of Keble College, Oxford University), 'Reassessing the Life of Isaiah Berlin'

Ross Terrill (Research Associate in Government, Harvard University), 'R. H. Tawney's Vision of Fellowship'

Juliet Fleming (University Lecturer of English, Cambridge University), 'The Ladies' Shakespeare'

Elizabeth Fernea (UT English and Middle Eastern Studies), 'The Victorian Lady Abroad: In Egypt with Sophia Poole and in Texas with Mrs. E. M. Houstoun'

Richard Schoch (University of London), 'The Respectable and the Vulgar: British Theater in the Mid-Nineteenth Century'

Ferdinand Mount (Editor, *TLS*), 'Politics and the *Times Literary Supplement*'

Fall Semester 1999

Round Table Discussion on the Boer War, 1899–1902: Barbara Harlow (UT Professor of English), John Lamphear (UT History), and Roger Louis (UT Kerr Professor)

Sharon Arnoult (Assistant Professor of History, Southwest Texas State University), 'Charles I: His Life after Death'

Kenneth O. Morgan (Fellow of The Queen's College, Oxford and former Vice Chancellor, University of Wales), 'Lloyd George, Keir Hardie and the Importance of the "Pro-Boers"'

Richard Cleary (UT Architecture), 'Walking the Walk to Talk the Talk: The Promenade in Eighteenth-Century France and England'

Keith Kyle (Journalist and Historian), 'From Suez to Kenya as Journalist and as Historian'

Malcolm Hacksley (Director of the National English Literary Museum, Grahamstown, South Africa), 'Planting a Museum, Cultivating a Literature'

Ben Pimlott (Warden of Goldsmiths College, University of London), 'The Art of Writing Political Biography'

Geraldine Heng (UT Associate Professor of English), 'Cannibalism, the First Crusade, and the Genesis of Medieval Romance'

A. P. Martinich (UT Philosophy), 'Thomas Hobbes: Lifelong and Enduring Controversies'

Round Table Discussion on Lyndall Gordon's *T. S. Eliot: An Imperfect Life*: Brian Bremen (UT Associate Professor of English), Thomas Cable (UT Blumberg Professor of English), Elizabeth Richmond Garza (UT Professor of Comparative Literature), and Thomas F. Staley (Director, HRHRC)

Shula Marks (Professor of History, School of Oriental and African Studies, University of London), 'Smuts, Race, and the Boer War'

Round Table Discussion on the Library of the British Museum: William B. Todd (English), Irene Owens (Library and Information Science), and Don Davis (Library and Information Science and Department of History).

Henry Dietz (UT Professor of Government), '*The Hound of the Baskervilles*'

Spring Semester 2000

Susan Napier (UT Associate Professor of Asian Studies), 'The Cultural Phenomenon of the Harry Potter Fantasy Novels'

Round Table Discussion on *Dutch: A Memoir of Ronald Reagan:* A Chapter in the 'Special Relationship?': Roger Louis (UT Kerr Professor), Harry Middleton (Director of the LBJ Library), and Elspeth Rostow (LBJ School)

Norman Rose (Chaim Weizmann Chair of International Relations, Hebrew University, Jerusalem), 'Harold Nicolson: A Curious and Colorful Life'

Charlotte Canning (UT Theater History and Theory), 'Feminists Perform Their Past'

John Ripley (Greenshields Emeritus Professor of English, McGill University), 'The Sound of Sociology: H. B. Tree's *Merchant of Venice*'

Sergei Horuji (Russian Academy of Sciences), 'James Joyce in Russia'

Janice Rossen (Biographer and Independent Scholar), 'Philip Toynbee'

Max Egremont (Novelist and Biographer), 'Siegfried Sassoon's War'

Paul Taylor (Professor of International Relations, London School of Economics and Political Science), 'Britain and Europe'

Lord Selborne (President, Royal Geographical Society), 'The Royal Geographical Society: Exploration since 1830'

Craig MacKenzie (Department of English, Rand Afrikaans University, Johannesburg), 'The Mythology of the Boer War: Herman Charles Bosman and the Challenge to Afrikaner Romanticism'

Peter Catterall (Director, Institute of Contemporary British History, London), 'Reform of the House of Lords'

Bernard Porter (Professor of Modern History, University of Newcastle), 'Pompous and Circumstantial: Sir Edward Elgar and the British Empire'

Craufurd D. Goodwin (James B. Duke Professor of Economics, Duke University), 'Roger Fry and the Debate on "Myth" in the Bloomsbury Group'

Jamie Belich (Chair in History, University of Auckland), 'Neo-Britains? The "West" in Nineteenth-Century Australia, New Zealand, and America'

Round Table Discussion on Norman Davies, *The Isles:* Sharon Arnoult (Midwestern State University, Wichita Falls), Raymond Douglas (Colgate University), Walter Johnson (Northwestern Oklahoma State University), David Leaver (Raymond Walters College, Cincinnati), and John Cell (Duke University)

Fall Semester 2000

Round Table discussion on Paul Scott, the Raj Quartet, and the Beginning of British Studies at UT—Peter Green (UT Dougherty Professor of Classics), Robert Hardgrave (UT Professor of Government and Asian Studies), and Roger Louis (UT Kerr Professor)

Suman Gupta (The Open University), 'T. S. Eliot as Publisher'

Jeffrey Cox (University of Iowa), 'Going Native: Missionaries in India'

Kevin Kenny (Boston College), 'Irish Nationalism: The American Dimension'

Joseph Kestner (University of Tulsa), 'Victorian Battle Art'

James E. Cronin (Boston College), 'From Old to New Labour: Politics and Society in the Forging of the "Third" Way'

Gerald Moore (Mellon Visiting Research Fellow, HRHRC), 'When Caliban Crossed the Atlantic'

Richard Howard (Shakespearean Actor, London), '"Health and Long Life to You": A Program of Irish Poetry and Prose Presented by an Englishman, with Anecdotes'

Stephen Foster (Northern Illinois University), 'Prognosis Guarded: The Probable Decolonization of the British Era in American History'

Frank Prochaska (University of London), 'Of Crowned and Uncrowned Republics: George V and the Socialists'

Robert H. Abzug (UT History and American Studies), 'Britain, South Africa, and the American Civil Rights Movement'

Paula Bartley (Visiting Research Fellow, HRHRC), 'Emmeline Pankhurst'

Thomas Jesus Garza (UT Associate Professor of Slavic Languages), 'A British Vampire's Christmas'

Spring Semester 2001

Betty Sue Flowers (UT Distinguished Teaching Professor), 'From Robert Browning to James Bond'

Larry Carver (UT Professor of English), 'Feliks Topolski at the Ransom Center'

Oscar Brockett (UT Distinguished Teaching Professor), 'Lilian Baylis and England's National Theatres'

Linda Levy Peck (George Washington University), 'Luxury and War'

R. James Coote (UT Architecture), 'Architectural Revival in Britain'

Adam Roberts (Oxford University), 'Britain and the Creation of the United Nations'

Mark Southern (UT Professor of Germanic Studies), 'Words over Swords: Language and Tradition in Celtic Civilization'

Round Table discussion on Ben Rogers *A Life of A. J. Ayer:* David Braybrooke (UT Government and Philosophy), Al Martinich (UT History and Philosophy), David Sosa (UT Philosophy), and Paul Woodruff (UT Plan II and Philosophy)

Bartholomew Sparrow (UT Government), 'British and American Expansion: The Political Foundations'

Jose Harris (Oxford University), 'Writing History during the Second World War'

Charles Loft (Westminster College), 'Off the Rails? The Historic Junctions in Britain's Railway Problem'

Dan Jacobson (University of London), 'David Irving and Holocaust Denial'—Special Lecture

Dan Jacobson (University of London), 'Self-Redemption in the Victorian Novel'

George S. Christian (UT British Studies), 'The Comic Basis of the Victorian Novel'

Paul Taylor (London *Independent*), 'Rediscovering a Master Dramatist: J. B. Priestley'

Fall Semester 2001

Round Table Discussion on Ray Monk's Biography of Bertrand Russell, *The Ghost of Madness*—Al Martinich (UT History and Philosophy), David Sosa (UT Philosophy and British Studies), and Paul Woodruff (UT Plan II and Philosophy)

Alex Danchev (Keele University), 'The Alanbrooke Diaries'

Robert M. Worcester (LSE and Market Opinion Research International), 'Britain and the European Union'

Martha Ann Selby (UT Associate Professor of Asian Studies), 'The Cultural Legacy of British Clubs: Manners, Memory, and Identity among the New Club-Wallahs in Madras'

Roger Owen (Harvard University), 'Lord Cromer and Wilfrid Blunt in Egypt'

James Loehlin (UT Associate Professor of English), 'A Midsummer Night's Dream'

Jeffrey Meyers (Biographer), 'Somerset Maugham'

Elspeth Rostow (UT LBJ School), 'From American Studies to British Studies—And Beyond'

Nicholas Westcott (British Embassy), 'The Groundnut Scheme: Socialist Imperialism at Work in Africa'

Round Table Discussion on 'The Anglo-American Special Relationship': Gary Freeman (UT Government), Roger Louis (UT Kerr Professor), Elspeth Rostow (UT American Studies), and Michael Stoff (UT History)

Christopher Heywood (Sheffield University), 'The Brontës: A Personal History of Discovery and Interpretation'

James Bolger (New Zealand Ambassador and former Prime Minister), 'Whither New Zealand? Constitutional, Political, and International Quandaries'

R. J. Q. Adams (Texas A&M University), 'Arthur James Balfour and Andrew Bonar Law: A Study in Contrasts'

Ferdinand Mount (Editor, *Times Literary Supplement*), 'British Culture since the Eighteenth Century: An Open Society?'

James Loehlin (UT English), 'A Child's Christmas in Wales'

Spring Semester 2002

Round Table Discussion on Adam Sisman, *Boswell's Presumptuous Task:* Samuel Baker (UT English), Linda Ferreira-Buckley (UT English), Julie Hardwick (UT History), and Helena Woodward (UT English)

A. G. Hopkins (UT History), 'Globalization: The British Case'

Susan Napier (UT Professor of Asian Studies), 'J. R. R. Tolkein and the Lord of the Rings: Fantasy as Retreat or Fantasy as Engagement?'

Wilfrid Prest (Adelaide University), 'South Australia's Paradise of Dissent'

Tom Palaima (UT Professor of Classics), 'Terence Rattigan's *Browning Version*'

Alan H. Nelson (University of California at Berkeley), 'Thoughts on Elizabethan Authorship'

Penelope Lively (London), 'Changing Perceptions of British and English Identity'

Hans Mark (UT Professor of Aerospace Engineering), 'The Falklands War'

David Butler (Oxford University), 'Psephology—or, the Study of British Elections'

Robert L. Hardgrave (UT Professor of Government), 'From West Texas to South India and British Studies'

Geoffrey Wheatcroft (London), 'The Englishness of English Sport'

Eileen Cleere (Southwestern University), 'Dirty Pictures: John Ruskin and the Victorian Sanitation of Fine Art'

Jamie Belich (Auckland University), 'A Comparison of Empire Cities: New York and London, Chicago and Melbourne'

Churchill Conference—Geoffrey Best (Oxford), Sir Michael Howard (Oxford), Warren Kimball (Rutgers), Philip Ziegler (London), Roger Louis (UT Kerr Professor)

Catherine Maxwell (University of London), 'Swinburne's Poetry and Criticism'

Round Table Discussion on Churchill and the Churchill Conference: Rodrigo Gutierrez (UT History), Adrian Howkins (UT History), Heidi Juel (UT English), David McCoy (UT Government), Joe Moser (UT English), Jeff Rutherford (UT History), Bill Livingston (UT Senior Vice-President), and Roger Louis (UT Kerr Professor)

Fall Semester 2002

James K. Galbraith (UT LBJ School of Public Affairs), 'The Enduring Importance of John Maynard Keynes'

Michael Green (University of Natal), 'Agatha Christie in South Africa'

Sumit Ganguly (UT Asian Studies), 'Kashmir: Origins and Consequences of Conflict'

Margaret MacMillan (University of Toronto), 'At the Height of His Power: Lloyd George in 1919'

Douglas Bruster (UT English), 'Why We Fight: *Much Ado About Nothing* and the West'

John Darwin (Oxford University), 'The Decline and Rise of the British Empire: John Gallagher as an Historian of Imperialism'

Kevin Kenny (Boston College), 'The Irish in the British Empire'

David Wallace (University of Pennsylvania), 'A Chaucerian's Tale of Surinam'

Peter Bowler (Queen's University, Belfast), 'Scientists and the Popularization of Science in Early Twentieth-Century Britain'

Bernardine Evaristo (London), "A Feisty, Funky Girl in Roman England'

Frank Moorhouse (Australia), 'Dark Places and Grand Days'

David Cannadine (University of London), 'C. P. Snow and the Two Cultures'

Round Table Discussion on 'Edmund S. Morgan's Biography of Benjamin Franklin'—Carolyn Eastman (UT History), Bruce Hunt (UT History), Roger Louis (UT Kerr Professor), Alan Tully (UT History)

Mark Lawrence (UT History), 'The Strange Silence of Cold War England: Britain and the Vietnam War'

Tom Cable (UT English), 'The Pleasures of Remembering Poetry'

Spring Semester 2003

Round Table Discussion on 'W. G. Sebald—*Rings of Saturn*': Brigitte Bauer (UT French and Italian), Sidney Monas (UT History and Slavic Languages), Elizabeth Richmond-Garza (UT English and Comparative Literature), Walter Wetzels (UT Germanic Studies)

Diana Davis (UT Geography), 'Brutes, Beasts, and Empire: A Comparative Study of the British and French Experience'

Colin Franklin (Publisher), 'Rosalind Franklin—Variously Described as "The Dark Lady of DNA" and "The Sylvia Plath of Molecular Biology"'

Sidney Monas (History and Slavic Languages), 'A Life of Irish Literature and Russian Poetry, Soviet Politics and International History'

Neville Hoad (UT English), 'Oscar Wilde in America'

Selina Hastings (London), 'Rosamond Lehman: Eternal Exile'

Bernard Wasserstein (Glasgow University), 'The British in Palestine: Reconsiderations'

Anne Chisholm (London), 'Frances Partridge: Last of the Bloomsberries'

Philip Morgan (The Johns Hopkins University), 'The Black Experience and the British Empire'

Jeremy duQuesnay Adams (Southern Methodist University), 'Joan of Arc and the English'

Didier Lancien (University of Toulouse), 'Churchill and de Gaulle'

Avi Shlaim (Oxford University), 'The Balfour Declaration and its Consequences'

Martin J. Wiener (Rice University), 'Murder and the Modern British Historian'

Winthrop Wetherbee (Cornell University), 'The Jewish Impact on Medieval Literature: Chaucer, Boccaccio, and Dante'

Philippa Levine (University of Southern California), 'Sex and the British Empire'

Summer 2003

Donald G. Davis, Jr. (UT History and School of Information), 'Life without British Studies is Like . . . '

Kurth Sprague (UT English and American Studies), 'Literature, Horses, and Scandal at UT'

David Evans (UT Astronomy), 'An Astronomer's Life in South Africa and Texas'

Tom Hatfield (UT Continuing Education), 'Not Long Enough! Half a Century at UT'

Fall Semester 2003

Richard Oram (HRHRC), 'Evelyn Waugh: Collector and Annotator'

Round Table Discussion on 'Booker Prize Winner James Kelman: Adapting a Glasgow Novel for the Texas Stage': James Kelman (Glasgow), Mia Carter (UT English), Kirk Lynn, and Dikran Utidjian

Simon Green (All Souls College, Oxford University), 'The Strange Death of Puritan England, 1914–1945'

Elizabeth Richmond-Garza (UT English and Comparative Literature), '*Measure for Measure*'

Lewis Hoffacker (US Ambassador), 'From the Congo to British Studies'

A. P. Thornton (University of Toronto), 'Wars Remembered, Revisited, and Reinvented'

Deryck Schreuder (University of Western Australia), 'The Burden of the British Past in Australia'

Robert Mettlen (Lamar Centennial Professor), 'From Birmingham to British Studies'

Paul Schroeder (University of Illinois), 'The Pax Britannica and the Pax Americana: Empire, Hegemony, and the International System'

Ferdinand Mount (London), 'A Time to Dance: Anthony Powell's *Dance to the Music of Time* and the Twentieth Century in Britain'

Brian Bond (University of London), '*Oh! What a Lovely War:* History and Popular Myth in Late-Twentieth Century Britain'

Wendy Frith (Bradford College, England), 'The Speckled Monster: Lady Mary Wortley Montagu and the Battle against Smallpox'

Harry Middleton (UT LBJ Library), 'The Road to the White House'

Jeremy Lewis (London), 'Tobias Smollett'

Christian Smith (Austin, Texas), 'Christmas Readings'

Spring Semester 2004

Round Table Discussion on 'The Pleasures of Reading Thackeray': Carol Mackay (UT English), Judith Fisher (Trinity University), George Christian (British Studies)

Thomas F. Staley (HRHRC), '"Corso e Recorso:" A Journey through Academe'

Patrick O'Brien (London School of Economics), 'The Pax Britanica, American Hegemony, and the International Order, 1793–2004'

Michael Wheeler (former Director of Chawton House Library), 'England Drawn and Quartered: Cultural Crisis in the Mid-Nineteenth Century'

Walter Wetzels (UT Germanic Studies), 'Growing Up in Nazi Germany, and later American Adventures'

Kathleen Wilson (State University of New York, Stony Brook), 'The Colonial State and Governance in the Eighteenth Century'

Elizabeth Fernea (UT English and Middle Eastern Studies), 'Encounters with Imperialism'

Chris Dunton (National University of Lesotho), 'Newspapers and Colonial Rule in Africa'

Miguel Gonzalez-Gerth (UT Spanish and Portuguese), 'Crossing Geographical and Cultural Borders—and Finally Arriving at British Studies'

Peter Stansky (Stanford University), 'Bloomsbury in Ceylon'

Round Table Discussion on *The Crimson Petal and the White:* John Farrell (UT English), Betty Sue Flowers (LBJ Library), Roger Louis (UT Kerr Professor), Paul Neimann (UT English)

Ann Curthoys (Australian National University), 'The Australian History Wars'

Martha Ann Selby (UT Asian Studies), 'Against the Grain: On Finding My Voice in India'

Steven Isenberg (UT Visiting Professor of Humanities), 'A Life in Our Times'

Summer 2004

Carol Mackay (UT English), 'My Own Velvet Revolution'

Erez Manela (Harvard University), 'The "Wilsonian Moment" in India and the Crisis of Empire in 1919'

Scott Lucas (Birmingham University), '"A Bright Shining Mecca": British Culture and Political Warfare in the Cold War and Beyond'

Monica Belmonte (US Department of State), 'Before Things Fell Apart: The British Design for the Nigerian State'

Dan Jacobson (London), 'Philip Larkin's "Elements"'

Bernard Porter (University of Newcastle), ''Oo Let 'Em In? Asylum Seekers and Terrorists in Britain, 1850–1914'

Fall Semester 2004

Richard Drayton (Cambridge University), 'Anglo-American "Liberal" Imperialism, British Guiana, 1953–64, and the World Since September 11'

David Washbrook (Oxford University), 'Living on the Edge: Anxiety and Identity in "British" Calcutta, 1780–1930'

Joanna Hitchcock (University of Texas Press), 'An Accidental Publisher'

Alan Friedman (UT English), '*A Midsummer Night's Dream*'

Antony Best (London School of Economics), 'British Intellectuals and East Asia in the Inter-war Years'

John Farrell (UT English), 'Beating a Path from Brooklyn to Austin'

Christopher Middleton (UT Liberal Arts), 'Relevant to England—A Reading of Poems'

Gail Minault (UT History and Asian Studies), 'Growing Up Bilingual and Other (Mis)adventures in Negotiating Cultures'

Roger Louis (Kerr Professor of English History and Cultures), 'Escape from Oklahoma'

John Trimble (UT English), 'Writing with Style'

Niall Ferguson (Harvard University), 'Origins of the First World War'

James Hopkins (Southern Methodist University), 'George Orwell and the Spanish Civil War: The Case of Nikos Kazantzakis'

James Currey (London), 'Africa Writes Back: Publishing the African Writers Series at Heinemann'

Sidney Monas (UT History and Slavic Languages), 'A Jew's Christmas'

Geoffrey Wheatcroft (London), '"In the Advance Guard": Evelyn Waugh's Reputation'

Spring Semester 2005

Katharine Whitehorn (London), 'It Didn't *All* Start in the Sixties'

Gertrude Himmelfarb (Graduate School of the City University of New York), 'The Whig Interpretation of History'

Kurt Heinzelman (UT English and HRHRC), 'Lord Byron and the Invention of Celebrity'

Brian Levack (UT History), 'Jesuits, Lawyers, and Witches'

Richard Cleary (UT Architecture), 'When Taste Mattered: W. J. Battle and the Architecture of the Forty Acres'

Edward I. Steinhart (Texas Tech University), 'White Hunters in British East Africa, 1895–1914'

Don Graham (UT English), 'The Drover's Wife: An Australian Archetype'

A. C. H. Smith, (London) 'Literary Friendship: The 40-Year Story of Tom Stoppard, B. S. Johnson, and Zulfikar Ghose'

Paul Woodruff (UT Philosophy and Plan II), 'A Case of Anglophilia—And Partial Recovery: Being an Account of My Life, with Special Attention to the Influence of England upon My Education'

Toyin Falola (UT History), 'Footprints of the Ancestors'

Robert Abzug (UT History) 'Confessions of an Intellectual Omnivore: The Consequences on Scholarship and Career'

Deirdre McMahon (Mary Immaculate College, University of Limerick), 'Ireland and the Empire-Commonwealth 1918–1972'

James Coote (UT Architecture), 'Building with Wit: Sir Edwin Lutyens and British Architecture'

Jay Clayton (Vanderbilt University), 'The Dickens Tape: Lost and Found Sound before Recording'

Christopher Ricks (Oxford University), 'The Force of Poetry: Shakespeare and Beckett'

Summer 2005

Blair Worden (Oxford University), 'Poetry and History of the English Renaissance'

Robert Bruce Osborn (British Studies), 'The Four Lives of Robert Osborn'

Alessandra Lippucci (UT Government), 'Perseverance Furthers: A Self-Consuming Artifact'

William H. Cunningham (former President of the University of Texas), 'Money, Power, Politics, and Ambition'

David V. Edwards (UT Government), 'Friendly Persuasion in the Academy'

Elizabeth Richmond-Garza (UT English), 'A Punk Rocker with Eight Languages'

Richard Lariviere (UT Liberal Arts), 'Confessions of a Sanskritist Dean'

Fall Semester 2005

Celebration of 30th Anniversary and Publication of Yet More Adventures with Britannia

Robert D. King (UT Jewish Studies) , 'T.S. Eliot Reconsidered'

Round Table Discussion on 'The London Bombings': James Galbraith (LBJ School), Elizabeth Cullingford (UT English), Clement Henry (UT Government), Roger Louis (UT Kerr Professor)

Dolora Chapelle Wojciehowski (UT English), 'The Erotic Uncanny in Shakespeare's *Twelfth Night*'

Karl Hagstrom Miller (UT History), 'Playing Pensativa: History and Music in Counterpoint'

James D. Garrison (UT English), 'Translating Gray's *Elegy*'

Miguel Gonzalez-Gerth (UT Spanish and Portuguese), 'Another Look at Orwell: the Origins of *1984*'

Round Table Discussion on 'The Imperial Closet: Gordon of Khartoum, Hector McDonald of the Boer War, and Roger Casement of Ireland': Barbara Harlow (UT English), Neville Hoad (UT English), John Thomas (HRHRC)

Guy Ortolano (Washington University in St. Louis), 'From *The Two Cultures* to *Breaking Ranks:* C.P. Snow and the Interpretation of the 1960s'

Catherine Robson (UC Davis), 'Poetry and Memorialization'

Round Table Discussion on 'Britain and the Jewish Century': Lauren Apter (UT History), Robert D. King (UT Jewish Studies), Sidney Monas (UT History and Slavic Languages)

Hans Mark (UT Aerospace Engineering), 'Churchill, the Anglo-Persian Oil Company, and the Origins of the Energy Crisis: From the Early 20th Century to the Present'

Randall Woods (Arkansas), 'LBJ and the British'

Spring Semester 2006

Richard Gray (London), 'Movie Palaces of Britain'

Samuel Baker (UT English), 'The Lake Poets and the War in the Mediterranean Sea'

Thomas F. Staley (HRHRC), 'Graham Greene and Evelyn Waugh'

Gary Stringer (Texas A&M), 'Love's Long Labors Coming to Fruition: The John Donne Variorum Donne'

Caroline Elkins (Harvard), 'From Malaya to Kenya: British Colonial Violence and the End of Empire'

Grigory Kaganov (St. Petersburg), 'London in the Mouth of the Neva'

Graham Greene (London), 'A Life in Publishing'

John Davis (Oxford), 'Evans-Pritchard: Nonetheless A Great Englishman'

Barry Gough (Wilfrid Laurier University), 'Arthur Marder and the Battles over the History of the Royal Navy'

Ivan Kreilkamp (Indiana), '"Bags of Meat": Pet-Keeping and the Justice to Animals in Thomas Hardy'

James Wilson (UT History), 'Historical Memory and the Mau Mau Uprising in Colonial Kenya'

Anne Deighton (Oxford), 'Britain after the Second World War: Losing an Empire and Finding a Place in a World of Super Powers'

Steve Isenberg (UT Liberal Arts), 'Auden, Forster, Larkin, and Empson'

Harriet Ritvo (MIT), 'Animals on the Edge'

Peter Quinn (NY), 'Eugenics and the Hour of the Cat'

Dan Jacobson (London), 'Kipling and South Africa'

Fall Semester 2006

Michael Charlesworth (UT Art and Art History) and Kurt Heinzelman (UT English), 'Tony Harrison's "v."'

Peter Stanley (Australian War Memorial), 'All Imaginable Excuses: Australian Deserters and the Fall of Singapore'

Selina Hastings (London), 'Somerset Maugham and "Englishness"'

James W. Vick (UT Mathematics), 'A Golden Century of English Mathematics'

John O. Voll (Georgetown), 'Defining the Middle East and the Clash of Civilizations'

James Loehlin (UT English), 'The Afterlife of Hamlet'

Daniel Topolski (London), 'The Life and Art of Feliks Topolski'

John Darwin (Oxford), 'The British Empire and the British World'

David Cannadine (University of London), 'Andrew Mellon and Plutocracy Across the Atlantic'

John Lonsdale (Cambridge), 'White Settlers and Black Mau Mau in Kenya'

Kate Gartner Frost (UT English), 'So What's Been Done about John Donne Lately?'

John Summers (Harvard), 'The Power Elite: C. Wright Mills and the British'

Marrack Goulding (Oxford), 'Has it been a Success? Britain in the United Nations'

Priya Satia (Stanford), 'The Defence of Inhumanity: British Military and Cultural Power in the Middle East'

Don Graham (UT English), 'Burnt Orange Britannia: A Missing Contributor!'

Spring Semester 2007

Bernard Porter (Newcastle University), 'Empire and British Culture'

Paul Sullivan (UT Liberal Arts Honors Program), 'The Headmaster's Shakespeare: John Garrett and British Education'

Round Table Discussion on 'The Queen': Elizabeth Cullingford (UT English), Karen King (UT American Studies), Roger Louis (UT Kerr Professor), Bryan Roberts (UT Sociology)

Martin Francis (University of Cincinnati), 'Cecil Beaton's Romantic Toryism and the Symbolism of Wartime Britain'

Susan Crane (Columbia University), 'Animal Feelings and Feelings for Animals in Chaucer'

Michael Charlesworth (UT Art History), 'The Earl of Strafford and Wentworth Castle'

Adam Sisman (London), 'Wordsworth and Coleridge'

Jenny Mann (Cornell University), 'Shakespeare's English Rhetoric: Mingling Heroes and Hobgoblins in *A Midsummer Night's Dream*'

David Atkinson (Member of Parliament), 'Britain and World Peace in the 21st Century'

Bertram Wyatt-Brown (University of Florida), 'T. E. Lawrence: Reputation and Honor's Decline'

Roger Louis (UT Kerr Professor), 'All Souls and Oxford in 1956: Reassessing the Meaning of the Suez Crisis'

Indivar Kamtekar (Jawaharlal Nehru University), 'India and Britain during the Second World War'

Cassandra Pybus (University of Sydney), 'William Wilberforce and the Emancipation of Slaves'

Stephen Howe (University of Bristol), 'Empire in the 21st Century English Imagination'

Geoffrey Wheatcroft (London), 'The Myth of Malicious Partition: The Cases of Ireland, India, and Palestine'

Charles Rossman (UT English), 'D. H. Lawrence and the "Spirit" of Mexico'

Kenneth O. Morgan (House of Lords), 'Lloyd George, the French, and the Germans'

Fall Semester 2007

R. J. Q. Adams (Texas A&M), 'A. J. Balfour's Achievement and Legacy'

Robin Doughty (Geography), 'Saving Coleridge's Endangered Albatross'

Caroline Williams (University of Texas), 'A Victorian Orientalist: John Frederick Lewis and the Artist's Discovery of Cairo'

Susan Pedersen (Columbia University), 'The Story of Frances Stevenson and David Lloyd George'

Eric S. Mallin (UT English), 'Macbeth and the Simple Truth'

Mark Oaten, M.P., 'How "Special" is the Special Relationship?'

Dan Birkholz (UT English), 'Playboys of the West of England: Medieval Cosmopolitanism and Familial Love'

Jeremy Lewis (London), 'The Secret History of Penguin Books'

Matthew Jones (Nottingham University), 'Britain and the End of Empire in South East Asia in the Era of the Vietnam War'

Martin Wiener (Rice University), '"Who knows the Empire whom only the Empire knows?": Reconnecting British and Empire History'

Book Launch: *Penultimate Adventures with Britannia* (Follett's Intellectual Property)

Hermione Lee and Christopher Ricks (Oxford), 'The Elusive Brian Moore: His Stature in Modern Literature'

Gabriel Gorodetsky (Tel Aviv University), 'The Challenge to Churchill's Wartime Leadership by Sir Stafford Cripps (the "Red Squire")'

Helena Woodard (UT English), 'Black and White Christmas: The Deep South in the Eighteenth Century'

Spring Semester 2008

Roundtable discussion on Tim Jeal's biography, *Stanley: The Impossible Life of Africa's Greatest Explorer,* Diana Davis (UT Geography), A. G. Hopkins (UT History), Roger Louis (UT History)

Elizabeth Richmond-Garza (UT English and Comparative Literature), 'New Year's Eve 1900: Oscar Wilde and the Masquerade of Victorian Culture'

Robert Hardgrave (UT Government), 'The Search for Balthazar Solvyns and an Indian Past: The Anatomy of a Research Project'

Lucy Chester (University of Colorado), 'Zionists, Indian Nationalism, and British Schizophrenia in Palestine'

Michael Brenner (University of Pittsburgh), 'Strategic and Cultural Triangulation: Britain, the United States, and Europe'

Roger Morgan (European University, Florence), 'The British "Establishment" and the Chatham House Version of World Affairs'

Jason Parker (Texas A&M), 'Wilson's Curse: Self-Determination, the Cold War, and the Challenge of Modernity in the "Third World"'

Stephen Foster (Northern Illinois University), 'The American Colonies and the Atlantic World'

A.G. Hopkins (UT History), 'Comparing British and American "Empires"'

James Turner (Notre Dame University), 'The Emergence of Academic Disciplines'

Dror Wahrman (Indiana University), 'Invisible Hands in the Eighteenth Century'

Narendra Singh Sarila (Prince of Sarila), 'Mountbatten and the Partition of India'

Pillarisetti Sudhir (American Historical Association), 'The Retreat of the Raj: Radicals and Reactionaries in Britain'

Keith Francis (Baylor University), 'What Did Darwin Mean in *On the Origin of Species*? An Englishman and a Frenchman Debate Evolution'

Fall Semester 2009

'Ted and Sylvia'—Round Table Discussion, (UT English), Judith Kroll, Kurt Heinzelman, Betty Sue Flowers, Tom Cable

Roby Barrett (Middle East Institute), 'The Question of Intervention in Iraq, 1958–59'

John Kerr (San Antonio), 'Cardigan Bay'

Sue Onslow (London School of Economics), 'Julian Amery: A Nineteenth-Century Relic in a Twentieth-Century World?'

John Rumrich (UT English), 'Reconciliation in *The Winter's Tale:* The Literary Friendship of Robert Greene and William Shakespeare'

Richard Jenkyns (Oxford), 'Conan Doyle: An Assessment beyond Sherlock Holmes'

Theresa Kelley (University of Wisconsin), 'Romantic British Culture and Botany in India'

Sir Adam Roberts (Oxford), 'After the Cold War'

Geoffrey Wheatcroft (London), 'Churchill and the Jews'

Sir Brian Harrison (Oxford), 'Prelude to the Sixties'

Eric Kaufmann (LSE), 'The Orange Order in Northern Ireland'

Robert McMahon (Ohio State University), 'Dean Acheson: The Creation of a New World Order and the Problem of the British'

Mark Metzler (UT History), 'Eye of the Storm: London's Place in the First Great Depression, 1872–96'

James Loehlin (UT English), Christmas Party, reading passages from Charles Dickens, *A Christmas Carol*

Spring Semester 2009

Margaret MacMillan (Oxford University), 'The Jewel in the Crown'

Bernard Wasserstein (University of Chicago), 'Glasgow in the 1950s'

Dominic Sandbrook (London), 'The Swinging Sixties in Britain'

Karl Meyer and Shareen Brysac (*New York Times* and CBS), 'Inventing Iran, Inventing Iraq: The British and Americans in the Middle East'

Albert Lewis (R. L. Moore Project), 'The Bertrand Russell Collection: The One That Got Away from the HRC'

Sir David Cannadine (Institute of Historical Research, London), 'Colonial Independence'

Linda Colley (Princeton University), 'Philip Francis and the Challenge to the British Empire'

George Scott Christian (UT English and History), 'Origins of Scottish Nationalism: The Trial of Thomas Muir'

Roy Foster (Oxford), 'Trevor-Roper and Scotland'

Warren Kimball (Rutgers University), 'Churchill, Roosevelt, and Ireland'

R. J. Q. Adams (Texas A&M), 'A. J. Balfour and his Critics'

Dan Jacobson (London), 'Hardy and Eliot'

John Darwin (Nuffield College, Oxford), 'Britain's Global Empire'

Saul Dubow (Sussex University), 'Sir Keith Hancock and the Question of Race'

Weslie Janeway (Cambridge), 'Darwin's Cookbook'

Julian Barnes (London), 'Such, Such Was Eric Blair'

Cassandra Pybus (Visiting Fellow, UT Institute of Historical Studies), 'If you were regular black . . . ': Slavery, Miscegenation, and Racial Anxiety in Britain'

Summer 2009

Peter Green (UT Classics), 'Drink and the Old Devil'